Chippendale's classic Marquetry Revealed

Jack Metcalfe

For Gloria

Born 8th October 1939 in Farnley Hall, Otley, in the octagonal bedroom,
with neo-classical décor by Joseph Rose.
An avid diarist for 59 years, devoted mother for 47 years,
her love everlasting …

ACKNOWLEDGEMENTS

The marquetry and related applications displayed throughout this book could not have happened without the host of professional and non-professional organisations and individuals who gave their time and expertise, all in the quest of knowledge. This book is richer in content thanks to their valued contributions.

Organisations
The Chippendale Society
Newby Hall
Temple Newsam House
Nostell Priory
Renishaw Hall
V&A London
Burton Constable Hall
Firle Place Trust
Leeds Museums and Galleries
Harewood House Trust
Country Life Library UK
Leonardo di Vinci Museum, Milan, Italy
Sotheby's Auction House, London
Colonial Williamsburg Foundation, USA
Swedish International Museum, Stockholm
Hildesheim University, Germany
Forum 2000 Horsforth, Leeds.

Individuals (in no specific order)
The Late Tommy Limmer – My teacher, friend and mentor.
Ted Clements – Photographer.
Hugh Hillyard-Parker – Editor and book designer.
Dr Heinrich Piening – Furniture conservator, dye analytics specialist.
Ian Fraser – Furniture conservator, Leeds Museums & Galleries.
Thomas Lange – Furniture restorer, Ronald Phillips Ltd, Mayfair, London.
The late André Jacob Roubo – Le Menuisier Ébéniste, Paris, France.
Jürgen Huber – Furniture Conservator, Wallace Collection, London
Lucinda Compton – Artistic conservation, furniture and fittings.
Stuart Gill – Director, Newby Hall and Gardens.
Melissa Gallimore – Freelance curator and formerly Curator, Harewood House.
Peter Metcalfe – Dearest brother and fellow marqueteur.
Lorraine Trickett – Friend and proof reader.
Mike and Joan Camm – My long standing friends and loyal supporters throughout.
Will Lawton – Friend, English literature graduate, and proof reader.
Dr David Bower – Writer and friend.
Tony Forster – Director, SPA Laminates, Leeds.
Malcolm Long – Engraver.
Malcolm Slater – Marqueteur.
Patrick Dingwall – Director, Sothebys Auction House.
Simon Banks – Furniture restorer, Dingwall and Banks.
Simon Feingold – Specialist polisher and dyer.
Philippa Barstow – Furniture polisher/teacher.
Deborah Gage – Curator, Firle Place Trust.
Chris Blackburn – Curator, Nostell Priory.
Alexandra Sitwell – Owner, Renishaw Hall.
Leela Meinertas – Senior Curator, Furniture, V&A London.
Kelly Marie Wainwright – Curator, Burton Constable Foundation.
Dr Adam Bowett – Furniture and wood historian.
James Lomax – Hon Curator, Chippendale Society.
Hans Michaelsen – Furniture conservator and dye researcher, Germany.
Dr Todd Stewart – CAD drawings, Leeds University.
Emeritus Professor Joyce Hill – Anglo-Saxon Language, Leeds University.
Quentin Smith – Chairman, Staffordshire Marquetry Group UK.
Andrew Cox-Whittaker – Furniture restorer and Webmaster, Chippendale Society.
Martin Speak – Former lecturer and polisher at Leeds College of Art & Design
Alison Monk – Former student at Leeds College of Art & Design
Simon Brock – Former student at Leeds College of Art & Design

and Neil Metcalfe – My loving son and guiding light.

First published in the United Kingdom by
Jack Metcalfe
Yorkshire
England

Copyright © Jack Metcalfe

The moral rights of the author have been asserted.

The author can accept no legal responsibility for any consequences arising from the application of information, advice or instructions given in this publication.

Front cover photographed by Ted Clements, with kind permission by Newby Hall, Ripon, North Yorkshire.

All photographs of furniture which appear in this publication and are held in the following locations – Firle Place, Harewood House, Newby Hall, Nostell Priory, Private Collection, Renishaw Hall, Temple Newsam House – are the sole copyright © Ted Clements.

All rights reserved. No part of this publication may be reproduced, store in a retrieval system, or transmitted in any form or by any means electronic, mechanical, photocopying, recording or otherwise, without the prior written permission of the copyright owner.

Design and typesetting by Hugh Hillyard-Parker, Edinburgh, hugh@hillyard.org.uk

CONTENTS

CHAPTER 1 • INTRODUCTION

Thomas Chippendale   9
Chippendale in London • Chippendale's *Director* • Chippendale's innovations

UV-VIS spectronomy   12

André Jacob Roubo   13

Neo-classicism and its canonic status   15
The classic style

Chippendale, marquetry and the classic style   18
Chippendale's approach • Chippendale's collaborators • List of Classic motifs used in the marquetry format

CHAPTER 2 • MATERIALS & TOOLS

Introduction   23

Materials   25
Harewood • Holly • Other materials used • Inherent timber problems • The changes • Veneer production • Why and how are veneers so thinly cut? • Why did they want veneers so thin? • Animal glue • Fish glue

Tools   33
Fretsaw invention • Marquetry cutter's bench • The reciprocating treadle saw • Aluminium table-mounted treadle saw • Computer Aided Design (CAD) images showing dimensional construction • Extra wide floor-standing treadle saw • Treadle saw summary • Chevalet or marquetry donkey • Advantages of the chevalet • Disadvantage of the chevalet • Bevel cutting • Fretsaw blades • Knife cutting • Inlay knife • Shoulder knife • Hollow punches • Veneer hammer and other presses • Veneer hammer • Hot sand bags • Penwork or artwork

CHAPTER 3 • TECHNIQUES

Introduction   51

Inlay   52
Inlay technique • Shoulder knife

Creating line drawings in the 18th century   56
Prick and pounce

Packet fretsawing technique   58

Two-part fretsawing or the classic method   60
On-the-line, off-the-line • The first part • The second part • Satinwood's inherent problem experienced

Bevel cutting   64

Stick-as-you-go technique   65
Discovering two-part fretsawing and stick-as-you-go on a Chippendale commission • Assembling the marquetry and backgrounds using the stick-as-you-go method • Stick-as-you-go • How is the border constructed? • Mass production • Building a Greek key design • Building Greek key using a mitre box

The template method   77

The window method   80

Making berries with a punch   81

Constructing stringers and decorative bandings   82

Discovering a new inlay technique through application of artwork   83
Domed door technique applied to the Diana and Minerva commode

Pen-work – or should I say 'artwork'?   85
Artwork versus engraving

Who supplied and performed all the marquetry and finishing work, in London, from c.1760?   87

CONTENTS

CHAPTER 4 • DYES AND DISCOVERY

Introduction 89
England's alum trade 90
Alum-houses
Discovering dyes 93
Making dyes for the reproduction door panel of the Harewood library writing table • Dyeing the colours • Green-dyed holly • Recipe No 1 • Red dyes • Natural holly • UV-VIS Spectronomy • The tests • Results (summary)
Dye tests at Schloss Nymphenburg 103
Results
The basics of dyeing 104
Acidity/alkinity • Mordants • Modifiers • Mordants – alum and tin • Quantities • Alkaline elements • Neutral • Acidic elements • Alum (aluminium potassium sulphate) • Tin chloride
Recipes 106
Barberry • Young fustic and wig tree • Weld • Curcuma • Saffron • Kamala • Brazilwood • Henna • Madder • Cochineal • Campeachy • Indigo • Indigo-carmine • Green
Harewood 119
Making harewood • Chippendale's silver/grey harewood • Weber recipe
Tannin treatment 121
Tannin treatment of pear wood to make mock-ebony
Making indelible ink 122
Preparation • History
Synthetic dyes 123
Conclusion 124

CHAPTER 5 • BUILDING A REPLICA 1: DOOR PANEL OF THE HAREWOOD LIBRARY WRITING TABLE

Introduction 125
Investigation 126
Restoring damaged marquetry 128
Acanthus leaves • Chippendale's near calamity creates a defining moment • Laurel leaves • First evidence of dyes • Berries and ribbons • The central vase • Indian rosewood
Building a replica marquetry door panel 134
Acanthus leaves • Plumage • Central vase assembly • Central column • Making the central floret • Guilloche • Anthemion • Laurel leaf swags • Acanthus flower • Satinwood banding • Outer crossbanding • Penwork
The completed panel 147
In conclusion 148

CHAPTER 6 • BUILDING A REPLICA 2: DIANA & MINERVA COMMODE

Introduction 149
Preparatory work 150
Sourcing the timbers • Discovering the dyed colours used on the original • Identifying marquetry techniques • Creating line drawings • Tools for the construction
The marquetry begins: covering the nine drawers 154
Building the laurel leaf swags, drops and ribbons

Building the marquetry for the two outer doors — 157
Building the four corner fans • Laurel leaf garland

Making the long and short fascia panels — 161

Building the two incurved end panels — 162
Building the challenging guilloche

The commode top — 167
Creating a line drawing • Building the central fan • Creating four matching acanthus leaf elements • Making the decorative diamond • Making two acanthus leaves that sit either side of the fan • Ready to commence installation of all elements My new treadle saw • Fretsawing background veneers outside the diamond • Forming circular stringers • Fitting the green-dyed borders and tulipwood crossbanding • Gluing and sanding the top • Images of the top panel and its original, scientifically proven colour scheme

Today's marquetry technique — 184

Decorating the domed door — 185
Inlaying and hammer-veneering • The dome door construction • Practice model • Step 1. Hammer-veneering eight satinwood segments to the dome • Step 2. Building the half-round fan • Step 3. Fretsawing the laurel leaf swags and drops • Steps 5, 6 & 7. Using the inlay knife • Step 8. Building the two triangular designs on the fascia panel • Step 9. Central 16-fluted circular white fan • Steps 10 & 11. Fitting the tulipwood crossbanding and gluing to door • Step 12. Building the raised arch that sits above the dome • My dilemma • Redrawing new swags and drops

Commode finished, complete with brass mounts — 201

CHAPTER 7 • BUILDING A REPLICA 3: PIER TABLE TOP

Introduction — 203
Amazing historical events • A second restoration programme • Discovering engraving work • Discovering dyestuffs and paints used on the original table • Filming the work while building the replica

Investigation and preparation — 207
Engraving • The project team and plan • Creating a life-sized paper template of the marquetry top • Cutting the solid wood substrate • Creating an exact line drawing of the marquetry work • Testing for dyestuffs using UV-VIS spectronomy • Creating colour drawings based on Heinrich's findings • Veneers for the marquetry work • Making 'harewood' • Hammer veneering harewood background veneers to the substrate

Dyeing and installing the green and blue stringers — 213

Installing the garland of 80 laurel leaves and swags — 214

Acanthus flowers made with berberis wood — 216
Building the flowers

Building the two end panels — 218
Building the central fans using the template method • Cutting the harewood background to the outer panels • Installing the swags of laurel leaves • Using fish glue and a new applicator • Fitting tulipwood crossbanding around the table • Building the corner decorations

Rebuilding the central plumage — 227

The replica table top complete — 228

CHAPTER 8 • GALLERY OF CHIPPENDALE'S MARQUETRY FURNITURE

Introduction		231
8.1	Pembroke 'games' table ~ Nostell Priory, 1769	233
8.2	Harrington commode ~ c.1770	236
8.3	Bureau dressing table ~ Harewood House, 1770	241
8.4	Commode ~ Nostell Priory, c.1770	243
8.5	Pier tables (pair) ~ Harewood House, 1770	246
8.6	Library steps ~ Harewood House, 1771	248
8.7	Library writing table ~ Harewood House, c.1771	250
8.8	Sideboard pedestals (pair) ~ Harewood House, c.1771	252
8.9	Pier tables (pair) ~ Music room, Harewood House, 1771	254
8.10	Pier tables (pair) ~ Dining room, Harewood House, 1771–2	257
8.11	Salon commode ~ Harewood House, c.1772	259
8.12	Dressing commode ~ Harewood House, 1772	264
8.13	Fall-front secretaire ~ Harewood House, c.1772	266
8.14	Pier table ~ Harewood House, 1772	269
8.15	Pier tables (pair) ~ Harewood House, 1772	272
8.16	Horseshoe table ~ Burton Constable Hall, 1772	275
8.17	Diana & Minerva commode ~ Harewood House, 1773	277
8.18	Panshanger cabinets (pair) ~ Firle Place, 1773	279
8.19	Pembroke table ~ Newby Hall, 1775	285
8.20	Renishaw commode ~ Renishaw Hall, c.1775	288
8.21	The 'Lunar' table ~ Harewood House, 1775	293

INDEX   300

CHAPTER 1

INTRODUCTION

THOMAS CHIPPENDALE

Thomas Chippendale was baptized on 5th June 1718 at the Parish Church, Otley, a small market town situated in Wharfedale, Yorkshire, England. We do not know the date of his birth, since recording births was not either available to or patronised by the working classes. We know that children were baptized very soon after birth, since infant mortality was very high at this time, so parents wanted their children recorded in the church of their choice.

Thomas was the only child of John Chippendale, joiner, and his first wife Mary, daughter of Thomas Drake, stonemason, of Otley. John Chippendale re-married and had seven more children.

Thomas Chippendale probably received an elementary education at Otley Grammar School, followed by a formal apprenticeship during his formative years. It is believed he received this from the York-based carver and cabinetmaker, Richard Wood. This can only be speculation, but strong links with the York-based firm continued throughout his working life. Richard Wood ordered eight subscription copies of Chippendale's 1st edition *Director*. One of Wood's apprentices – William Benson – became foreman in Chippendale's London workshop. Despite all this, and following registration of his baptism, Chippendale disappeared without trace for the following 30 years.

Chippendale in London

The next record we have of Chippendale is when he registered his marriage to Catherine Redshaw on the 19th May 1748 in St George's Chapel, Mayfair, London. Their marriage produced nine children – five boys and four girls with the first-born, Thomas (always known as Chippendale 'the Younger') eventually being schooled in the business.

In 1754, two momentous events were to transform Chippendale's life. First, he moved into premises in the heart of the fashionably paved shopping area of London at 60, 61 & 62 St Martin's Lane. The property provided for workshops where every aspect of his business could be based, and also allowed him living quarters for his wife and family. He also acquired a new business partner, James Rannie, who injected capital into the business and lived next door to his partner, at no 62. Rannie, of Scottish descent, was a wealthy merchant with fishing interests and capital to invest. He employed Thomas Haig, a bookkeeper, who probably looked after the accounts of the business.

History proves James Rannie to have been a sound and faithful business partner. Without his loyalty and financial backing, Chippendale, on his own, could not have survived. Clearly, Rannie believed in Chippendale's talents and skill; he

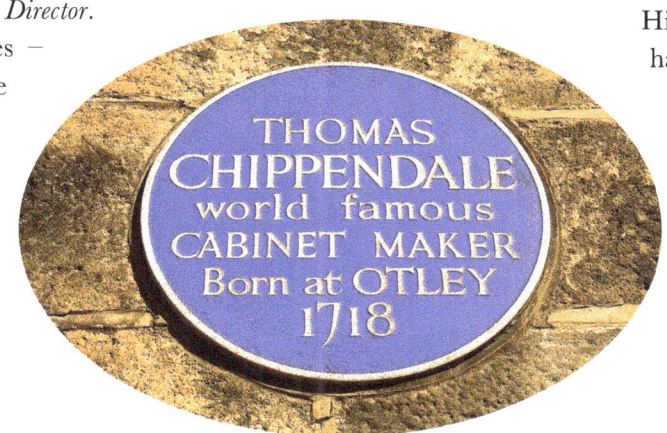

Figure 1.1 Blue plaque celebrating Chippendale's birth

constantly backed him when further and regular financial inputs became necessary.

The workshops at the back of the front units were accessed by a yard which led into a chair shop, cabinet-makers' workshop, carpet, glass and feather rooms, a large upholsterers' shop, timber stores, workshops and a counting house. They named their new premises 'The Cabinet and Upholstery Warehouse' and adopted a chair as their shop sign.

Other furniture makers of the time also owned properties in St Martin's Lane; these included John Channon, William Hallett, William Vile and John Cobb. Unlike Chippendale, other furniture makers chose not to use signs to advertise their business, considering it undignified. They preferred to rely on word of mouth to gain business. Clearly, Chippendale was determined to lead from the front, even if it meant breaking with protocol. While moving to such a high-profile address was a bold move for any aspiring tradesman to make, the second event proved even more momentous.

Chippendale's *Director*

Some years prior to 1754, when he perhaps received formal training from an associate – Matthias Darly, an engraver and qualified drawing master – Thomas Chippendale had the courage to publish a detailed catalogue of designs, something only reserved for professional artists and architects of the day. The 161 plates eloquently displayed 'Elegant and Useful Designs of Household Furniture in the Gothic, Chinese and Modern Taste'.

He called his publication *The Gentleman and Cabinet Maker's Director*, copies of which were distributed, as the dual appeal of the title intended, to the nobility and fellow tradesmen. No other 'tradesman' had ever published his own designs of this magnitude and scale, and the outcome was astounding. Nearly all his commissions started from that publication, which was an immediate sell-out. Thomas Chippendale's journey had begun.

Starting from humble beginnings, his journey takes him into a world that most mortals could only dream about. With no academic qualifications to support him, young Chippendale had to rely on his raw talent of artistry and craft, coupled with an unshakeable belief in his own abilities. I have good reason for this bold declaration about his persona. His talents and self-confidence are clear for all to see when reading the bold statement he made at the beginning of the *Director*, as it came to be known, where he states *"what ever design you may chose, I will make it better"*.

These qualities, these skills, coupled with his unshakeable self-belief were to bring him to the pinnacle of his trade and allow his genius to enter the world of nobility and aristocracy on the grandest scale. The *Director* immediately transformed and elevated his reputation as a supreme furniture designer and cabinet-maker both in Britain and Europe – and eventually in America and Canada. Today, Thomas Chippendale is a household name across the world.

Figure 1.2 Chippendale's groundbreaking 'Director'

Chippendale's innovations

The *Director* was filled with an eclectic array of furniture and household fittings, encapsulating the most expressive designs ever to grace England's stately homes. The birth of the taste for Gothic and Chinese styles led eventually to Chippendale's authorship of the newly-founded neo-classical movement, bringing with it a collection of marquetry masterpieces that reveal new techniques, new wood species, new tools, each shaped by invention, skill and experience, and not least by fashion. We first need to examine the past, to see how and why marqueteurs worked in the way they did. Through this examination, I have been able to build a knowledge base by applying my own marquetry skills to uncover the secrets lurking beneath the polished surfaces.

By 1758 Chippendale had already produced the first two editions of his famous portfolio *The Gentleman and Cabinet-Maker's Director*, and was, at this time, working on the third and final edition, which was published in stages between 1759 and 1762. The first twelve years of his post-*Director* career (1758–70) involved making furniture and household fittings, which did *not* include marquetry. As the cover of the *Director* states, he was intending to make furniture in the Gothic, Chinese and the Modern taste. While no marquetry designs exist in the *Director*, the motifs that make up the medium appear as carved images, which he successfully applied to his furniture and household fittings.

A new and exciting architectural style was sweeping across Europe in the middle of the 18th century, which was made more visible to Chippendale by the celebrated architect Robert Adam, who had returned from a four-year 'Grand Tour' of France and Italy in 1758. Adam had been able to study, among other things, the findings in the Roman ruins of Herculaneum and Pompeii, following the rediscovery of artefacts unearthed from the devastation caused by the volcanic eruption of Vesuvius in 79 AD. Adam brought back with him drawings of local plants, flowers, household earthenware, and decorative emblems of Roman and Greek origins.

Perhaps the one symbolic image that depicted neo-classicism more than any other was the vase, and both Adam and Chippendale displayed many versions of it, used in plaster casts, wood and metallic carvings and, of

Figure 1.3 Statue of Thomas Chippendale outside the Manor House in Otley

course, marquetry. It's also worth noting here that Josiah Wedgwood, considered the greatest potter that ever lived, also used the same vase designs on his 'cream ware' ceramics, which were supplied to the same clientele as Chippendale's.

CHAPTER 1 | INTRODUCTION

UV-VIS SPECTRONOMY

In 2007 a remarkable scientific break-through came my way by a chance meeting. I was invited to present a paper on neo-classical marquetry at an International Marquetry Symposium held in Vadstena, Sweden. Also at that conference was a German conservator and scientist, Heinrich Piening, who presented a paper on UV-VIS Spectronomy (ultra-violet, visual spectronomy), a scientific way of detecting dyestuffs used on antique marquetry work.

I immediately saw the opportunity that Heinrich's pioneering work presented me, and I invited him to come over to England and discover what dyes were used to colour the marquetry elements on Chippendale's collection. A full analysis of the dyestuffs and the recipes that were available at the time allowed me the opportunity to reproduce the range of colours that make up the original marquetry work.

Thanks to Heinrich's pioneering discovery and willingness to apply his science to my research, I gained a wealth of information, which provides the backbone of this publication. For the first time ever, you will see precisely what Chippendale's furniture looked like when it was first made, not only through computer graphically produced images, but also through working on three reconstruction projects with talented colleagues, resulting in ambitious replicas of Thomas Chippendale's classic masterpieces.

The first is a door and drawer panel from the famous 'Harewood Library writing table'. The second is a complete replica of Chippendale's most celebrated work 'the Diana and Minerva commode' made for Harewood House, Leeds, in 1773. The third and final piece is a marquetry table made for the then circular dressing room at Harewood House in 1772.

Each of these projects feature within this book, showing stepped construction of the replicated techniques, plus the use of dyed veneers depicting the colours identified during Heinrich Piening's scientific analysis. Additionally, other marquetry commissions, which Heinrich tested and identified, are colour matched using digital reproduction techniques, using Photoshop.

Chapter 4 describes my visit to Heinrich's laboratory at Schloss Nymphenburg, Munich in 2009. The chapter includes replications of all the 18th century dye recipes, discovered on Heinrich's previous visit to test the Chippendale marquetry. Each dye produced during my stay unfolds ancient recipes, which you may find useful in your own workshops or research. The visit, as recorded in Chapter 4, forms the foundation to my studies, in the knowledge that science, and not guesswork, lights the way in glorious technicolour.

Figure 1.4* Heinrich Piening performing tests at Harewood House on a pier table while I log the readings

* Reproduced by kind permission of the Trustees of the 7th Earl of Harewood Will Trust and the Trustees of the Harewood House Trust

ANDRE JACOB ROUBO

History has repeatedly provided the torch to light the path of knowledge during my long research of this book. One significant example of this is the production of an 18th century classic five-volume treatise titled *L'Art du Menuisier* ('The Art of the Carpenter'), written by a third-generation Parisian-born woodworker – André Jacob Roubo.

Commissioned by the Academy of Science in Paris between 1769 and 1774, Roubo wrote five volumes on the tools and techniques of specialist subjects including carpentry, furniture making, marquetry and parquetry, carriage-building and garden structures. Each volume is expertly enhanced with exquisite engravings, with each plate illustrating either tools, offered in scale and dimensional size, or techniques so eloquently drawn that very little text is needed to enhance the illustration. The drawings, created by Roubo himself through his declared skill as a draughtsman, illustrate the depth of his talent in addition to his writing skill.

The only drawback is that the volumes are only available in the French language. That was the case until the early part of 2008, when I was fortunate to show the book to a friend who had just retired from a lifetime teaching schoolchildren French and German language.

My friend, who wishes to remain anonymous, only needed one sight of the classic tome to convince her that this was an opportunity to reignite her love of 18th century French language. She was, in her own words, 'back home' and began translating with skill, and unquenchable enthusiasm. The volume she worked on (Volume 3), covers the tools and techniques of marquetry, entitled *L'Art du Menuisier – Ébéniste*. The facsimile version, still available from selected booksellers today, consists of 277 pages, plus 60 plates of engraved drawings (see Figure 1.6).

The translation proved difficult in two areas. The first was the 18th century language, which includes words and phrases unrecognised in today's modern French tongue; the second was the use of colloquial words and phrases to describe woodworking jargon. While my friend saw the former as a challenge, the latter needed someone with knowledge of 'local' woodworking jargon, not always recognisable today, especially in an area away from Roubo's immediate surroundings. Local jargon within trades can differ in areas only a few hundred miles apart, let alone in a different country and separated in time by more than 240 years.

Figure 1.5 André Jacob Roubo

It's ironic that the six-year period taken by Roubo to write the five volumes matches the same six-year period Chippendale spent making his collection of marquetry masterpieces. The woodworking

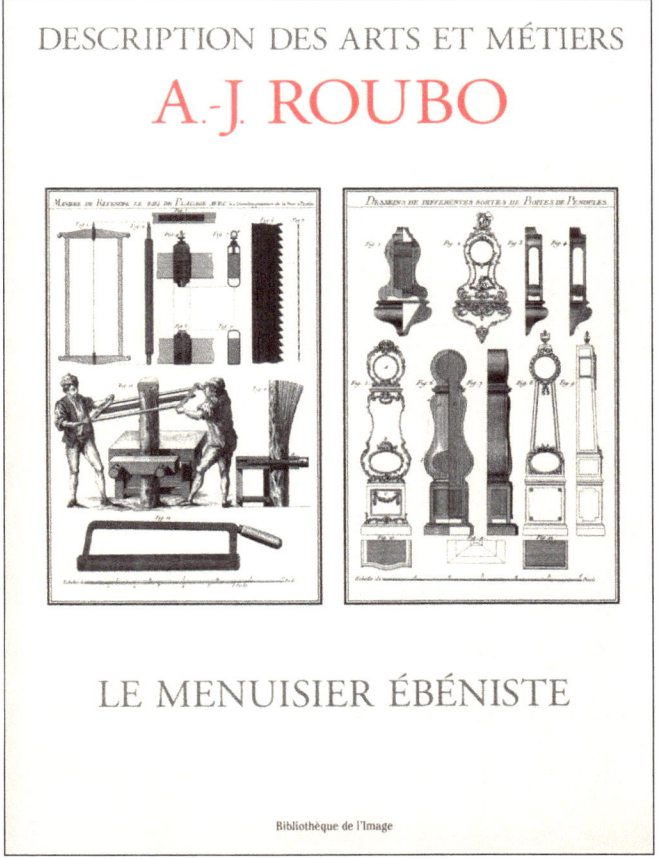

Figure 1.6 Le Menuisier Ébéniste

CHAPTER 1 | INTRODUCTION

and furniture history fraternity throughout the world reveres Roubo's treatise. His engravings, expertly drawn by the author and reproduced by the Academy of Science in Paris, have influenced historians, restorers and wood-working enthusiasts for over 240 years.

The complete, unabridged text of Volume 3, 'Marquetry', now translated into English, reveals further evidence of the tools and techniques upon which 18th century European furniture makers depended to create their masterpieces.

However, I will not be relying on my own copy of Roubo's translation to define techniques undertaken by English marqueteurs. This is because Roubo, in my opinion, either misled his readers or was himself misled by French *ébénistes*, so that his theoretical explanations were either misleading or sometimes wrong. In fairness to the author, I fully suspect Roubo was deliberately misled by the marquetry workshop from whom he was attempting to gain knowledge. Roubo himself declared he was new to marquetry, and we know that workshop secrecy was paramount in those highly competitive days of French marquetry furniture.

It is fortunate that parallel to our translation, an American publisher also produced an English translation of the marquetry volume. The Lost-Art Press under stewardship of Christopher Swartz, with technical input by Donald C Williams, Michele Pietryka-Pagán and Philippe Lafargue, published this work, which is now available under the title: *To make as Perfect as Possible, Roubo Translation*.

I am delighted to merge Roubo's theoretical teachings, where applicable, with Chippendale's applied techniques, each contribution underpinning the other. For my part, replica tools and techniques are used in this book to reproduce authentic marquetry practices in a step-by-step fashion.

We have to remember that both men, separated only by the English Channel, a distance seldom bridged by the average man in those days, would most likely have been unaware of each other's work produced over the same period. This makes me doubly grateful for the sterling work performed by my friend in bringing Roubo's work to my attention and opening up hidden secrets that had previously been unattainable.

Figure 1.7* Page from Roubo's 'L'Art du Menuisier'.

* Courtesy of Colonial Williamsburg Foundation USA

NEO-CLASSICISM AND ITS CANONIC STATUS

Neo-classicism is the name given to a quite distinct movement in the decorative and visual arts. 'Neo' comes from a Greek word meaning 'new', and the 'neo'-classical movement embraces theatre, music, poetry, architecture and furniture. This movement occurred at different times across Europe between the 18th and 20th centuries.

What any neo-classicism depends on most fundamentally is a consensus about a body of work that has achieved canonic status. I'm not referring to the ecclesiastical meaning of the word, although there are similarities between them. For something said to be 'canonic' can be interpreted to mean that the work must have symmetry, yet also obey rule, order, form and law, thus retaining perfect control of an artistic expression. The classics are considered to be art, theatre, poetry, music and architecture (the latter embracing both external and internal architecture) and of course furniture design.

Ideally, neo-classicism is essentially an art of an ideal; an artist, well schooled and comfortably familiar with the 'canon' does not repeat it in lifeless reproductions, but synthesizes the tradition anew in each work. It's abundantly clear from his work that Chippendale followed the form of the canon within his designs and understood fully the neo-classical concept. Through this idiom, his skill as a supreme designer came to the fore, and he found himself building images full of grace, style and symmetry, yet retaining the rule, order and form that the movement demanded. Here was an opportunity to achieve an eclectic style, based on earlier revival work of the Greek and Roman movements, yet motivated by his own design inspirations.

Adam had provided Chippendale with the ammunition he needed to fulfil his ultimate dreams. What followed set the standard for all to admire and emulate.

The classic style

Before venturing any further, let me suggest that the term neo-classical be known, from now on, as 'classic'. This is because marquetry practitioners, like myself, use the term 'classic' for this type of marquetry application.

After reading and absorbing Chapters 2 and 3 in particular, you will appreciate that the tools and techniques point to a new and unique methodology. Coupled with that, one design characteristic seen in marquetry creations – namely symmetry – requires a specific application to achieve symmetrical exactness. You could say that symmetry creates its own marquetry rules, as laid down in the canon, and for that reason Chapters 2 and 3 obey and teach the classic style.

Another and perhaps more relevant reason for the change follows my visit to Ravenna in 2015, where I found classic motifs in abundance, produced in the sixth century and made with tiny mosaics applied to the ceilings, walls, floors and decorative panels of the city's cathedral and basilica. Examples are shown in Figures 1.8 to 1.12.

Figure 1.8 Sixth century classic mosaic designs in the Cathedral, Ravenna, Italy
Note the blue and gold half-round fan above the pillars.

Figure 1.9 Classic mosaic three-dimensional fan seen on the incurved domed ceiling.
Cathedral, Ravenna, Italy

Here was the classic style in all its colourful glory. Fans, urns, vases, guilloche, acanthus leaves, ribbons, Greek key and anthemions were laid out before me in full colour, matching perfectly those produced twelve centuries later by Adam and Chippendale. Robert Adam made his historic grand tour in the 18th century, and witnessed similar classic drawings on the walls of the ruins of Pompeii and Herculaneum. We do not, however, know if he visited these earlier hand-made examples in Ravenna.

That apart, I feel more drawn to the existence of the art and craft mosaic work, which talented artisans of the sixth century AD produced. I fully appreciate the discoveries and introductions that Adam made, and without which architectural changes would not have happened on the scale we witnessed. However, from my point of view, speaking as a marquetry practitioner, the final answer is to support the actual production as seen in the images given here.

Figure 1.10 This two-tone half-round fan built in mosaics echoes the design produced on Chippendale marquetry work. A stylised guilloche is seen below the fan.
Cathedral, Ravenna, Italy

Figure 1.11 It is amazing to see this half-round mosaic fan built in the 6th century as a floor design. Turn it into a circle and build it in marquetry and it fits perfectly on top of the Diana and Minerva Commode (see Chapter 6).
Cathedral, Ravenna, Italy

Figure 1.12 This panel was mounted on a wall as a display of typical mosaic motifs used in the period. It shows: top centre, a guilloche, as seen on Chippendale marquetry in this book; right, a Greek Key design eerily imitating a swastika; on the left, a stylised Guilloche; and bottom centre, perhaps the most compelling image of the 18th century – the vase. The panel is bordered throughout with rows of berries. I could not introduce the classic images that flood this book and my research more dramatically – all of which proves that history leads our way into the future. These powerful sixth-century classic motifs still provoke our artistic needs to this day, some 1500 years later.

CHAPTER 1 | INTRODUCTION

CHIPPENDALE, MARQUETRY AND THE CLASSIC STYLE

Chippendale's marquetry furniture symbolises all that is best of the classic period, and over 20 known pieces, made over a six-year period (1769–75) are identified, catalogued and analysed in revealing detail. As you will see in this book, Chippendale took up this new methodology while constructing a writing table and building the marquetry on its four matching doors. Chapter 5 highlights a mistake still visible on each door panel, and gives clear evidence of a planned switch from the old method of building marquetry using the 'packet fretsawing' technique, to a controlled methodology we now call two-part fret sawing or the 'classic style'. Working methods were never documented, or if they were, they did not survive, leaving me to discover the techniques through close scrutiny, using my own experience and knowledge of 18th century techniques. Some of the discoveries are written about in Roubo's marquetry volume, as you will read about in following chapters.

As a practising marqueteur, I have a distinct advantage over others, both from living almost on the doorstep of Chippendale's greatest Yorkshire-based commissions, and by spending the past 20 years reproducing and teaching his timeless designs. This has provided the opportunity to replicate his techniques and reproduce his eclectic array of classic motifs. The knowledge I have gained from seeing and analysing the marquetry laid before me has allowed me to fully illustrate and explain his working methods. Only when I have seen evidence for myself, have I then made searches for written confirmation from the same period. In that way, you as a reader can check my conclusions by seeing my illustrations and reasonings contained within – or indeed visit the said furniture pieces (where possible) to see the evidence for yourself.

Previous claims about techniques and methods of working practices are shrouded in controversy, mainly because they lack conclusive evidence, opening up opportunities for conjecture. In my case, where I have not been able to gather proof that a practice was indeed followed, I will clearly declare it, allowing you the reader to form your own conclusions. The latter scenario does occur, but only exceptionally.

My book describes the tools and materials used during Chippendale's period. Early hand fret saws, plus the mechanical reciprocating fret saws are detailed, both in construction and use. Packet and the classic fret sawing methods are illustrated and explained in detail.

Fret sawing methods form the cornerstone of this book, and my discoveries give conclusive evidence of 18th century treadle fret saws, which were used in larger London-based marquetry workshops. The findings finally lay to rest any misconceptions that may have been previously held. Veneers, sawn from the log, produce startling revelations which many restorers will find hard to accept, but prove how marqueteurs and their contemporaries across Europe led the field in innovative thinking and skill. The range and type of veneers used are detailed, including the dyes that were used to produce the array of colours used with artistic panache. Adhesives, also common to the period, as well as other materials teach you how to prepare and assemble marquetry and veneering work.

Chippendale's approach

Chippendale described himself as an 'upholder', implying that he was capable of supplying every aspect of furniture and fitting which his customers required. These included floor furniture, wall furniture, wallpapers, curtains and blinds for windows and carpets for the floors. He was the supreme entrepreneur, capable of supplying sumptuous creations for formal staterooms, as well as providing more basic furniture for servant accommodation.

He preferred large commissions where he could supply every need for every room, from attic to basement. He had a workforce of approximately 50 journeymen in his St Martin's Lane workshops, and any number of contractors whom he deployed from time to time. During his time, over 700 items of household furniture and fittings emerged from his London workshops, a figure far in excess of his contemporaries operating in the same vicinity. His clientele ranged from titled personages to famous and influential businessmen, both within the capital city in which he worked and the provincial cities and towns across England and Scotland.

During the 1750s and 1760s he supplied furniture in the Gothic and Chinese style but, by 1769 he had found a need for making and supplying marquetry-decorated furniture. It's this period where this book commences. From 1769 towards the end of his working life in 1775, he was finally able to supply furniture which for the very first time, included the full range of colour. He embraced the medium with consummate artistry and style on a scale that, in my opinion, has never been equalled.

Over the intervening years, sadly, the dyed colours he used have all but disappeared, and we have become accustomed to viewing his creations in their current ghostly mid-brown state. We have to remind ourselves that while colour was desirable in an artistic sense, it also had a practical application, because it brightened up interiors, which had to rely on illumination from candles and open fires. Shades of green, red, gold, yellow, and purple collectively created reflective images, both in natural daylight and under night-time illumination. In the mid-18th century, colour was the order of the day, both in furniture and fittings as it was in room decor on ceilings and walls.

Chippendale's collaborators

Thomas Chippendale spent the majority of his time working with the celebrated architect Robert Adam. Adam's plasterwork to ceilings and walls complement the decor on furniture and fitting supplied by Chippendale, which the former skilfully supplied, in the Yorkshire houses of Harewood, Newby Hall, Burton Constable Hall, and Nostell Priory.

Adam worked with the celebrated Yorkshire plasterer Joseph Rose, whose supreme skills complemented in style and colour all that Chippendale supplied, and the collective results bear witness to the successful collaboration the three men enjoyed. While today the plasterwork has, in the main, lost its initial impact of colour, we have to remind ourselves that a total polychromatic programme was achieved by Adam, Rose and Chippendale on each of their joint commissions. Examples of Adam and Rose's work are shown in Figures 1.13 and 1.14.

It's at this stage that I have to introduce you to a fourth member of the team, a man who specialised in marquetry and a master of 18th century working practices, whose exquisite marquetry occurs time and again across the collection. Throughout this book you

Figure 1.13 Ceiling by Robert Adam at Harewood House, with plasterwork by Joseph Rose

will see for yourself why it is possible to recognise the hand of one individual as clearly as looking at his signature. Sadly, we will perhaps never know his name, or anything about his personal life. What I do know, however, is that he was a highly talented mature marqueteur, a thinking man, displaying exceptional skill and dexterity gained, I imagine, through years of experience. From that evidence alone we can see he was a proud and disciplined man.

Tradesmen today often complain that the designer who created the work overshadows those who perform the work. In this case 'the designer' – Thomas Chippendale – deserves all the plaudits I can bestow on him. As you will find out in this book, not only was he the accomplished designer, but he clearly also understood technically the work his skilled workforce

Figure 1.14 Close-up of the ceiling by Robert Adam in the Gallery at Harewood House

was performing, inasmuch as he actually intervened on a number of occasions to make their tasks possible. Without his personal intervention the techniques I first discover, then describe and replicate, could not have happened.

List of classic motifs used in the marquetry format

Knowing the range of motifs Chippendale and Adam used when they created their interior designs helps our own understanding of the style and harmony they achieved. Seeing the motifs will help you understand why they became and still remain standard bearers of architectural artistry.

A motif can be one of many things: vases, urns, female figures, goats' heads, rams' heads, satyr masks, griffins, sphinxes, fans, acanthus leaves, paterae, berries, laurel leaf swags, ribbons, scrolls, guilloches, Greek keys and perhaps the most repeated motif of all (particularly by Adam), the anthemion or, as we call it today, the honeysuckle. These can be displayed singularly to make an artistic statement, or collectively to add style and flow to a creation. In marquetry they are sometimes used both artistically and technically – the two requirements being interdependent. Examples of the technical versus artistic requirement became evident during my research of the marquetry work, as detailed in this book, and during construction of the replica Diana and Minerva commode, described in Chapter 6.

It's clear that Chippendale did not produce all his own art and design work, and certainly the strong union with Robert Adam, which saw them working together on most of the large commissions, points to a collaboration of skills. There is also evidence of artistic recruitment from the continent, when the Swiss artist Angelica Kauffmann (1741–1807) was employed by Adam to paint ceilings and mural decorations in many of his houses. It's also possible that her work provided the inspiration for medallions found on furniture. Whether that includes marquetry artwork such as the two medallions – Diana and Minerva – and the painted medallion on the matching Secretaire remains unproven. Kauffman married the Venetian artist Antonio Zucchi (1726–95), who also worked for Adam and had joined him previously on his tour of Italy.

As I write here in 2017, I realise my journey spans over twenty years. When I started out, little did I realise that I would encounter such a diverse collection of historical masterpieces and witness ground-breaking events on such a grand scale. During this enthralling journey, I have been constantly reminded of the galaxy of eminent people whose genius I have touched, savoured and learned from, and which I humbly acknowledge. These talented men, with their fertile minds, dexterous hands and seductive creations, have given me the greatest marquetry masterclass I am ever likely to receive in my lifetime.

So join me on my journey of discovery, as you travel through the pages of this book meeting men, named and unnamed, of celebrity status or unknown.

I trust my long and fruitful research will satisfy your intellectual curiosity.

CHAPTER 2

MATERIALS AND TOOLS

INTRODUCTION

In order to understand how and why mid-18th century English marquetry furniture evolved as it did, we need to look in detail at both the materials and the tools that made this evolution possible. While we enjoy and admire Chippendale's classic designs, it will help to understand fully how his journeymen transformed those designs into the marquetry images that inspire us today. Identifying and understanding each individual process, and discovering the materials and tools used to create them, are fundamental to each stage of production.

This chapter takes us inside a London marquetry workshop of around 1769, where newly-developing working methods were emerging. These methods, driven mainly by the need to produce images in the new and exciting style, led to the use of new materials in the form of newly-found exotic veneers arriving from foreign lands, both east and west of London. The new array of marquetry motifs also demanded vibrant colours to highlight and bring realism to the images that our designer artistically introduced on his furniture. These multi-coloured images called for the introduction of dyed veneers. In addition, glues, and the tools needed to lay the veneers to their substrates, are covered in depth in this chapter, both from my own experience of working with hot animal glue and from the images and English text of Roubo's marquetry translation.

New tools had to be made and used in order to skilfully craft the cutting and shaping of motifs that the classic marquetry introduced. We will examine the different types of fretsaws available for the purpose of cutting intricate patterns, in many cases cutting multiple copies from one packet of one veneer type.

One type of fretsaw, namely the treadle saw, plays a major part in my reproduction of classic marquetry work, bringing me to a firm conclusion as to its presence and use within the walls of the London workshop.

The craft knife also plays a major part in producing classic style motifs, such as building fans using a jig, which we call the 'template method'. Another craft knife was made to 'inlay' marquetry motifs into a veneer already glued to the substrate, and I will be showing clear evidence of the use of both knives in Chapter 3.

Hand-made hollowed punches made it possible to produce uniform small-to-medium size round berries. Each hollowed punch was made fit-for-purpose to match the sizes shown on the designs.

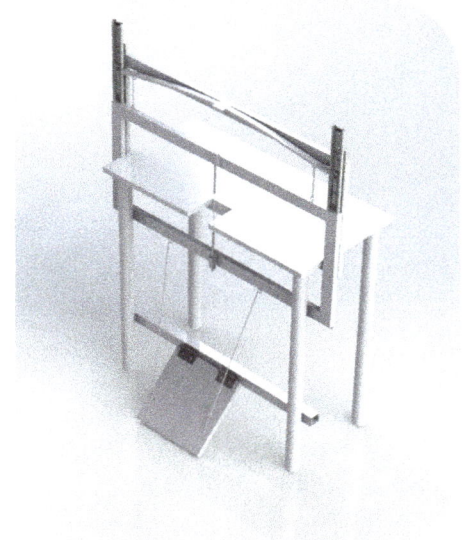

Chapter 2 | Materials & Tools

During the six-year period (1769–75) when we see Chippendale's marquetry collection emerge, we also see a cessation of techniques and working practices that had previously been deployed. Out went the well-used 'packet' method of cutting marquetry patterns, initiated and used successfully by André-Charles Boulle (1642–1732), and with it came the end of his famous *'premier-partie'* and *'contre-partie'* (positive and negative) matching marquetry work. Boulle mastered this technique, which dominated European furniture making for almost a century, while encouraging his counterparts to mimic his style.

In addition, out went the method of inlaying marquetry directly into the solid wood substrate. This method, to be fair, preceded Boulle's packet fretsaw method, dating back as far as the 14th century, when marquetry panels first started appearing in monasteries and churches across cities in and around northern Italy. In its place came another form of inlay, where marquetry was inserted onto a background veneer already glued to the substrate. This practice, using a small inlay knife, was widely used not only on Chippendale furniture but also by other firms across the city. We have evidence of such a firm being deployed as a contractor to the Chippendale workshop (see Figure 3.8 in Chapter 3, page 54).

Finally, out went parquetry as a geometric background design, as used profusely on French cabinet work during the reigns of both King Louis XIV and XV. Across Britain, the classic style was the new design concept, demanding new materials, new tools and an innovative and talented workforce to match. Eighteenth-century marqueteurs achieved these conceptual changes and with them, in my opinion, produced a collection of English marquetry furniture still unrivalled to this day.

The materials and the tools the marqueteurs introduced, along with the techniques explained in Chapter 3, provide the backcloth to understanding the rest of this publication. Knowledge gained from these two chapters will greatly amplify your 'stewardship' of the marquetry and, with it, allow a better realisation of the skills, artistry and pleasure the collection offers when reading the chapters that follow.

I have tried, where possible, to separate material-type subjects from tool subjects, but there are instances where it is not possible to cover one subject without talking about the other. Similarly, it's not always possible to talk about a certain tool or a type of material without showing or talking about the *technique* they were used on. For this reason some overlapping will occur, but I have tried to aim for clarity in the topics I write on. I trust you will forgive the minimal amount of overlapping that occurs during this and the next chapter.

MATERIALS

Veneer selection was paramount to the success of the new marquetry-veneered furniture that was to emerge during the 1770s. This was a new and exciting concept in Chippendale's already acclaimed solid-carved-wood medium. Finding and retaining the right selection of veneers did not come to him immediately though, and, as we will see in Chapter 8, early experiments had to be shelved. However, within a couple of years (1769–71), he established a set of veneers that were to stay with him for the rest of his working life.

The choice of background veneers for which marquetry would be displayed essentially consisted of two species: West Indian satinwood (*Zanthoxylum flavum*) found in Florida Keys and the West Indies, and East Indian rosewood (*Dalbergia latifolia*), found in Burma and India. On rare occasions Chippendale used sycamore (*Acer pseudoplatanus*) treated with iron sulphate to create harewood (see below) and, in three instances, holly (*Ilex aquifolium*).

Satinwood and rosewood, however, dominated the selection, and it's also worth noting that our designer used these woods to reflect the gender of the person they were intended for. If the item of furniture was intended for a gentleman, such as a library writing table, then the dark coloured Indian rosewood was used. If the piece was intended for a female member of the house, such as a dressing table, then the lighter gold-coloured satinwood was selected.

To border both of these species, he selected South American tulipwood (*Dalbergia frutescens*) every time. This is a vivid multi-coloured stripy veneer perfect for cross banding borders.

Within the designs he introduced a small range of other tropical hard woods, shown in Table 2.1:

Figure 2.1 East Indian rosewood

Figure 2.2 West Indian satinwood

Figure 2.3 South America tulipwood

Figure 2.4 East Indian padauk

Figure 2.5 Indian/ Sri Lankan ebony

Figure 2.6 South America purpleheart

Table 2.1 Tropical hardwords introduced by Chippendale

Common name	Botanical name	Origin
Padauk	*Pterocarpus dalbergiodes*	Andaman Islands
Ebony	*Diospyrus ebenum*	India and Sri Lanka
Purpleheart	*Peltogyne pubescens*	South America

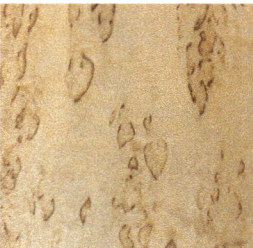

Figure 2.7
Ash

Figure 2.8
Birch (Masur)

Figure 2.9
Boxwood

Figure 2.10
Maple

Figure 2.11
Sycamore

Table 2.2 Temperate hardwords introduced by Chippendale

Common name	Botanical name	Origin
Ash	*Fraxinus excelsior*	UK & Europe
Birch (Masur)	*Betula pendula*	UK & Europe
Boxwood	*Buxus sempervirens*	UK & Europe
Maple	*Acer platinoides*	UK & Europe
Sycamore	*Acer pseudolatanus*	UK & Europe

Like the tropical woods, a small selection of temperate hardwoods were also added, listed in Table 2.2 and illustrated in Figures 2.7–2.11.

Harewood

One other veneer to add to the list is 'harewood'. This is essentially sycamore or maple veneers immersed into a bath of iron sulphate, which changes the colour of the white woods to silver/grey. Chippendale used harewood as a background foil on two commissions which I will be covering in later chapters.

The name harewood creates much confusion, especially within the pages of this book, since the longest commission of Chippendale's working life was spent at Harewood House in my home county of Yorkshire. That apart, it's important at this early stage to explain the origin of the name.

I am indebted to Dr Adam Bowett (furniture and wood historian) for his researches and discovery. The first occurrence of the term is 'airewood' mentioned by the 16th century diarist John Evelyn, who refers to wood of the maple tree called airewood, used for making musical instruments, mainly lutes. When Thomas Chippendale delivered a pier table made for the circular dressing room in Harewood House in 1772, he described the table in his bill as being constructed from 'airwood', which may have been his interpretation from the earlier spelling. What still remains unsolved is the change of spelling to 'harewood', which is what the process is known as today.

I am also indebted, this time, to Professor Joyce Hill, former lecturer on Anglo-Saxon history at Leeds University. Professor Hill was able to confirm:

> "*Har wudu* (adjective + noun) thus literally means 'a grey wood' – that is to say, most probably a wood that is not dense enough to be called 'dark'. There is no instance of a compound noun *harwudu* referring to a particular kind of wood, or indeed of the separate adjective + noun being so applied. The only way to interpret *har wudu* is as a description of a wood in the sense of a substantial stand of trees."

While that does not mean the name identifies one particular type of tree or the colour of the timber or the bark, it does mean that a group of trees would be called *'Har Wudu'* meaning 'grey wood'. This is interesting because we know the Harewood family name was changed from Harwood to Harewood at some time in the past, and that would account for the link with the

Figure 2.12
Maple

Figure 2.13
Sycamore

Figure 2.14
Figured sycamore

Anglo-Saxon meaning of the name *'har'* grey and *'wudu'* wood. Is the change of spelling the link to the title of the treated sycamore we now call harewood? In Adam Bowett's book, *Woods in British Furniture Making 1400-1900*, on page 94, he writes: "The transition from airwood to harewood seems to have occurred at the turn of the 18th and 19th centuries."

This follows the earlier use of treated sycamore veneers, by 18th century furniture makers such as Ince and Mayhew, Gillows of Lancaster, and Chippendale, who each displayed the silver/grey stained veneers on selected furniture. You will find 'harewood' used by Chippendale on selected commissions covered in this book.

Holly

Finally, I have to talk about the most important veneer of all. I refer, of course, to holly (*Ilex aquifolium*), with its origins in the UK and Europe. Over 175 different species grow around the world. In each case the heartwood is creamy-white, sometimes found with grey mineral casts and consisting of little or no figuring.

Holly trees should be cut in winter, sliced into veneers immediately and dried before the summer, in order to avoid discolouration of the timber. The grain tends to be irregular, but has a fine even texture. Its velvety touch in the veneer form makes it a marqueteur's joy to work with, being perhaps the softest hardwood available. The ability to cut and shape veneers with a small craft knife is an important feature of this wood, helping marqueteurs to achieve the highest standard of workmanship when making such items as fans.

Holly, however, holds a more important attribute for the make-up of marquetry work: the molecular structure and even texture of holly, coupled with its natural white colour, make it ideally suited to dye penetration. For this reason it was used extensively for producing the dyed colours that added vibrancy to Chippendale's creations. Some of these colours are shown in Figure 2.15. Dye specialists in London and across Europe used the species during 1770–80 when marquetry-decorated furniture was at its prime.

Other materials used

Over and above veneers, ivory was selectively used on Chippendale's more important works. The ivory was always skilfully engraved to complement his design elements (see Figure 2.16).

Figure 2.15 Natural holly and different colours of dyed holly veneers.

Figure 2.16* Ivory head skilfully engraved.

* *Private collection – reproduced by kind permission*

The marquetry work was further enhanced with the addition of sandshading and artwork applied with a fine artist's brush and not, as initially claimed, with a pen. I will cover pen/artwork in Chapter 3.

Chippendale also used brass mounts on his marquetry furniture instead of ormolu (gilded bronze), thus understating the overall effect, yet proving that his choice of metal balanced perfectly with his marquetry themes.

Inherent timber problems

One aspect that most observers of Chippendale's marquetry furniture will not appreciate, unless they have first-hand experience, is the enormous challenge that tropical hardwoods presented to his journeymen. Working with these timbers, compared to working with temperate hardwoods obtained across Europe, required a whole new approach to sawing from the log, fretsawing, knife cutting, gluing, sanding and finishing.

The reasons are many, but the overriding one is the extra hardness of the tropical species and, since they were used mainly as backgrounds for the softer temperate woods, they were always present and required special attention. For instance, it is not possible to cut satinwood, rosewood, tulipwood, padauk, purpleheart and African ebony freehand with a small craft knife. With these six woods, it is always prudent to use a veneer saw against a straight edge when cutting straight lines, either with or against the grain. Sawing with a fretsaw requires that tropical veneers are always placed between other veneers in the packet, to prevent the timbers breaking at tight turns in the marquetry work.

Indian rosewood is unique because of the inherent wax found in the cells of the timber, which has to be removed prior to cutting and assembling; otherwise the oil leaches into adjacent veneers and stains them permanently.

Padauk leaks red dust and ebony black dust, both when sanded and later when polished. Both species must always be sealed to prevent this happening; otherwise the two colours (red and black) leach into adjacent lighter coloured veneers and stain them permanently. Today, a composite sanding sealer is brushed into these species prior to sanding and polishing, so as to prevent leaching.

It's worth noting, however, that I have never observed any leaching from either padauk or ebony on any of Chippendale's work. This is because all veneers, prior to use, were treated by brushing on hot animal glue to the 'face' sides and covering with plain white parchment paper, before being placed between two flat boards and clamped overnight, or until they were needed. The glue acts as a sealant by filling the grain of the wood, so that any subsequent leaching is prevented. However, this practice was not performed solely to prevent coloured dust leaching across species, but also to make the veneers more stable during cutting and fretsawing.

I doubt whether the leaching problem was ever noticed by 18th century marqueteurs, because pre-sealing with hot glue and parchment paper was a matter of standard working practice. To put this to the test, I performed an exercise with a group of marqueteurs at the Leeds Marquetry Group some years ago. I set them the task of making two sets of table mats, one set consisting of two contrasting veneers, padauk and sycamore, and the other half making the same mats with ebony and sycamore. Both groups were asked to pre-seal the face sides of each veneer with plain paper glued on with hot animal glue. For them, this was their first

Figure 2.17 Padauk on sycamore.

Figure 2.18 Sycamore on padauk.

introduction to classic marquetry techniques and they were impressed with the process – so much so that the Leeds group invested in a gluepot. Each group made up a fretsawing packet, consisting of padauk and sycamore for group A, and ebony and sycamore for group B, and pasted the same fretsaw design to the top veneer. I then asked the two groups to carry out 'packet fretsawing' which is not part of the classic methodology, as you will see later in this chapter. Packet sawing belongs to the Boulle period, which was replaced during the mid-18th century.

On completion, and when the two contrasting but matching tablemats were glued to a substrate, they were sanded and polished without adding any sanding sealer to prevent leaching. The results of both the ebony and the padauk (the latter seen in Figures 2.17 and 2.18) were totally free of colour leaching.

The changes

Chippendale's design requirements called for a new practice in veneer production, producing thinner veneers than had ever been previously achieved. Without this, none of what was to follow could have occurred. It called for a new and untried approach to dyeing veneers in the sheet form, as against dyeing small pre-cut elements as used by European cabinetmakers of the same period. It called for a fretsaw with a turning-throat capable of sawing panels up to 450 mm (18 inches) long, and stable enough to accurately cut multiple layers of veneers which, when stacked together, measured anything between 6 and 9 mm (1/4 – 1/3 inch) thick. It called for a new practice of constructing duplicate copies of motifs from a pre-formed template using a small craft knife. It called for bending and pressing assembled marquetry panels around compound angles and, finally, it called for the ability to mass-produce marquetry motifs to meet some of Chippendale's more ambitious commissions.

Each of these changes I will examine closely in the following pages, starting with the most important product that would determine whether the other changes could be achieved or not – namely the ability to produce the thin veneers that were to become the trademark of Chippendale's creations during the following six years.

Veneer production

The most compelling evidence I discovered during my research finally convinced me of a practice I had initially discounted, simply because it sounded too incongruous to be true. I discovered, through my personal inspection, that throughout Chippendale's entire marquetry collection the veneers (where marquetry work existed) consistently measured 1 mm thick! Veneers on other parts of the furniture, where marquetry was not needed, tended to be 2 to 2.5 mm thick. This was an unmistakable indication that the marquetry veneers and the background veneer that surrounded them had been purposely thinned.

Two questions immediately sprang to mind – how was that achieved and why did the veneer need to be that thin?

Why and how are veneers so thinly cut?

I had read articles about 18th century sawyers who could saw ten leaves of veneers per inch from a log. These sawyers had a 'lifetime's experience' and were clearly acknowledged by receiving recognition in Roubo's Volume 3 on marquetry techniques. The engraving from Roubo, in Figure 2.19, shows two men sawing a log with the two-handled frame-saw.

If we consider this task of producing ten veneers to one inch, it's perhaps easier in metric calculation, where 25 mm equals 1 inch. This relates to each veneer being (25/10) 2.5 mm thick. However, half of the thickness is lost in sawdust because of the waste generated from the kerf of the saw, thus leaving each veneer about 1.2 to 1.3 mm thick. My previously-established evidence that the finished thickness of veneers on Chippendale's furniture is 1 mm provides confirmation, with the additional thickness lost through final sanding and leveling after laying and pressing the veneers to the substrate. Clearly these journeymen sawyers became known by reputation, because their unique skill is noted by Roubo who stated, somewhat disapprovingly, that the veneers were '*très mince*' (very thin), but then qualified that by adding: *"presqu' rien lorsque l'ouvrage est fini; ce qu'il faut absolument éviter, quoique cela soit d'usage à présent"*, which translated means *"almost nothing when the work is finished, which is absolutely necessary to avoid, even though that is the custom at present"*.

Chapter 2 | Materials & Tools

Figure 2.19* *Two men with a lifetime's experience sawing ten veneers to the inch from the log. The frame-saw (Roubo's Fig. 6) has no set on the teeth. The small hacksaw (Roubo's Fig. 12) is used to accurately register the cuts on the top of the log prior to using the frame-saw.*

* *Courtesy of Colonial Williamsburg Foundation USA*

Roubo's five volumes were written in Paris between 1769 and 1775, and the technique just described was witnessed in Paris by the author. We can only assume, therefore, that either sawyers with the same skills operated in London, or that the Parisian-based sawyers moved to London where their skills were in demand, or that the thin-sawn veneers were exported from France to London. We do know that marqueteurs started using thin-sawn veneers from 1769, but I have also been able to measure veneers used by other furniture makers prior to that year who operated from London workshops. A pair of matching commodes at Aske Hall in North Yorkshire, made by the French cabinetmaker Pierre Langois, who had workshops in Tottenham Court Road, London, and operated at the same time as Chippendale, used veneers of the same thickness.

A completely different picture evolves in furniture made in France and in Germany during the same period. French furniture made by Riesener and Leleu shows veneers of thicknesses between 1.5 and 2 mm, but there is evidence that these two makers did re-sand the veneers on more than one occasion to revive the dyed colours. Riesener was so obsessed with maintaining the dyed colours that he was known to have sanded one piece three times. Measurements in areas where secondary sanding would not have been made (areas out of sight on the cabinet) measured 2.5 to 3 mm thick.

David Roentgen, the celebrated German cabinetmaker and marqueteur, used veneers at about 3 mm thick, but he used a completely different technique in adding dyed veneers to his marquetry work. After cutting out a piece intended for a picture, he would stain (dye) it and allow it to dry, before inserting it into the picture. Each piece was meticulously built up in this manner. In Germany also, the problem of producing thinner veneers was compounded by the rules of the cabinet-makers' guild operating during the mid-18th century. Only two foreign journeymen could be employed in any one workshop. The only exceptions to this were workshops operating within large cities, such as Berlin and Munich, which were allowed more.

Why did they want veneers so thin?

By using my own knowledge of veneering and marquetry, and through examination of London-based marquetry furniture, I can confidently offer the answer to this second question. My five principal reasons are as follows:

1 The ability to dye 'sheets' of veneers, as against small marquetry samples, thus speeding up colour penetration evenly across the sheet.

2 To veneer furniture across concave and convex surfaces: the thinner the veneer, the more easily it bends.

3 To permit use of a small craft knife to cut and build marquetry motifs.

4 To produce multiple sets of classic-style motifs from one sawing, which creates the all-important symmetry to the new design medium.

5 To achieve tight marquetry joints, without the inherent saw kerf of the past.

The two main contributing factors for making these tasks possible were the discovery of holly and the ability to saw it into very thin veneers. The ability to saw other veneers thinly also made task 2 possible.

Animal glue

An adhesive created from skins, bones and tendons of horses by prolonged boiling, this glue is formed through hydrolysis of the collagen, a protein of fibrous connective tissue readily turned into gelatine. The word collagen itself derives from the Greek '*kolla*' – glue. These proteins form a molecular bond with the glued object.

The glue is applied hot, typically with a brush, and then pressed into place with a 'veneer hammer'. The glue is kept warm in a glue pot and kept at the right consistency by the addition of water. The temperature should be maintained at a constant 140°F. Today thermostatically controlled gluepots maintain the temperature for us, but in the 18th century the glue was held in a pot, which in turn was immersed in another pot holding hot water (see Figure 2.20). Maintaining a constant temperature of the water relied on experience.

Two things had to be avoided:

1 The glue should never be allowed to reach boiling point.

2 The consistency of the glue should be maintained with water, so that the glue flowed from the brush in a steady stream – not lumpy or watery, but with a smooth even consistency.

CHAPTER 2 | Materials & Tools

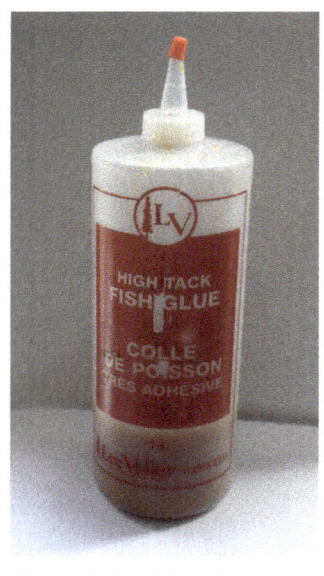

Figure 2.20 Glue pot in a bain marie

Figure 2.21 Fish glue

Since marqueteurs used this method of preparing their glue on a daily basis, it became second nature to prepare and maintain the glue correctly when a gluing session was about to commence. I had personal experience of this when working as an apprentice upholsterer in a workshop in Leeds (D. Fielding & Sons, Cabinetmakers and Upholsterers – sadly no more) during the 1950s. Gluepots, without thermostats, were used every day by the cabinetmakers for gluing up furniture joints, applying veneers and laying leather to tops of writing tables, etc. The water in the outer pot was heated on a small electric hot plate, set on a low setting, so that the temperature of the glue and the water in the outer pot was maintained throughout the day.

Fish glue

Initially, fish glue was made from the heads, bones and skin of the fish, but this glue tended to be too thin and less sticky. Through time, it was discovered that the air bladders of a sturgeon produced satisfactory glue that was white and tasteless. It eventually was named 'isinglass', meaning a pure transparent form of gelatin. It was used in glue and jellies and as a clarifying agent. It is sometimes referred to as ichthyic, meaning 'fishlike'.

Today's modern fish glue, seen in Figure 2.21 in the liquid form, is made from an extract of cod fish skins. I buy mine from Lee Valley Tools in Canada since, so far, I have not been able to source a supplier in the UK.

The glue can be applied either cold or hot, and is water-resistant. The glue is ideal for antique restoration and successfully glues glass, ceramics, metal, wood, cork, paper and leather. I only ever use the glue in the cold state. Like animal glue, this product is fully reversible, and application of water and a hot iron softens the glue, releasing its bond with the substrate.

It was used during the 18th century where longer 'open times' were needed, to position and secure materials in place. The open time of fish glue is about one and a half hours, whereas hot animal glue grabs almost instantly. The setting or pressing time is also much longer, usually around 12 hours, thus requiring clamps to hold materials in place during that period.

Fish glue was used to glue non-wood type veneers in the 18th century, such as tortoiseshell, brass, and pewter. While these types of veneers were not used on Chippendale's furniture, brass mounts and ivory were, and perhaps fish glue was preferred to animal glue for these materials – I have not had the opportunity to lift any existing brass mounts or ivory veneers to see whether this is the case. The glue is also perfect for sanding, offering the finest and flattest surface of all glues I have ever experienced. Added to that, in-situ repairs to small damaged areas in wood can be effectively repaired using sanded particles of the wood that match the affected area: mix the sanded dust with a small amount of fish glue to produce a thick, woody-type glue, and work it into the damaged area. After the glue and its wood dust has fully dried, sand the area back to the level of the surrounding areas and the damage disappears.

My use of fish glue is quite sparse, since most of my work is glued with hot animal glue. Occasionally, if I have a large marquetry panel that covers, say, a 'shallow' incurved area, and I want to glue the panel down in one piece, I would select fish-glue and use a vacuum bag to apply the pressure. The long open time allows plenty of time to position the panel in place, before pressure is applied. I used fish glue on the two end panels of the replica Diana and Minerva commode because they were incurved only slightly and allowed the entire panel to be positioned perfectly prior to applying pressure. Conversely, the domed door on the same commode has a deep incurved surface and can only be glued with hot animal glue, using the stick-as-you-go and piece-by-piece method. Chapter 6 illustrates both gluing processes. I discuss the stick-as-you-go method in Chapter 3.

TOOLS

Having the right tools for the job was just as important to 18th century journeymen as it is today. In most cases, they would 'manufacture' their own, and shape and fashion them to their own personal needs. I know from researching their work what type of tool performed the job in hand, and in most cases, there is sufficient evidence from engravings of the size, shape and material used to manufacture them.

For marquetry work, the range of tools is relatively small when compared to those used by, say, a cabinet maker or a wood carver, but despite this, the tools had to be made with precision and purpose. While most of the tools are readily documented, leaving no doubt as to which were used, there is very little recorded about the introduction and use of the most important tool of all – the fretsaw. The only type shown in 18th century documents is the hand-held fretsaw, seen in Figure 2.22, which shows Roubo's detailed illustrations of its construction, leaving us to conjecture about the use of other more sophisticated models.

Despite my extensive research to try and find records relating to mechanical-type saws, I have not been able to prove that the reciprocating treadle saw was used during the 18th century. I am nevertheless convinced that a type of treadle saw was operational. With such scarcity of information I have had to try and evaluate the type of machine that would have been needed to perform the type of marquetry cutting Chippendale's technique demanded. It is from this most unstable beginning that my evaluation takes place, and I trust you will hear all the arguments and reasonings as I try to 'make a case' for one type of saw over the other. My judgements are based on practical experiences as a marquetry cutter, specialising in Chippendale's working methods, over the past twenty years.

Fretsaw invention

Throughout Europe, the fretsaw provided the primary means for cutting marquetry shapes. The size, shape and design of the fretsaw frame may have altered over the years, as well as the manufacture of the blade, but as a tool it still remains unchallenged today as the most versatile and adaptable instrument available to

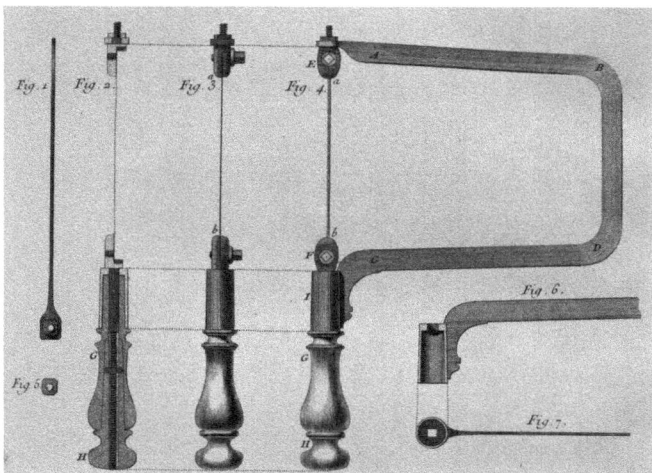

Figure 2.22* Roubo's engraving of a hand-held fretsaw.

marqueteurs. With its introduction, a change of technique took place and intarsia (to inlay) practised during the 15th and 16th centuries across northern Italy was replaced in the early part of the 17th century with marquetry (to overlay).

The invention of the fretsaw is attributed to an unnamed German clockmaker, who first filed teeth along a stretched-out clock spring, to create the first fretsaw blade. The date of this invention is unknown, leaving us to guess at a period somewhere in the early part of the 17th century. The blade, clamped across the ends of a wooden frame and held in tension, allowed metals to be pierced out for clock components. It's interesting to observe that fretwork, in solid wood, often adorns clock casements, suggesting that carriage and pendulum clocks were the first 'cabinets' to be decorated in this manner. Its uses for other applications soon grew, and before long wood in the veneer form was being cut and shaped, producing elaborate marquetry designs.

Figure 2.23 shows an early means of holding a veneer flat while allowing a marqueteur to fretsaw within the 'V' shaped cutout, holding the saw in one hand while the other turns and hold the veneer.

Early fretsaws had a limited use, due mainly to the design of the saw frame, with the first models having a throat of only 75 mm to 100 mm (3 to 4 inches) (the throat is the distance between the blade and the back of

* *Courtesy of Colonial Williamsburg Foundation USA*

Chapter 2 | Materials & Tools

Figure 2.23

the saw frame). The depth of throat determines the size of material one can cut. Since the tool was primarily intended for sawing out tiny clock parts, the short throat was not a limiting factor. However, as marquetry patterns for decorating furniture panels increased in size, so the need for a fretsaw frame that could accommodate such panels became apparent.

Marquetry cutter's bench

Making larger fretsaws, however, only provided half the cutters' needs. A table or vice to hold the material in position while sawing was required. Early solutions ranged from a simple flat board clamped to a bench (as seen in Figure 2.23) to a more elaborate wooden frame housing a seating platform, with a mechanical device to clamp and release the wood during sawing.

The design requirements of the wooden bench were clearly defined from the outset, but in reality, I imagine that trial and re-adjustments occurred before the bench finally served all the cutters' needs. First, the bench had to be portable, so it could be placed under a window to catch maximum daylight. Since candle light was the only means of illumination in the 18th century, cutting intricate patterns with a fine blade required good vision.

Secondly, the vice or clamp, attached to the bench, had to be at eye level to offer the cutter the best view of the work. Finally, the vice had to have a 'foot-controlled mechanical device', which would allow the mating faces of the vice to be closed together, under foot pressure, leaving both hands free to control and rotate the veneers during cutting. Once these design requirements were achieved, the forerunner of marquetry's most recognised and documented tool was born. At this stage it was known as the 'marquetry cutter's bench' (shown in Roubo's eloquent engraving in Figure 2.24) and was in use from about 1620.

The marquetry cutter's bench and the independent hand-held fretsaw served marqueteurs for the next 140 years. Certainly, prior to and during the productive years of André Charles Boulle (1642–1732), who developed packet fretsawing to a level not previously seen, these tools were combined with immense skill.

Somewhere around the mid-18th century, however, it became apparent that the hand-held saw coupled with packet fretsawing produced an inescapable flaw. It was almost impossible to keep the hand-held saw totally perpendicular to the material held in the vice, and packet sawing produced a permanent visible kerf between two mating pieces, equal to the thickness of the saw blade. The inability to maintain the saw at 90° to the veneer surface resulted in acute angles and bad joints when two contrasting angles were brought together, while the gap caused by the kerf had to be filled to disguise it. This in turn produced a dark 'engraving' line around all mating

Figure 2.24* Roubo's engraving of a marquetry cutter's bench.

* *Courtesy of Colonial Williamsburg Foundation USA*

pieces. It is this line that is the trademark of packet fretsawing, and it is present on the majority of Boulle work and on marquetry work by his contemporaries.

The reciprocating treadle saw

The only documented fretsaw recorded to be in use in the mid-18th century is the hand-held type illustrated in Figure 2.24, and mentioned in Roubo's treatise. However, I firmly believe that a modified 15th century reciprocating saw was available and was used to good effect to produce the marquetry work for decorating Chippendale's furniture. This may appear a bold statement to make, but there is sufficient evidence available of its existence.

To get that evidence, we have to go back in time to around 1480, when a hydraulic reciprocating saw was commonplace in cities in northern Italy. The drawing in Figure 2.25, made by Leonardo da Vinci, shows a water-driven auto-feed reciprocating saw (this is a drawing of a working machine seen by Leonardo in Milan sawing a plank of wood). You can see clearly how the paddled wheel (bottom centre), when turned by a force of water, operates a drive shaft, which in turn forces the saw to reciprocate vertically up and down through the timber. The timber, in turn, is carried on a wooden chariot with wheels, allowing the timber to be pulled through the saw blade by means of a rope fastened to the front of the chariot and extended to a small ratcheted wheel, which increments ratchet-by-ratchet as the timber advances through the saw blade.

The key part of this mechanism is the design of the frame supporting the saw blade. Notice the rectangular wooden structure to which the top of the blade is fixed and the larger rectangular wooden frame that surrounds it. These two frames provide the control to the reciprocating action.

The drawing produced by Leonardo prompted the Leonardo da Vinci Museum in Milan to build a replica model of the saw to show how it worked. This model, shown in Figure 2.26, clearly illustrates how the flow of water would generate movement on the paddled wheel, forcing the drive shaft to move the saw blade through the log. The two wooden rectangular frames provide the all-important support and reciprocating movement for the saw blade, and it is this frame arrangement that led to the invention of the first treadle-operated fretsaw.

If we now consider the saw shown in Figure 2.27, we can see the precise arrangement of two rectangular frames giving support to a fretsaw blade. Like the earlier hydraulic versions, the reciprocating action is identical.

It is clear that the saw went through a transition from being hydraulically driven to foot-driven, while retaining the same two-framed structure. The mechanical transition also explains, perhaps, why no patent records exist for its introductory use as a fretsaw. After all, by 1770 the saw had already been in use in the hydraulic mode for approximately 300 years.

Another clue to its design features is the marquetry cutter's bench shown in Figure 2.24. That arrangement made use of a pedal to control the jaws of the vice, which clamped the marquetry packet in place during sawing. If we put together the hydraulic saw arrangement and add the cutter's bench controls, we begin to see how the treadle saw evolved.

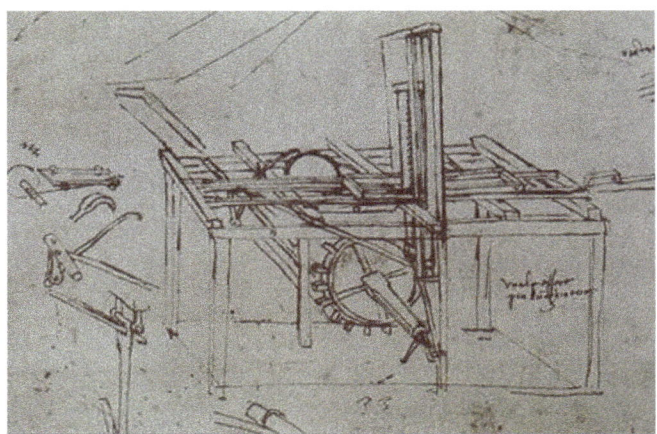

Figure 2.25* *Leonardo's sketch of a water-driven auto-feed reciprocating saw.*

Figure 2.26** *Modern reproduction of the saw in Leonardo's sketch.*

* *Courtesy of Leonardo da Vinci Museum, Milan*
** *Courtesy of National Museum of Science and Technology 'Leonardo da Vinci', Milan*

CHAPTER 2 | Materials & Tools

Figure 2.27

As Figure 2.27 shows, the saw allows the operator to sit at a horizontal table and, under downward pressure of one foot (left or right) on the foot treadle, the inner wooden frame is pulled downwards, causing the fretsaw blade to travel downwards through the small hole in the table. As the treadle reaches its maximum downward movement, the operator removes pressure with the foot causing the frame to be moved upwards under pressure of the return spring, which is provided by the lath of wood (oak, ash or yew) suspended across the top of the inner frame and simply attached by two lengths of string. The saw blade moves through the table again, but this time in an upward direction.

This simple yet effective reciprocating action provides the most perfect sawing control one could hope for. Total control of the saw and precise cutting is achieved almost immediately. As I use this tool, I become more and more convinced of its use during the 18th century. My cutting technique has improved beyond all expectations to a point where perfection is achieved at every visit. I find it so rewarding to follow a line drawing with consummate precision. Surely this was the reason for such exquisite marquetry work, not just on Chippendale's furniture, but throughout Europe during the same period?

If it can transform me (now in my late 70s), from a mediocre sawyer using a power-driven fretsaw, into a competent operator after only a few sessions, then it tells me that it's the tool and not the man that makes the transformation!

The model shown in Figure 2.27 is constructed in wood, with simple metal blade holders and a throat of just 300 mm (12"). The blade sits 'mid-point' between the inner frame; therefore the throat is measured from the blade to either of the two sides of the frame.

An important aspect, however (not always evident to designers until the saw is used), is another, more important 'throat' inherent in every saw of this type, namely the distance between the blade and the operator himself, seated at the table. Since you always have to be close to where the saw is cutting, in order to achieve accuracy, the operator's midriff limits the distance which a veneer can be turned around the saw blade. If, like me, expansion of that part of the anatomy in inches matches the years it has taken to develop, you may find yourself well restricted.

Joking apart, I have seen claims of a reciprocating saw built with an 'endless throat', because the upper frame is linked to the lower frame only by the saw blade, making the claim that the throat is only limited by the size of the room it is housed in. This type of arrangement can only apply to a machine having a very stout and strong blade, suitable for ripping solid timbers. A delicate fretsaw blade would not support such an arrangement. Furthermore, as just discussed, the operator must be able to see the blade and the pattern being cut at very close quarters.

The only modern fittings added to this saw are two metal drawer runners, shown in Figure 2.28. The runners include ball-bearing units to assist a smooth action. Since no such facility existed in the 18th century, it is perhaps likely that the original versions may have included wooden channels made from lignum vitae for

Chapter 2 | Materials & Tools

Figure 2.28

the front frame to pass through. Lignum vitae is a very dense, hard and heavy timber, containing its own wax, which makes it ideal for self-lubricating movement between the two frames during the reciprocating action. As well as its lubricating and durable properties, it is impervious to water penetration, and so was used during this period, for example, to produce paddles on watermills. Lignum vitae was also used by the celebrated clockmaker John Harrison during the 18th century to construct his pendulum, and early marine chronometer clocks, which subsequently led to him winning the coveted longitude prize. His clock movements relied on lignum vitae bushes to provide the all-important self-lubrication which maintained the clocks' unprecedented accuracy.

Aluminium table-mounted treadle saw

After using the first saw (which was expertly made for me by marqueteur and friend Malcolm Slater), I have started using a second model, again built by Malcolm, which is table-mounted and, instead of being constructed from wood, is made of boxed aluminium. (see Figures 2.29 and 2.30). The saw is clamped to a trestle made from boxed steel, which in turn is secured against a wall. A simple angle iron leg provides the final fixing point to prevent any vibration during sawing.

Because the frames are aluminium, the saw is extremely light in weight, while retaining all the strength of the wooden version. Its capacity to stand and be secured in any part of a workshop makes it both portable and less hungry on precious workshop space. Nearly all my fretwork in the production of the marquetry for the

Figure 2.29 Footplate hinged at the heel end.

Diana and Minerva Commode (described in Chapter 6) was performed on these two versions.

It is worth noting that while I own a modern 'top of the range' electric variable-speed fretsaw, the two 'home-made' reciprocating treadle saws out-perform the former in every aspect. The problem with electrically-controlled fretsaws is that they are essentially designed for cutting solid timber, where the strength of the timber around the blade provides stability and control during cutting.

Figure 2.30 Footplate hinged at the toe end.

In marquetry, the veneers are flimsy and the designs are mostly complex, involving many acute bends and twists, which make it difficult to achieve accuracy when the blade movement is outside the control of the sawyer.

Another remarkable comparison between the modern electric saw and the treadle saw concerns the number of blades that break. By design, marquetry-cutting blades have to be thin and hence fragile, and the electric saws do break blades, sometimes with irritating regularity, whereas breakage is a very rare event indeed on the treadle saw. The reason for this lies in the design of the two machines. All modern electric saws are controlled by a 'front-to-back' frame structure with the blade held at the front of the frame. Unfortunately, this design always permits some sideways movement at the front of the frame where the blade is clamped; the tiniest of movement to the side puts strain on a fine blade, particularly evident when fretsawing around tight turns. Consequently, under this condition blades do break. Conversely, the treadle saw is controlled by a left-to-right frame structure, with the blade held centrally within the frame. Sideways movement is impossible because of the rigidity of the two interlocking frames. Making turns while sawing either to the left or the right puts no pressure on the blade whatsoever, and so blade breakages are virtually nil.

You can probably gather my enthusiasm for the treadle saw, and you are right. Having worked with them for a number of years and produced cutting which surpasses anything I have ever achieved before, I strongly recommend conservators, restorers and marquetry enthusiasts to make their own machine, following the detailed plans given on these pages. It amazes me that the left-right frame structure was subsequently replaced with the front-back arrangement, but as already discussed, perhaps the fretsaw manufacturers are aiming the machine at those who shape solid timbers.

You will note in Figure 2.30 that the treadle plate is designed to be used by either the left or right foot. Also, the plate is hinged at the 'toe end', so that when the ropes are attached, the operator presses on the plate with the heel of the foot not the toe. This makes a remarkable difference, because it removes leg muscle strain completely. I found during trials that the first foot plates, seen in Figure 2.29 and hinged at the heel end, did result in slight calf muscle strain after sawing sessions.

Computer Aided Design (CAD) images showing dimensional construction

The illustrations and photos in Figures 2.31–2.36, plus the descriptions in Table 2.3, give you a complete picture of the construction of a treadle saw.

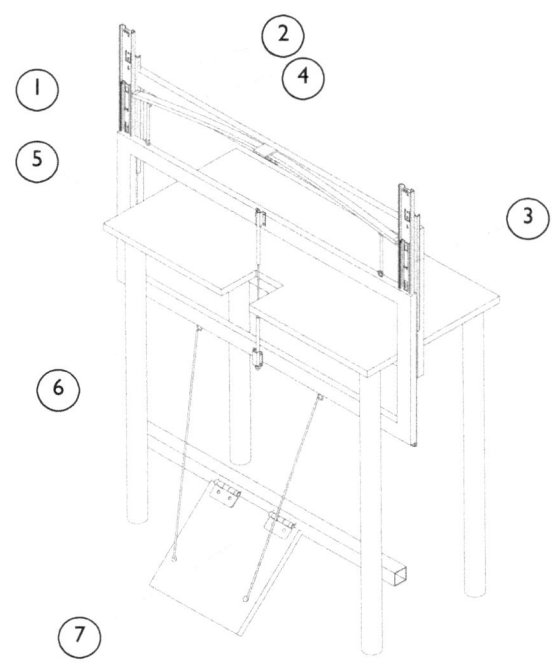

Figure 2.31 Plan view showing the 7 parts from Table 2.3.

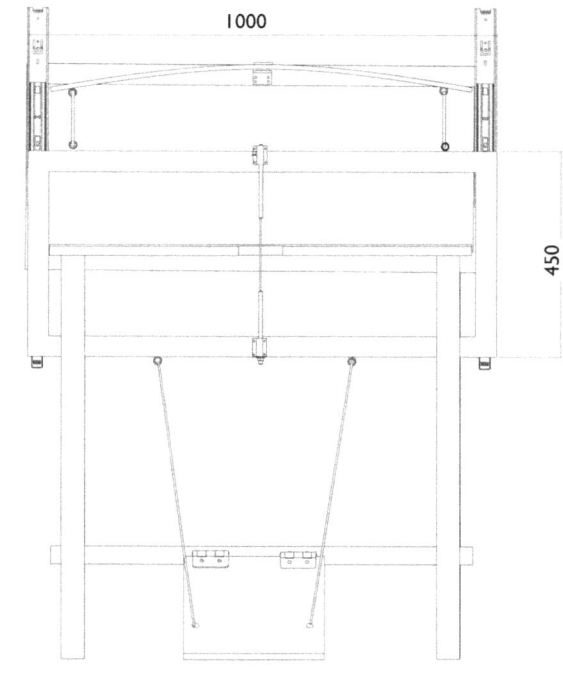

Figure 2.32 Front elevation with external dimensions.

CHAPTER 2 | Materials & Tools

Table 2.3 Components of a treadle saw (key to elements numbered in Figure 2.31)

Item	Description
1	Front-boxed aluminium frame, which floats vertically by attachment to the two drawer sliders (**3**).
2	Rear aluminium boxed frame, fixed to the table.
3	Linear bearing drawer sliders, seen left and right; connects frame (**1**) allowing front frame to move vertically relative to fixed rear frame. Sliders also shown in Figures 2.28 and 2.29.
4	Wooden lath acting as a spring to lift moving frame (**1**) upwards. Clamped in centre of rear frame with a 90° metal clamp held in place with small bolts or screws.
5	Wooden (MDF or Ply) table top, approx 12 mm thick with front insert cutout to allow blade changing. The insert should slide in place by two grooves either side of cutout. The insert is best made from a piece of perspex, with a tiny hole made for the blade to pass through.
6	Fretsaw blade held by moving frame (**1**). It is clamped and tensioned top and bottom with metal clamps and held in tension with threaded nuts. See Figures 2.35 and 2.36.
7	Heel press foot plate held in place with two hinges attached to the table and connected to the lower front frame with two strings.

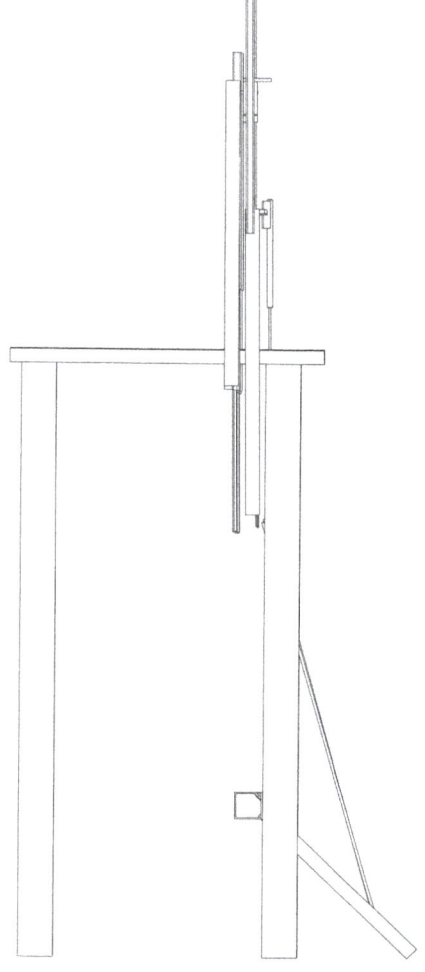

Figure 2.34 Side elevation

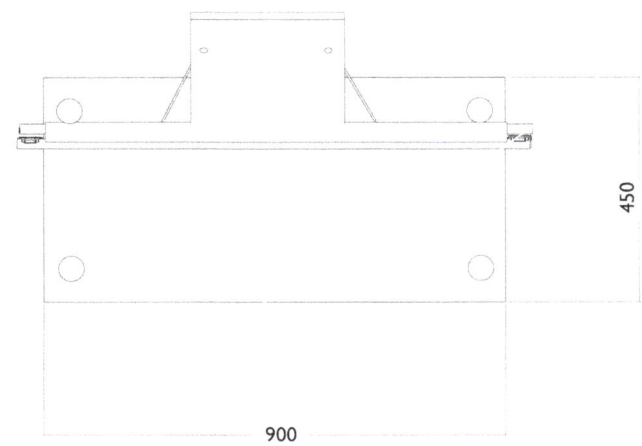

Figure 2.33 Top elevation with internal dimensions.

Figure 2.35 Threaded blade clamp (top and bottom) is tensioned with threaded nuts.

Figure 2.36 Blade clamp fitted above and below the blade showing drilled hole for tightening rod (not shown).

CHAPTER 2 | Materials & Tools

Figure 2.37* Front view

Figure 2.38* Front angled view

Extra wide floor-standing treadle saw

On these two pages we see images of a floor-standing treadle saw copied from an original saw held in a small museum in Karlsruhe, Germany. Students of the University of Applied Sciences and Arts, Hildesheim, Germany, built this replica copy. It is currently held in the museum at Hildesheim.

The saw is 189 cm (6 ft 2.4 inch) high, and 153 cm (5 ft) wide. The table has a working high of 99 cm (3 ft 3 inch). The table size is 66 cm (2 ft 2 inch) x 153 cm (5 ft). Clearly the saw was made to be operated in the standing position, hence its table height as given above. The saw throat, measured from the central blade to both the left and right of the frame is approximately 61 cm (2 ft) either side.

The sawyer has control of the reciprocating action by using either foot on the treadle plate. The advantage the sawyer has in the standing position, against the sitting position, is that the sawyer can move sideways either left or right when the packet being sawn has to pass across their body. I am sure the sawyer would have been highly dexterous in manipulating their stance to allow a packet of veneers to pass across the front of their body while maintaining the sawing action.

The images in Figures 2.37 to 2.43 show construction features to assist in understanding the design. In Figure 2.42 we see how the inner frame is held in place and allowed to slide up and down. In Figure 2.43 note how the metal bracket wraps around the fixed metal plate, but clearly leaves space for the bracket to slide freely in the reciprocating action.

Figure 2.39* Front top half

* Permission of Hildesheim University, Germany

CHAPTER 2 | Materials & Tools

Figure 2.40* Front bottom half

Figure 2.41* Blade holder close-up

The timber used for the construction is beech, but any temperate hardwood would suffice. Steel banding is used to connect the inner frame to the top and bottom elements of the treadle saw, but thin ropes would have the same effect. The central fretsaw blade passes through a drilled hole in the table, shown in Figure 2.41. It is clearly well aligned and small enough to prevent small pieces of sawn marquetry parts from falling through.

Figure 2.42* Detail wire links

Figure 2.43* Locking bracket detail

* *Permission of Hildesheim University, Germany*

CHAPTER 2 | Materials & Tools

Treadle saw summary

Having sung the praises of the treadle saw, it would be only right to point out two possible limitations that the machine may have caused marquetry cutters in the 18th century.

* **Light source** – In the 18th century there was no electricity to illuminate the work, and so a cutter would need as much natural daylight as possible in order to produce accurate cutting. The saw's table, being low down (particularly the seated version), may have been lower than the windows in a workshop, and not in the best position to gain maximum light. Certainly working under candlelight would have been difficult, but we have to remind ourselves that very accurate cutting was achieved by marquetry sawyers during that period.

* **Standing position** – In my view the treadle saw's main failing in the 18th century was the position of the sawyer. I believe that the standing type, seen in Figure 2.37, was ergonomically unsuitable when used for long periods. Stooping over the work while standing on one foot, with the other operating the treadle, would have caused great strain on the back and legs. I think it was for this reason alone that the next invention took place: the introduction of the chevalet, which I discuss next.

Figure 2.44 Chevalet showing the bench seat and treadle foot plate, for use with either left or right foot.

Chevalet or marquetry donkey

I have already highlighted the limitations of the treadle saw, and perhaps it was for these reasons that the next step in the history of the fretsaw evolved. This was the advent of the chevalet, derived from the French word *cheval*, meaning horse. Another name for the bench was 'saw horse', but its most affectionate and romanticised label has always been the 'marquetry donkey'.

As Figures 2.44 and 2.45 show, the horizontal arm is adjusted so that it is maintained at 90° to the jaws of the donkey. This ensures that when two sawn elements are brought together, the mating faces always provide a square joint. To ensure square cutting, the horizontal arm has two adjustments at the two ends of the saw frame. One end allows horizontal adjustment, while the other controls the vertical. The sawing arm is moved forward and backwards along a rod which slides between two bushes. Because the sawing arm cannot move, other

Figure 2.45 The chevalet arm with saw frame holding the blade that spans across the jaws of the vice.

CHAPTER 2 | Materials & Tools

Figure 2.46 Horizontal adjustment

Figure 2.47 Vertical adjustment

Figure 2.48 Side elevation showing the vice and sawing arm arrangement.

Figure 2.49 The author showing the seated arrangement.

than forward and backward, it provides the marquetry cutter with total concentration when cutting intricate shapes. He only has to think about following the lines on the pattern before him. He does this by moving the material around the saw blade as the pattern demands.

However, the most important advantage of the chevalet versus the treadle saw is that the cutter is now seated! How utterly delighted the 19th century cutters must have been to use this saw with its comfortable seating arrangement. Notice I say the 19th century and not the 18th. This is because the chevalet emerged at the early part of the 19th century, well after the productive period of the mid to late 18th century, both in Britain and in the rest of Europe.

Advantages of the chevalet

The advantages of this saw over the treadle type just discussed are as follows:

- A larger sized panel can be accommodated because the throat depends on the length of the horizontal arm plus the depth of the donkey frame below the mechanical vice. Unlike the treadle, the operator's body does not interfere when turning the marquetry packet during cutting. On the chevalet the packet turns in front of the operator like an aeroplane's propeller.
- The marquetry being cut is elevated much higher than on the treadle's flat table, thereby gaining more natural light for the work during sawing.
- The donkey is free-standing, allowing sawing to take place in any location.

Disadvantage of the chevalet

- There is less control of the work during cutting than with the treadle saw, because only one hand is free to hold the packet, whereas both hands are free on the treadle type.

Bevel cutting

Purely for clarification, I am honour bound to clear up the burning question that I imagine, by now, will be on the lips of some readers, especially my many friends and marquetry colleagues across Europe, and in America and Canada. The treadle saw with a rectangular frame and horizontal table does not permit bevel cutting, simply because there is insufficient space within the rectangular frame to gain the amount of tilt the table requires, usually between 12 to 15 degrees.

However, the main single reason why bevel cutting was never performed lies in the way 18th century classic marquetry was designed and produced, and in the next chapter, *Techniques*, you will learn how two-part fretsawing removed the opportunity to bevel saw. Bevel cutting only works where just *two* veneers are sawn together as a packet; however, the classic method requires *multiple* sheets of veneers, of one type and colour, held together in a packet and sawn simultaneously.

Fretsaw blades

Regarding fretsaw blades, it is interesting to compare the two images in Figures 2.50 and 2.51. In Figure 2.51 the blade used on the door panel is much smaller, meaning the marquetry shows decreased gaps on blind cuts. In comparison, in Figure 2.50, the gaps are significantly larger and clearly created with a much thicker blade, and perhaps by a different marqueteur. From evidence such as this, I can confidently state that the drawers for the Harewood Library writing table were farmed out to a different workshop. We will come across this departure on other similar commissions later in the book.

Fretsaw blades were most likely made within the marqueteur's workplace. They were constructed from sprung steel, normally intended for clock springs. After filing fine teeth along its length, teeth are 'set' by punching them alternately left and right along the length of the blade. The set determines the width of kerf through the wood: the finer the teeth, the narrower the

Figure 2.50* Note the 'blind cuts' seen centre of picture – these are where the fretsaw travels up the leaf, stops, while the packet is turned 360° around the blade. The resulting hole equals the width of the saw blade. This marquetry is from the drawer fronts of the Harewood Library writing table.

Figure 2.51* Like Figure 2.50 blind cuts are visible, but not as prominent. This marquetry was produced on the same piece of furniture, but on the door panels.

resulting kerf. For the most part, marqueteurs used two-part fretsawing when applying marquetry, but 'packet fretsawing' is evident on one particular piece – the Harewood Library writing table. By measuring the diameter of the resulting hole made by the saw blade, we can determine the width of the blade. In the case of Figure 2.51, which came from one of the door panels of the Harewood Library writing table, the blade used was about 2 mm wide. However, it is also clear that the same person did not make all the blades used, and it is likely that some marquetry was 'farmed out' to external firms. If we look at the drawer fronts (Figure 2.50) compared to the door panel (Figure 2.51), we can easily see that the quality of marquetry cutting is by far inferior on the drawer fronts. The width of the blade used for this work was about 3.5 mm.

Knife cutting

Most marquetry books, when talking about historical tools, tend to leave out the knife; I assume this is because it is not considered to have any use in marquetry construction of the 18th century. However, I have found clear evidence that knife cutting was used extensively to construct some of Chippendale's motifs. In support of this is the fact that the knife is clearly illustrated by Roubo, as shown in Figure 2.52.

The blade could well have been made from old hacksaw blades. You can see from Roubo's drawing that the blade is ground down to an acute angle, of about 30°, which is not too different from a modern scalpel blade used today. The width of the blade looks very thin, so it is easy to see that, providing the cutting edge and

Figure 2.53 The author's craft knife

point was retained, straight-line cutting of veneers would certainly be very successful. Clearly, the blade did eventually need replacing, which explains why the handle was made in such a way that the binding string could be undone to change worn blades. I use such a knife myself, shown in Figure 2.53, where straight line cuts are needed, particularly on very hard tropical woods such as those used on Chippendale's work. I can easily identify with their need for such homemade tools.

The advantage of such a knife over the modern scalpel is that it only requires one bevel, against bevels on each side of a scalpel. Like my 18th century counterparts, I have used an old sawn off hacksaw blade. In my case both handle and point are shaped from the same redundant blade. A few rolls of masking tape softens the handle during use.

Inlay knife

The inlay knife was a purpose-made knife used for a specific application. The knife, together with a small tack hammer, illustrated in Figure 2.54, was used to cut into veneers already glued to the substrate. Figure 2.55 shows two bevels, one ground to the front and one to the back of the point. The same was done on the other side.

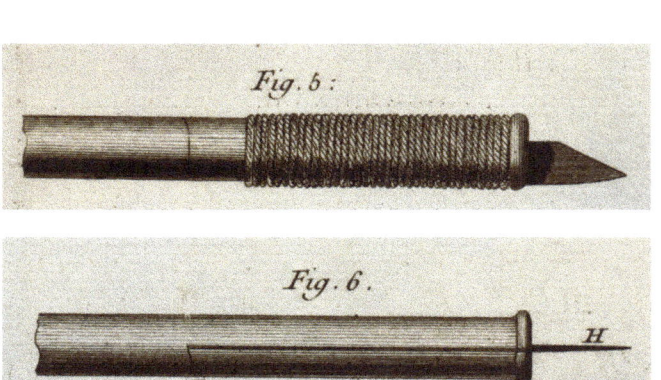

Figure 2.52* Craft knife used in the 18th century. Roubo's engraving shows a spliced wooden handle (as Fig. 6), tensioned with string (as Fig. 5).

Figure 2.54 Inlay knife together with a small tack hammer.

* Courtesy of Colonial Williamsburg Foundation USA

CHAPTER 2 | Materials & Tools

Figure 2.55 My inlay knife showing close up of bevels.

Figure 2.56 Inlay knife made by Simon Banks.

Figure 2.57 My home-made shoulder knife.

The back of the blade is flat to allow the hammer to tap it, allowing the knife to cut into the veneer.

I am indebted to furniture restorer Simon Banks of Dingwall & Banks, Antique Furniture Restorers, North Yorkshire, who made the knife seen in Figure 2.56. Simon made this knife after experiencing knife marks along glue lines when restoring antique furniture. The resulting bevels, equal on both sides, are based on Simon's experience and trials to establish the ideal shape for the job. Figure 3.8 on page 54 provides evidence of the inlay technique used in London during Chippendale's time.

Shoulder knife

The shoulder knife, seen in Figure 2.57, I made some years ago. The handle is mahogany and shaped to rest on the shoulder as intended. I ground the blade to produce a sharp point suitable for gouging out a solid wood substrate for letting in 'intarsia' work. Intarsia, from the Latin for 'to insert', was the name given to inlay work of the 14th and 15th century when intarsia was inlaid into church pews and the backs of choir stalls in cathedrals in Northern Italy.

Figure 2.58 shows a self-portrait of intarsia wood inlay artist Antonio Barili (1453–1516) from Siena, Italy. The knife rests on his shoulder, leaving his two hands free to control the point of the knife. The panel he is working on shows him inscribing his name and personal details. The intarsia work on the back panel was inlaid using the shoulder knife. Sadly the work was destroyed during the Second World War. I personally have never been successful with the knife, but perhaps I had, in the past, expected the tool to be a precision instrument capable of performing intricate tasks. The fact that Roubo described the knife as more of a tool for roughly digging out a substrate comforts me.

Figure 2.58 Self-portrait of Antonio Barili.

Hollow punches

One commonly used motif within the classic design is the inclusion of berries. These are found in the centres of guilloches, around the circumference of paterae, between laurel leaves and so on. The berries are always a uniform round shape, but vary in size depending on the type and size of the motif for which they are needed. This variation in size meant that hollow punches of different diameters had to be forged. Figure 2.60 shows my collection of 21st century punches, which, I imagine, would not be too dissimilar to those used 250 years ago. The main difference is that mine are made of high-speed steel, while carbon steel was the new, much softer metal available in the mid-18th century.

Berries were used for practical reasons too. When laurel leaves were fretsawn and placed onto a satinwood background veneer, the joints between leaf nodes was so small that the remaining satinwood broke away during sawing. Figure 2.61 shows arrows where holes are visible. It was impossible to prevent this, as I found out for myself while building a design for the Diana and Minerva commode (see Chapter 6). You could say that the inclusion of berries was a 'get out of jail card' both for the original marquetry cutter and for me. Bear in mind, too, that my fretsaw blade was much finer and uniform in shape than the one the marqueteur making the original panel would have used. My blade, size 2/0, is machine-made, whereas the equivalent blade used by my counterpart 250 years ago would have been thicker and hand-tooled with a three-cornered file to form the size and set of the teeth. Thankfully Chippendale, the designer, came up with this neat solution to overcome the problem.

Figure 2.59 Hollow punch used to create uniform berries.

Figure 2.60 Set of hollow punches.

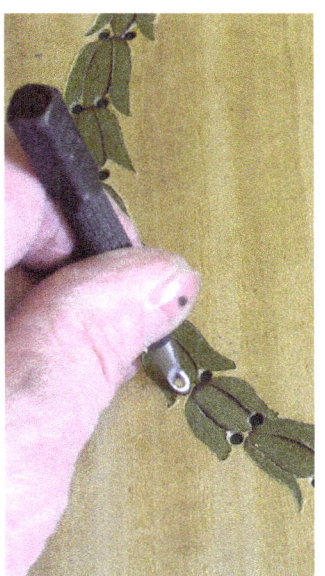

Figure 2.61 Arrows show holes in satinwood background veneer.

CHAPTER 2 | Materials & Tools

Veneer hammer and other presses

Pressing veneers to a substrate in the mid-18th century required many different approaches, using many different agents and tools to fix the veneers with their marquetry onto the furniture. Boulle work for instance, consisted of a mixture of woods, tortoiseshell and metals such as brass and pewter. While Chippendale mainly used wood veneers for his creations, he did occasionally use ivory. The glue available at the time was animal glue, also known as scotch glue or hide glue. Roubo referred to it throughout his writings as 'English Glue', saying it was the best glue available.

Veneer hammer

This tool has been in use as long as hot animal glue has been available. The name of the tool causes confusion because it's not a hammer in the true sense of the word, but more like a 'squeegee'-type hand press.

The tool has a broad rounded edge that is used to squeeze out glue from between the veneer and the substrate as the veneer is pressed into position, before the glue has time to gel and stick. A warm iron is also used with the hammer to keep the glue 'workable', and it's this combined use that demands skill and experience to work the veneer into place.

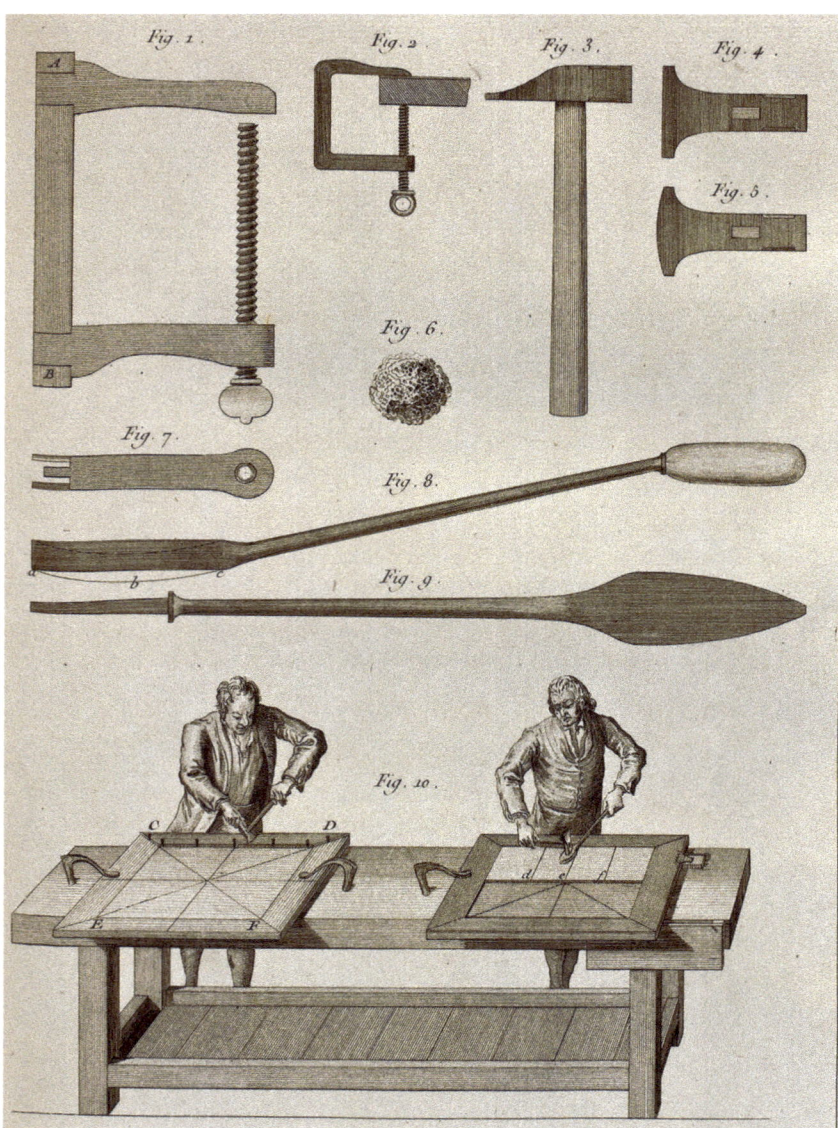

Figure 2.62* Roubo's engraving showing hammer veneering techniques.

* *Courtesy of Colonial Williamsburg Foundation USA*

Roubo's highly illustrative engraving (Figure 2.62) shows the tools and the processes needed to perform this highly skilled work.

- *Figs. 1 and 2* show two simple clamps that would be used to apply pressure on, say, outer borders of a panel.

- *Figs. 3, 4 and 5* show the hammer (*Fig. 3*) with its squeegee profile on the left and the hammer head on the right. *Fig. 4* shows the type of head used on flat surfaces, while *Fig. 5* shows the head shaped to match an incurved profile, thus allowing veneers to be pressed into an incurved panel.

- *Fig. 6* is a sponge used to apply hot water to a veneer to keep the glue workable during hammer veneering. This is an essential tool since the glue does cool, making pressing impossible. But since animal glue is reversible by application of heat and water, the sponge provides the perfect answer.

- *Fig. 7* shows the top profile of the bottom arm of the clamp at *Fig. 1*, showing the type of tenon joint used at point B in *Fig. 1*.

- *Fig. 8* shows the iron with its wood handle designed to prevent the heat transferring and burning the operator's hand.

- *Fig. 9* shows the tapered end which fits inside the wood handle.

- *Fig. 10* shows two men hammer-veneering veneers in a pre-determined order.

I cover this order in more detail in Chapter 3, pages 65–72, where I illustrate and describe, step by step, how a Chippendale table was glued down using the stick-as-you-go method.

Hot sand bags

For pressing veneered work on to curved surfaces, 18th century cabinet-makers had to rely on either hammer veneering, as just discussed, or on the use of hot or cold sand bags. Both hot animal glue and fish glue can be effectively pressed using sand bags. Figure 2.63 shows a Roubo plate of a sand bag applying even pressure to a curved surface. Hot animal glue requires heated sand bags, while the fish glue can be pressed with either hot or cold sand bags.

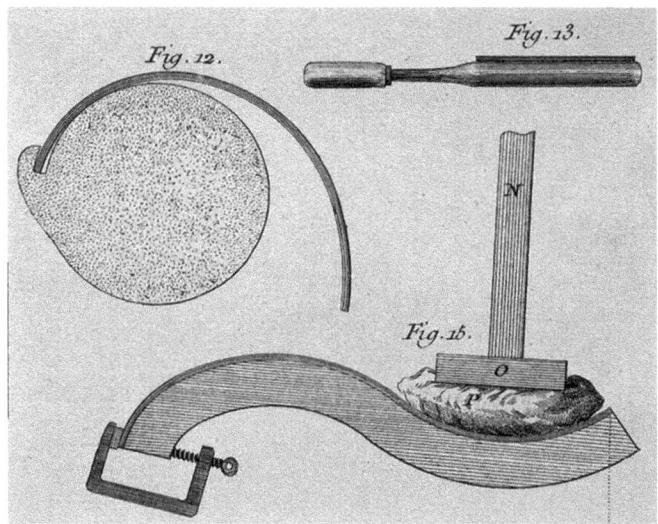

Figure 2.63 Roubo's engraving showing sand bag used on a curved surface.

Small bags, made from either hessian or calico and filled with sand were heated in an oven. Providing they were sewn up securely, a bag would last many years. Getting the right amount of filler into the bag, so that the bag remains firm yet spreads across the surface to be glued, came with practice. Too little sand and the heat is not retained long enough for the bag to be effective; too much and it won't spread sufficiently to cover the area under press.

Applying pressure to a concave surface is much easier than to a convex. The former can, in most cases, be secured with a flat board laid across the bag, pressing it down into the incurving recess. Applying pressure to a convex surface may have needed a shaped panel similar to the profile of the panel to be veneered – I say similar, because the sand bag will take up any discrepancies between the two panels once they are pressed together.

Penwork or artwork

While penwork or artwork is related to engraving, artwork does not involve marquetry type tools and so does not fit within this chapter. However, artwork is a matter of great importance as one of the techniques used to form the final decorations on many marquetry commissions; therefore the subject matter is discussed in Chapter 3 on pages 85–86.

* Courtesy of Colonial Williamsburg Foundation USA

This concludes my chapter on materials and tools, which leads me into Chapter 3, *Techniques*, in which I identify and describe the many techniques used in creating and building classic marquetry designs.

CHAPTER 3

TECHNIQUES

INTRODUCTION

This section of the book provides the all-important foundation to our understanding of 18th-century working methods. As a practising marqueteur specialising in Chippendale's marquetry, I am fortunate to have the skill and experience to recognise and be able to replicate the range of techniques that he and his skilled journeymen introduced. Having started the task of replicating, I was soon reminded, however, that marquetry qualifications on their own were not going to be enough to fully unravel the secrets that their marquetry work concealed. I also had to get inside the minds of those responsible for creating such exquisite workmanship; knowledge of the tools they used was only a halfway house.

After 20 years of detailed research, I feel I have finally got inside the minds of those who performed the technical processes. It is all too easy to pass the full acknowledgement on to Thomas Chippendale himself, even though he was mainly responsible for the production of his masterful designs. It is most certainly true that he relied on a skilled workforce to transform his designs into the finished product we all enjoy today. Marquetry always has been, and still is, specialist work, not generally performed by cabinet-makers, and therefore it is my firm opinion that the marquetry techniques were introduced and executed by unknown journeymen with skilled hands and inventive minds. Journeymen, as the name implies, moved around Europe during the mid to late 18th century seeking work in the best workshops of the time. Chippendale's introduction of marquetry furniture in 1769 would have attracted such skills. Whether marqueteurs worked directly for the designer or formed part of a separate specialist firm is open to conjecture.

In this chapter, I will be discussing the arguments for and against the existence of an established specialist workplace where all the veneering and marquetry techniques could have taken place. We have to take into account not just Chippendale's marquetry furniture, but those of his competitors across London, whose classic-style marquetry was almost identical in design to that of the great man. This collectively produced a substantial demand on marqueteurs to perform and deliver the work to a high level of skill.

This chapter deals with marquetry techniques, and it is important that you fully understand how they were executed. Whether you are a historian, curator, conservator, restorer or a dedicated marqueteur, I trust you will be more than impressed with the work of these classic practitioners.

There are no records of the men who performed this work, neither by name nor nationality, but we can admire their innovative talents. One such person, I am convinced, executed most of the marquetry that adorns Chippendale's creations. His skilful hands are visible time and again, and it is to this man, this unsung giant, that I dedicate this chapter.

INLAY

The term 'inlay' is perhaps the most overused term we have in marquetry circles. Too many commentators refer to marquetry work as inlay. Before proceeding to describe it, let me first define inlay as opposed to marquetry so we can see what the differences are and what we are dealing with.

- **Inlay** – is where a cavity is created in the groundwork, which can be either solid wood or a veneer pre-glued to the ground. A prepared marquetry motif is laid upon the ground and a fine line is scored around the motif. After removing the motif, an inlay knife is used to dig out the cavity, so that the inserted motif fits snugly into the cavity window. When sanded, the surrounding ground and the inserted inlay finish at the same level.

- **Marquetry** – is where a marquetry motif is constructed by first cutting each separate component part, then assembling the parts into a background veneer *before* it is glued to the ground. The assembled design, held together with tape, is glued across a prepared groundwork, either in one operation, or using the stick-as-you-go method. Hence marquetry is said to be 'overlaid'.

In the 18th century a form of inlay, as just defined, did exist in some cases. It occurred when the background veneer, used as the foil for the marquetry work, was glued to the substrate prior to the inclusion of the marquetry elements. The marquetry design, after being cut, was laid on the background and held in place temporarily with spots of glue or tapes. A line was scored around the perimeter of the marquetry elements and then lifted clear, revealing a scored line. A small 'inlay knife' (see Figure 3.1) was used to cut the background veneer along the scored line. By turning the knife with one hand to the left or right, determined by the scored line, and tapping the back of the blade with a small hammer in the other hand, the knife cuts through the veneer to the substrate below. The surplus veneer could then be released from its bond by applying heat from a small iron spatula with a wooden handle (perhaps in the 18th century heated in an oven adjacent to a fire) and warm water. Once the glue below softened, the background

Figure 3.1 Inlay knife

veneer was lifted clear of the substrate. This allowed the marquetry to be inlaid into the resulting cavity.

There are problems with the inlay method, however, which I suspect subsequently brought about its demise. The first is that the method leads to mistakes, which are evident on many examples of marquetry inlaid with this method. I refer to visible cuts at junctions where marquetry terminates at a point. Figure 3.2 illustrates 'v' shaped nicks into the background veneer, caused by hitting the inlay knife 'once too often' with the hammer and allowing the knife to penetrate the background, beyond the inlay line.

While an untrained hand might cause this, the repetitive evidence of 'v' shaped nicks on furniture made across Europe indicates that the mistake was allowed to remain. The alternative would have required lifting the background from its bond to the substrate, and gluing

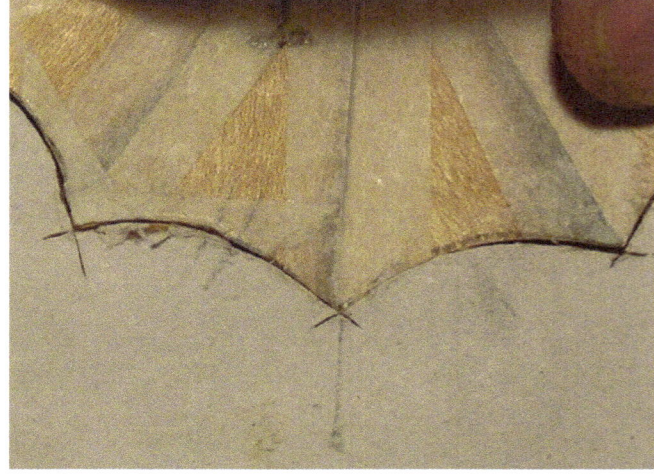

Figure 3.2 V-shaped nicks in background veneer from the inlay knife.

another veneer. This was a costly and time-consuming operation, which was clearly not an option.

Another and more serious problem, however, is the limitations of the knife itself. The artisan can follow a line and cut it accurately, providing the line is smooth, linear and does not consist of any sharp turns and twists. Chippendale's marqueteurs soon realised these hazards, which is why, I suspect, inlaying was used in only the most extreme cases, when two-part sawing was not possible. We will see later in this chapter when these instances occurred.

Inlay technique

Figure 3.3 shows the marquetry motif placed on the background veneer. A line is scored around the outside of the motif using a sharp knife. Figure 3.4 shows the use of a homemade inlay knife and small tack hammer to gouge a line into the background veneer while carefully following the scored line. For purposes of this illustration I have deliberately cut in two lines, one that follows the path of the scored line, and one set inside that line. In Figure 3.5 you can see a second set of scored lines waiting to be cut – we will see the reason for this in a moment.

Figure 3.3 Marquetry placed on the background veneer.

Figure 3.4 Using a homemade inlay knife and small tack hammer to gouge a line into the background veneer.

Figure 3.5

Figure 3.6

Figure 3.6 shows the marquetry inserted and good tight joints achieved. For purposes of this exercise I have deliberately not used any glue, because I want to show you the most compelling evidence restorers find of when an inlay knife has been used.

The final picture (Figure 3.7) shows two lines of knife marks, which are caused by my cutting in the lines with my knife. What I am showing you is simulation on my part, but these kinds of knife marks are often found during restoration work. Similarly, nicks at junctions as shown in Figure 3.2 are another clear indication of inlaying.

The final evidence is this painting of two marqueteurs working in a London workshop shown in Figure 3.8. Painted by Swedish artist Elias Martin in London in 1760, it shows one man seated at a marquetry cutter's bench, colloquially known as 'the donkey', fretsawing marquetry motifs. The other man is gouging out the background veneer on the table, using an inlay knife and small tack hammer, almost the image of my knife seen in Figure 3.1.

This picture fills me with hope and amazement, because they could well be the very two men whom Chippendale employed to inlay marquetry to drawer fronts on many of his commissions during the period 1769–75. Whilst this is perhaps a romantic notion on my part, we don't know how many small workshops like the one shown here were operating at this time. In Chapters 5 and 6, I talk about the London firm placing work to outside contractors and, in particular, small

Figure 3.8* Painting by Elias Martin, 1760

drawer fronts, which I have proved were inlaid using the method seen here. It is interesting to see a marquetry cutter's bench being used to fretsaw the motifs and not a larger treadle saw. Maybe this was simply a two-man operation with limited resources, yet skilled enough to perform the type of marquetry customers required. The painting offers the suggestion that space, or lack of it, was a limiting factor. I have been in such cramped workshops myself, especially in Sorrento, Italy, and those confinements did not distract or affect the quality of workmanship that emerged.

Shoulder knife

I cannot let the opportunity go by without a brief mention about theories that still abound today, that the shoulder knife was used during the 18th century to perform the cuts just described. Having made such a tool and practised using it, as suggested by some historical commentators and marquetry practitioners, I discount its use as a precision tool for cutting and shaping marquetry work.

Figure 3.7

* Courtesy of The Swedish National Art Museum, Stockholm

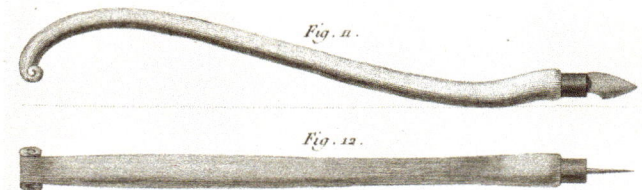

Figure 3.9* Roubo's illustration of a shoulder knife

Figure 3.10 My own homemade shoulder knife

The shoulder knife is a tool made for crude work, and was used initially in the 15th and 16th centuries by Italian monks practising *intarsia* work. It was used to gouge out wood when preparing cavities in substrates, and as such was never intended for fine precision work such as inlaying marquetry. Roubo himself, while he illustrates the knife (Figure 3.9) and how it was made, does not even suggest that the knife was used for intricate inlaying of marquetry, but as a tool for the initial removal of solid wood substrate to produce a cavity. My homemade shoulder knife is seen in Figure 3.10.

What perhaps could have happened is that it was used like a small inlay knife – in other words with the knife held upright and not leant against the shoulder, while tapping the back of the blade with a small hammer. However, it would have been awkward to control, and indeed *was* awkward as I found myself when I tried this method. Subsequently, the smaller controllable knife was made to replace it.

Following the knife, a gimbarde (Figure 3.11 – also known in France as 'old woman's tooth') was used to create a uniform cavity. Today we call such a tool a 'router', yet my late uncle and teacher, Tommy Limmer, used the same comical nickname when he taught me how to use it (see Figures 3.12 and 3.13). How wonderful that these nicknames travel across countries from one workshop to another, giving a clear indication that travelling journeymen not only brought skills, but also their local vernacular. Thanks to Roubo we know that this nickname has travelled across Europe over the past 250 years.

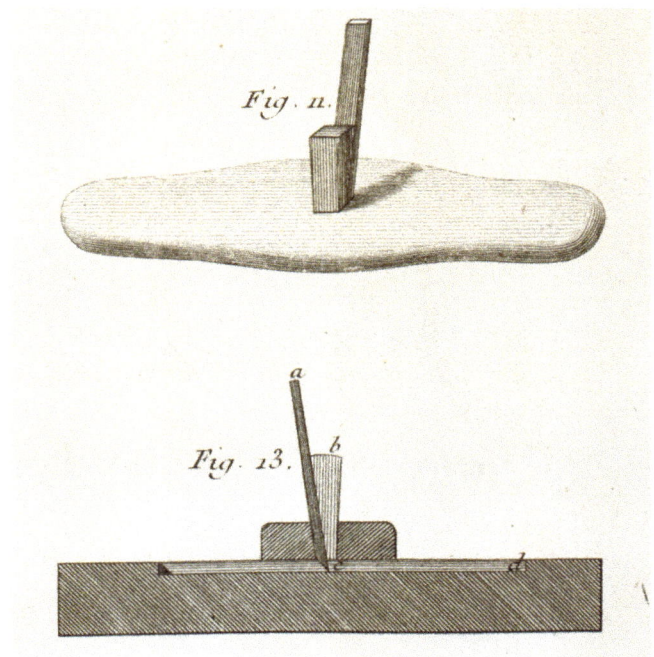

Figure 3.11* Roubo's illustration of a 'gimbarde' or router

Figure 3.12 Router showing blade or 'old woman's tooth' in the centre

Figure 3.13 Router creating cavity

* *Courtesy of the Colonial Williamsburg Foundation, USA*

CREATING LINE DRAWINGS IN THE 18TH CENTURY

Before starting to talk about the different techniques which I want to describe to you, I must add that none of them could commence without the production of accurate, repetitive line drawings. In the 18th century the accuracy of marquetry drawings was paramount. As you study the finished marquetry work in this book, you will begin to realise that accurate drawings must have been produced for the end results to be fully accomplished.

For me, in the 21st century, making copies of drawings is not a major problem. With the use of a modern photocopier I can quickly reproduce as many copies of a 'master copy' as I need. In the 18th century however, no such facility existed, and to replicate the original engraved drawing from which the marqueteur could work was a long process.

Prick and pounce

The first step is to trace an original drawing as shown in Figure 3.14. For this purpose I have selected the most common motif used on Chippendale designs, namely the acanthus leaf.

The next step is to prick a series of holes along the lines of the engraved drawing. As you can imagine, this slow process demanded patience and a steady hand, so as not to change the designer's initial creation. A hand held 'pricker' (shown in Figure 3.15) provided perfect control, and its metal spike ground to a sharp point allowed me to push to a depth that would leave holes of even diameter. I placed a padded card (approximately 3mm (16th inch) thick under the tracing to control the depth of the pricker.

Figure 3.14 Tracing acanthus leaves.

Figure 3.15 Using a fine pricker to punch holes along the tracing paper, which rests on padded card.

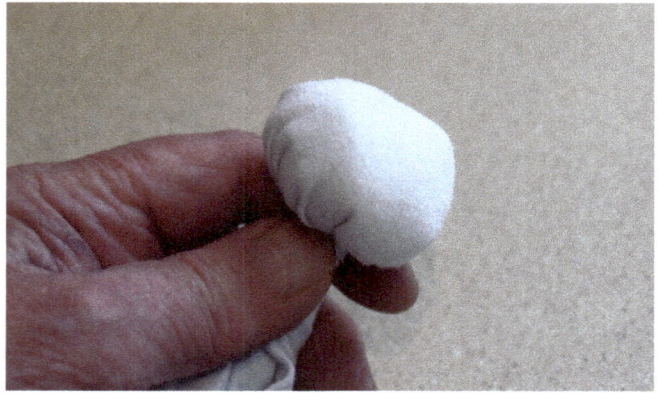

Figure 3.16 Pounce bag.

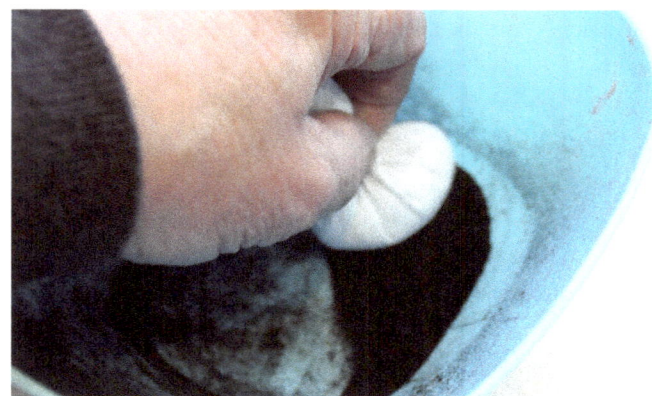

Figure 3.17 Rubbing the pounce bag into charcoal dust.

Figure 3.18 Pricked holes visible along the drawn motif.

Figure 3.19 Joining up the dots with a pencil.

I made a simple pounce bag consisting of a wad of cotton wool placed into a cotton handkerchief. Figure 3.16 shows the resulting pounce bag.

I had previously broken up a lump of charcoal into dust, then finely sieved it to achieve very fine dust particles. I pressed the pounce bag into the dust, as seen in Figure 3.17. This allowed me to transfer the dust into the holes of the tracing paper by passing the pounce bag in circular motions across the tracing paper. This had the effect of forcing black dust through the holes of the tracing paper, leaving clear lines of black dots along the paper design. Figure 3.18 shows the end result.

Because carbon is coal based, heat acts as its sealant, so the paper with its carbon dots was passed over a hot sheet of brass to fuse the dots in place. As many copies as desired could be reproduced in this manner, safe in the knowledge that each copy would match all previous copies. Finally, I was able to join up the dots with a pencil to produce a continuous line drawing to use as basis for fretsawing (see Figure 3.19).

It has to be noted here that while I have only shown a small example, we have to consider the size of the task when a whole panel has to be produced using this method. Imagine making a prick and pounce copy for the top of the Diana and Minerva commode, measuring over 2 metres (7 ft) long by over 600 mm (2 ft) wide (see Figure 6.58 on page 167). It is clear from this that whoever performed the prick and pounce work under Chippendale's employ was meticulously skilled. Conversely, marquetry work produced by Chippendale's rivals often fell short of his high standard of accuracy.

Chapter 3 | Techniques

PACKET FRETSAWING TECHNIQUE

This technique is mostly attributed to Andre-Charles Boulle (1642–1732), whose French furniture was flamboyantly decorated with marquetry work. While Boulle did not invent packet fretsawing, he took it to levels not previously seen. Not only did he use veneers of wood, but he also introduced the use of materials such as brass, pewter and tortoiseshell.

He was particularly famous for designing and making matching furniture pieces where one piece was decorated with the *premier-partie* (positive) elements of the packet materials, while the matching piece was decorated with the *contre-partie* (negative) element. By intermixing the materials he could provide the most impressive and sumptuous designs. The work became so famous that the technique of packet fretsawing was eventually known as 'Boulle-work' regardless of whether the work was attributed to him or to his many contemporaries. The illustrations below show the step-by-step method of packet fretsawing, as used by Boulle.

The technique requires that two materials, known as 'the packet' (see Figure 3.20), are held together with small pins. A design drawing is glued onto the top layer of the packet (Figure 3.21) and a small hole is drilled into one part of the drawing to give access for the fretsaw blade (Figure 3.22). By following the lines of the design, the marqueteur is able to fret out the pattern.

Figure 3.20

On completion, the sawn elements are assembled as you would a jigsaw puzzle. Two contrasting but exact copies of the design are produced, one positive and the other negative (shown in Figure 3.23). The resulting gap caused by the kerf of the saw blade is illustrated in Figure 3.24, where I have held it up to a window to highlight the gaps.

Essentially, this technique has the advantage of producing two assembled designs from just one sawing. Boulle and other European furniture-makers operating

Figure 3.21

Figure 3.22

Figure 3.23 Two contrasting but exact copies of the design are produced, one positive and the other negative

Figure 3.24

in the 17th and early part of the 18th century were quick to see the commercial advantage when two matching furniture items could be decorated from just one sawing process. For instance, Boulle could mix brass with tortoiseshell and, by doing so, produce one cabinet with brass as the background and tortoiseshell as the motif, while the matching cabinet showed the two materials in the opposite mode. Because they had been sawn from the same design, the two cabinets both matched and opposed each other, making the furniture very appealing to the wealthy patrons they attracted.

Despite its popularity, particularly across France, the technique did have one inherent fault. The 'packet' consisting of two materials sawn in one operation meant that the pieces when assembled together left a gap equal to the thickness of the fretsaw blade. Careful use of fillers made attempts to disguise the gap before the surfaces were varnished. Ebony was used regularly as a veneer because of its dark, almost black, colour meaning that dark fillers used to fill the gaps could not be detected. However, where metals (brass or pewter) were intermixed with tortoiseshell the gap was more difficult to conceal, and the obvious dark line around each motif became known as the 'engraving line'. The filler material presents long-term problems because, as it dries out, it breaks away from its surrounding marquetry. This is a major problem for conservators and restorers when modern central heating breaks down the materials. Once the filler is lost, the integrity of the marquetry is threatened, resulting eventually in damage and subsequent loss.

Before leaving this technique, I have to stress, I have seen work done by Boulle where gaps between mating edges did not exist. While these examples are rare, it does show that if clients were prepared to pay for the additional work, two-part fretsawing would be performed. This shows that the technique I am about to discuss was known and used, although exceptionally, by Boulle during his productive years, between 1680 and 1720.

TWO-PART FRETSAWING OR THE CLASSIC METHOD

As the name implies, the technique of two-part fretsawing requires two separate sawing exercises. The first part involves fretsawing the marquetry elements without the inclusion, at this stage, of the background veneer. This has a distinct advantage over packet fretsawing, because marquetry elements can be sawn either as a single element from just one veneer or, more fittingly, sawn in multiples to meet the repetitive and symmetrical – classic – movement. The latter requires multiple layers or 'stacks' of veneers of one species and colour appropriate to the motif. With the motif's design pasted to the top veneer, multiple copies can be produced from one sawing, each identical to each other.

You could say that this technique was born from the classic movement and there were immediate advantages both in better reproduction of repeat designs, as well as proving to be a great time-saving technique.

It became abundantly clear to me that we were also seeing here the birth of mass production. In today's terms the scale of such production looks relatively small, but put into the context of 18th century workshop activity, the introduction of this new technique was an important milestone. The technique became used firstly because of the 'repeat' nature of the classic design, and secondly to see the end of packet fretsawing and the undesirable gaps the old technique produced after assembling the marquetry.

A third and not so obvious reason for introducing the technique is 'management control'. We are going to see precisely when this technique was first performed and the reasons why it was performed when we examine the marquetry work carried out on the Harewood Library writing table given in Chapter 5.

On-the-line, off-the-line

Two-part fretsawing technique is also known (within the trade) as 'on-the-line, off-the-line'. I'm indebted to my colleague, furniture restorer Simon Banks for reminding me of this vernacular. It is a typical technician's description of what one would have to perform in order to perfect the technique. It simply means that, for the first part, you saw 'on-the-line' of the design, and for the second part you saw 'off-the-line' or up to the line of the design to be more precise. To illustrate this, I have produced four drawings showing the actions of the two parts and the result.

If we take a simple drawing, as seen here at **A**, with a line around it and we fretsaw 'on the line', the result is design **a**, where the line is removed.

If we now use the same-sized drawing shown at **B** and saw 'up to the inside of the line', we remove the coloured area, but leave the line intact, and we end up with a window **b**. You can see that **a** will fit perfectly into window **b**.

To help us understand this technique, the following set of illustrations taken by me during the production of two-part sawing provide detailed explanations of the steps necessary for its implementation.

The first part

Figure 3.25 shows one door of the Diana and Minerva commode, which I describe in more detail in Chapter 6. I am using the ring of laurel leaves that circle the central medallion as the two-part sawing technique.

In Figure 3.26, the line drawing is used to cut out two sets of leaves from the drawing. Figure 3.27 shows the drawings pasted onto a dyed-green veneer (in this case, two dyed-green leaves because there are two matching doors on the commode). I know the leaves are cut this way on the original because I have examined the grain direction on the original laurel leaves, and the grain

Figure 3.26

Figure 3.27

changes direction from leaf to leaf as they wrap around the circle.

The fretsawn leaves are placed so that they are laid out in the tray and numbered to aid location when I start to assemble them later (see Figure 3.28).

Figure 3.25*

Figure 3.28

* Reproduced by kind permission of the Trustees of the 7th Earl of Harewood Will Trust and the Trustees of the Harewood House Trust

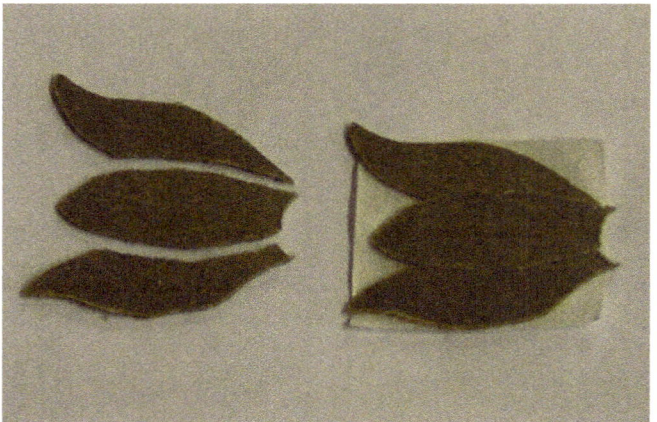

Figure 3.29

Figure 3.30

Each leaf consists of three separate parts and, when pushed together, any gaps are removed (see Figure 3.29). However, prior to that they have to be individually sand shaded (see Figure 3.30) to provide the all-important 3D effect.

It is worth noting here that, had packet fretsawing been used, and not two-part, the grain of all the leaves would have pointed in the same direction. The technique is already showing this distinct advantage to improving the finished artistic effect.

The second part

The laurel leaves, now sand shaded and held together to form single leaves, are placed on the background satinwood veneer, which is used for the commode door. Keeping the leaves in number order is paramount and Figure 3.31 shows the upper and lower rings correctly orientated.

The upper ring of leaves is spaced correctly around the circle, which will eventually be filled by the medallion. The satinwood background veneer is covered in protective paper, glued on with hot animal glue. This was standard practice in the 18th century, since the paper helped to protect and stabilise veneers during fretsawing.

It is worth reminding you at this stage that tropical hardwoods, such as satinwood, tulipwood, ebony, padauk, purpleheart and the full range of rosewoods, have inherent characteristics that can, without protection, cause sawyers a number of problems. These include oily substances in ebony, padauk and many rosewoods which, unless correctly treated, can leak out into surrounding veneers. The applied animal glue and paper play a great part in avoiding these problems. The other reason is that all the veneer types given here are hard, and sometimes too brittle, to be sawn by any other than a fretsaw. I was soon reminded of this very problem during this exercise.

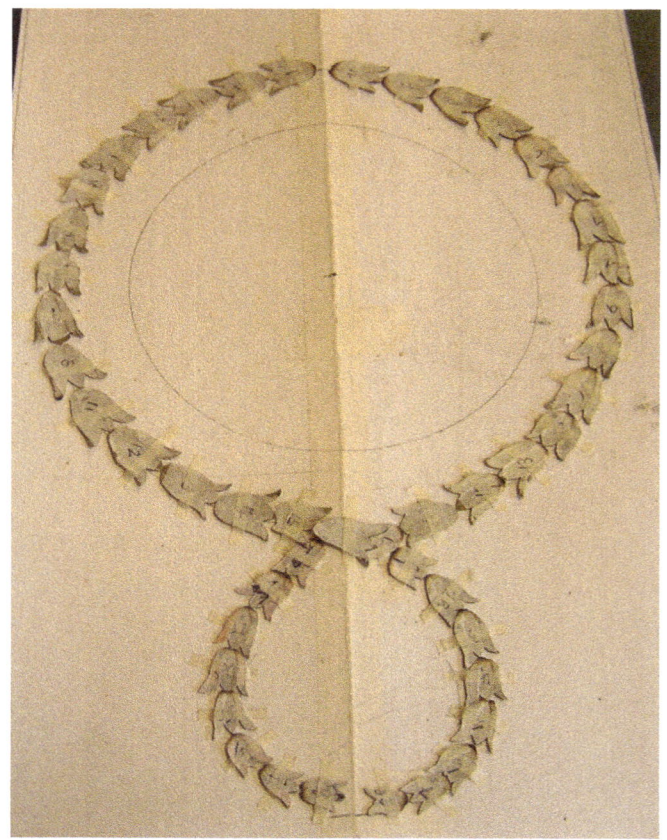

Figure 3.31

Figure 3.32

Figure 3.33

With the leaves held in place, a line is scored around each leaf using a sharp knife. The leaves are then replaced in number order back into their tray. The scored line is used as a guide to fretsaw up to. Figure 3.32 shows the scored line while Figure 3.33 shows me fretsawing 'up to' the line `but not on it. This illustrates the accuracy of the treadle saw.

Satinwood's inherent problem experienced

After inserting the leaves into their sawn windows, I found that holes appeared where leaves converged together – see the arrows in Figure 3.34. The small amount of satinwood left after fretsawing is not enough to keep the veneer intact and tiny breakages occur. I quickly realised, to my relief, that it was not my standard of fretsawing but the fact that the tiny amount of veneer was not strong enough to hold in place.

It became obvious to me at the same time that this problem was also experienced by the marqueteur sawing the original work. Clearly he would have had to consult the designer, and the remedy was to place two red berries into joints where leaves met. Fortunately, berries form part of the classic movement, so the canon was still obeyed.

I found on all the original Chippendale marquetry furniture where berries were added that they were sometimes large, sometimes small, but were always constant and circular. It was obvious that a type of hollow steel punch was made. Technically, this was not a problem in the mid to late 18th century.

Figure 3.34

As Figure 3.71 later in this chapter illustrates, I used a similar tool to punch the holes and punch out red berries from a sheet of red veneer.

BEVEL CUTTING

After perfecting the two-part sawing method, as we have just seen, the next natural progression would have been to adopt a method that allows both the inserted motif and its surrounding background to be sawn simultaneously without resulting in gaps between the mating edges. Such a method is now, in modern times, available and is called 'bevel' cutting. For the most part, I have been able to prove that two-part sawing was much preferred by marqueteurs of the period we are dealing with, since it allowed multiple cutting of the marquetry elements that made up the designs., thereby achieving the all-important symmetry that the classic design demands. This is a feature that is not possible with bevel cutting.

As the name implies, bevel cutting is performed by fretsawing two veneers at a pre-determined angle (bevel), so that one veneer (the smaller) drops into the cavity of the other (the larger) without leaving any gaps between the mating edges.

The bevel or angle is determined from the following formula:

$$\Theta = \operatorname{Sin}^{-1} t/w$$

where $t =$ the thickness of the blade measured over the set
$w =$ the thickness of the veneer.

Bevel cutting can only be used when working with just two veneers. Classic designs invariably required multiple cutting of 2, 4, 6 and even, in one case, 9 veneers, and so is not suitable for this technique.

As mentioned earlier, fretsaws and their respective frames and tables did not allow for bevel cutting, and it is my opinion that bevel cutting is a 'modern' advancement brought about following construction of 'front-to-back' framed fretsaws as against the types covered in Chapter 2. We are probably looking at the early to middle 20th century before such a practice was adopted.

STICK-AS-YOU-GO TECHNIQUE

Perhaps the least documented technique of all is 'stick-as-you-go', mainly because, I suspect, it is the least understood, or the least researched. I also think that the technique suffers the misconception of being referred to, all too often, as inlay work. While the title may belong to a modern-day vernacular, the technique, used in the mid to late 18th century, was the standard method of gluing marquetry and its background veneer to the substrate.

The technique requires the operator to have the skill and application of hammer veneering. The two techniques are dependent on each other and, in the period we are discussing, it became the main method of securing veneer work to a substrate. The reason for this is that in the mid 18th century large items of furniture were being produced, resulting in large panels of marquetry and veneering work, much too large to glue down any other way. As platen presses had not been designed on the scale that were needed, hammer veneering became the main technique to glue the veneers down.

Roubo produced a very clear illustration in one of his drawings (see Figure 3.35). Roubo's 'Figure 10' shows two men at a workbench hammer veneering a panel. The man on the left is hammer veneering the outer border at *C D*. You will note he is holding the hammer in his left hand while applying downward pressure with his right hand. In this way he can work the hammer from the centre of the border to the outer edges, left and right.

It is also worth noting that he has placed veneer pins or tacks along the inner edge and the mitred ends where he wants the border to lay once it is in place. It was standard practice across Europe to lay the outer borders first, before laying the inner panels, which you can see taking place on the picture on the right. Here the four outer borders are glued, mitred on each corner and, by following the precise lines shown on the left-hand picture, they are 'square' to the frame to which they are applied. Providing these measured lines are followed precisely, the pre-measured centre will fit perfectly.

The man on the right is applying heat from the iron, held in his left hand, while applying pressure to the iron with the hammer, held in his right hand. In the case of the illustration, panels *d*, *e* and *f* are hammer veneered in

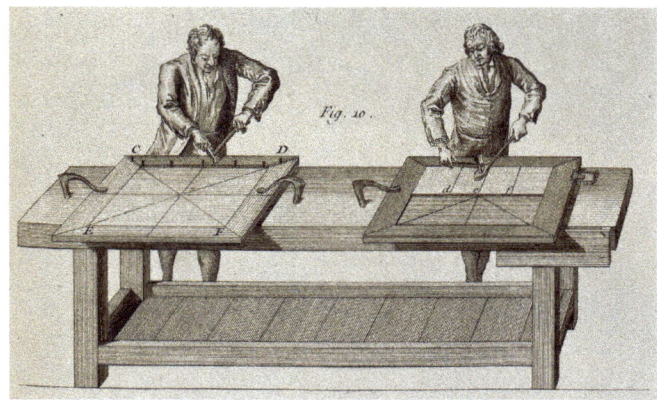

Figure 3.35* *Roubo's illustration of hammer veneering*

that order. The central panel could well be a marquetry design and in this case it would be laid in stages, working from the borders to the centre, using the 'stick-as-you-go' or 'piece-by-piece' method as it's also called. Chapter 2 shows the hammer and other tools needed to perform the technique (see Figure 2.62 on page 48).

The following explanations and illustrations should further illuminate where the stick-as-you-go technique was effectively and widely used across UK and European furniture-makers from the mid 17th century and continuing throughout the 19th century. Marqueteurs used the technique, as we will see throughout this book, with the exceptions being when the inlay method was more appropriate. Unlike English marqueteurs, who used one veneer type as the background foil for the inclusion of marquetry, the leading European cabinet-makers consistently created parquetry designs to act as background foils into which central medallions of marquetry were inlaid. Despite these different artistic styles, the technique of stick-as-you-go was the same.

Stick-as-you-go: a step-by-step example

The construction method is best explained by the following step-by-step illustrations, (see Figures 3.36 to 3.47), which show the highly popular 'Louis Cube' design, much used by some of the European contemporaries I have just mentioned.

I have not fitted the borders prior to sticking the centre panel of parquetry, which is what would have taken place in the 18th century. However, I did install

* Courtesy of the Colonial Williamsburg Foundation. USA

CHAPTER 3 | TECHNIQUES

Figure 3.36 Substrate showing measured borders.

Figure 3.37 Battens fixed with nails to two adjacent sides.

Figure 3.38 I start laying the cubes to create a balanced design both left to right and top to bottom of the panel.

Figure 3.39 Close-up of building cubes.

Figure 3.40 All cubes in place and perfect balance achieved to opposite sides of the design. This is because I measured the pattern before starting the build.

Figure 3.41 Marquetry motif laid in place across cubes.

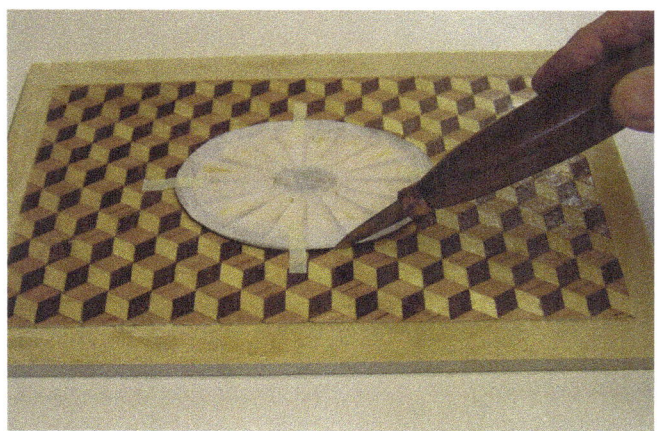

Figure 3.42 Line scored around the motif, which is then lifted clear.

Figure 3.43 Close-up picture showing scored line just visible.

Figure 3.44 Inlay knife used to cut through veneers to the substrate below.

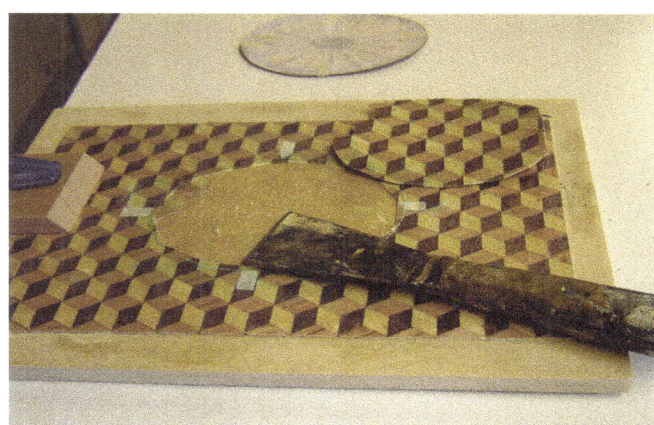

Figure 3.45 After applying hot water with small brush to soften the animal glue, the insert is lifted clear.

Figure 3.46 The remaining pieces are cut away with the inlay knife and tack hammer. Note: I deliberately cut two lines around the insert so that the inner knife marks would show on the photo

Figure 3.47 Motif glued in place. Borders needed to be installed to frame the work

two borders (battens seen at Figure 3.37) to align the central panel and register where the parquetry should start.

This small illustrative explanation of the stick-as-you-go technique does not however, explain the more demanding work of laying marquetry and background to a full sized table of, say, 2100 mm (7 ft) in length. Tables and cabinets of this scale were commonplace to Chippendale and other furniture makers of the time.

Discovering two-part fretsawing and stick-as-you-go on a Chippendale commission

Figure 3.48 shows one of a pair of pier tables *en suite* with matching pier glasses (called 'pier' when they are placed between windows and stick out into the room) made for the music room at Harewood House. These became a focus of my attention when I first visited the house. It was not just the splendid beauty of the carvings to the legs, plinths and mirrors that struck me, nor the flamboyant marquetry that adorned the two tables. I was more intrigued as to how the veneers and the marquetry was first cut, and then glued to the substrate. Following numerous visits and studying photographs I eventually found the answers.

Throughout this book, you will find instances where technical necessity outplays artistry. It is part and parcel of building designs and satisfying the practical needs of marquetry construction. Both the matching top panels were cut and laid using two-part fretsawing and not, as I first thought, laid by the inlay method. There are tiny clues that confirm my findings, and it is through these clues that I am able to provide the secret of how these large panels were assembled.

In addition, using my knowledge of marquetry construction techniques, I deduced what method was used to build the elaborate and splendid borders that surround each table. I was able to work out how the borders were cut, assembled and finally glued to the baseboard.

I will start with the central panels and, with the aid of photographs and Photoshop illustrations, explain the techniques that were used to cut and lay both the marquetry and its background veneers to their respective baseboards. I am indebted to my talented photographer Ted Clements for his skill with both camera and Photoshop to make the illustrative reproductions look realistic.

Figure 3.48* Pier table in Harewood House

The photograph in Figure 3.49 shows the flair and artistry we have come to expect from our eminent designer. The first point to note about the tops are their physical size. The overall dimensions of each measure 1780 mm (6 ft 7") long and 748 mm (2 ft 5½") wide, making them the third largest marquetry surface in the collection, beaten only by the two commodes of similar dimensions, namely the Diana and Minerva and the Renishaw. The dimensions of the Indian rosewood forming the background veneers (discounting the decorative border around the table) measures 1600 mm (5 ft 3") long, by 570 mm (1 ft 10½") wide. This area is covered by two leaves joined together lengthways down the centre, resulting in each leaf measuring 1600 mm (5 ft 3") long and 285 mm (11¼") wide.

The first and most obvious point to note is that veneers of this size are far too large to fit into the throat of a fretsaw. The physical dimensions of the two leaves mean that only two techniques would have been possible: the first option would have been to inlay, which means gluing down the two background veneers to the substrate first, then inlay the marquetry using an inlay knife. Because the marquetry consisted of floral work of very elaborate acanthus leaves with jagged and pointed edges, I was not convinced the inlay knife could have handled

* *Reproduced by the kind permission of the Trustees of the 7th Earl of Harewood Will Trust and the Trustees of the Harewood House Trust*

Figure 3.49* Inlay on the Harewood House pier table

such a complex design. On first inspection I thought the only way I could prove the inlay knife was used would be to look for knife marks in the background veneers. As you will recall knife marks occur at junctions where a leaf turns direction and the inlayer hits the knife once too often making a nick into the background veneer that's impossible to hide. I searched both tables and not one unwanted knife mark was found, meaning either a very skilful inlayer was ultra-careful in his technique, or another method was used.

This other method would be to use two-part fretsawing and the stick-as-you-go hammer veneering techniques. However, my immediate rejection of this method was because the two background veneers were clearly two matching leaves of Indian rosewood each measuring over 1500 mm (5 ft) long, and on the face of it fully intact. It was then I spotted the answers, which revealed physical unplanned cuts to the rosewood backgrounds.

You can see in Figure 3.49 that the acanthus leaves appear to touch the top and bottom edges of the rosewood background veneers, where they meet with the surrounding borders. On close inspection I noticed tiny cuts 'across the grain' of the rosewood where the acanthus leaves had fallen short of their intended target. The three images in Figure 3.50 are macro photographs highlighting the cuts. Black lines about 6 mm (¼") long signify the cuts. One cut impossible to hide is one made across the grain. I found these cuts along both the top and bottom edges and on both tables. These clues gave me the answer to the technique used.

Figure 3.50*

* Reproduced by the kind permission of the Trustees of the 7th Earl of Harewood Will Trust and the Trustees of the Harewood House Trust

Figure 3.51*

The illustrations on the following pages showing how the central panels were first cut with the two-part method and then glued to the substrate, using hammer veneering, are given with the aid of Photoshop.

Figure 3.51 shows the two rosewood background veneers broken up along the lines where the marquetry pieces separate each section. You will note that the panel now has four identical quadrants: top left and right, and bottom left and right. There are two small background pieces numbered 4L (left) and 4R (right), making a total of six pieces in each quadrant. I have left the bottom veneer free of numbers because you can see that the bottom veneer is a mirror image of the top and as such is broken up in the same way. This means we have a total of 24 separate pieces, not counting the central area where the oval fan resides, which impacts on all four quadrants. In total, therefore, there are 25 separate pieces.

We have to imagine, for the purpose of these illustrations, that the background veneers were first covered with plain parchment paper, stuck down with animal glue.

To carry out two-part fretsawing, the marquetry is first sawn, and so let us imagine the first stage is complete. Each marquetry element is then placed on the two matching rosewood background veneers (while they are still in two large unbroken sheets) and, when in place, held with spots of animal glue. Using a small craft knife, lines would be scored around each marquetry element and the marquetry then lifted from the background.

It is at this stage that the two unbroken rosewood background veneers would be cut into the segments as shown at Figure 3.51. This is achieved by drawing a continuous line down the centre of the marquetry pieces, where a 'window' will be sawn. By doing this, the rosewood background is cut into manageable sizes to fit the fretsaw throat, without compromising the windows. If you imagine cutting a complete horizontal line along the centre of the design, you will create two equal panels. Cutting continuous lines in the vertical marquetry elements further reduces the size of each panel. Now each segment can be fretsawn following the scored lines, in the knowledge that each piece will fit within the throat of the saw.

Assembling the marquetry and backgrounds using the stick-as-you-go method

First of all, in the 18th century we learn that the border veneers were glued to the substrate first, as already described by Roubo (see Figure 3.35). Therefore, the central panel and all the borders are completed, and the whole assembly is held together with tabs of glued paper placed on the face side. If we imagine that the image

* Reproduced by the kind permission of the Trustees of the 7th Earl of Harewood Will Trust and the Trustees of the Harewood House Trust

*Figure 3.52a**

*Figure 3.52b**
Stage 1 *of the 'stick-as-you-go' process*

shown at Figure 3.52a is covered in paper glued to the marquetry, and that the completed assembly is lined up so that it fits the table top perfectly, then small metal tacks are driven into the table top along the lines where the four borders meet the central panel (see Figure 3.52a).

The central panel is then removed from its borders by cutting through the paper which holds them together. The resulting Photoshop images are shown in Figure 3.52b and on the next page.

The central veneers and marquetry are lifted clear without disturbing the tacks, shown in blue. Each border is glued separately using the hammer veneering technique shown on Figure 3.35. Once the glue has dried and the borders are secure, the tacks can be removed. Since the tacks were driven in place before the central panel was cut free of the four borders, we know that the central panel will now fit the space perfectly.

Stick-as-you-go

All that remains is to stick the rosewood background veneers and the associated marquetry using the stick-as-you-go and hammer veneering techniques. Stages 2 to 7 show step-by-step Photoshop images as to how I imagine the stages were carried out.

While I have not performed hammer veneering on this scale myself, I have used the technique on much smaller work and it works very well. The main secret is to get the outer border perfectly in place, and metal nails

* Reproduced by the kind permission of the Trustees of the 7th Earl of Harewood Will Trust and the Trustees of the Harewood House Trust

Chapter 3 | Techniques

Stage 2: *Working from each of the four corners, the background pieces and marquetry are glued in place using the hammer veneering technique.*

Stage 3: *Acanthus leaf, C scrolls and background are added to each corner.*

Stage 4: *Marquetry foliage is glued and inserted down the centre of panel. This would have produced tight joints on both sides.*

Stage 5: *Four more C scrolls are added along with surrounding backgrounds.*

Stage 6: *Final foliate sections are glued in place.*

Stage 7: *Central fan is added to complete the process.*

* *Reproduced by the kind permission of the Trustees of the 7th Earl of Harewood Will Trust and the Trustees of the Harewood House Trust*

(as shown at stage 1) ensure this happens. The main advantage is that, throughout the process, you the 'layer' are totally in control, and can stop and rest at any stage. If glue sets where marquetry and veneers have not yet been placed, application of water and heat quickly softens it and allows you to carry on gluing. The overriding secret of hammer veneering is the consistency of the glue. Only experience teaches you the technique; Chapter 2 explains the process.

What you have just witnessed was a fortunate discovery, which allowed me to determine the process just described. As I said earlier, I made another discovery, but this time by studied analysis using my knowledge and experience in this field of classic marquetry. I refer to the way the elaborate border surrounding the table was constructed.

How is the border constructed?

I thought that finding the clue as to how the marquetry top and associated background was laid was a bonus, but then to have the benefit of discovering how this very elaborate border was produced surpasses even that.

The simulated results produced using Photoshop (see Figure 3.53), show one corner of the table and its proven colours, taken from the analysis of dyestuffs identified by Heinrich Piening using his UV-VIS Spectronomy (Chapter 4 covers this aspect in detail). A section of the border is seen here.

The repeat border design consists of six elements, which are, commencing at the bottom corner far right: back-to-back 'S' scroll in pink; green acanthus leaf standing on a red berry; a blue strap linking the two S scrolls and finally a green bud supporting a green laurel leaf. The pattern then repeats around the circumference of the table.

In each corner a burgundy anthemion covers the mitred corners. The rosewood background matches the background used on the top, but in the case of the border the grain points at right angles to the central background, forming a cross-banding effect. An inner banding of satinwood with white stringing separates the border from the inner veneers, and tulipwood cross-banding is fitted around the outside of the table.

Mass production

Each element is repeated 82 times around the table, and therefore a number of packets would have been fretsawn to produce multiple copies, minimising the amount of sawing and provide uniformity. It took me some considerable time to work out how often the design repeated itself around the border. On-site visits to Harewood House combined with studying photographs revealed the answer. The pattern repeats every fourth element. On first inspection it is not obvious that the repeat is happening, but it is revealed by the slight change in the way the craftsman saws the elements. I had the advantage of on-site studies looking at the borders on both tables, bearing in mind that the two tables match exactly.

The four-element match is achieved by sawing two sets back-to-back, or 'book-matching' as it is known. This is achieved by inserting every other coloured veneer in the packet reversed from its neighbouring veneer. When assembling the four-element match, every other set is opened up like a book to form a mirror image of its neighbouring set. In this way it makes identifying the repeats difficult, which is intentional.

Figure 3.53* *Proven colours of dyestuffs used to dye each marquetry element.*

* *Reproduced by the kind permission of the Trustees of the 7th Earl of Harewood Will Trust and the Trustees of the Harewood House Trust*

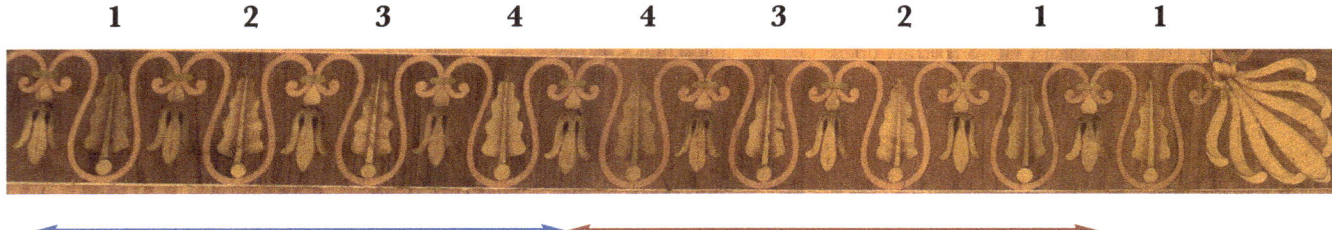

Figure 3.54* Sample border showing repeat pattern every fourth element, shown by arrows and numbers here

To illustrate this, in Figure 3.54, I have numbered the sets **1** to **4** with its book-matched set alongside numbered **4** to **1**. The second set is the inverted set of the first. This rule applies regardless of whether you view this right-to-left, or left-to-right.

Figure 3.55 shows the base pattern used to make multiple copies. The upstanding acanthus leaves and laurel leaf drops, plus the dyed pink back-to-back S scrolls are each repeated four times. Looking at the mathematics, we know each element is repeated 82 times. We also know the pattern repeats every four elements, meaning 82/4=21 repeats (rounded up) are needed. The extra repeat will accommodate the odd element that occurs on the long sides.

Clearly there is a limit to the number of veneers one can saw in one packet. I have to remind you that this technique requires 'two-part' sawing, resulting in one set for the elements, and one set for the background veneers.

Now we have to consider the different colours needed in the sets which provide the different elements. In each set we have to include green and pink veneers. The blue strap will be sawn separately due to its miniscule size. The red berry will be added after construction by using a hollow punch. My experience proves that a maximum of 12 veneers (plus two wasters) in one packet is manageable with a treadle fretsaw. Therefore four separate packets, each consisting of six green and six pink veneers plus two wasters, will produce 24 repeat elements.

For the rosewood backgrounds, two separate packets, each consisting of 12 veneers (six face side up and six reverse side up) plus two wasters will provide 24 background veneers ready to receive the marquetry elements from the first packets.

Figure 3.55*

To complete both tables we double these figures, resulting in eight packets of the dyed veneers and four packets of rosewood background veneers. This leaves ample spares if needed. Eight anthemions sawn from one packet of eight purple dyed veneers and one packet of eight rosewood veneers solve the eight corners on the two tables.

Building a Greek key design

The Greek key design stretches back through history and relates to a design signifying meander. The design took its name from the river Meander, with many twists and turns and mentioned by Homer in *The Iliad*. Meander was the most important symbol in Ancient Greece, symbolizing eternal flow. In more modern times it is also believed that the garden-maze found today in public parks originates from the design.

In furniture, the geometric design is generally used as a border arrangement, and has always intrigued me as to how it was originally constructed. Chippendale used it when he designed the two matching pedestals and the side table for the dining room furniture at Harewood House.

To help me solve the construction technique, I am helped to some degree by Roubo. He illustrates its construction and describes how it is put together, and I

* Reproduced by the kind permission of the Trustees of the 7th Earl of Harewood Will Trust and the Trustees of the Harewood House Trust

refer you to the English translation created by the Lost Art Press under the title: *To Make as Perfectly as Possible – Roubo on Marquetry*.

I found Roubo's illustrations very helpful, but struggled to stay with his narrative. It required many attempts to read through and fully digest his explanations. During his narrative I started to doubt his logic and eventually formed the opinion that he perhaps did not understand the processes he was trying to describe. This could have been because the person showing him wanted to conceal the methodology in order to protect workshop practices; this happened regularly during that period. After all, competition was everything; so why give away your working methods to an outsider? Roubo must have come across these professional obstacles, particularly with marquetry techniques, which, as a carpenter, were new skills to him.

Building Greek key using a mitre box

As an alternative, I have compiled my own method using a jig I introduced in my first marquetry book *The Marquetry Course*.

The history of the mitre box is unknown. I was introduced and taught to build and use it by my late uncle, Tommy Limmer, and the success of the tool since I introduced it in my book has been encouraging. Its simplicity is the key to its success and may well have been used in the 18th century on both sides of the English/French channel.

My mitre box could most certainly be used to cut the Greek key stock by setting up the box with adjustable stops and two saw cuts set at 45° and 90° angles. If we consider the Greek key design as seen on the pedestals supplied by Chippendale for Harewood House, we see how many different parts are needed and at what angle the cuts have to be made. It is just a matter of measuring each part and counting how many are repeated on the four corners shown at Figure 3.56. The resulting production list is achieved.

Here we see the full panel showing all four corners of the Greek key design. Each element within the design can be measured, compared with other parts for shape, size and repeat. From this, a full count can be made of each matching component.

To make matters easier, in Figure 3.57 I have shown one corner of the above panel, with all components

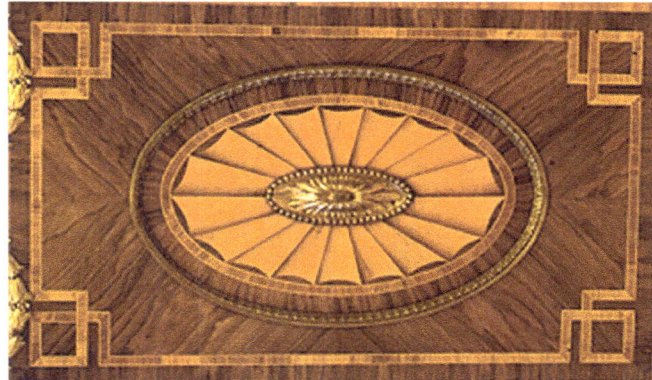

Figure 3.56*

clearly labelled so that we can easily do a count of stock needed to make the panel, thus:

- **a** = 2 parts, both ends having same mitre of 45°
- **b** = 1 part, one end mitred at 45° and the other at 90°
- **c** = 1 part, both ends mitred at 45°
- **d** = 1 part, both ends mitred (In line) at 45°
- **e** = 1 part, one end mitred at 45° and one end at 90°
- **f** = 1 part, both ends mitred in line at 45°, but opposite to **d**

In total, seven parts are needed for one corner, but altogether we need 8 × **a**; 4 × **b**; 4 × **c**; 4 × **d**; 4 × **e** and 4 × **f**. Add to that the two long vertical parts that link top to bottom, plus the two shorter horizontal parts that link left to right. Each of these parts is mitred at each end by 45°.

Clearly, I have not applied any measurements to these stock items – that would be done if I were actually making this design. From this we know how to arrange the mitre box so that all the stock can be produced so that each part is cut precisely the same for each type.

One point to observe, parts **d** and **f** have opposite, but equal, mitres set at 45° at both ends. To cater for this

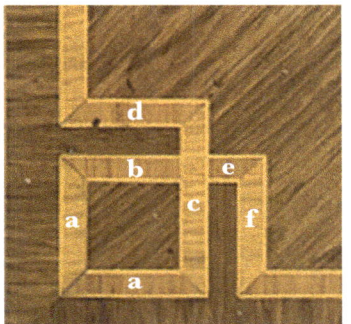

Figure 3.57*

* *Reproduced by kind permission of the Trustees of the 7th Earl of Harewood Will Trust and the Trustees of the Harewood House Trust*

change without changing the angle of the mitre on the mitre box, we simply turn one banding over and cut from the reverse side, then turn it back to lay it in place.

The mitre box seen in Figures 3.58 and 3.59 is made with two slots for cutting the 45° and 90° angles needed to build the Greek key design shown in Figure 3.57. I constructed the box from a flat piece of hardwood measuring 28cm (11 inch) by 10cm (4 inch) by 2.5cm (1 inch) thick.

I then made two hardwood strips. I cut the two angles on my chop saw, thus making sure the cuts were precisely the angles I needed. My chop saw blade creates a wide gap, so after making the cuts, I finished up with three sections which I simply placed together on the flat board of the box and pushed together to trap the ultra-thin mitre saw blade, which I use to cut the bandings. In this way I get a tight accurate mitre slot, which provides straight vertical sides essential for producing accurate parts.

The adjustable central stop-block allows for distance setting and a simple clamp holds it in place. I placed the whole assembly in a bench vice to maintain stability while sawing. I believe this would have been the type of jig that 18th-century marqueteurs could have constructed. Home-made jigs like the template board used to construct repetitive fans of different shapes and sizes were clearly used, as already seen in this chapter.

The mitre box is just another example of a simple jig built for purpose. It is capable of producing any geometric repetitive pattern such as Greek key, Louis cube, chess board squares plus any number of repetitive decorative bandings.

In Figures 3.58 and 3.59, we see one decorative banding being sawn after a stop-block is placed so that the required length of the part is maintained. The stop-block is a small piece of wood, cut to the correct angle and held in place with a clamp. One stop-block is made with one end cut at 45° and the other end at 90°.

The way to align the piece to be cut is to first place the mitre saw into the slot, place the banding up to the saw blade, then measure the length backwards from the saw blade to the point that equals the measurement you need. Place the stop-block at that point and clamp in place. Re-check your measurements and adjust if necessary; accuracy is paramount.

Figure 3.58 Mitre box with 45° slots

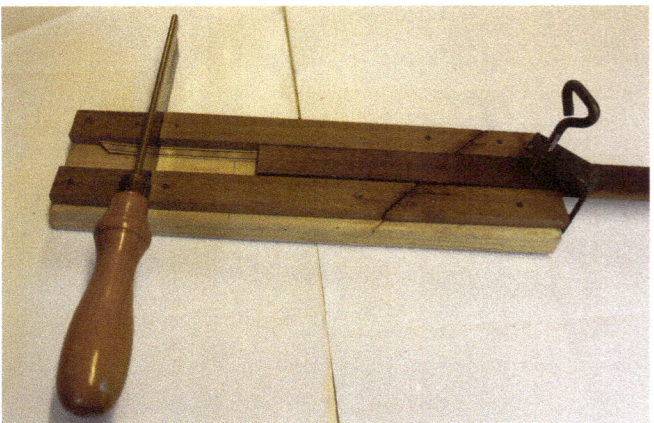

Figure 3.59 Mitre box showing 90° slots

THE TEMPLATE METHOD

This marquetry technique is one I have been teaching students for over 20 years and one that I feature in my first book *The Marquetry Course*. It is the one technique that relies solely on cutting veneers, not with the fretsaw, but with a knife. It is one of the reasons why marqueteurs wanted veneers sawn as thinly as possible from the log, so they could cut and assemble some motifs with a small knife.

For most of the motifs we see built by the template method, holly was used because, although it is botanically classed as a hardwood, the texture is soft and free of any grain or figuring marks and accepts dyes readily, which was the other reason for needing thin veneers. The motifs concerned were fans or patera, which our designer mainly presented in a dyed-pink or red colour. It is worth noting at this stage that dyed veneers were purchased from specialist dyers, most likely operating in and around London and supplying a range of dyed veneers to London-based furniture makers of the time. (I explore this aspect at the end of this chapter.) The dyed veneers were holly and produced in sheet form. Typically, sizes could range from 300 mm² (1 ft²) to perhaps as large as 600 mm x 300 mm (2 ft x 1 ft).

Figures 3.61 to 3.69 take you through the stages of construction and, as you will see, the name 'template' becomes obvious, as the fan is made up using a pre-drawn pattern on a flat board. Regardless of the shape of the fan, pre-drawn templates can be reused time and again with the knowledge that each assembled motif will result in a perfect match to those built previously.

While no evidence exists of this method from the 18th century, after many years of study and examination of the numerous fans displayed across Chippendale's furniture, I have no doubt that this was the way fans were constructed. Each and every one displayed straight-line knife cuts on each flute that made up the fan, using a straight edge to cut against. Each flute was a separate piece of veneer with its grain pointing towards the centre. The scallops at the ends of each fan were either cut by hand using a knife, or cut with a half-round carver's chisel of the appropriate profile.

The final clue is where repeat fans exist. Each fan is a perfect copy of the rest, proving that a template was used to build multiple copies. That does lead to the one disadvantage because only one fan at a time can be built. While this is slower than multiple fretsawing, the extra time taken to construct a fan is more than compensated by the perfect accuracy the method offers. The hardest cut to make 'accurately' with a fretsaw is a long straight line, which is another reason why the flutes of fans were always knife cut.

Figures 3.61 to 3.69 show the step-by-step process used to make one replica half-round fan for the drawer fronts of the Diana and Minerva commode, as detailed in Chapter 6. There were three drawers across the front of the commode and two dummy drawers across each of the two end panels. In total nine identical fans were

Figure 3.60 Draw the template on a flat board, using compass and protractor to set dimensions.

Chapter 3 | Techniques

Figure 3.61 *After cutting each dyed veneer for the eight flutes, each one has to be sand shaded along one edge.*

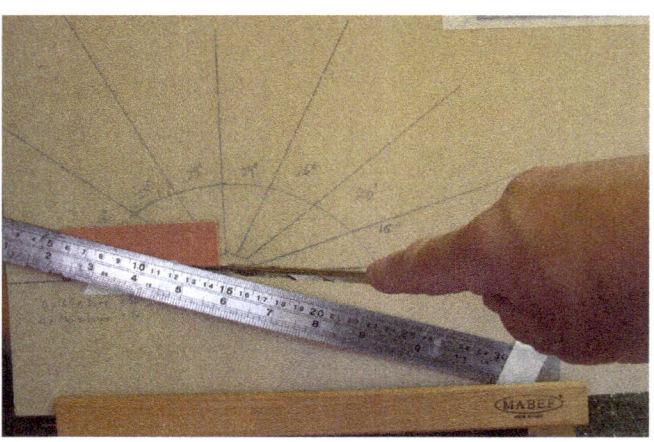

Figure 3.62 *Each flute is placed on the template and a rule lined up to the template line of the first flute. A knife is used to cut the veneer.*

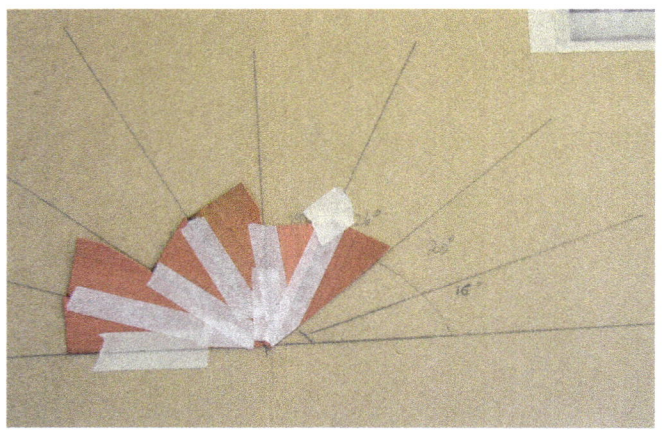

Figure 3.63 *Build up each flute in turn as shown. Hold together with veneer tape.*

Figure 3.64 *Using the shapes template, score lines to outer and inner edges, using a pencil.*

Figure 3.65 *Using the scalloped template, draw around each scallop as shown.*

Figure 3.66 *Fan ready for some knife cutting.*

CHAPTER 3 | TECHNIQUES

Figure 3.67 Cut complete and already looking 3-dimensional.

Figure 3.68 A white border attached and ready to cut the stringer.

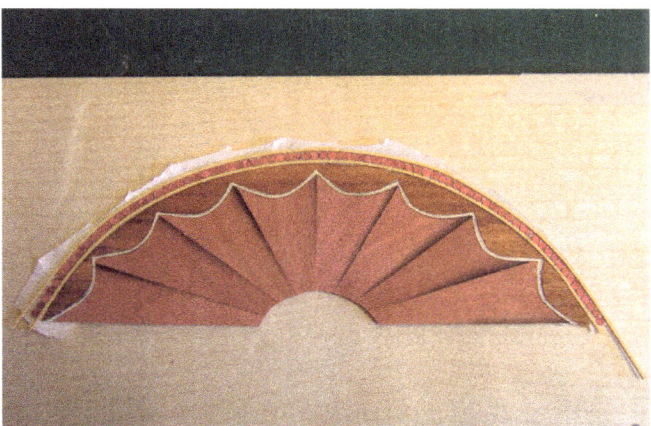

Figure 3.69 Fan complete and decorated with a padauk border and row of berries trapped between two stringers.

needed to complete this part of the construction. The template, as you see it drawn out in the following stepped illustration, was used to construct all nine fans in turn.

I trust you can see that other shapes of fans can be constructed in the same manner. Corner fans and circular fans follow the same procedure, once you have drawn the template for the size and shape. The only one that slightly differs is the two-part circular fan and I have shown this in the next subject – the Window Method.

Additionally, I show an alternative method in Chapter 6 when building the two-tone circular fan on the top of the Diana and Minerva commode.

THE WINDOW METHOD

I know this is going to surprise many modern-day marqueteurs, because until now the window method has always been considered a 20th-century innovation. I was led to believe that it was discovered and introduced during the mid-20th century by hobbyists in the UK to construct marquetry pictures. Discovering the use of this method, it is yet another example of the innovative mind of a very talented and forward-thinking journeyman working on Thomas Chippendale's furniture. I come across this man time and again, where his 'skilled hands and fertile mind' are clearly visible. Our journeyman performed the most intricate parts of the marquetry work during the six years' employment. *'Oh that such a talent can inspire us, yet we never know his name.'*

During my research, I have come across two separate instances where clearly the method was chosen deliberately, because it best fitted the situation. The first was a circular fan made for the Horseshoe Table built for Burton Constable Hall in Yorkshire. The fan was constructed from one sheet of veneer, possibly ash or sycamore, with the fan design drawn directly on to the veneer. This was probably the first circular fan used by Chippendale, which explains the chosen method of construction. The proof of the use of one sheet of veneer is the distinctive grain pattern, which can just be seen in the borders that surrounds each flute. The grain 'runs through' each flute from top, starting at about 1 o'clock, and running through to about 4 o'clock at the bottom of the illustration. Similarly, the grain on the left-hand-side runs from about 10 o'clock down to 7 o'clock (see Figure 3.70).

After gluing the template pattern directly on to the sheet of perhaps ash or sycamore, each flute is cut out, revealing the windows behind which dyed holly was placed, before the joints were scored around with a craft knife then removed and cut through with the knife, free hand, following the scored line. Each flute was then sand-shaded before being placed into its relevant window. Even the splits to the borders to the right-hand-side follow the direction of grain as just described.

The second occasion was again on a circular fan, but this time showing that 'our journeyman' had developed a better way to build the initial flutes of the fan by discovering the template method, then adding the second stage with the window method.

The difference between the fan built for the Diana and Minerva commode in 1773 and the fan built for the horseshoe table a year earlier demonstrates the learning curve that the marquetry motifs were presenting to those practicing the newly-found methodology. The Burton Constable fan in Figure 3.70 was built from one sheet of veneer, whereas the circular fan on the Diana and Minerva commode was built from individual strips of wood, pre-cut and built following the template drawing.

Figure 3.70* Circular fan on the Horseshoe Table at Burton-Constable Hall, constructed by the window method.

* *Courtesy of the Burton Constable Foundation*

MAKING BERRIES WITH A HOLLOW PUNCH

Berries dominate Chippendale's marquetry work, providing artistic relief to his motifs. While we may well see the inclusion of berries as being solely artistic, it is revealing to see and perhaps surprising to learn that they were also added as a practical necessity. They also suffered the all too often unfortunate misinterpretation of being displayed by penwork (or, as I prefer to call it, artwork), which I will explain after this technique.

Berries were usually expressed in dyed red, as in nature's form. Hollowed metal punches were made in different sizes to cater for the range of berries on Chippendale's designs. Tiny berries of approximately 4 mm diameter surrounded fans, while larger sizes, ranging from say 6 mm to 8 mm, were used on various other aspects of his designs. Figure 3.71 shows a 4 mm punch in use.

There were many occasions where berries were deliberately added to hide damaged veneers caused during the construction of certain elements. I refer in particular to leaf joints, where laurel leaf joints leave small areas of background veneer, which break at the joint where two leaf nodes converge. In most cases the background was satinwood, a very brittle wood that usually breaks away under these conditions, as I found myself when reconstructing them. It was obvious to me that despite the care I took to avoid the breakage shown in Figure 3.72, inevitably the satinwood chipped away leaving a gap at the leaf nodes. Without doubt, Chippendale's marqueteurs also had the same problem, because two berries are strategically placed in each leaf node to overcome the same problem I had encountered. Had I not had the opportunity to replicate this work, the problem and the enforced disguise would have certainly escaped me. It clearly demonstrates the close association Chippendale 'the designer' had with his trusted marqueteur in overcoming a practical problem by providing an artistic solution.

To make berries, the punch first punches out a berry from a sheet of dyed-red veneer. Then, using the same punch, the background veneer is punched to accept the berry. Before the berry is inserted, it is necessary to slightly increase the diameter to compensate for the thickness of the punch. To achieve this, all that's required is to hit the berry 'flat-on' once with a hammer to slightly enlarge the size. It sounds crude, but it works, because the berry when punched out, slightly 'cups' inwards, thus reducing its diameter. A tap by the hammer restores it to the correct size. Obviously one cannot prove that this technique was used, but we have to give credence to the possibility, particularly when we see the inventive minds of the journeymen at work on the more elaborate techniques clearly laid out before us.

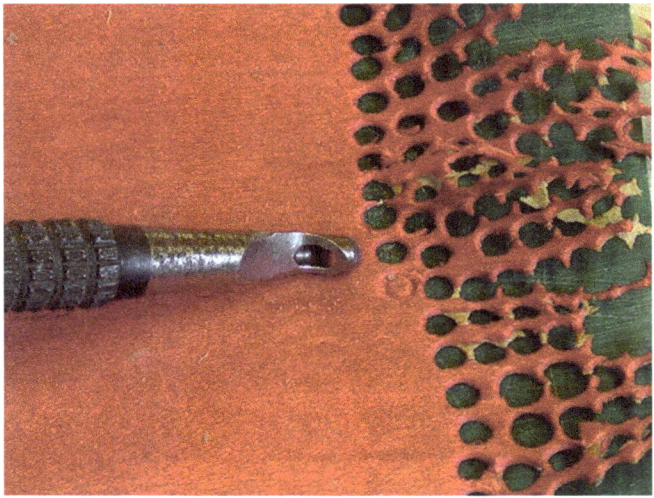

Figure 3.71 Sheet of dyed red veneer and hollow punch used to punch out berries.

Figure 3.72 Holes punched out where satinwood breaks at leaf nodes, thus hiding the inevitable problem, yet providing an artistic solution.

CHAPTER 3 | TECHNIQUES

CONSTRUCTING STRINGERS AND DECORATIVE BANDINGS

Marquetry stringers and bandings form part of the classic movement and standard designs existed and were used by all the London furniture makers.

Stringers existed in both the flat and square structure and were offered in widths consisting of 1 mm, 1.5 mm, 1.8 mm, 2.7 mm, 3.4 mm and 6 mm.

Stringers also came in two basic colours: ebony and white. White stringers could be supplied from sycamore, boxwood or holly. Exceptionally, wide stringers would be made, but they were then called 'flat lines' and usually dyed green. There are examples of such green lines on a number of Chippendale designs, usually 6 mm wide. On one isolated work I discovered blue stringers used on the curved table made for the circular dressing room at Harewood House. Like the original marqueteur, I had to dye some white stringers to achieve the blue colour. Chapter 7 shows the process.

Bandings were standardised during the classic period of marquetry furniture design. A banding consists of a filler enclosed by two or more stringers, and is generally constructed in the following widths: 5, 10, 20 and 30 mm. The stringers were, in most cases, white, but exceptionally ebony could be used. The infill materials were commonly satinwood, tulipwood, padauk, kingwood, boxwood and ebony. In almost all cases, satinwood, tulipwood and padauk were constructed with the grain across the width of the banding, therefore creating a cross-banding effect.

To make these additional trimmings, marqueteurs in the mid 18th century build simple jigs to cut and create 900 mm (3 foot/1 yard) long strips of stringers and bandings.

DISCOVERING A NEW INLAY TECHNIQUE THROUGH APPLICATION OF ARTWORK

While working on the replica Diana and Minerva commode, as described in Chapter 6, I discovered an example of artwork which led to finding another working method I had not envisaged. The evidence was without doubt unchallenged and led to a technique which answered the one vital question I had been asking myself since I started work on this project: "How was the marquetry on the dome constructed?"

The commode is renowned for its amazing incurving domed door, as seen in Figure 3.73. The dome slopes in three directions simultaneously, creating compound angles both vertically, horizontally and diagonally, which oppose each other. What makes the dome so challenging is that it is covered in veneer and marquetry, begging that one question. The answer was staring me in the face, as I noticed the artwork on the drawer front above the domed door.

Figure 3.74 shows artwork worn away, revealing the truth about how the swags were cut and then inserted into the background. Figure 3.75 offer a close-up picture of the swags, clearly revealing the eroding of the artwork over many years, but showing without doubt that the swags and drops were each sawn as one solid piece of dyed green veneer. The artwork was added during the polishing process to give the impression that three separate petals were cut for each leaf. Where artwork has not worn away, it clearly resembles sand-shading, giving the same impression that three veneers represent one leaf.

Figure 3.73* The domes door construction dilemma, with the solution staring me in the face as given on this picture!

* *Reproduced by the kind permission of the Trustees of the 7th Earl of Harewood Will Trust and the Trustees of the Harewood House Trust*

Figure 3.74*

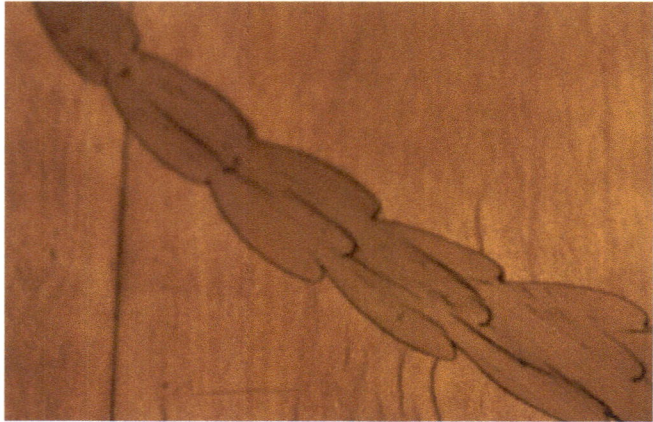

Figure 3.75*

Firstly, I need to explain how the left-hand drops and swags, as seen in Figures 3.74 and 3.75, were worn away. If we look at Figure 3.74 and imagine the long central drawer above the domed door is open and the lady of the house is sitting at the commode to perhaps write a letter or do some sewing, her clothing would rub against the opened drawer front. Over a long period (100 years and more) constant rubbing along the drawer front by successive owners has caused the artwork to erode. This is an amazing yet perfectly explainable social reason.

Despite previous theories that this commode was purely intended as a showpiece, in reality it was a well-used working piece of furniture and, as such, wear and tear occurred. I am indeed fortunate that it did, otherwise I may have missed the discovery of an otherwise hidden technique I now wish to reveal.

Throughout my research I have come to the conclusion that drawer fronts were nearly always 'farmed out' to external contractors. The skill level always suffers when compared with the rest of the two-part sawn technique used on the remaining panels. However, the most compelling evidence lies in the design of the swags shown at Figure 3.74. They are very simple and I believe that this was a deliberate ploy on part of the designer. The reason why the laurel leaves don't have sharp points to their outer petals is due to the constraints of the inlay knife and its operator. By rounding the edges of the petals it makes it easier to cut out the shapes with the inlay knife and avoid the problem of making nicks into the background veneers where they are not needed, as shown at Figure 3.2 of this chapter.

Domed door technique applied to the Diana and Minerva commode

Discovering the inlay technique was like lifting a dark veil from my eyes because I now had the answer about how the veneers and the marquetry were laid across the complex compound angles that make up the Diana and Minerva domed door.

If we look at Figure 3.73, we can see that the dome consists of a central fan surrounded by eight equal segments traversing the dome, starting on the left and arching across the dome to the right-hand side. Each of the eight segments is of equal size. Eight marquetry swags bisect each segment, by running across the direction of grain, while eight marquetry drops are placed along the joints of the segments being laid in line with the grain. Eight tiny daisy-type flowers are placed where two segments meet at the top of the dome. This was a vital and practical way of hiding gaps, which occur between the segments as the opposing pull caused by the compound angles on each joint. A small gap always occurs, as I found for myself when I replicated this panel (Chapter 6). This is yet another example of our marqueteur's practical knowledge of inlaying techniques coming to the rescue with a modified design.

Pre-veneering panels to substrates which are either concave or convex is the only solution to keeping the work under control and achieving desired results. The inlay knife makes inlaying fully controllable, achieving tight joints throughout the working process.

To see how the task of applying the satinwood background veneers and inlaying the marquetry was achieved, a full step-by-step illustrated procedure is given in Chapter 6.

* Reproduced by the kind permission of the Trustees of the 7th Earl of Harewood Will Trust and the Trustees of the Harewood House Trust

PENWORK – OR SHOULD I SAY 'ARTWORK'?

The term 'penwork' has long been associated with the 17th and 18th century practice of applying Indian ink to marquetry work using a quill pen.

I have to confess that had I not found myself having to apply penwork on some of the replica work seen in this book, I would not have questioned the assumed application technique. In reality I found it very difficult to use the pen to apply Indian ink to the marquetry work, simply because the pen would not bend and flow when attempting to draw curved lines.

In the end I consulted a colleague who works professionally as a decorator of antique furniture with artistic 'penwork' to see what tools were favoured. Lucinda Compton is a furniture restorer regularly applying artwork to Chinese decorated furniture as well as antique marquetry work. Lucinda assured me that she always used a fine artist's brush since, like me, she found the pen does not bend to allow the ink to flow on curved lines Because of this I will, from now on, refer to the process as 'artwork'. Ultra-fine artist's brushes provide the perfect tool for the work. Much of the artwork on Chippendale's marquetry is seen on acanthus leaves, where long curved lines give the impression of fine veins running along the leaves. If the artwork is correctly applied, it enhances the overall effect, but over-enthusiasm can ruin the finished appearance. Unfortunately, we all too often experience a short cut that slightly diminishes the completed work. One such motif is berries. Instead of using real berries punched out of veneer, berries are far too often displayed by use of the artist's brush.

Artwork was a fashionable addition to 18th century marquetry decoration and in most cases Chippendale's artisans used it to good effect, adding artistic expression to marquetry foliage in particular. Acanthus leaves become more flamboyant with the addition of artwork; laurel leaves become three-dimensional as accent lines are added; and plumages become more life-like.

The application of artwork requires the surface to be first sanded flat ready to accept a polish. One or two coats of base polish are applied and allowed to dry. The artwork requires a paint that will not be dissolved by further coats of polish and although I have not had any existing paint analysed, one would imagine water-based

Figure 3.76* Two rams' heads and torchere flames on two matching display cabinets showing fine artwork.

paint to be the most appropriate, since either spirit, lacquer or wax based polishes were adopted in the 18th century.

In Figure 3.77, we see the use of colour, with red paint used on a torchere to represent flames. Evidence of black paint can be seen on the leaves above the flames.

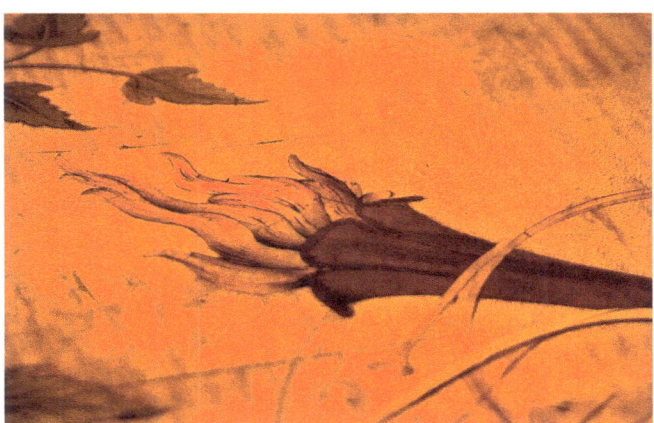

Figure 3.77* Torchere showing red paint to depict flames. Commode supplied by Chippendale to Nostell Priory.

* *Kind permission of the Firle Place trust*

This is part of a commode supplied by Chippendale for Nostell Priory, but not made by him.

Artwork versus engraving

We have seen an example of adding artwork to marquetry in the previous pages when discussing the drawer fronts of the Diana and Minerva commode. When performed skilfully, artwork adds an acceptable medium, giving realism to the foliage and surrounding motifs. It is relatively quick and inexpensive to apply and was used extensively on the majority of Chippendale's commissions.

Conversely, on more prestigious commissions, our designer opted to use the elaborate and expensive medium: engraving. Removing thin slivers of veneer from a motif and filling the resulting gap with a dark wax to embellish marquetry work is achieved by the engraving technique. It is a highly specialised skill and, to that end, expensive.

Of the known commissions given in this book, only four works were decorated with this medium. Our designer used it only on the most prestigious commissions, and each made for Harewood House. These include the Diana and Minerva commode, the two matching pier tables made for the drawing room, the 'Lunar' table made for the yellow drawing room (now in a private collection) and the pier table made for the, now removed, Circular Dressing Room (now the property of the Chippendale Society).

Figure 3.80*

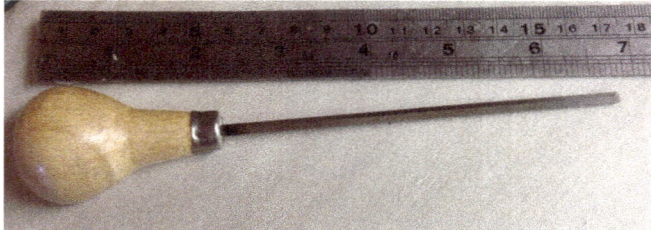

Figure 3.78 Engraver's tool, or 'burin'

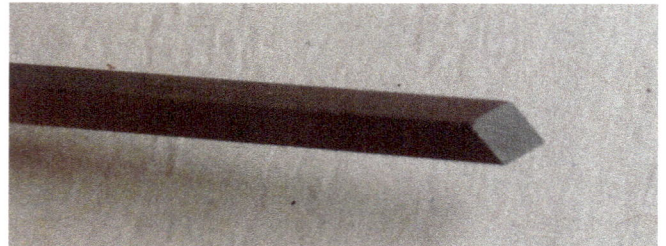

Figure 3.79 V-shaped notch on engraver's tool

An engraver's skill is not born overnight but through a given aptitude for the medium, amplified by extensive training. A fully accomplished engraver must be capable of working on many different materials, which include metals such as brass, pewter, silver and bronze. Engraving ivory was applied, as we have seen on, the Diana and Minerva commode as well as on the Lunar table (see Chapters 6 and 8 respectively).

In addition to engraving ivory, the marquetry work also received the same application. The technique offers much finer accent lines than that achieved by artwork applied by a brush, resulting in much classier lines of embellishment. The engraver's tool, sometimes referred to as an 'engraver' or a 'burin', is seen in Figure 3.78. The tiny 'v' shaped notch at the end of the tool (see Figure 3.79) allows the engraver to dig out slivers of material. In marquetry work, slivers of wood are taken from veneers, mainly to represent veins in foliage work. Other slivers provide artistic embellishment across different motifs within the design concept.

The overall result greatly enhances the finished marquetry work, achieving the all-important classic appearance. Figure 3.80 shows extensive engraving work to the curved back table featured in Chapter 8.

* Reproduced by the kind permission of The Chippendale Society

WHO SUPPLIED AND PERFORMED ALL THE MARQUETRY AND FINISHING WORK, IN LONDON, FROM C.1760?

This is a very thorny subject, which has puzzled historians for many years. Both the supply of marquetry materials in all their forms and the processes needed to apply the required skills are easy to see and quantify. The problem is that there are no records showing who performed them, or where they were carried out. We do know that many London-based rival firms were making and supplying similar classic marquetry decorated furniture from c.1760. There was certainly a work demand of such magnitude to warrant centralisation.

We have always known that marquetry is a specialised skill, not readily akin to cabinetwork. The training of marqueteurs is again extensive and lengthy if all aspects of the trade are to be realised. The French call the marqueteur an *ebeniste*, which embraces all the finishing processes needed to complete the furniture after the cabinetwork is complete. This makes sense since each of the processes and skills are specialised, and as such are better centralised with one company.

To establish and run a central business to meet the demands of a thriving marquetry trade across London at this time would include:

- understanding woods and all their individual characteristics
- sourcing woods from home and abroad
- storing timbers waiting to be sawn
- sawing veneers from the trunk to produce stock
- storing veneers to maintain the right environment
- dyeing veneers to produce the necessary colour palette for the classic marquetry work of the day
- providing the skills of fretsawing, knife cutting and inlaying marquetry work
- providing skills of hammer veneering and stick-as-you-go
- providing techniques of book and quarter matching veneers and applied marquetry
- providing sandshading technique
- producing standard stringers and decorative bandings to meet the classic demand
- making repeat designs by the prick and pounce method
- knowing how to use and apply different glues for securing veneers and other materials
- knowledge and skill of finishing, including levelling and sanding veneers and marquetry
- applying artwork by brush
- application of engraving
- polishing
- making and fitting brass mounts for furniture decoration

Discovering the basic two types of surface decoration (inlay versus two-part fretsawing) poses more questions than answers, but does provide a clue as to where marquetry work was carried out. We know marquetry work is a specialised skill and can be carried out, in most cases, independent of the cabinetwork; marqueteurs are capable of preparing line drawings to use as working templates. Making replica drawings by using the prick and pounce method was common practice to them. Purchasing timbers for sawing into veneers, both for use as background foils as well as dyed veneers for depicting marquetry images, forms part of a marqueteur's stock. We know that all the designs used, not only by Chippendale, but also his contemporaries, were very similar to each other. They each followed the same classic designs, using similar, and in most cases the same, background veneers to build the panels. The dyed woods were the same colours across all makers and were produced using the same dye materials.

We know there are just four different methods of construction when it comes to cutting marquetry motifs. These are the inlay method, two-part fretsawing, the template method and the window method. (The inlay method is highlighted in Elias Martin's painting seen in Figure 3.8.) As the painting suggests, this is a very small operation, consisting of perhaps two or three marqueteurs, and perhaps only a small number of firms offered this type of construction. Two-part fretsawing, however, needs a larger operating establishment, each requiring at least one large treadle saw to cut the veneer motifs and matching background veneers. This company would also need skilled artisans who could apply the stick-as-you-go and hammer veneering techniques.

We know that two conflicting methods of applying 'surface decoration' effectively split the industries into two distinct operators, one method applying artistic brush work and the other engraving the surfaces. It is clear from my own research, as detailed in this book, that where inlay work was performed, the artistic decoration was always applied by brush. Conversely, where two-part fretsawing occurred, both brush work and/or engraving was used.

We also know that both operating companies sometimes worked on the same commissions, each performing their own individual methodology. An example of this is the Diana and Minerva commode, where the three drawer fronts were clearly inlaid and art/brush work applied to provide the final surface decoration. In contrast, the rest of the commode was cut and laid using two-part sawing plus the template method, followed by the addition of engraving to the marquetry and the two ivory flesh parts of the figures Diana and Minerva. This joint working arrangement occurred whenever drawers formed part of the furniture piece. It was simple and safe to send off the drawers to a different, and smaller, operative, while the main unit was with a larger marquetry specialist.

It is also worth considering the production of dyed veneers and the making of stringers and decorative bandings. We know all the London furniture makers used the same dyed colours and the same stringers and decorative bandings. It was part of the classic medium to stick to the same materials, therefore forming the reasoning for central production under one firm.

Additional fitments such as brass work could not, in most cases, be fitted to the furniture until the marquetry work was completed. In the case of the Diana and Minerva commode for instance, brass berries form long strips that fit on top of marquetry work on the eight columns between the doors, drawers and curved side panels. It's usually part of the marqueteur's skill to get the brass mounts made and to fit them when delivered from the brass foundry. As already mentioned, in France the marqueteur, titled *Ebeniste*, is usually responsible for all additional attachments required over and above cabinetwork. I imagine the same operating divisions of responsibility applied in London during this period.

The company, if it existed, would need a sizable set of workshops to hold all the materials and perform the processes listed above. These workshops would have to include the following accommodation to effectively operate:

- a timber shed for raw timbers
- a space for sawing timbers into veneers
- a room for storing sawn veneers
- a room(s) for dyeing veneers and holding the necessary materials and equipment
- a room for holding treadle saw(s) and large assembly work tables
- space to perform sand shading
- space for preparing, making and storing stringers and decorative bandings
- space for applying engraving work
- room(s) for polishing and finishing processes
- room(s) for producing brass mouldings.

My final opinion as to who performed the work on Thomas Chippendale's marquetry work is based on what I have already stated above. Yes, our designer deployed two distinct, yet different cutting and laying techniques, most likely performed from two different workshops. However, I am convinced the same marqueteur performed most, if not all, of the classiest aspects of the marquetry work.

My overriding belief remains: the same highly talented marqueteur worked on the great man's commissions. Whether that was as a Chippendale employee or employed by a central London based marquetry workshop just described is not known. Perhaps one day, like me, another passionate researcher will find evidence of these working arrangements within the capital city.

I trust this chapter and the previous chapter on materials and tools have been of educational benefit and have provided you with enough information into workshop practices as carried out in London establishments. I hope the following marquetry projects I feature will be better understood with the information about the range of materials, tools and working techniques revealed in these two all-important chapters.

CHAPTER 4

DYES AND DISCOVERY

INTRODUCTION

Today's antique furniture sadly lacks the real impact of colour that was originally evident. As a result mainly of exposure to sunlight and atmospheric pollution, particularly in city environments, the true colours of the woods have, in most instances, been reduced to differing shades of brown. Had it been possible to prevent exposure, which in almost all cases it was not, we would today be enjoying furniture made during the last millennium that displayed the rich colours of the tropical hardwoods they were constructed from, as well as the vibrant addition of dyed veneers used in the marquetry work.

Until recent times, the only way to find out what dyed colours lurked beneath the surface of the polish was to either remove lock escutcheons to reveal veneers hidden from light or to actually lift and remove marquetry elements from their location. The latter is only possible where damage to the work is sufficient to warrant intervention. Conservation carried out on the Harewood Library writing table, discussed and revealed in Chapter 5, illustrates such action.

However, because of a new and exciting scientific invention, I am able to reveal the dyes that were used on other furniture items, where physical intervention is prohibited. Each application process is discussed and illustrated in this important chapter, giving you a unique insight into the secrets of how 18th century dyed veneers were first sourced and then applied.

In this chapter, I show how coloured marquetry was first identified and subsequently recreated, allowing me to build a reproduction door and matching drawer panels on the Harewood Library writing table. The problem with this conservation exercise, as I detail in Chapter 5, was that it had to rely on guesswork as to which dyes were used to create the colours we revealed.

In stark contrast, I show a new technique which came about through a chance opportunity while presenting a paper at an International Marquetry Symposium held in Sweden in 2007. Also at the same event was a German conservator scientist, Heinrich Piening, who had developed a technique of identifying dyestuffs that had been used on antique furniture without harming the integrity of the original marquetry. This was groundbreaking and came to my attention at such an opportune time.

However, before we embark in detail on these two important events, it is perhaps useful to understand the history behind the manufacturing of dyes in England.

The main ingredient necessary to make a successful and lasting dyestuff, in the 18th century, is the mordant, which make dyes 'bite' into the material they are applied to and stay permanent. Without a mordant, dyes would simply wash away when in contact with water or polish. The discovery of one type of mordant and the subsequent production of it in England, during the early part of the 17th century, provides an amazing, yet true, story embracing chemistry, engineering, royal monopoly and government legislation but, most of all, over 250 years of unparallelled human endeavour.

ENGLAND'S ALUM TRADE

Alum, or 'aluminium potassium phosphate' as it is chemically known, was first discovered in Italy during the early part of the 15th century. Roman foot soldiers first noticed that their white socks turned yellow when in contact with a certain type of loose crystal and that no amount of washing would remove the colour. It was further discovered that if the crystals were dissolved in water and mixed with vegetable dyes, the colours remained in the cloths. Similarly, they found that the solution worked to keep leather permanently soft.

From these discoveries, Italy generated its own cloth dyeing and leather softening industry which soon attracted trade with other European countries, including England. However, this precious trade was abruptly halted when King Henry VIII (1491–1547) wanted to divorce Catherine of Aragon and marry Anne Boleyn. The Catholic Church would not allow it, in response to which King Henry broke off all communications with the Pope and the Vatican and ceased overseas trading with Italy. He set up his own church – the Church of England – and created his own laws to suit his own needs.

Unfortunately, the cessation of the alum trade with Italy caused England to look elsewhere for another supplier. A similar dyeing works was operated in Flanders (Belgium) and English cloth manufacturers traded with them, but the dyes were not very reliable and therefore the search was on across England to find a raw mineral to produce their own mordant.

The north coast of Yorkshire provided the answer. The Jurassic rocks along the coast both to the north and south of Whitby held a mineral that, after 30 years of experimentation, proved to be capable of making alum. Unlike the Romans, who had natural alum present in the form of crystals, the English version had to be manufactured. Natural alum exists where previous volcanic action has occurred, which provided the clue as to how to make it from an 'unnatural' source.

As with most national logistical problems, the answer to the supply was solved at the highest level. Thomas Chaloner of Guisborough, North Yorkshire, a Member of Parliament, campaigned for government support for the 'chemical' industry. Alum was now so important to the country's economy that Chaloner was given complete autonomy of the whole process by King James 1 of England. He opened the first alum works in 1604 and, by 1609, alum became a 'Royal Monopoly'.

In total, 30 alum works were opened along the Yorkshire coast and, at the height of the industry, the county was producing almost 5,000 tons of alum a year. The mineral was one of the most highly prized products in Europe with a value so great that efforts to secure its monopoly sparked off intensive trade wars, including raids by French, Dutch and Spanish pirate ships who tried to storm the sites along the coast. Farmers and fishermen fired muskets from cliff tops to fight off invading pirates and at Ravenscar a cannon was erected on the cliff top.

It became obvious that the scarcity of the raw mineral increased its market value, as its use now included such products as making paper, tanning leather, dyeing fabrics, fixing watercolours and, most importantly, medicines. It was used as a treatment for eczema, chilblains, bleeding and even as a contraceptive. Wood dyeing was to benefit much later.

It is thought that Chaloner visited Italy and persuaded two 'Italian alum workers' to return to England with him to teach the manufacturing processes. First, the dark grey shale had to be hacked from the cliff face using picks, hammers and chisels. The shale was heated by huge bonfires measuring some 15 metres high and 30 metres across and initially fuelled by brushwood.

Figure 4.1 Remains of the Peak Alum Works at Ravenscar, showing the outlines of two steeping pits now covered in grass.

Figure 4.2 Red shale

Eventually, as production increased and wood became a spent commodity, coal was shipped in from mines in Durham and Sunderland. The fires burned non-stop for a year, with rain and snow providing a welcoming coolant.

After this, 'liquor men' washed the shale in steeping pits to produce the alum liquor. Pitmen emptied the pits and dumped the now unwanted red shale (shown in Figure 4.2) on spoil heaps; these can be seen even today, rising up to 50 feet high. Remains of two such spoil heaps are seen in Figure 4.3 covered in red gorse.

The alum liquor had to pass through more stages of cleansing with water, a commodity which had to be caught and stored in reservoirs central to the alum works. Some alum sites had as many as six steeping pits, where the shale was transferred from pit to pit to assist cleaning and separation. Wooden channels were built into the ground for the mineral to trickle down from the final steeping pit to the alum-house, allowing gravity to control its journey.

Alum-houses

The liquefied mineral provided the first ingredient for making alum. While the processes within the alum-houses, at the time, remained top secret, we now know that potassium and ammonia had to be added during production. Potassium was obtained by toasting seaweed. Since the alum works were all centred along the north-east coast, the North Sea provided an abundance of seaweed which was collected in fleets of ships along the coast and delivered to the alum sites. The nearby port of Whitby gained a boost to their ship-building industry. Toasted seaweed provided the all-important liquor obtained from the burnt seaweed ash. It took 20 tons of burnt seaweed to produce one ton of ash. One important by-product from this chemical process was Epsom salts, used nationally both as a fertiliser and production in medicine.

However, providing ammonia was not as straight forward, since it had to be obtained from human urine! Initially, local farmers and their families were invited to contribute daily into buckets placed outside the farmsteads but, not before long, demand outstripped the supply and the industry looked for help. The demand for ammonia was such that the collection of urine was carried out on a grand scale. Receptacles were placed on street corners in the east coast cities of London, Hull and Newcastle and the public were invited to contribute. It was preferable to gather urine from the working classes, since it was proven that samples from rich personage contained impurities as a result of high intakes of wines and spirit.

Chaloner had such faith in the production of alum and its value to the country that he told his servants *'they could sell his urine for a penny a firkin'*. The urine was transferred weekly into barrels and shipped along the north-sea to the coastal towns of Whitby and Ravenscar, North Yorkshire, where they were offloaded onto shale beaches. Wooden sleepers (tracks still visible today) were laid into the shale for the barrels to roll up the beach till they reached the cliff face. Snake-like tracks were cut into the cliff face for pony and cart to transport the

Figure 4.3 Cliff face today, with its raw grey-coloured mineral and two remaining red spoil heaps in front.

barrels up to the alum-house, situated on the cliff top. Similarly, barrels were used to carry the completed alum down to the boats for onward distribution.

The conditions in bleak winters, with biting easterly winds and the stench of ammonia permanently in the nostrils, were appalling and it is hard to imagine the wretched life the workers had to endure. It is generally believed that the term 'taking the piss' originates from this very activity! To this day, the city of Hull claims to be the first city in the world to build the first outside public lavatory.

Inside the alum house, the brewer would test the alum liquor after all ingredients were added. The gravity was finally tested by dropping a hen's egg into the mixture to see whether it floated, which would indicate that the concentration of liquor was correct to allow the resulting alum to set into crystals without formation of ferrous sulphate.

The most amazing fact to emerge from this phenomenal operation is that England produced its first chemical industry some 150 years before chemistry was formally discovered.

Production of alum continued for 250 years along this coastline until 1855, when the discovery of coal gas provided the by-product 'aniline' as an alternative mordant. The alum industry finally came to an end. Today, the spoil heaps, the steeping pits, the ruins of the alum-house and the wooden sleepers along the beach at Ravenscar are ghostly images retained as a national museum for all to see and relive the unrelenting determination of man's quest to overturn adversity into an international industry of epic proportions.

DISCOVERING DYES

Dyeing is a process steeped (forgive the pun) in history. The first written record of dyestuffs was set down in China in 2600 BC. In more recent times and applicable to wood dyes, it is recorded in 1641 when dyeing cloth 'in the wood' was introduced in England, using dye extracts from trees such as madder, weld, logwood and fustic. After this, more of nature's products have increased the range of vegetable dyes, including brazilwood dust, barberry root, wig tree, indigo and many more.

The mineral product iron sulphate increases the range of colours available to the dyer, together with animal extracts from the female Mexican beetle – cochineal. The all-important mordant is needed to retain the dye into the material it is applied to. Mordants used in 18th century come in four different forms and each will be discussed in this chapter.

Making dyes for the reproduction door panel of the Harewood library writing table

The first method used to discover what and where dyes were used on Chippendale's furniture was when I was asked to replicate one of the door panels on the famous Harewood Library writing table, now held at Temple Newsam House in my home city of Leeds. Chapter 5 deals with the details of that project, showing the step-by-step process of constructing the marquetry work.

The project team who produced the initial investigation into the woods used on the writing table and produced the first computer facsimile showing what the panel may have looked like when first made, consisted of: Conservator Ian Fraser, Leeds Museums and Galleries; Dr Adam Bowett, Furniture and Wood Historian; Simon Feingold, Restorer and Antique Finisher; plus myself.

The work was carried out in 2003 in Ian's workshop and studios at Temple Newsam House, Leeds. These were exciting and, for us, pioneering days, but I have to remind you that the only evidence we had to work on, before we started, were the colours we discovered when we lifted marquetry elements on the door panels shown in Chapter 5, plus a set of known 18th century recipes which may or may not have been used to dye the colours. When we looked at the options during the 18th century to produce, say, a red dye, more than half a dozen dyestuffs were available. Similarly, four or five dyestuffs were available to produce yellow. Despite the shortage of proof as to which dyestuffs produced the colours we found, the important task was to reproduce the colours to the nearest tonal quality.

Recipe selection was another challenge, since availability was both wide yet conflicting in make-up from one author to another. Dyers bestowed great secrecy to their methods and guarded their own personal recipes, including amusing comments aimed to get that 'special effect' like 'boil it tenderly' and 'take your smet' and finally the mind-provoking instruction 'add a quarter or a little less piss'.

Dyeing the colours

To replicate the dyed colours, we used recipes from an 18th century document held in the British Library and titled:

> *The Cabinet-Maker's Guide to the whole art of Dyeing, Staining Varnishing & Beautifying of WOOD by PETER WEBER. Cabinet-maker and Ebonist. Second Edition*

In total, six different tones of colours were identified: three shades of green and three shades of red. These, together with the natural white colour, were all produced from holly veneer (*ilex aquifolium*). The green shades ranged from a darkish tone for the acanthus leaves, through mid-green for the laurel leaves, to a lighter green for the stringing surrounding the satinwood banding. The latter bordered the central marquetry panel.

The red shades consisted of a burgundy-red for the lower central vase, a pinkish-red for the upper portions of the central vase, and a scarlet-red for the berries and ribbons which adorn most of the elements within the design. Similarly the theme continued for the drawer fronts, where dark green was used for the acanthus leaves, light green for the stringing around the circular fans and pinkish-red for the flutes of the fans. On both the door and drawer fronts, white holly was artistically and selectively used for contrast and harmony.

During the following dyeing processes and as the colours emerged, the elements of Chippendale's design began to unfold and, for the first time, we realised we were revealing a polychromatic masterpiece.

Green-dyed holly

Weber's recipes for producing green-dyed holly could not have been more straightforward. On the following pages are (un-edited) extracts from his manuscript, given in italics.

> ### Safety Note
> If using the following products, safety precautions are vital, since the substances can be dangerous if not handled correctly.
>
> - **To avoid contact with skin, use rubber gloves to protect the hands and safety glasses to protect the eyes.**
> - **To protect clothing, a rubber or cotton apron should be worn.**
> - **Always use 'inert' vessels to mix and heat the dyes, such as ones made of copper, earthenware or glass.**
> - **Do not use iron or aluminium vessels, as this can adversely affect the chemical balance.**
>
> Remember that 'oil of vitriol' is known today as sulphuric acid, and must only be added to water.
>
> **Never add water to sulphuric acid – it will EXPLODE.**

Recipe No 1

For a Fine Blue Dye

Take a clean glass bottle, into which put one pound of oil of vitriol, then take four ounces of the best indigo, pounded in a mortar into small lumps; put them in the vitriol (take care to set the bottle in a basin or glazed earthen pan, as it will ferment); after it is quite dissolved, provide an earthen or wooden vessel, so constructed that it will conveniently hold the veneers you mean to dye; fill it rather more than one third with water, into which pour as much of the vitriol and indigo (stirring it about) till you find the whole to be a fine blue dye, by trying it with a piece of white paper or wood; put in your veneers; let them remain till the dye has struck through.

Figure 4.4 Adam Bowett adopting safe practices

Chapter 4 | Dyes & Discovery

To Dye Yellow

Take of the roots of barberry four pounds, reduce it by sawing to dust, which put in a copper or brass trough, add four ounces of turmeric, to which put four gallons of water, then put in as many white holly veneers as the liquor will cover, boil them together for three hours, often turning them; when cool, add two ounces of aquafortis [today known as nitric acid], *and you will find the dye strike through much sooner.*

Figure 4.5 Barberry root and turmeric

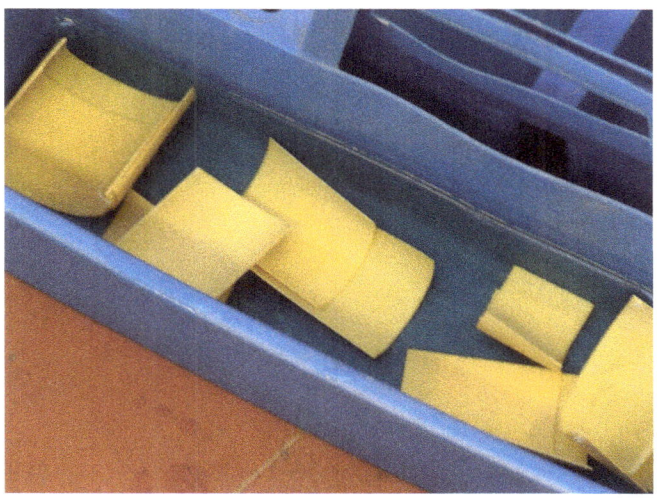

Figure 4.6 The resulting holly veneers, dyed yellow

However, the following recipe must be read also to fully understand the complete process.

To Dye Green

Proceed as before to produce a yellow, but instead of aquafortis, add as much of the vitriolated indigo as will produce the desired colour.

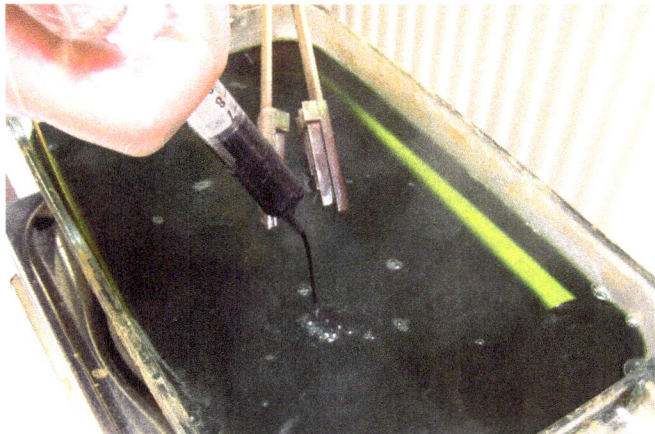

Figure 4.7 Adding vitriolated indigo

Figure 4.8 Results of dyeing holly with barberry root and turmeric: three green samples

CHAPTER 4 | DYES & DISCOVERY

The dye and vitriol quantities specified in the recipes were greatly reduced for our purposes, since we only needed to produce small amounts of green veneers. The different shades of green were achieved by reducing or increasing the amount of indigo to the yellow veneers. It was a question of trial and error on our part, and eventually we produced the required three shades of green shown in Figure 4.8. Three green samples illustrated show the dark green (right) for the acanthus leaves, the mid-shade (centre) for the laurel leaves and the light green (left) for the stringing.

Red dyes

We identified three shades of red, each needing a different recipe to achieve the desired shade.

Burgundy-red

Burgundy-red was produced from brazilwood and logwood chips (campeachy). The tiny marquetry triangular samples (see Figure 4.9) compare perfectly in colour to our dyed veneer shown on the right of Figure 4.9. We were supremely confident that they had used the same recipe to produce this colour. Later evidence was to confirm our belief as you will witness when the panel is cleaned up prior to polishing – as described in Chapter 5.

The burgundy colour was only used on the lower central vase, and therefore only a small quantity of holly was dyed.

Weber's recipe for making purple listed the following:

Take some chip logwood and crush brazilwood chips into dust and heat up both with one pint of water. Add as many veneer pieces of holly as required. Add two ounces of alum, and six ounces of pearl-ash, and let them boil two or three hours every day until the colour strikes through. Keep adding water to compensate for losses due to evaporation.

Dragon's blood

The pinkish-red colour surrounding the line of white columns was achieved with a resin extracted from the dragon tree, so called because of its barbed branches resembling a dragon's mane. This is one vegetable dye product that does not need a mordant to 'fix' it.

The resin, shown in Figure 4.11a, is a very sticky substance and will only dissolve in alcohol. The resin provides its own built-in mordant. I had to boil the dye on a low heat, for 2–3 hours every day for a week in

Figure 4.9 Brazilwood dyed sample (right) with original veneer (left)

Figure 4.10 Central part of vase showing burgundy colours obtained from brazilwood. Also the central column top centre, with white and pink/red columns provided the second red dye to be made using dragon's blood.

Figure 4.11a Resin extracted from the dragon tree

Figure 4.11b Dyed veneer sample showing dragon's blood pink colour

order to achieve full penetration. Figure 4.11b shows the veneer sample after dyeing. It gives a very pleasing pinkish/red colour ideal for the rounded column above the central vase.

The same dyed holly was used for the fans on the drawer fronts which I constructed later. I found the colour sandshaded very well, which is generally unusual for dyed veneers.

Red berries (cochineal)

The third and final red we produced was for the numerous red berries that adorn many of the elements on the panel. Red berries appear in clusters between the laurel leaves and surrounding the compass roses and small rosettes; they are used to decorate the roundels of the guilloche. Additionally, they provide the ribbons which bunch the white plumages together. Figure 4.12 shows one scarlet red berry removed from one of the original door panels.

To match this colour, we elected to use cochineal. The small female insect (*Dactylopius coccus*) feeds on cacti in Mexico and the West Indies. The Mexican species that we used provides the more scarlet colour.

The small dried black bodies (see Figure 4.13) are used today for colouring foodstuffs. When the bodies are heated in water, a bright scarlet red dye is released. After many trials (and failures) with different mordants to get the dye to penetrate fully through the veneers, we eventually found that tin chloride gave us complete penetration of the colour.

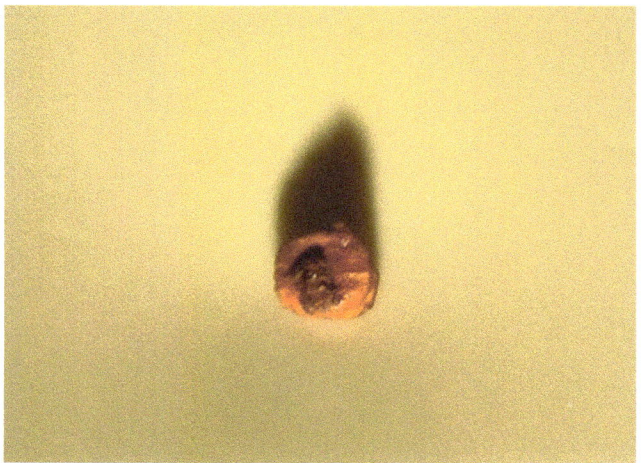

Figure 4.12 Original bright red berry removed from one of the door panels

Figure 4.13 Cochineal ready for dyeing the red berries

CHAPTER 4 | DYES & DISCOVERY

Figure 4.14 Holly soaking in tin chloride

Figure 4.15 Cochineal soaked for three days

First the veneers were soaked in tin chloride for one day (see Figure 4.14). This mordant was the key to achieving full penetration of the cochineal, where alum had previously failed.

Cochineal was added to the mordant mixture and heated on a low setting two hours a day for three days (see Figure 4.15). Finally, the colour we were looking for emerged, a deep scarlet red with a classic regency appearance (see Figure 4.16).

That completed all the dyeing, giving us the range of colours needed to commence the marquetry work (see Figure 4.17). Using 18th century recipes and dye products that were certainly in use during production of this work gave us a good feeling that we were repeating and experiencing the same practical problems encountered by our predecessors.

Natural holly

Holly is one of nature's whitest woods, which is one reason why it is ideal for dyeing. We found that natural holly was used throughout the design. While the natural white has darkened slightly with age, it is still clearly visible on the panel.

Having completed our investigation, we were able to create a 'map' of the design to produce a master template to work from. Chapter 5 deals with the construction of the dyed veneers to rebuild the classic marquetry that make up the replica door and drawer panels on the Harewood Library writing table.

Figure 4.16 Deep scarlet colour achieved

Figure 4.17 A range of dyed veneers, illustrating our experiments

UV-VIS Spectronomy

Discovering the dye colours on the Harewood Library writing table required us to lift the original marquetry work, thus exposing the hidden dye colours below. Using 18th century recipes, we reproduced those colours to our satisfaction. The problem with this approach was the failure to identify which dye substances were used to create a particular colour. All we could do was to follow one original recipe from that period in the hope that we were using the same dyestuff that was used to colour the original. The following scientific approach proved that (in hindsight) we did get some right, and some wrong.

A ground-breaking scientific method came my way when I was invited to lecture at an International Marquetry Symposium in Vadstena, Sweden, in 2007. Also at that venue was a German conservator from Munich, Heinrich Piening, who gave a lecture on his recent research into obtaining evidence of dyestuffs used on antique marquetry work without any intrusion to the integrity of the original work.

UV-VIS Spectronomy (Ultra-violet Visual) is a scientific technique that produces a white light across the specimen of veneer under test at opposing angles of 0° and 45° for a period of 50 milliseconds, whereupon some of the white light is absorbed and some is reflected. The reflected light is detected and split by a spectrometer. This in turn produces a unique wavelength, which can later (back at the laboratory) be run against a computer library of known dye pigments until a matching wavelength is obtained.

Between my first meeting with Heinrich in Sweden and his visit to me a year later, he completed his 'Doctorate of Science' studying the same subject matter. Heinrich (now Dr Piening) arrived in London in February 2008 to first carry out tests on a roll-top desk made by Jean-Henri Riesener, dated 1769. The desk, made for the Comte d'Orsay (Count d'Orsay) c.1770, is held at the Wallace Collection, London. Heinrich also gave a lecture to an invited audience at the London collection before travelling up to Leeds the following morning.

Tests at Temple Newsam House on a table made by the London-based French cabinet-maker Pierre Langlois, were repeated on Chippendale's celebrated Library writing table made c. 1770. I chose the latter piece because of our dye experiments discussed earlier in this

Figure 4.18* Heinrich performing tests at Harewood House on a pier table while I log the readings

chapter – I was curious to learn whether our selection of dyestuffs was correct or otherwise. In total, about 90 scans for dye pigments took place on the two pieces.

On the third and final day of testing, Heinrich and I visited Harewood House, where we tested a selection of Chippendale's pieces: one of the two large pier tables made for the Music Room (see Figure 4.18), followed by the world famous Diana and Minerva commode and the Library steps, the latter made to match the library writing table tested the previous day at Temple Newsam House.

The final Harewood piece was the celebrated pier table made in 1775, which I refer to as the 'Lunar' table and consider to be England's finest marquetry work (see Figure 4.19). I was particularly excited to learn about the dyestuffs on this table because the green dyes are very clearly still evident on the acanthus leaves, ribbons and laurels.

In the afternoon, a visit to Newby Hall in North Yorkshire allowed us to test three pieces: a card table (one of a pair), the dining table and one of its matching pedestals. These three pieces, made by Thomas Chippendale the Younger, were chosen purposely to get a spread of time between items made at the start of the firm's marquetry production (c.1770) and nearing the end (c.1778).

In total, 286 scans were made and stored on the computer with pictorial images annotated to show where and at what point of the marquetry the scans took place.

* Reproduced by the kind permission of the Trustees of the 7th Earl of Harewood Will Trust and the Trustees of the Harewood House Trust

Chapter 4 | Dyes & Discovery

Table 4.1 Items of furniture tested using UV-VIS spectronomy

Furniture item	Maker	Period	Location
Pier table	Pierre Langlois	c.1776	Temple Newsam
Harewood Library writing table	Thomas Chippendale	c.1771	Temple Newsam
Pier table (music room)	Thomas Chippendale	c.1772	Harewood House
Diana and Minerva commode	Thomas Chippendale	c.1773	Harewood House
Library steps	Thomas Chippendale	c.1771	Harewood House
Pier table	Thomas Chippendale	c.1775	Private collection
Card table	Thomas Chippendale the Younger	c.1778	Newby Hall
Pedestal for dining table	Thomas Chippendale the Younger	c.1791	Newby Hall
Dining table	Thomas Chippendale the Younger	c.1791	Newby Hall

By using these pictures and computer data sheets, Heinrich would be able to correlate the results once they were matched to known dyes.

The tests

In total, over two days, we tested five items made by Chippendale, three by Chippendale the Younger, and one French piece made by Pierre Langlois in his workshop in Tottenham Court Road, London. The items are listed in Table 4.1. The selections I made were intended to spread the usage of dyes over as long a period as possible. By doing so I hoped to see a pattern emerge. I was not certain what type of pattern, but hopefully the finding would lead to some firm conclusion as to the way dyeing was performed and, more importantly, by whom. With a spread of 21 years (c.1770–1791), one would perhaps hope to see either consistency of selection of dyestuffs used or see intentional changes.

For each piece, I had pre-prepared data sheets cross referenced to black/white pictures of each marquetry panel I had chosen. In that way Heinrich and I had a two-way audit trail: (1) to match each marquetry element to its black/white picture, and (2) to match the reference number awarded by the computer for each test made, cross referenced to the same number I entered on the pictures. This provided Heinrich with a full data trail necessary to provide the end results. For example, when testing, say, the Diana and Minerva commode, the computer would start at HAR1 (HAR to indicate the test was held at Harewood and 1 being the first test), with the numbering running sequentially for all pieces tested at Harewood.

Results (summary)

As I expected, the range of dyes used by Chippendale and identified through UV-VIS Spectronomy analysis was relatively small. However, it is true to say that the types of dyestuff used were a mixture of predictable and surprising. The predictable dyestuffs included those that have a long history of use, stretching back, in some cases, thousands of years. Table 4.2 describes the range, giving the dyestuff name, colour, origin, common name and botanical name.

Figure 4.19* Tests on Chippendale's and England's finest marquetry piece

* Private collection – reproduced by kind permission

CHAPTER 4 | DYES & DISCOVERY

Table 4.2 Results of UV-VIS spectronony tests, showing the range of dyestuffs identified

Dyestuff	Colour	Origin	Common name	Botanical name
Berberis	yellow	Worldwide	barberry	*Berberis vulgaris*
Weld	yellow	Worldwide	weld	*Reseda luteola*
Curcuma	yellow	Asia	turmeric	*Curcuma aromatica*
Young fustic	yellow	Worldwide	wig tree	*Cotinus coggygria*
Saffron	yellow	Asia	crocus flower	*Crocus sativus*
Madder	red	Asia	dyer's madder	*Rubia tinctoria*
Cochineal	red	Mexico	lac beetle	*Dactylopius coccus*
Henna	red	Asia	henna	*Lawsonia inermis*
Brazilwood	burgundy	S. America	brazilwood	*Caesalpinia echinata*
Kamala	orange	India	kamala	*Mallotus philippensis*
Campeachy	purple	West Indies	logwood	*Haematoxylum campechianum*
Indigo	blue	Madagascar	indigo	*Indigofera tinctoria*
Indigo carmine	blue	(manufactured colour made with indigo and sulphuric acid)		
–	green	(manufactured colour made up from a mix of yellow and blue dyes)		

Table 4.3 Table of dyes found on each piece of furniture tested

	Pierre Langlois table, Temple Newsam	Library writing table, Temple Newsam	Pier table, Music Room, Harewood House	Diana and Minerva commode, Harewood House	Library steps, Harewood House	'Lunar' pier table, private collection	Card table, Newby Hall	Pedestal, Newby Hall	Dining table, Newby Hall	Curved pier table, Temple Newsam
Berberis	■	■	■	■	■	■	■			■
Weld			■	■						
Curcuma				■		■				
Young fustic	■	■				■	■	■		
Saffron		■								
Madder						■		■	■	■
Cochineal		■		■						
Henna				■						
Brazilwood	■	■	■	■	■	■	■		■	■
Kamala						■				
Campeachy		■				■				
Indigo			■							■
Indigo carmine	■	■	■	■	■	■	■		■	■

It is immediately clear from Table 4.2 that five different plants were used to produce yellow dye and three different plants and the Lac beetle (cochineal) were used to produce red dye. This in itself is sufficient evidence to suggest that Chippendale did not produce his own dyes, but most certainly purchased the veneers already dyed from an external source.

To support this theory, we found that the source dyestuff for both yellow and red changed from one marquetry work to the work immediately following. There were even cases where different sources of yellows and reds were used on the same marquetry commission (see Table 4.3, which shows the results of all ten tests). Had Chippendale produced his own dyes, he would not have used five different sources of yellow, particularly when, as we found, the difference between the tonal values was minimal. The same argument applies to the three reds.

I am now convinced that veneer dyeing was centralised and that London workshops, including Chippendale's, purchased veneers which were already dyed. Specialist dyers would almost certainly have had access to the full range of dyestuffs coming into the country and would experiment with each product. Commercially this makes sense: dyeing woods is a very specialist subject, but it is also costly to set up the various source materials and equipment necessary to achieve large-scale production. Apart from the full range of dyestuffs, mordants and moderators (both acidic and alkaline) had to be sourced and stored. Small, medium and large inert vessels were essential for use as dye baths. In the 18th century, copper would most likely have been used for this purpose, since it did not affect the chemical balance and it is a good conductor of heat. A heat source was essential, just as was demineralised water to maintain pH levels.

A very pleasing aspect of the dye tests was to witness the precision given by Chippendale to depict and use the colours that perfectly matched the object. In particular, he made sure that flowers used in his designs were given the correct dye to match nature's colours. For instance we know that anthemions (honeysuckle flowers), prior to fully opening into full flower, have burgundy 'fronds or fingers'. It is in that pre-opening state that Chippendale and Robert Adam drew the motif, and from these tests we discover the dyestuff 'campeachy' (burgundy) used to represent these motifs. Similarly, acanthus flowers, in nature, have contrasting leaves of white and lilac or pink (depending on species) and the spectronomy results identified these colour pigments.

DYE TESTS AT SCHLOSS NYMPHENBURG

Schloss Nymphenburg (see Figure 4.20) is a Baroque palace situated in Munich, Germany. It was the summer residence of the rulers of Bavaria, and is now a state museum and workplace where Heinrich heads a team of furniture conservators. I had the privilege to work with him in his laboratory at Nymphenburg in the summer of 2009. In a most inspiring visit, Heinrich performed dye processes for each of the results he had previously discovered during his visit the previous year. Heinrich, shown in Figure 4.21 in his dedicated laboratory, gave me the most perfect hands-on masterclass of 18th century dyeing techniques.

What you read in this chapter is a result of that experience expressed, hopefully, in a coherent and basic style, without attempting to break into scientific dialogue. As a practising marqueteur without any previous experience in this subject, I have to produce the results in a factual and concise manner, understandable to all readers. I make no apologies to academic students if this chapter fails to answer scientific questions. My aim is to illustrate the results that Heinrich achieved, giving suggestions of dye recipes that may or may not have been used to produce the range of coloured veneers we know were available at the time.

Results

The best way to show the results is to list each dye identified, giving the source (animal, vegetable or mineral) of the dye, the chemical compound within the

Figure 4.21 Heinrich in his laboratory making blue dye

species that creates the dye colour, and then a recipe that may have been used to produce the end result.

Before doing that however, we need to look at the basics of dyeing and learn why we need to control the process and the materials used to make up the dyes. Without establishing and fully understanding the ground rules and the reasons for them, we cannot hope to achieve successful results.

Figure 4.20 Schloss Nymphenburg, Munich

Chapter 4 | Dyes & Discovery

THE BASICS OF DYEING

Before outlining the recipes for each of dyestuffs, there are three basic aspects of dyeing it is important to look at: acidity/alkinity, the use of mordants and the use of modifiers.

Acidity/alkinity

pH (power of Hydrogen) is a method of measuring the acidity or alkalinity of any given solution on a scale ranging from 1 (acid) to 14 (alkaline). In dyeing, we must aim to perform the process in a neutral or as near to neutral scale (7) as possible. For instance, the first basic ingredient we have to use in almost all dye recipes is water. Pure water has a pH of 7 (neutral), therefore it is essential that we use pure, demineralised water for dyeing. Sometimes referred to as de-ionised water, this is water that has had all mineral contents removed by being passed through a bed of ion-exchange resin which removes mineral salts.

This process is provided in professional dyeing laboratories by constructing filter plants into the incoming water system. For small to medium-scale users, demineralised water can be purchased in various container sizes to fit user consumption.

Other materials needed in the dye recipes given in this chapter each have their own pH level, as illustrated in the pH chart in Figure 4.22, which lists the various products, including the necessary mordants and modifiers.

Mordants

The term 'mordant' comes from the French word *mordre*, 'to bite', so 'mordant' means 'biting'. Mordants are mineral salts that bind dyes into fibre. They can directly affect light and wash-fastness, prevent colour leaching and make some colours brighter.

In the 18th century the main mordants used were alum (aluminium potassium sulphate), iron sulphate, tin chloride and copper.

Modifiers

Modifiers are chemicals that assist dyeing; they can help fix colour into fibre but are not strong enough in themselves to be considered mordants. Their main use is to maintain as near equilibrium to the pH state by

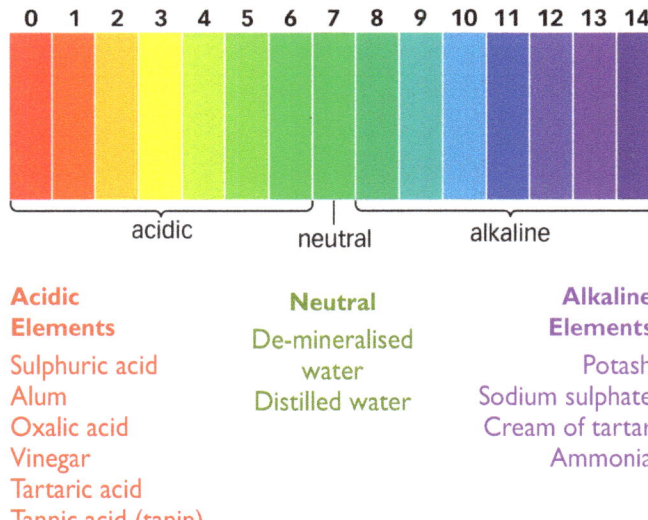

Figure 4.22 pH chart

balancing or counterbalancing dye baths from acid to alkali (and vice versa). Modifiers should be added according to individual dye recipes. Apart from alum, the acidic and alkaline products listed in Figure 4.22 are all modifiers.

Mordants – alum and tin

All the dye recipes given in this chapter rely on pre-mordanting the veneer samples. I will cover this procedure first. Mordants on their own can create an imbalance in the pH level and modifiers are used to correct this.

Quantities

It should be noted that the quantities given throughout this chapter are purposely kept to a minimum. This is because, during my brief visit to Nymphenburg, we had to complete all the processes for each colour in five days (including a weekend). To help achieve this we produced the dyed colours on samples of holly measuring approximately 25 mm². The samples were deliberately kept small to allow us to complete each recipe and achieve colour saturation during the short visit. The samples, produced solely for this publication, provide a coherent record and realistic illustration of the colours used.

Alum (aluminium potassium sulphate)

Recipe

8g alum
2g cream of tartar
100 ml water
Add veneer samples and warm to dissolve. Leave fully immersed for 24 hours, as shown in Figure 4.27. Take the veneers out and allow to fully dry naturally.

Figure 4.23 Alum   *Figure 4.24 Alum dissolved in water*

Tin chloride

Recipe

0.5g tin chloride
0.5g oxalic acid
0.5g cream of tartar
500 ml water
Take 400 ml water, warm to 40°C and dissolve the cream of tartar and the oxalic acid. Take 100 ml water, boil it and dissolve the tin chloride. When dissolved, put both solutions together. Add the veneer samples as shown below.

Figure 4.25 Tin chloride   *Figure 4.26 Tin chloride dissolved in water*

Veneer samples are shown soaking in alum and tin in Figure 4.27. Note the glass weights on top of the veneers to keep the samples submerged. Samples were left submerged overnight to achieve full penetration of veneer thickness. All veneer samples were saw-cut to thicknesses of 1–1.5 mm. Half were maple and the other half holly, so that we would see if any significant differences occurred between the two samples both after mordanting and after dyeing.

Figure 4.27 Veneer samples soaking – alum on the left and tin chloride on the right

RECIPES

The recipes given for each of the following dyestuffs are based on dyeing approximately six veneers, each measuring 25 mm². In practice and for large quantities of dyeing, the quantities needed should echo those given in whatever recipe selected.

My aim in this book is to identify the dyestuff, then reproduce the colour using that product. I am more than satisfied that the reproductions achieved with Heinrich, and given in this chapter, match the original dyed colours as close as one could possibly wish to achieve.

Barberry

Latin: *Berberis vulgaris*
Family: *Berberidaceae*
Origin: Europe, Asia, North America and Canada

Barberry is a shrub native to most parts of the world. It is a deciduous shrub growing up to 4 m high. The leaves are small, oval, 2–5 cm long and 1–2 cm broad, with a serrated margin (see Figure 4.28); they are borne in clusters of 2–5 together, subtended by a three-branched spine 3–8 mm long. They have yellow flowers and the fruit consists of oblong red berries, which ripen in late summer or autumn; they are edible but sour, and rich in vitamin C.

The bark shaved from small branches provides the main dye stock, as shown in Figure 4.29. The chief colouring agent is *berberine*, a yellow, crystalline, bitter alkaloid. Berberine can also be extracted from the ground root by boiling in water.

Figure 4.28 Barberry

Recipe

10g barberry
300 ml water
10 ml vinegar acid
Boil for 30 minutes.
Add 10g sodium sulphate
Mordant: alum see recipe on p. 105

Figure 4.29

Figure 4.30 Sample of bright yellow veneer obtained from barberry

Young fustic and wig tree

Latin: *Cotinus coggygria*
Family: *Anacardiaceae*
Origin: West Indies, South America

Before going any further, let's clear the confusion over tree and dye names. When talking about some yellow dyes in the 18th century, four names come into conversation: fustic, old fustic, young fustic and wig tree. At first, it suggests four different trees when it is only two! Luckily, the Latin botanical names help to solve the confusion.

1. Fustic (also called 'old fustic') (*Chlorophora tinctoria*) is a tree producing yellow dye and yellow-coloured timber.
2. Wig tree (also called 'smoke tree') (*Cotinus coggygria*) is a shrub producing yellow dye, which on production is called young fustic (*Rhus cotinus*).

Remembering these rules should help you to follow any recipes found in the future and not, as I experienced, get confused as to which name belongs to which plant or dyestuff. In the rest of this chapter I only deal with the dyestuff extracted from the wig tree, namely young fustic. Fustic or old fustic was used by Chippendale, but only in the solid timber form (see Chapter 8, pages 233 and 234). Fortunately, Chippendale was oblivious to this confusing nomenclature since he simply referred to all of it as 'yellow wood'.

The wig tree is so named as the spring flowers resemble a lady's wig. However, it does not end there because another common name is 'smoke tree' because, in autumn, the flowers turn scarlet and look like balls of smoke, as seen in Figure 4.31. The tree is native to a large area from southern Europe, east across central Asia and the Himalayas to northern China. It is a shrub, growing to 3–5 m tall with an open, spreading, irregular habit, only rarely forming a small tree. The shavings from the heartwood provide the colour, obtained from the chemical property *fisetin*, a hydroxyflavone present in the wood.

Figure 4.33 also shows the dried flower looking like a lady's wig!

Figure 4.31 The wig tree   *Figure 4.32*

Recipe

10g fustic
300 ml water
10 ml vinegar acid
Boil for 30 minutes.
Add 10g sodium sulphate.
Pre-mordant with alum

Figure 4.33 Dried flower of the wig tree

Figure 4.34 Sample of bright yellow veneer obtained from wig tree

Weld

Latin: *Reseda luteola*
Family: *Resedaceae*
Origin: Europe, America and Asia

This Mediterranean herb is the oldest yellow dye plant in the world. Weld is a more concentrated yellow dye than most dye flowers. The leaves have the most intense dye, but the whole plant (except roots) contains dye.

With an alum mordant, weld makes lightfast orange-yellow. With tin mordant it makes a lemon-yellow; with iron, a greenish-olive; with copper, a yellow-green.

The main chemical colouring matters are *luteolin* and *apigenin*.

Recipe

30 grams dried leaves and seeds
Soak overnight in 300 ml water
Next day boil the broth and allow to cool
Pre-mordant with alum and/or tin chloride
Filter the dyebath through filter paper (see Figure 4.38) and add veneer samples to the yellow liquid. Leave overnight to allow colour saturation.

Figure 4.35 Weld plant

Figure 4.36 Weld flowers and leaves crushed after drying

Figure 4.37 Soaking overnight

Both alum and tin samples shown in Figures 4.39 and 4.40 have the same yellow tonal value.

Figure 4.39 Sample of weld-dyed veneer with tin

Figure 4.40 Sample of weld-dyed veneer with alum

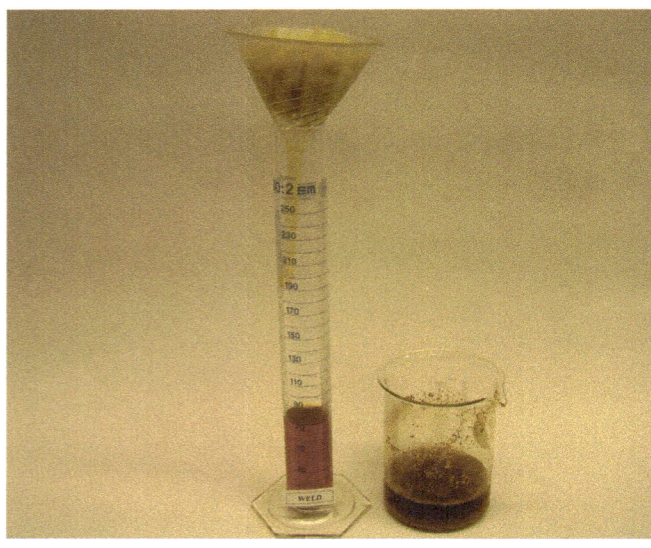

Figure 4.38 Filtering the dye bath

Curcuma

Latin: *Curcuma longa*
Family: *Scitamineae*
Origin: India, Sri Lanka, Java, West Indies & Africa

Curcuma is a dyestuff better known as turmeric – the spice used in cooking and food colouring, but also used to dye textiles and woods as far back as the 17th century.

The main colouring matter is *curcumin* obtained from tubers bearing many rhizomes in the plant's root system. The plant, when fully grown forms a small perennial herbaceous bush.

Recipe

Curcuma is solvable in both water and ethanol.
4.5g curcuma
300 ml water
4.5g in ethanol
stand overnight
Mordant: alum

(Source: Schweppe, p.664, Recipe 2)

Figure 4.41 Curcuma plant

Figure 4.42 Tubers crushed into powder and dried to produce dyestuff.

Figure 4.43 Sample of curcuma-dyed veneer

Saffron

Latin: *Crocus cartwrightianus*
Family: *Crocus sativas*
Origin: Iran

Saffron is a spice obtained from the flower of the *Crocus sativas*. Saffron crocus grows up to 20–30 cm (8–12 in) and bears up to four flowers, each with three vivid crimson stigmas called threads (see Figure 4.44). These are collected and dried to be used mainly for seasoning and as colouring agents in food (see Figure 4.45). Saffron, long among the world's most costly spices by weight, was first cultivated in Greece.

The saffron crocus, unknown in the wild, probably descends from *Crocus cartwrightianus* which originated in Crete. The saffron crocus is a triploid that is 'self-incompatible' and male sterile; it undergoes aberrant meiosis and is hence incapable of independent sexual reproduction. All propagation is by vegetative multiplication via manual 'divide-and-set' of a starter clone or by interspecific hybridization. If *C. sativas* is a mutant form of *C. cartwrightianus*, then it may have emerged via plant breeding, which would have been selected for elongated stigmas, in late Bronze Age Crete.

Saffron's taste or hay-like fragrance results from the chemicals *picrocronic* and *safranal*. It also contains a carotenoid pigment, *cronin*, which imparts a rich golden-yellow hue to dishes and textiles.

Its recorded history is attested in an Assyrian botanical treatise from the 7th century BC, compiled under King Ashurbanipal, and it has been traded and used for over four millennia.

Iran now accounts for approximately 90% of the world's production of saffron.

Figure 4.44 Saffron crocus showing the vivid crimson stigmas

Figure 4.45 Stigmas from the saffron

Recipe

0.4 grams saffron stigmas
100 ml cold water
Mix together and steep for 2 hours or until colour is achieved.
Mordant: alum Note: A mordant is not essential when dyeing with saffron as it is colour fast. Figure 4.46 shows the results of dyeing veneers with and without a mordant.

Figure 4.46 Samples of saffron-dyed veneer: yellow with alum (left) and orange without alum (right)

Kamala

Latin: *Mallotus phillippinensis*
Family: *Euphorbiaceae*
Origin: South America, India and the Caribbean

Kamala dyestuff is obtained from the fruit of the bush or tree, which can grow to a height of 5–10 metres.

The fruit *Bixa orellana* with its seeds and pulp are crushed in water and left to ferment. After filtering the resulting mash, it is placed over heat till evaporation leaves the pure dye to be dried in the sun.

Today kamala dye is available in powder form, as seen in Figure 4.48, or in small cakes. The chemical colouring matter is *bixon*, which is easily soluble in alkalis and warm alcohol.

Figure 4.47 Fruit and seeds of the Mallotus phillippinensis

Recipe

10g kamala
300 ml water
45g sodium carbonate
Boil together. Add cream of tartar to the brew while still hot.
Mordant: alum

The resulting colour with alum mordant is orange as seen in Figure 4.49

Figure 4.48 Kamala dye in powder form

Figure 4.49 Sample of kamala-dyed veneer

Brazilwood

Latin: *Caesalpinia echinata*
Family: *Fabaceae*
Origin: South America, especially Brazil

Early Portuguese explorers called the tree *'Pau Brazil'* – *pau* is Portuguese for 'wood', and *Brazil* is said to have come from *brasa*, Portuguese for 'ember'. The wood is used for violin bows and has a red or purplish dye.

The chemical compound is *Brazilin* found in the heartwood. Small shavings as seen in Figure 4.51 produce a natural red colour.

Recipe 1

10g brazilwood – rasped
500 ml water
Soak overnight; then filtrate.
Mordant: alum and tartaric acid. Heat to 80°C.
Mix the two solutions together and soak the veneers in the solution overnight.
(Source: Schweppe, p.671, Recipe 20)

Recipe 2

125g brazilwood, rasped
500 ml ethanol
Mix and let it stand overnight. Then filtrate and take 500 ml water instead of ethanol.
Filtrate and put the solution together.
Mordant: alum
(Source: M. Beschormer, pp.17–18, in: Michalesen/Buchholz, p.457)

A bright natural red colour achieved (see Figure 4.53).

Figure 4.50 Caesalpinia echinata in the Botanical Gardens of São Paulo, Brazil

Figure 4.51 Shavings of brazilwood   *Figure 4.52*

Figure 4.53 Sample of brazilwood-dyed veneer

CHAPTER 4 | DYES & DISCOVERY

Henna

Latin: *Lawsonia inermis*
Family: *Lythraceae*
Origin: India, now found in the tropics and sub-tropics

Lawsonia inermis is a small shrub whose dried leaves dissolved in water provide a dye that ranges in colour from black through red to orange - its neutral state. Historically, henna was used for dyeing hair and nails and staining hands and feet in preference to dyeing clothing.

The main colouring matter is *Lawsone* and is soluble in either water or alcohol. Today, Henna is available as a hair dye.

Henna extract powder (see Figure 4.55) produces orange dye when mixed with alum. The result is shown in Figure 4.56.

Recipe

25g henna powder wrapped in cotton cloth
300 ml water
Add dye into water and soak overnight.
The next day bring water to boil; then let it stand for 1 hour at 80°C.
Transfer into 300 ml of fresh water.

(Source: Schweppe, p.668, Recipe 13)

Figure 4.54 Lawsonia inermis

Figure 4.55 Henna extract powder

Figure 4.56 Sample of henna-dyed veneer

113

Madder

Latin: *Rubia tinctoria*
Family: *Rubiaceae*
Origin: Southern European countries across the Mediterranean

In order to obtain the best dyestuff content, the quality of the soil that the tree grows in is important. A soil very rich in alkali (mainly calcium) is required. In the 13th century madder roots came from Flanders in Belgium and another species *rubia peregrina* came from Turkey and the Middle East.

The part of the plant used for the dye is the tuber type roots. After drying, the roots are ground into powder and put in a pot with water. This should be heated to extract the bright red dye. The use of alum as a mordant will give a deep red colour on wool. If a copper dye vat is used, the colour will be brighter.

The main chemical compounds that produce the colours are *alizarin* and *purpurin*. These are present in the root system of the tree, but only alizarin is present in freshly cut roots. Purpurin develops as the roots dry out. The two compounds differ in concentration – alizarin will give a more orange-red, whereas purpurin is more violet in colour.

Depending on the temperature of the preparation of the dyestuff, it is possible to extract more of purpurin or alizarin. The colour of alizarin and purpurin is sensitive to pH. Normally wood is acidic. Mordanting with alum will get a brick-red colour, with tin, a pink colour; and with iron, a violet colour. It is difficult to get a repeatable colour under these conditions.

The only dye sample I have from a madder dye process is the strip of cotton shown in Figure 4.59.

Figure 4.57 Madder plant showing the red roots

Figure 4.58 Dried madder roots

Recipe

| 10g madder powder |
| Soak in 600 ml water for 12 hours. |
| Then slowly heat the brew and allow to boil for 10 minutes. |
| Remove from heat and allow to cool. |

Schweppe, page 670, Recipe 16

Figure 4.59 Piece of cotton dyed with madder

Cochineal

Dyestuff obtained from the female beetles
Dactylopius coccus
Country of origin: Mexico – found on different varieties of cacti

Cochineal was first imported into Europe in 1518 following its discovery in Mexico. For harvesting, the insects are collected twice a year in May and July and killed with hot steam or vinegar, before being dried in the sun.

The main chemical compound – carminic acid - is easily soluble in water or alcohol. Both alum and tin mordants can be used.

Recipe

3g cochineal
300ml water
Mix and stand overnight.
Then boil for 15 minutes.
Filtrate then warm up to 90°C
Mordant: alum and tartaric acid or tin chloride.

(Source: Schweppe, p.668, recipe 14)

Figure 4.62 shows a sample using alum and tartaric acid. The result is a bright crimson red colour, ideal for depicting berries on Chippendale's classic images.

Figure 4.60 Dried cochineal beetles

Figure 4.61 Solution of cochineal

Figure 4.62 Sample of veneer dyed with cochineal

Campeachy

Latin: *Haematoxylum campechianum*
Family: *Fabaceae*
Origin: Central America and West Indies

Also called 'logwood', the campeachy tree grows to heights of 9–15m with a short crooked trunk; small yellow flowers grow in clusters from the leaf stems. The dyestuff is obtained from the heartwood.

The chemical compound is *haematoxylin* and is an acid-based indicator, which – depending on additions of moderators – will produce colours ranging from red to violet.

Recipe

3g logwood
Boil the wood chipping in 300 ml water for 1.5 hours.
Add 4g of potash.
Add mordanted samples and leave overnight.

Figure 4.66 shows a sample produced using alum (burgundy); a tin mordant produces violet.

Figure 4.63 Campeachy or 'logwood' tree

Figure 4.64 Campeachy powder

Figure 4.65 Solution of campeachy

Figure 4.66 Sample of veneer dyed with campeachy

Indigo

Latin: *Indigofera tinctoria*
Family: *Legume (Pea)*
Origin: India, Japan, China, Central and Latin America, West Africa

The plant grows to 1–2 metres high and is often referred to locally as 'three-leaved-indigo' as the picture here illustrates. The leaves, after being dried, are wetted and through fermentation (which removes the sugar) indigo is produced.

The chemical compound is *indigotin* and is soluble in water or ethyl alcohol and dilute acids.

Figure 4.67 Indigo leaves

Recipe

| 3.8g indigo powder |
| 23.2 ml sulphuric acid |
| Mix the two together constantly for 15 minutes. |
| Then stand overnight. This stage removes the grain in the powder. Mix with a glass rod (see Figure 4.70). |
| Using a 'dropper', put some drops into water (see Figure 4.71). |
| **NB: Do not add water to the sulphuric acid – it will explode!** |
| Mordant: alum |

Indigo-carmine

Indigo-carmine is the term used for indigo dye with sulphuric acid added.

Begin with extracted indigo from the *Indigofera tinctoria* as described above.

Figure 4.68 Indigo powder   *Figure 4.70 Indigo carmine*

Recipe

| 3.8g indigo carmine |
| 250 ml water |
| Mordant: alum |

Indigo carmine can be purchased from pharmacies, although it is very expensive.

Figure 4.69 Sample of veneer dyed with indigo

Figure 4.71 Adding drops of indigo carmine to water. Here the five stages illustrate the change from water to ink colour.
NB: DO NOT ADD WATER TO SULPHURIC ACID – IT WILL EXPLODE!

The five pictures shown in Figure 4.71, taken in sequence, illustrate the effect of adding indigo carmine to water. Note how the water quickly turns into ink.

By using a glass 'dropper', small quantities of the blue mix are added drop by drop until a blue ink effect is achieved. If the water does not turn into 'ink' but the indigo carmine remains solid in the water, then the indigo has not been mixed enough with the sulphuric acid.

Dye wood samples are soaked (either cold or hot) over some days. The sample shown in Figure 4.72 was left in the bath for two days.

Green

Commence with veneers already dyed yellow. In our case we chose veneer dyed with barberry. After the yellow-dyed veneers have fully dried, immerse them into the indigo-disulphate mix as explained above. Leave for about three days. The result is shown in Figure 4.73.

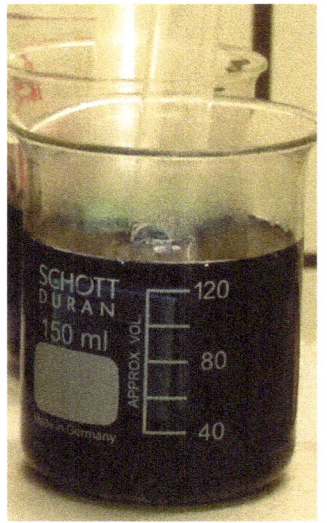

Figure 4.72 Wood samples soaking in indigo-carmine 'ink'

Figure 4.73 Sample of green veneer created by immersing barberry-dyed veneer into indigo-disulphate mix

HAREWOOD

Achieving colours for dyes does not rely solely on natural plant or animal extracts. Minerals play their part as well. Iron sulphate is a natural mineral compound which, when immersed in water, produces a chemical agent that influences everything on contact. Its effect is to turn objects blue, grey, brown or silver in colour. The colour change is dependent on the object in question. We know that the hydrangea flower can be influenced with sulphate of iron to turn its natural pink flowers blue. With wood veneers we know that certain white woods change colour when they are immersed in the solution: maple veneer turns grey, as does birch, beech, ash and holly. Poplar turns sandy brown, but sycamore uniquely turns silver/grey. We call these treated veneers 'harewood' – see Chapter 2, page 26, for the history of the name.

Figure 4.74 Sulphate of iron crystals

Making harewood

To create harewood, all that is needed is some sulphate of iron and water – any garden centre should stock it. The blue crystals seen in Figure 4.74 are immersed in warm water in a flat, inert vessel. I use a plastic emulsion tray (unused) shown in Figure 4.75.

Various veneer samples are immersed in the bath and left to soak overnight. The samples you see are maple, sycamore, plane, birch, ash, beech and holly. Other woods that respond to the treatment are poplar, masur birch and pear – the latter I will discuss shortly.

I never measure the amount of sulphate, but just put a small amount to cover the palm of my hand. Add about two cupfuls of warm water to help dissolve the crystals, after which the cold bath effects the chemical change.

Figure 4.75 Veneer samples immersed in a bath of iron sulphate and water

Figure 4.76 Ten veneer samples after treatment with sulphate of iron to convert them to harewood

You will have observed that I do not measure either the water or the crystals, and so far I have had nothing but total success with this casual approach. I find this really pleasing following the strict regime that surrounds the use of dyes.

The ten pictures in Figure 4.76 illustrate the range of harewood samples after treatment. I have only witnessed the use of sycamore by Chippendale (see Chapter 7).

You will note that different woods turn different colours. Maple and beech turn grey, birch, ash and poplar turn different shades of brown. Holly ranges from light to mid grey. Sycamore is always the odd one out, since it consistently turns silver/grey in colour, and was used by Chippendale on a number of his marquetry commissions.

Chippendale's silver/grey harewood

Harewood was used, as a background veneer, on a pier table made for the circular dressing room at Harewood House in 1772. I show a detailed reproduction of that table in Chapter 7.

In November 2015, Heinrich Piening visited me and applied UV-VIS spectronomy tests on the harewood and discovered two dyestuffs. Iron sulphate and logwood (campeachy) dyes were present. These combinations produce a lovely vivid silver/grey colour when ripple sycamore veneers are used.

Working with Ian Fraser (conservator Leeds Museums and Galleries), we performed a selection of tests using different quantities of the two dye elements, iron and logwood, with each test soaked in 200 millilitres of cold distilled water and left soaking for 24 hours. The test that gave us the best silver/grey colour consisted of 15 grams of iron sulphate crystals and 2 grams of logwood chips.

I use a very knowledgeable and educational website for my dye supplies – www.wildcolours.co.uk. In the 18th century, iron sulphate would not have been available and in its place dyers would have used rusty nails soup. Soaking iron nails and washers etc. in rainwater creates the perfect iron soup liquid for the dye bath. Logwood chips would have been produced by chopping up small lumps of the campeachy tree heartwood into small shaved samples. Logwood on its own produces a purple dye colour, but when mixed with iron, the silver/grey colour results. Iron, as well as a dye, is also a mordant, and therefore the silver grey is colour fast without adding any external mordant.

Weber recipe

The only historic written evidence of a dye recipe for making harewood appears in a recipe written by German cabinet-maker, ébéniste, Peter Weber. The Cabinet-Makers Guide was written and printed for the author in London, in 1809. This publication is labelled 'second addition'. There is no known record of a first edition, leaving one to speculate its existence.

The second edition clearly postdates Chippendale's period of harewood production during the 1770s, and while both iron and logwood appear as ingredients in Weber's recipe, his other ingredients were not found when Heinrich Piening produced tests on the original harewood background veneer.

Figure 4.77 Harewood made from sycamore dyed with campeachy and iron sulphate

Heinrich and I did reproduce Weber's recipe during his visit in November 2015, but we did not produce a silver/grey colour. The recipe given below produced a dark brown to black colour.

Weber's recipe – To dye the Silver Grey

Take a cast-iron pot of six to eight gallon, and from time to time collect old iron, nails, hoops, etc. etc. expose them to the weather until they are covered with rust, add one gallon of vinegar, and two of water, boil all well for an hour, then have your veneers ready, which must be of air-wood (not too dry), put them in the copper you use to dye black, and pour the iron liquor over them; add one pound of chip logwood, two ounces of bruised nut-galls, then boil up another pot of the iron-liquor to supply the copper with, keeping the veneers covered and boiling two hours a day.

The recipe is misleading and leaves one confused as to the procedures. The cast iron pot is used for holding the rusty iron nails etc. The pot and its iron contents are exposed to the weather until they are rusty. One has to assume that the pot allows rainwater to enter, therefore creating the right conditions to make the iron rusty. Then vinegar and water are added and boiled for one hour. The veneers are placed into a copper pot and the iron liquor is poured over them, and chip logwood and nut-galls. Finally, the recipe says, keep the veneers covered and boil for two hours a day. It fails to say for how many days.

Since we were unable to reproduce a silver grey colour, one has to question the accuracy of this recipe. Fortunately, I have the advantage of Heinrich's scientific findings taken from the original harewood veneer, where the harewood used on the Chippendale table was treated with only iron and logwood. Our reproduction of these two dyes produced the perfect silver grey result.

TANNIN TREATMENT

The term tannin, from tanna, of the oak or fir tree as in Tannenbaum, refers to the use of wood tannins from oak, which is how we find the terms tan and tanning for leather treatment. Tannins are found in leaf, bud, seed, root, and stem tissues of trees and plants. In the oak tree, high concentrated tannin is found in the gall nuts, or oak apple as it is also called. An adult female wasp lays single eggs in developing leaf buds. The larvae feed on the gall tissue resulting from their secretions. The nuts shown in Figure 4.78 are found on the underside of oak leaves.

Oak galls have been used in the production of ink since at least the time of the Roman Empire. In the early 20th century, iron gall ink was the main medium used for writing in the western world.

Another form of high concentrated tannin is found in the seeds of the red grape, grown for making red wine. The ancient practise of treading the grapes was not an image to promote a romantic practice, but a necessity to prevent the seeds from breaking. Human feet, it was found, were not firm enough to break the seeds, so while the juice was extracted, the seeds remained intact. The red grape itself has enough tannin in it to give the effect of a dry mouth, but had the seeds been punctured the resulting wine would have been undrinkable.

Tannin treatment of pear wood to make mock-ebony

Pear wood which has previously been immersed in sulphate of iron to produce harewood, as just explained, can be further treated with a solution of tannin, using oak gall nuts (see Figure 4.78).

Figure 4.78 Nut galls found on underside of oak leaves

The end result is a 'natural' black veneer, which imitates ebony. Pear has been used throughout the late 18th and 19th century to replicate ebony. Its lack of figure, straight even grain and soft texture make it an ideal replacement for the real ebony which itself presents many problems, namely availability, difficulty sawing and colour leaching into adjacent lighter coloured marquetry work. Here I have found a quick and simple way to stain pear.

The gall nut seen in Figure 4.78 is extremely hard and should be crushed with a hammer, between sheets of paper. Once crushed into tiny particles, place them into a solution of warm tap water and stir the contents around. Leave the solution to stand and the tannin to react for an hour and you will see the water turn into black ink, as shown in Figure 4.79. Immerse a sample of pear (treated previously into harewood) into the solution and leave overnight – Figure 4.80 shows the colour sample after soaking.

Figure 4.79 Oak nut-gall soaked in warm tap water. Note the black ink water.

Figure 4.80 Pear wood veneer after overnight soaking

MAKING INDELIBLE INK

Writings found in ancient manuscripts are found as early as the 4th century and continued in use across Europe into the 20th century. They use an ink that remained permanently etched onto the parchment paper it is applied to. We know this ink was produced using the nut gall that grows on the backs of oak leaves, as mentioned earlier.

The small, round, hard nut that, when broken and crushed, produces a purple-black or brown-black ink when mixed with iron salts and tannic acid. To bind the ingredients together 'Gum Arabic' is used as the binding agent. Once the ink is applied with a pen and dried, it cannot be removed through any normal means. The only way to remove the ink is by scraping away a thin layer of the writing surface.

Another feature of this type of ink is that age darkens the ink even blacker, as shown on many ancient manuscripts.

Preparation

The ink is generally prepared by adding iron sulphate ($FeSO_4$) to a solution of tannic acid, but any iron donor, such as rusty nails or any iron scraps, can be used along with the addition of vinegar. Preferably rain water is added to prevent unwanted elements which tap water may hold. The Gallo tannic acid was usually extracted from oak galls, hence its name. Fermentation of the extract releases tannic acid, which yields a dark black ink. Gum Arabic binds the ingredients together.

Figure 4.81 Nut gall or oak apple

History

This basic recipe was used by scribes throughout Europe. The oldest known Bible, *Codex Sinaiticus*, dating back to the middle of the fourth century, was thought to be written using ferrous oak gall ink. The ease of making iron gall ink, and its permanence and water resistance, made it the favoured choice.

Alternative inks were made from lampblack or other carbon based materials, neither of which are permanent or waterproof.

Iron gall ink continued to be used into the middle of the 20th century especially for writing up formal documents that required permanence, such as at registry offices for writing up birth, marriage and death certificates. Iron and gall-nut formula became the industry standard for over 1,400 years. Its demise came when other waterproof products became available, especially for writing on modern paper. Today, iron gall ink is only used by artist enthusiasts for reviving original methods.

SYNTHETIC DYES

I am compelled to mention dyes which were not even known about in the 18th century, simply because they were not discovered. At that time there were only three basic source components available to dyers: animal, vegetable and mineral. Each of these sub-products has been thoroughly represented in this chapter and need no further discussion. Today, we see dyers moving away from these traditional dye products and instead using chemical components to achieve results that produce lightfast and colourfast dyes.

Synthetic dyes were preceded by aniline dyes, the latter being a by-product of coal gas discovered in 1855 and used as a mordant. Synthetic dyes are man-made. These dyes are made from petroleum, sometimes in combination with chemically derived components. The first human-made organic aniline dye, 'mauveine', was discovered by William Henry Perkin in 1856, the result of a failed attempt at the total synthesis of quinine. Other aniline dyes followed, such as fuchsine (Fuchsia), safranine (Saffron), and induline (indigo) which produced a bluish dye and was one of the first synthetic dyes, discovered in 1863 by J. Dale and Heinrich Caro.

Today, the chemical dye industry has further developed a full range of colour, and in Milan, Italy, companies are producing dyed veneers, which, I suspect, are products of synthetic compounds. Their recipes are kept top secret, but they do boast their products are colourfast for life. Synthetic dyes can include dangerous and toxic components in the manufacturing processes, which can be harmful to the human body. This is not a process for the untrained enthusiast to undertake. In Chapter 7, I made use of veneers, which were synthetically dyed, and while the colours will stay firm for the future (I am led to believe), the veneer I used (magnolia) presented me with many marquetry problems. These were not only due to the synthetic dye, but to the open grain of the wood as well. All is revealed in Chapter 7.

Sadly, the Italian firms only dye a restricted range of veneers. None of their chosen species match up to the quality of holly veneers as used by our 18th century counterparts. So while my work, as seen at Chapter 7, will remain in colour indefinitely, I would have been able to produce a replica more akin to the original had the same veneer species (holly) been dyed with synthetic components. This highlights a lesson I trust veneer dyers take on board, such that future marquetry work can achieve colour permanency, while maintaining high-quality work.

Discovering synthetic dyestuff used on the replica Diana and Minerva commode

I write this paragraph some ten/eleven years after constructing much of the marquetry work for the replica Diana and Minerva comode, described in the early part of Chapter 6. I refer mainly to the drawer fronts, two outer doors, and the columns between the drawers and doors. As I write this additional text here in 2018, between eight and ten years have elapsed since the dyed veneers were first laid onto their respective substrates. Noticing that the colours are as bright and crisp in colour as the day I laid them, I began to question the source of the dyed veneers I first purchased in 2007 from a UK veneer supplier (at the time) called Art Veneers. The firm sold me the green and pinky/red veneers, which are sycamore. The tonal values were perfect for use on this replica and I considered myself a lucky man to obtain them. However, not knowing the source of the dyes, nor where they were dyed and by whom, presented questions I needed answers to.

In 2018 I sent both samples off to Heinrich Piening in Munich for analysis. Within days he told me that both the red and green samples were dyed with synthetic dyes. It was the answer I expected and indeed welcomed. Heinrich went on to say: *"The results with my spectra library do not fit exactly, but the colour class and family will fit. Red is an athrachinone, similar to the natural cochineal. The green belongs to indanthren-colour group, a product from BASF (Baden Aniline and Soda Factory). The green also fits to the original Chippendale green in the colourmetry of my system. Both colours are normally used for dying textiles."*

By pure chance I had built coloured marquetry work that would last perhaps for many, many years and would not (as dicussed in Chapter 5 on pages 147–48) lose their dyed colours within ten years after exposure to ultraviolet sunlight.

CONCLUSION

Ancient dyes are an absorbing subject (no excuse for any intended pun this time), and I hope this chapter has stimulated your interest into how dyes came to be available, allowing Chippendale to fulfil his desire to produce colourful masterpieces in the selected range of dyes available to him at the time.

While the dyed colours must have been impressive when first delivered to his customers, one has to remember that those dyes did not stay fast for too long. My experience in making and using such dyed veneers from ancient recipes has allowed me to measure the life of the dyes from first exposure. I refer to the replica marquetry work as shown in Chapter 5. That period was only ten years. By that time the colours had turned brownish and certainly the impact from when they were first new had all but disappeared.

This chapter also raises the more important question regarding the operation of dyeing and by whom. We have seen the technical knowledge that dyeing processes demand and the materials and equipment needed for successful application. We also now appreciate the space the processing needs to dye veneers in sheet form with anything up to ten different colours being dyed simultaneously.

I am convinced that a specialist firm or firms within the capital city carried out these processes. As I have already stated at the end of Chapter 3, perhaps the same specialist firm performed other finishing processes. For more discussion of this, see Chapter 3 pages 87–88.

CHAPTER 5

BUILDING A REPLICA 1: DOOR PANEL OF THE HAREWOOD LIBRARY WRITING TABLE

INTRODUCTION

Initially made for Harewood House, Leeds, c.1771, Thomas Chippendale's Library writing table, shown in Figure 5.1, was sold at auction by Christie's in 1965 for £43,050, a then world-record price for a piece of furniture. It was purchased by a consortium of businessmen, including the Montague Burton Group, a Leeds-based family tailoring firm. The writing table was purchased on behalf of the City of Leeds Museums and Galleries. It consists of four doors (two on either side), each displaying the same highly acclaimed neo-classical design. The table epitomises all that is best of the period and is considered to be one of Chippendale's most prestigious works. Since its purchase, the piece has been on public display at Temple Newsam House, Leeds, where it still resides today.

Figure 5.1* Harewood Library writing table, made initially for Harewood House, c.1771, and now held at Temple Newsam. House, Leeds

* *By kind permission of the Leeds Museums and Galleries*

INVESTIGATION

It is over 230 years since the writing table was first made and, during this time, the veneers have faded as a result of exposure to air and the sun's ultraviolet rays. In general, dark woods lighten with exposure, whereas light woods darken. The door panel shown in Figure 5.2 illustrates this very well: the background veneers were much darker when new, whereas the woods used for the marquetry design were lighter. In pre-digital photographic terms, the whole panel has transformed to resemble a 'negative' of its former appearance.

In the year 2000, the table made a brief return to its former home, Harewood House, to help celebrate the Chippendale Millennium Exhibition. The move provided an opportunity to investigate surface damage to the marquetry veneers on each of the four doors caused, in each case, by movement of the oak substrates. This investigation provided a valuable insight into the techniques, tools and materials used during construction. The findings described in this chapter provide conclusive evidence of how the neo-classical masterpiece evolved. In total, two door panels and matching drawer fronts were reproduced to illustrate how the table looked when it was first made.

Each door panel consists of a central background veneer of Indian rosewood with all the marquetry work created using the native wood, holly. Surrounding the central panel is a narrow banding made of West Indian satinwood bordered on each side by green stringing. Outside the banding, a wider crossbanding border of South American tulipwood completes the design.

It is worth pointing out here that Chippendale used Indian rosewood as the foil for the marquetry if the piece was to be made for the male member of the house. Clearly this writing table was made for Edwin Lascelles, later 1st Baron Harewood. By contrast, if furniture was intended for the lady of the house, he mainly used gold-coloured satinwood.

A project as important and ground-breaking as this needed personnel with the skill and knowledge to oversee the objectives. As a practising marqueteur who, for the past 15 years, has taught, written about and constructed classic designs, I was keen to establish not only the colours of the veneers which made up the work, but to prove conclusively the techniques used to cut, assemble and lay the marquetry. The following investigative work provided an opportunity to gain that information and prove or disprove the varying theories that have been aired and contested for many years by conflicting authorities, including furniture makers, restorers, historians and, of course, marqueteurs. I was fortunate to have the opportunity to work under Ian Fraser, senior conservator at Leeds Museums and Galleries, who headed the project team. Dr Adam Bowett, renowned furniture historian and wood specialist, and Simon Feingold, specialist polisher and dyer of antique surfaces, completed the team.

The project brief was to establish the quantity of damaged or loose veneers on each of the panels and make them secure for the foreseeable future. An added objective was to discover which colours were used on the various marquetry elements. Using dyestuffs that were available in the 18th century, we aimed to dye veneers to provide polychromatic samples of the type of colours that would have been used on the original work.

My challenge was to reproduce two replica door panels and matching drawer panels, using the same background veneers used on the original, and to recreate the marquetry using the dyed colours identified during the restoration exercise.

CHAPTER 5 | Building a Replica: Door Panel of the Harewood Library Writing Table

Figure 5.2* One of four matching door panels showing the classic vase design. Note that the dark background veneer of Indian rosewood has turned lighter in colour, whereas the lighter dyed veneers that make up the marquetry design have darkened. The overall effect is to make it appear as a negative of its former self.

* By kind permission of the Leeds Museums and Galleries

RESTORING DAMAGED MARQUETRY

Following the initial brief, we set about locating and lifting damaged marquetry elements, thus allowing us to rescue them before further damage occurred. This chapter describes the various marquetry elements we worked on, showing the state prior to restoration work followed by the discoveries we made after lifting the elements from the substrate. I was also able to use my knowledge of marquetry techniques to establish how each element was sawn and laid into the background. You will see, like me, that not just one, but two fretsawing techniques were deployed in the construction of the door panels. This disclosure led to a ground-breaking discovery, forced on the maker by a mistake, which led to a change of construction method that was to continue for the rest of Chippendale's working life.

Acanthus leaves

If we look first at the acanthus leaf shown at the far left hand side of Figure 5.3, it is clear that it was cut into the background veneer as a 'packet' using a fretsaw.

Figure 5.3* The acanthus leaf shown far left and top right of picture illustrates the visible black lines between leaf and background veneer, equal to the thickness of the fretsaw blade.

Providing you ignore the engraving (that is, the long thin tapered black lines running upwards from the base of the leaf), then the proof of packet fretwork is three-fold:

- First you can see where the fretsaw blade has travelled down into the leaf from each curved 'leaf node', leaving a 'kerf mark' (the gap caused by the thickness of the blade) – labelled 1 in Figure 5.3.

- The second and most telling sign is where the saw stops part way into the leaf and the packet is turned 360 degrees around the blade to return back out of the leaf (labelled 2). The second node up on the leaf clearly shows the telltale black circle caused by turning the packet around the blade.

- The final clue is the constant kerf that appears around the outer edges of all the acanthus leaves, being consistent with the thickness of the fretsaw blade (labelled 3).

Chippendale's near calamity creates a defining moment

While studying the original door panels, I noticed that two elements of the marquetry design had been cut short. Figure 5.4 shows where the scrolling acanthus leaf that meets the top left-hand side border has been reduced in length by approximately 10 mm (⅜"). You can see how it should have finished by looking at the scrolled leaf above and to the right of it. The classic design for the door represents a vase, which has matching handles that mirror left to right, and the scrolled leaf is also missing on the opposite side. The same applies to the other three doors.

To unravel the reason for this unplanned event – and it certainly was unplanned – we need to look at the technique used to cut this part of the classic vase.

The reason for scrolled acanthus leaves being cut short is very clear. The marquetry was prepared outside the control of the cabinet-maker making the table, and when it was delivered and placed on the door panel, it proved to be too big. The door and the cabinet shell were already constructed, and the tulipwood border that was to surround the marquetry had to be maintained at a

* *By kind permission of the Leeds Museums and Galleries*

predetermined width so that the panels balanced throughout the construction. This meant that the cabinet-maker had two choices:

- Ask for the marquetry design to be reduced in size and cut again.
- Cut the finished panel short and hope it would not be noticeable.

The first option would have been costly and time-consuming, making it an unviable option. The second option, while certainly not the more attractive, bearing in mind the constraints the firm was placed under to get commissions delivered on time, was in the end a *fait accompli*. The action that had to be taken in order to cater for the mistake does lend weight to the theory that this marquetry work was carried out by external contractors outside the control of the cabinet-maker. The latter had no alternative but to reduce the marquetry panel.

We can imagine the confrontations this mistake would have generated! Chippendale was a perfectionist and demanded the same from his journeymen. It was just a possibility that it was this very act that prompted the furniture maker to employ his own marqueteur. While this is mainly conjecture, I do show throughout my research that I frequently recognise the hand of one skilled marqueteur producing high-class work across a range of commissions.

You could say he had learned a hard lesson, but what emerged was a change of technique that was to prove a master stroke on his (Chippendale's or an unknown marqueteur's) part. It was decided to use a method of fretsawing that allowed the marquetry to be cut by the marqueteur, but controlled at an intermediary point by the cabinet-maker, before final placement into the background veneer took place. The adopted method was two-part fretsawing, sometimes referred to as 'piece by piece', the 'classic method', or 'on-the-line, off-the-line'. Despite the plethora of names, the technique was not new, but used for the first time on our designer's marquetry.

Historically, two-part fretsawing was used during the Boulle years (see Chapter 1), providing the customer paid enough for the marquetry materials to be sawn twice. I have seen three examples of Boulle marquetry where gaps between mating pieces do not exist. Chapter 3 discusses the two-part fretsawing technique and its many titles in more detail.

Figure 5.4* *Acanthus leaf, far left of design, cut short to accommodate the crossbanding border.*

* By kind permission of the Leeds Museums and Galleries

The outcome of the mishap is, however, abundantly clear: Chippendale never used packet fretsawing again. You could say that uncovering this mistake was 'the defining moment' in my research, allowing me to identify how a near calamity heralded a better technique, which was to be employed on nearly all future commissions. The alternative method was inlay, as described in Chapters 3, 7 and 8.

Laurel leaves

The laurel leaves are those leaves shown traversing across the panel from top left to bottom right in Figure 5.3. Here the cutting technique is not immediately obvious. Visibly, each leaf consists of three sections which are placed side by side, without evidence of any kerf. Also, each leaf was clearly laid onto the background independently of its adjacent leaves, because the grain direction changes from leaf to leaf. Had the leaves been cut from a packet, the grain direction would have been in the same direction across all leaves.

This early observation told me that the laurel leaves were cut out with a fretsaw from one sheet of dyed-green holly, and not as a packet to include the background veneer, as occurred with the acanthus leaves. After cutting out each leaf, the three sections that form the leaf are pushed together, thus eliminating the gaps. The three parts are held together with tape; marqueteurs of the time would have used parchment paper and hot animal glue. Figure 5.5 shows the back of one laurel leaf, which I cut and assembled as described. Note that the central part has been sandshaded to give depth.

What I could not determine at this stage was how the laurel leaves were let into the background veneer. To find the answer to this question I needed to remove a leaf from one of the doors. Fortunately, as Figure 5.6 shows, the surface crack on this particular door panel travelled through one leaf, making it easily accessible. All three parts of the leaf were removed, as well as one of the red berries surrounding the leaf.

This was, without doubt, the most revealing evidence of the techniques used during construction.

With the oak substrate exposed before me I looked for signs of 'inlay' work, where the laurel leaf would have been 'let in' to the background veneer had it been pre-glued to the substrate. Had this occurred, knife marks would have been clearly visible in the oak substrate, caused by digging out the background veneer. As I fully expected, there were no knife marks present; in fact, apart from the surface crack, which is clearly visible, the oak base was clean, level and undisturbed. It is therefore clear that the marqueteur did not 'inlay' any of the marquetry on this piece of furniture.

Figure 5.5* One laurel leaf with the central petal sandshaded using hot sand.

Figure 5.6* One laurel leaf and berry removed, showing no sign of knife marks on the substrate, or sloping edges caused by bevel cutting.

* By kind permission of the Leeds Museums and Galleries

The second sign I looked for was evidence of how the leaf was sawn into the background veneer, bearing in mind that the laurel leaf had already been fretsawn from one sheet of green dyed holly. Two ways of sawing the laurel leaf into the rosewood are possible: one is to saw a vertical cavity and the other a bevelled cavity (known as conical sawing or bevel sawing). The latter, had it been deployed, would have shown a bevelled edge to the sides of the cavity walls shown at Figure 5.6. On inspection, it was clear that the cavity walls were perpendicular to the substrate, proving without doubt that vertical sawing and not bevelled sawing was performed.

However, this poses another question of how the joints between the leaves and the rosewood background are consistently tight. The answer is as follows: Figure 5.7 shows laurel leaves spot-glued onto their respective parts of the design, the individual leaves are numbered to aid correct positioning, as those to the left side of the picture show, S2, S3, S4 (Swag 2, Swag 3, etc.).

With the use of a sharp pointed craft knife (today we use a scalpel), a line was scribed around the edge of the leaf. After that, the leaf was removed by softening the glue with a heated knife. I have drawn a biro line around the scribed knife mark purely for your illustration, so you can see how I have fretsawn inside the pen line but, more correctly, inside the scribed line. The fretsaw blade is visible and is perpendicular to the veneer being sawn. By sawing 'up to' the scribed line 'accurately', the resulting cavity provides a perfect fit for the laurel leaf. In marquetry terms, this technique is today known as 'the reverse window method'. I imagine that in the 18th century it was simply called either two-part fretsawing or 'on-the-line off-the-line', the latter description referring to the use of two copies of the design, one to saw on-the-line to produce the leaf and the other to saw off-the-line to create the window in the background veneer so that the leaf fits perfectly.

My approach seen at Figure 5.8 uses a slight amendment to this method, inasmuch as I scribe around the sawn leaf, using it as the template instead of using a second copy of the design. The end result is the same.

In this instance, there are three logical reasons for performing two-part sawing:

1 The marqueteur achieved the desired artistic appearance by changing the grain direction as each leaf followed the swags of the design.

Figure 5.7 fretsawing cavity to insert laurel leaf.

2 It was more economical to cut the leaves out individually, both for technical and cost reasons. Dyed veneered holly would not have been cheap and, while we don't know the cost, it can be safely assumed that it would have been a relatively high figure, due mainly to the specialist materials and many processes required to achieve the range of colours. We have re-enacted these processes, as described in Chapter 4.

3 The third and most important reason was to finally cease operating the packet fretsawing technique, which dominated the previous hundred years by the 'Boulle' method. This method always resulted in a gap between marquetry and background, which had to be filled with a dark filler in an attempt to disguise it. As I stated earlier, Boulle did perform two-part sawing, but only on highly prestigious works for wealthy customers.

First evidence of dyes

Figure 5.8 on the next page shows the reverse side of a veneer after lifting it from its substrate, showing one section of a laurel leaf with its distinctive green dye. We also lifted another section to find a lighter shade of green. Clearly Chippendale wanted to maximise the artistic appearance and by choosing two different shades of green, he would have achieved his objective.

We found a lighter green used on the stringing, which fortunately is still evident today. This was a stroke of luck because we could not lift any of the stringing as it would

Figure 5.8* *One section of a laurel leaf showing green dye.*

Figure 5.9* *Red dye exposed after lifting this berry from the door panel.*

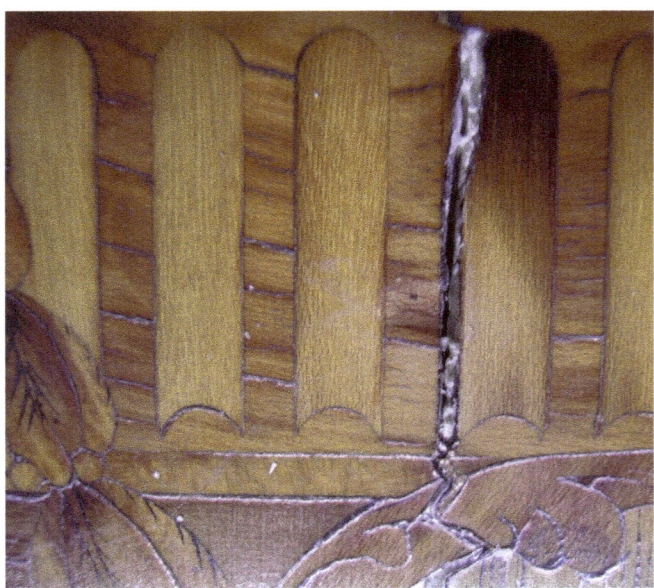

Figure 5.10* *Veneers seen sinking into the substrate on the central vase, providing the opportunity for some restoration*

have damaged them had we attempted to. These stringers retained their colour because they were dyed with the dyestuff saffron, which happens to be colour-fast and light-fast, meaning that the dye is not affected by exposure to ultraviolet light as other dyestuffs are.

It is worth noting at this juncture that I had not made this discovery when this project was taking place. Chapter 4 highlights that discovery. See Table 4.3 on page 101.

Berries and ribbons

Across the panel, tiny berries are used to embellish many of the elements. They appear as clusters around the laurel leaves, form uniform rings around the rosettes, and provide a central berry for the smaller rosettes and inside each curved shape of the central guilloche. In each case the berry is the same size – approximately 2 mm ($1/16$ inch) diameter. It was clear that a hollow punch of predetermined diameter was used to create the uniform berries, a method I was able to replicate, as you will later see when the reconstruction commences.

Additionally, the ribbons used to tie the white plumages together were dyed the same red colour – as seen on the berry shown in Figure 5.9. It was important to achieve a very bright crimson red shade to gain maximum impact, particularly when set against the white holly.

The central vase

The central vase consists of many contrasting elements and we fully expected to discover more colours as we removed selected veneers. In Figure 5.10 you can see the damage affecting the central vase with its arched vertical white columns. The veneer to the left centre of the surface crack is beginning to collapse inward and therefore an opportunity was available to lift the veneer, inspect its colour and rebuild the underneath so that it could be replaced level with its mating components. Further evidence of packet fretsawing can be seen on the bottom right-hand corner where the acanthus leaves clearly show the uniform kerf of the saw.

The veneer we lifted to the left of the surface crack revealed a pink-red colour, as shown in Figure 5.11. Excitement in the team was mounting as each discovery revealed secrets never before seen. It must be pointed out at this stage that on no account did we compromise the final integrity of the marquetry and veneering work on the classic piece. The veneers needed to be lifted, as you have seen on the photographs, because they were in danger of further damage and possible loss unless they were reglued to the substrate. We were fortunate because, on each of the four door panels, surface cracks and damaged veneers existed in four different parts of the design, and that allowed us to lift and examine enough elements to complete the investigation and produce an accurate 'map' of the colour spectrum applied to the classic masterpiece.

CHAPTER 5 | Building a Replica: Door Panel of the Harewood Library Writing Table

Figure 5.11* Pink-red sample from part of the central vase.

Figure 5.12* Small sample from part of the central vase, lifted to expose a burgundy dye. Note how I have wetted the sample (top left) to bring out the colour.

Burgundy

The lowest element of the central vase provided another surprise. A small triangular piece, shown on the bottom of the photograph in Figure 5.10 was lifting on one of the other panels and, when lifted (Figure 5.12), it revealed a remarkable burgundy colour. This small sample looked almost colourless when first removed, but you can see where I wetted the piece to reveal the burgundy dye. As these discoveries were being made, it was becoming increasingly clear that not only was Chippendale's classic panel brilliant in design, but the dramatic use of colour and shade had been planned for maximum impact.

Indian rosewood

The final veneer to assess was the Indian rosewood used as the background for the marquetry. This species produces a dark purple-brown colour with darker purple-black lines which provide the perfect foil to show off the classic marquetry work. While the original wood on the front of the door panels has faded to a light brown colour, the insides of the door panels, also veneered with the same wood but shielded from light, have retained the original colour. Another inherent property of Indian rosewood is that it has black oil traces in its vessels, which leach out into adjacent woods when polish is applied. Through our own experience working with Indian rosewood, it was clear that we had to remove the oil prior to use, otherwise oil deposits would bleed out during the final polishing process. We decided to degrease the leaves prior to commencing the assembly. For this we used acetone as the agent (Figure 5.13), a substance not available in the 18th century; perhaps they would have used Fullers Earth, natural clay mixed with water, which would remove the oil quite adequately.

Acetone is a highly flammable substance and we had to ensure strict safety precautions prior to using it. As you can see, we lined a large earthenware sink with heavy duty polythene to keep the acetone enclosed. It took only minutes to remove the oil deposits from the woods. Figure 5.14 shows the resulting ruby-red colour of the once-clear acetone. The rosewood leaves dried out instantly after removing them from 'the bath' as the acetone quickly evaporated.

Our initial investigation was now complete. We thought at the time that we, the project team, were the first people ever to see the evidence of dyed veneers on Chippendale's furniture. I was later able to witness two other restoration projects carried out much earlier than ours which highlighted the use of dyed woods. Those two projects were carried out by the same restorer, David Hawkins, and are reported in detail in chapters 7 and 8.

Figure 5.13 Rosewood veneers soaking in solution of acetone

Figure 5.14 Ruby-red acetone before disposal

* *By kind permission of the Leeds Museums and Galleries*

BUILDING A REPLICA MARQUETRY DOOR PANEL

This unique project, in addition to offering me the opportunity to closely examine the techniques, tools and materials used to construct the original marquetry, also allowed me to build a replica. For the most part, I used modern materials and tools to construct the marquetry, while maintaining the techniques Chippendale's craftsmen applied to the original work.

Some restorers may be surprised to see me using today's thinly sliced veneers and not producing my own sawn thicker veneers. The answer to that is simple: thin sliced veneers will give exactly the same finish and appearance as the thicker sawn types, but at a fraction of the cost and time. If I were repairing existing marquetry on a period piece of furniture, then I would have to saw my own veneers to match the existing thicknesses, but this panel is being built as new.

Acanthus leaves

I used the fretsawing 'donkey' (chevalet) with its horizontal arm for some of the work, because at the time the work took place I assumed (which later research proved quite wrong) that this was the type of saw in use at the time. My research, as detailed in Chapter 2, reveals that the chevalet did not, in fact, appear until the latter end of the 18th century, some 25 to 30 years after Chippendale's marquetry was produced.

As already discussed in this chapter, the acanthus leaves were fretsawn using the packet method. The evidence is easily identified by the clear gap (kerf) between the leaves and the surrounding background veneer. For two reasons, I decided to start the construction by fretsawing the acanthus leaves:

- First, the leaves 'framed' the design, giving me reference points to work to when adding the other elements;
- Second and more importantly, the acanthus was the only part of the design that repeated itself from the left-hand side of the design to the right-hand side. It's partly because of this that they were packet-sawn, allowing both sides to be cut in one sawing. The other reason for cutting them as a packet is due to the complexity of the design. The edges of the acanthus are a mixture of sharp curves and points, and because of this (one can only conjecture here) it was probably felt that it would have been difficult to maintain mating edges if two-part fretsawing was attempted. However, I do prove later that two-part sawing was adopted on the remaining elements of the design, where mating edges are not so complex.

Figure 5.15 illustrates how I made up the packet. The two veneers with the designs pasted on are two green-dyed veneers for the acanthus leaves. Two Indian rosewood veneers are also seen split down the centre to form two halves of the design. By splitting the design down the centre and inverting the two sides we form a packet, mirror-imaged, so that when opened up like a book the two sides with their respective marquetry elements are facing the correct way. This method is called 'book-matched fretsawing'.

Figure 5.15 The contents of the 'packet' for the acanthus leaves: two green-dyed veneers with the design pasted on, plus two Indian roseweood veneers.

Figure 5.16 shows the two halves prior to inverting them to form one packet.

Figure 5.17 shows the horizontal 'chevalet' sawing arm making a perpendicular cut into the packet, thus providing a square joint between mating pieces.

Figure 5.18 shows two matching pairs opened up and the packet-sawn marquetry let into the resulting backgrounds now joined down the centre. Some sandshading was done prior to insertion as you can see.

The assembled acanthus leaves exactly replicate the position reached on the original work when they discovered that the marquetry was too big to fit the door panel. We know now that the decision was taken to cut the leaves short, both left and right sides of the design, by about 10 mm and I intend to replicate this mistake. However, also like them, I will perform two-part fretsawing on the remaining design elements.

Figure 5.17 The horizontal 'chevalet' sawing arm making a perpendicular cut into the packet.

Figure 5.16 The two halves of the packet before inverting to form one packet.

Figure 5.18 The two matching pairs opened up and the packet-sawn marquetry let into the resulting backgrounds now joined down the centre.

Plumage

The white plumes are added next. These are positioned to the top and bottom of the design, and require fretsawing (Figure 5.19) and sandshading (Figure 5.21). Natural white holly is used for the plumes, while red ribbons of holly, dyed with cochineal, tie the plumes at the centres.

The packet, prepared independently of the panel, consists of two white holly veneers and one red veneer, surrounded by 'wasters' above and below. The design is pasted on top, so that the plumes are in line with the grain of the white veneers. Each component part is placed in a tray (see Figure 5.20), keeping the parts in pairs ready to assemble two matching plumages. The two red pieces are shown between the rows of plumes.

Figure 5.19 The packet for the white plumes ready for fretsawing

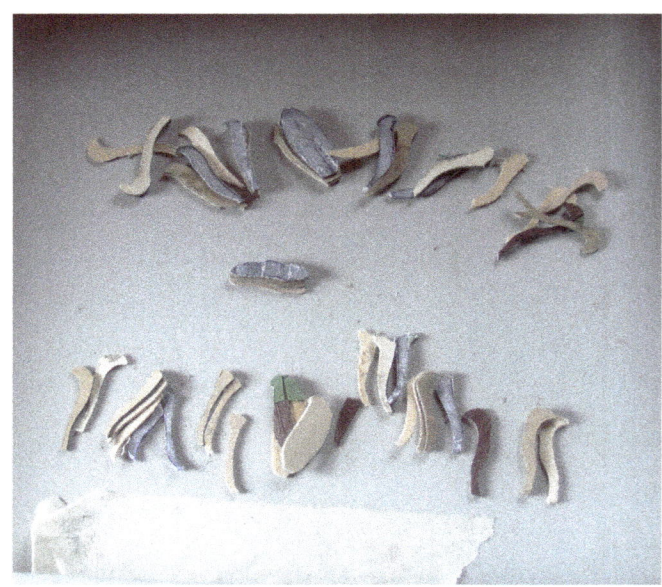

Figure 5.20 Plumage parts in pairs ready for assembly

Figure 5.21 sandshading veneers for the plumes

Figure 5.22 Fretsawing the window ready to accept the plumage

CHAPTER 5 | Building a Replica: Door Panel of the Harewood Library Writing Table

Figure 5.23 The assembled plumes are positioned on the background veneer and a line is scored round the outside

Delicate sandshading is required to give the all-important three-dimensional effect to each plume. I like to leave a shallow layer of sand since I find it better to control the amount of exposure and direct it where I want it without affecting the rest of the veneer. Using deeply-layered sand on tiny pieces like these makes it hard to direct the shading where it is needed.

After assembling the plumes, they are positioned on the background veneer (Figure 5.23) and, using a sharp knife, or in my case a scalpel, I score a line around the plumes onto the background veneer. Following the scored line, I fretsaw the window out ready to accept the plumage (shown in Figure 5.22).

These sets of images amply illustrate the two-part fretsawing technique that was to become the standard approach used over the next five years. Smaller white plumage pieces are cut and assembled in the same manner, and Figure 5.23 shows one set of plumes cut, sandshaded and assembled into the appropriate part of the design. Similarly, you will notice I have already sawn and cut in more acanthus leaves above and below the plumage. These were done by two-part sawing.

Central vase assembly

Working vertically up the panel I next needed to cut the central vase in. This required the use of one veneer dyed purple (brazilwood) and one veneer dyed green (indigo-berberis) for the acanthus leaves which encroach onto the vase.

Figure 5.24 shows the two veneers, purple and green, held in place with tape (I used masking tape) to prevent them slipping. Nails or spots of animal glue would have been used to hold the packet together when the original sawing took place.

With the drawing pasted to the face side, I was able to fretsaw the vase and the integral acanthus leaves (see Figure 5.25). Note here that I am using my electric fretsaw for this sawing. I am also operating the 'packet' fretsawing method at this stage. This is because the acanthus leaves I am sawing here are independent of the

CHAPTER 5 | Building a Replica: Door Panel of the Harewood Library Writing Table

Figure 5.24 The purple and green veneers of the vase are held in place using masking tape

Figure 5.25 Fretsawing the acanthus leaves that wrap around the vase

acanthus leaves I first installed at Figure 5.18. However both sets were cut by the packet method on the original panel so I am correct to replicate the method here.

I had one advantage over my 18th century predecessors, in that I was able to use a much finer blade. The result for me, using a 6/0 size blade, is that the kerf (gap) is not noticeable. In latter days, saw blades may have been made from clock springs stretched out between two clamps, while teeth were cut into the spring with a three-cornered file. It's possible to measure the width of the blades that were used on the original marquetry work by measuring the ends of 'blind cuts' where a packet has been turned 360° leaving a circular hole.

In Figure 5.26 you see the purple vase installed into the Indian rosewood background and the acanthus leaves in place on either side.

Figure 5.26 Purple vase installed into the Indian rosewood background

Central column

The column located above the centre of the vase consists of a pink veneer, which we dyed with dragon's blood (see Figure 5.27). White columns are cut into the pink veneer, shown in Figure 5.28, and since I was working solely with holly veneer, I decided to build this component with a scalpel and use the window method. I was later in my research to prove that the window method was used to build other component parts on other commissions, which I cover in Chapter 8.

Making the central floret

The five images in Figures 5.29–33 show the steps needed to build the circular floret consisting of eight white petals and a red centre (see Figure 5.30 below).

The floret is further decorated with a ring of red berries, shown in Figure 5.32. Cochineal was used to dye the holly red. The centres of each petal are delicately sandshaded to give depth. Red-dyed holly and a hollow punch make perfect uniform berries. A similar tool would have been made in the 18th century I am sure.

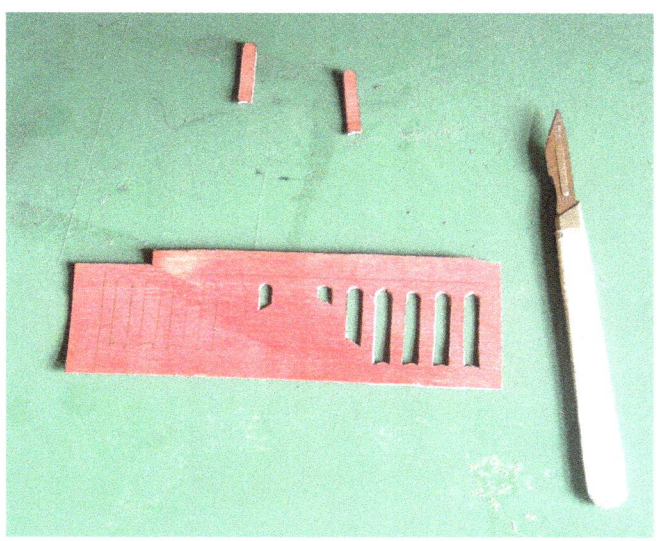

Figure 5.27 Cutting out windows in the central column using a scalpel

Figure 5.28 White columns being cut into the pink veneer

Figure 5.29 Cutting out the petals for the central floret

Figure 5.30 Assembling the central floret

Figure 5.31 A hollow punch is used to create the red berries

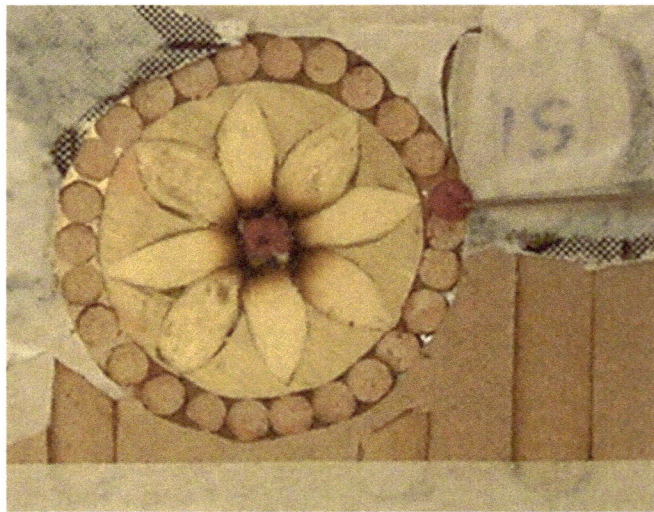

Figure 5.32 One red berry reversed to show the colour

Evidence of the uniform rounded berries on the original panel supports the use of a preformed tool. The marquetry is protected with paper at this stage, but I have reversed one berry to show you the red colour – shown in Figure 5.32.

The central column is set into the background veneers as shown in Figure 5.33. After that I have added the laurel leaf swags left and right of the floret, using two-part fretsawing technique.

Guilloche

Above the central column resides the most challenging design I ever had to build: the guilloche (pronounced gee-osh). In this case, the task was made much harder by its miniature size. The design consists of an intertwining rope surrounding a roundel. Here the rope is cut in white holly with red roundels. Figure 5.34 shows a suitable packet of white holly, red-dyed holly and two surrounding wasters.

It is hard to state what tools were used to build this challenging piece in the 18th century, but as you can see in Figure 5.35, I drilled the roundels out with a hand drill. An equivalent drill could have been used, or a hollow punch, as used to punch out berries. The 12-inch rule alongside the packet (Figure 5.35) indicates that the guilloche is 62.5 mm (2.5 in) long and 9 mm (⅜ in) wide.

Each piece is sawn and maintained in the correct order for reassembly later (see Figure 5.36). The separated packet, revealing the two veneers, red and white, and one brown waster is shown in Figure 5.37.

Figure 5.33 The central floret set into the background veneer

Figure 5.34 Packet prepared for creating the guilloche

Figure 5.35 Drilling out the roundels with a hand drill

Figure 5.36 Keeping the pieces in order for later assembly

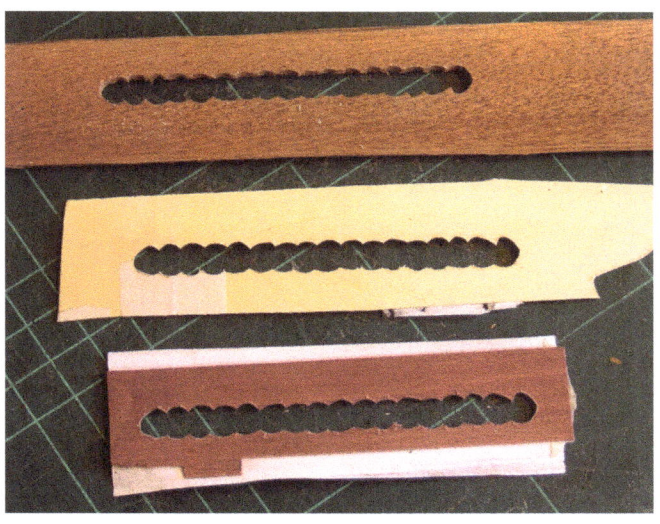

Figure 5.37 The packet separated, showing the two veneers, reed and white, and one brown waster

Figure 5.38 The completed guilloche, surmounted by the conical top, cut out using a scalpel and the window method

Very delicate shading is required; it is almost impossible to achieve uniformity, and I am beginning to question my sanity in taking on this challenge! I am not overly proud of my first attempt, but that is all part of the very steep learning curve I found myself in during this project. My promise to show every aspect of my work, 'warts and all', stands firm. I trust this helps to understand the challenges that the neo-classical motifs present. We have to remind those woodcarvers among us that while Chippendale carvers built many guilloches in solid wood, none of them had to build one as tiny as this one.

You can see the completed guilloche in Figure 5.38, together with the next stage of buildings above the guilloche. I cut this conical top to the central feature using a scalpel and the window method.

Anthemion

It was not possible to lift any part of the anthemion on any of the four door panels, simply because surface cracks did not occur there. We assumed the anthemion would have been depicted in white holly as the crowning glory to the vase. How wrong we were to be proved, when later we learned of the flower's true natural colour of burgundy, purposely selected by our designer to match perfectly.

Delicate sandshading was applied with a spoon to the tips of each petal (see Figure 5.40). The spoon was specially adapted by narrowing the end to allow the sand to flow directly where it was needed.

Figure 5.41 shows the anthemion after it has been let into the rosewood background, using the two-part method. Note how the small amount of sandshading separates the tips from the main petals giving the curled three-dimensional effects.

Of all the neo-classical motifs, the anthemion (honeysuckle as we know it today) is perhaps the most expressive, providing the shading is correctly applied. In plasterwork, as used on Robert Adam's ceiling designs, the anthemion was clearly his most used motif and perhaps his favourite. Set as a plaster cast in bas-relief (like looking inside an opened umbrella), the three-dimensional effect is achieved in ceilings and friezes. You can see some fine examples in Figure 1.14 in Chapter 1.

Figure 5.39 Cutting the anthemion

Figure 5.40 Delicate sandshading being applied with a specially shaped spoon

Figure 5.41 The anthemion set into the background veneer

Laurel leaf swags

The next stage is to cut in the laurel leaf swags and drops that hang between the central vase and the outer acanthus leaves. We proved during the investigation that these were cut using the two-part method. You can see in Figure 5.42 how I have laid the leaves along a length of green dyed veneer. By numbering each leaf, later identification is eased when I come to the final assembly stage. Each inner section of each leaf is sandshaded (see Figure 5.43). This proved a time-consuming exercise but without it, the leaf was lifeless. The outer sections are pushed up tight to the inner section, so that any gaps are eliminated. Figure 5.44 shows the shaded leaves (held together with tape) placed onto the design in the order they were fretsawn. Using a sharp knife, a line is scored around each leaf, leaving a clear line to fretsaw up to. The leaves are removed and kept in order while the second stage of sawing takes place.

The laurel leaves are let into the background (shown in Figure 5.45), beginning to show the classic vase effect for which this table is renowned.

The highly complex design is beginning to have a sense of order and symmetry and I eagerly await completion to see the whole picture before me. The colours are brilliant in their contrast to one another, even before any polish is applied, evident in Figure 5.45.

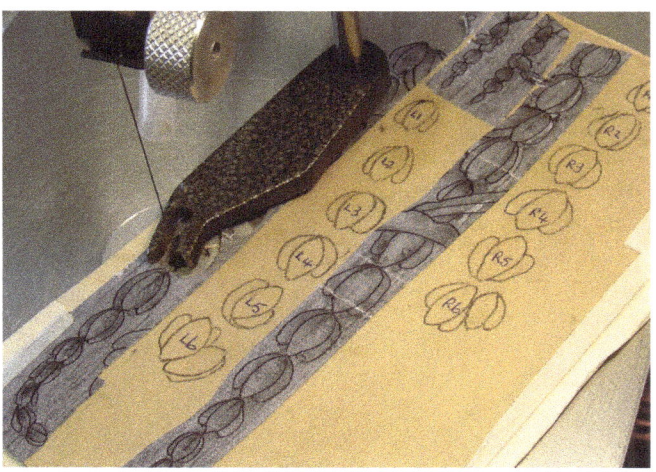

Figure 5.42 Cutting the laurel leaves

Figure 5.43 Sandshading is used on the central part

Figure 5.44 The laurel leaves are placed onto the background design in number order before being let in

Figure 5.45 The picture starts to take shape

CHAPTER 5 | Building a Replica: Door Panel of the Harewood Library Writing Table

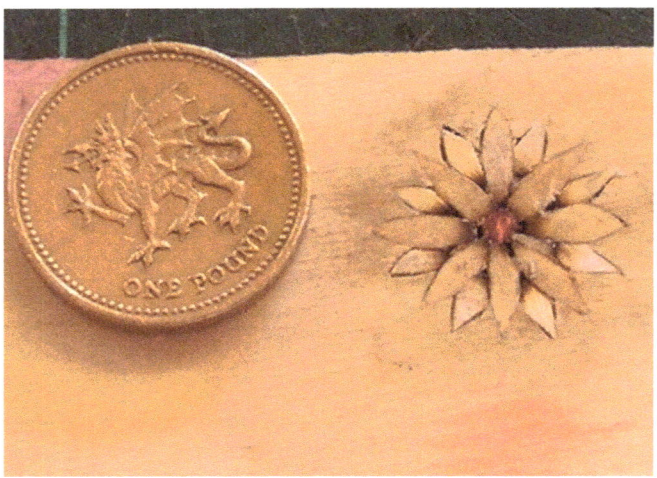

Figure 5.46 Acanthus flower, about the size of a £1 coin

Figure 5.47 The acanthus flower in situ

Acanthus flower

At the time this panel was built I did not realise that the motif, which terminated in the ends of the 'C' scrolls of the acanthus leaves, was a stylised representation of the plant's flower. In ignorance, I thought it was simply a small floret as produced earlier, and as such I produced it in natural holly with a red centre to show its artistic effect. Each petal is sandshaded to provide depth. Here, Figure 5.46, you can see the size of the flower against an old £1 coin.

We are to learn later that the acanthus flower consists of lilac and white petals and Chippendale used those colours to artistic effect. Again, because we could not lift any of these parts on the original work, we had to guess what colours they would have been. Our version shows all white petals, whereas the smaller petals would have been lilac, if nature and our intrepid designer's insatiable appetite for exactness is to be followed.

Satinwood banding

A satinwood crossbanding surround is installed, shown in Figure 5.48, surrounded by two green stringers.

For the first time, we have sight of the acanthus leaf deliberately 'cut short' at the top left-hand-side, just as it occurred on the original panel. Remember, it was this defining moment that led me to prove the types of cutting methods used on this panel and how they shaped the practices for the future. Because of that, I make a conscious decision to replicate the same mistake, in recognition of the dilemma they faced and the path they took which caused me to look closer for the conclusive answer.

Figure 5.48 All marquetry elements installed

Outer crossbanding

Tulipwood was used to crossband the outer panel (see Figure 5.49). Tulipwood (see close-up shown in Figure 5.50) is the most expressive wood available in terms of colour and figure. Stripes of salmon pink, yellow, orange, pale reds and burgundy make up this amazing timber.

I wish I could praise its physical attributes as much as I do its colours, but its dense, hard texture, coupled with its all-too-often tendency to splinter when attempting to saw it across the grain, provides a challenge that I could well do without.

You will notice I have tackled the mitred corners first, on the grounds that if I got these right, the infilling at the sides would be easier!

Notice I use a veneer saw to cut across the grain. A knife will not penetrate this wood, as it's far too hard. Even with the saw set up to a straight edge, many strokes of the saw are needed to get through the thickness.

To cut joints on overlapping veneers, I found the most effective tool was the blade of a wood plane, the width of the blade being enough to span the cut, as you can see in Figure 5.51. A cabinet-maker's block plane housing a steel blade was available in the 18th century. I have also made a simple blade by sharpening a wide wallpaper scraper. Remember, cabinet-makers and marqueteurs of that period were more used to making hand tools to solve problems. Replicating these tools to solve problems helps to get inside the minds of those talented craftsmen.

Figure 5.49 Tackling the mitred corners first

Figure 5.50 Close-up of tulipwood

Figure 5.51 Using the blade of a woodplane to cut joints on overlapping veneers

Figure 5.52 Crossbanding completes the inner panel

Crossbanding completes the inner panel, shown in Figure 5.52

Raised panels, also crossbanded in tulipwood, are fitted to left and right – shown in Figure 5.53 – and held in G-clamps till the glue sets.

Penwork

Students from Leeds College of Art and Design, Simon Brock and Alison Monks, provided the artistic hands necessary for applying the penwork (see Figure 5.54). Indelible Indian ink is applied after a base coat of polish. An open-nibbed pen adds artistry to foliage and 'C' scrolls. After application, the ink is trapped by application of the final polishing process. Figure 5.55 shows a practice panel before attempting the real item.

That said, I can now reveal that the final artistic decoration to the original marquetry work was actually performed by engraving. Our ignorance in not recognizing this technique – and my ignorance in particular can only be excused by admitting my/our naivety regarding this practice. I now know that Chippendale reserved the use of engraving for his most prestigious commissions; clearly this writing table, made for the master of the house at Harewood, fell into that category.

Furthermore, penwork was not used until the early part of the 19th century. The work I commissioned from Simon and Alison should have been performed with 'artwork' using artist paint bushes. Chapter 3 covers this technique in more detail.

Figure 5.53 Fitting the raised crossbanded panels

Figure 5.54 Simon Brock and Alison Monks from Leeds College of Art and Design

Figure 5.55 Practice penwork panel

THE COMPLETED PANEL

Here, in Figure 5.56, we see the panel complete. The polishing was carried out by Martin Speak, lecturer, teacher and polisher, at the time, for the Leeds College of Art and Design. Martin used French polish for the finish, whereas sandarac or best white polish would have been used on the original piece.

I had a scare when sanding the panel, because the burgundy dye on the central vase became blotchy, showing that the dye had not penetrated evenly through the thickness of the veneer. I was, however, comforted to find that the very same thing happened on the original (shown in Figure 5.57). If you look at the central purple vase on both the replica and the original, you will see the dark streaks that run across the veneers on both doors. This confirmed to us that we had used the same dye as was used on the original (brazilwood) and, as you can see, the same inconsistency is evident.

When I first saw this polished panel, I was totally speechless, despite the fact I had lived with it for over a year. The impact the whole writing table must have had when it was taken out of its wrapping on delivery to Edwin Lascelles, the owner of Harewood House in 1771, must have caused a similar reaction. It made me realise for the very first time what we are missing by not being able to maintain the dyed colours which the designer intended and achieved.

One door panel and one drawer panel have been on permanent display alongside the writing table since 2004 to allow visitors to see the original dyed colours. Over the past ten years the coloured veneers we produced for the project have darkened significantly, which is a measure of how quickly the original would have lost its initial impact.

Figure 5.56 The completed polished panel

Figure 5.57* One of the original panels

* *Reproduced by kind permission of the Trustees of of The Leeds Museums and Galleries*

The second door panel has been stored in the dark and has only ever seen the light of day when I have given talks. Even on that panel, oxidisation has reduced some of the tonal brightness that existed ten years earlier. Today's modern dyes are both light-fast and colour-fast, and had we used these to dye the veneers, the colours would have most certainly lasted many years longer.

Having said that, I believe our decision to dye our own samples was the right one, and, as you have seen, the purple brazilwood dye discovery would not have emerged had we purchased off-the-shelf coloured veneers.

IN CONCLUSION

I would like to express my thanks to the talented team who worked on this project: team leader Ian Fraser, furniture conservator, Leeds Museums and Galleries; Dr Adam Bowett, historian of English furniture and exotic woods; and Simon Feingold, specialist polisher and dyer of antique furniture.

Their collective skills made it possible not only to achieve the practical aspects of the marquetry work, but also to identify the initial dyes and colours, before advising on the replica design. The resulting reproduction is as near an exact replica as one could wish for.

Each team member's superb skills and professional contribution made it possible for me to reproduce a replica panel which illustrates the discoveries made and creative processes applied during this in-depth and revealing investigation. For my part, the discovery of the technical mistake formed the foundation of the processes I first identify then reveal in the chapters that follow.

CHAPTER 6

BUILDING A REPLICA 2: DIANA & MINERVA COMMODE

INTRODUCTION

If one were asked to name the top ten pieces of antique furniture in the world, it is almost certain that Thomas Chippendale's celebrated Diana and Minerva commode would proudly hold position at the upper end of that list. I could fill this book with the papers, studies, articles and historical journals that have praised this magnificent piece over the past two centuries. In 1986 the commode was sent to the world furniture exhibition held in Washington, USA. Needless to say, on my first visit to Harewood House around 1994, it was the commode that took my eye above all other pieces in the collection. Never in my wildest dreams did I imagine that ten years on, I would be involved in making a replica.

The decision to consider a remake came about following the formal launch of my first book *The Marquetry Course*. The Harewood House Trust very kindly allowed my publisher to hold the book launch at the house in 2003. Guests at that event included a retired woodworker who, like me, was captivated by the commode's style and grace, as well as the challenging details of its construction. My colleague prefers to remain anonymous, and I respect that choice. No further explanation is needed, except to say that his work befits the quality of the cabinet work he performed to get the carcass built and ready for the marquetry work to commence.

We discussed its construction at great length, while realising the challenges with which it presented us. The project began and a series of visits to the house, kindly coordinated by the curator at that time, Melissa Gallimore, allowed us to make detailed drawings and take copious photographs of every aspect of its construction.

Figure 6.1* The Diana & Minerva Commode, made for Harewood House, c.1773.

* *Reproduced by the kind permission of the Trustees of the 7th Earl of Harewood Will Trust and the Trustees of the Harewood House Trust*

PREPARATORY WORK

Sourcing the timbers

Chippendale's timeless creation was about to test our joint skills and knowledge to the very limit, not least by the use of tropical hardwoods for the main surface areas, both in the solid and veneer form. Satinwood in the solid proved just as much a challenge when it came to making the decorative mouldings that surround the work, as it did in the veneer that formed the ground. If that was not enough, tulipwood became an equal challenge, in trying to cut across the grain without suffering blistered fingers. This chapter takes you through ten years of design and build, replicating as near as possible those steps taken to build the original masterpiece.

I was fortunate to receive a generous contribution of the two main veneers; satinwood and tulipwood arrived through a local businessman and friend, Mark Forster, Director of SPA Laminates, based in my home city of Leeds. The company specialises in veneering panels for use by furniture manufacturers to make fitted units for kitchens, bedrooms and so on. I have known Mark for some years and, thanks to his interest and generosity, we received more than enough veneers to cover the background of the entire commode.

Other veneers were sourced from marquetry suppliers in the UK, which included the dyed colours. Because of the world restrictions on the use and reuse of ivory, we instead used ivorine for the flesh parts of the two figures, Diana and Minerva, a plastic substitute used by engravers on many works that originally included ivory. My colleague was ready to commence work following a few more visits to Harewood House to gain further detailed measurements and pictures.

Discovering the dyed colours used on the original

As you have already seen in Chapter 4, I was fortunate enough to meet Heinrich Piening, a German conservator and scientist who had developed a technique of identifying dyestuffs on antique furniture without harming the integrity of the veneers. The technique of UV-VIS Spectronomy is detailed and explained in Chapter 4, along with his findings. This chance meeting proved a major breakthrough for me, opening up an opportunity for Heinrich to visit me and examine the commode, and other pieces made by Chippendale, and so prove scientifically which dyestuffs had been used on the original marquetry to produce the range of colours.

Figure 6.2 Woods used in the construction of the commode.

Those findings have been replicated on this reproduction in every aspect of the marquetry work.

I have to say this is only a 'near perfect' match because it is not possible to reproduce the tonal values of colours. When we know from the spectrograph analysis results that, say, red or green dyestuffs were used, we have to accept that the tonal strength of such colours is guesswork. However, because I did have the added advantage of seeing marquetry elements lifted and exposed on the Library writing table detailed in Chapter 5, I know, for example, that berries were bright red in colour. Similarly, two different tones of green were also exposed when elements were lifted on acanthus leaves, compared to a lighter green used on laurel leaves. It is therefore possible to apply some sort of logic across different commissions to produce a colour spectrum that is near perfect. (**Please read page 123, 'Discovering Synthetic dyes used on the replica Diana and Minerva Commode'.**)

I thought the last project, reproducing the door panel of the Library writing table, described in Chapter 5, was a mighty task, but it proved a mere stepping-stone to the challenges and the learning process we went through to recreate both the cabinet work and the accompanying marquetry for the Diana and Minerva Commode. Join me on a fascinating journey that shows the highs, the lows, the discoveries and the evidence that support this reproduction.

I can now reveal something about the cabinet-maker who made the original commode: he was an Englishman. That may seem an obvious discovery, but we are looking at a period when 'journeymen' travelled across Europe seeking to work for leading workshops, and firms like Chippendale's would have attracted only the very best tradesmen. The evidence was found during a photography session, when we were examining the construction methods of the three drawers above the coved door. Under each of the two outer drawers we found hand-written words in manuscript and in lead pencil. The words 'left' and 'right' clearly identify which drawer belonged to which opening (see Figures 6.3 and 6.4). While this is a fairly standard practice of marking component parts, it is the only time I have found any writing on a Chippendale commission. Frustratingly, the designer never signed or stamped his name or initials on any of his work, making identification sometimes speculative if a bill of sale is not available. We do know that this commode was invoiced to the Harewood commission, so to have the added benefit of written words adds a personal touch.

Identifying marquetry techniques

Based on experience gained from making two previous Chippendale marquetry works, I was able to establish a host of marquetry methods used to construct the various elements. These, at the time, ranged from template work to construct the many fans, two-part fretsawing to produce the acanthus and laurel leaves and knife work using the window method to build the two ladies – Diana and Minerva. I have to declare, at this stage, that a further technique (inlay) was used on both the drawer fronts and laurel leaves that decorate the domed door. This new discovery did not become obvious until after I had completed building the marquetry on the three

Figure 6.3*

Figure 6.4*

* *Reproduced by the kind permission of the Trustees of the 7th Earl of Harewood Will Trust and the Trustees of the Harewood House Trust*

Figure 6.5* Monochrome image of the commode top.

drawers. I was later able to prove that the laurel leaves on each of the three drawers were constructed by the inlay technique. Unfortunately, by the time I discovered this, I had already built them using the two-part fretsawing technique, but fortunately, as you will see later in this report, I did use the inlay technique when I began building the laurel leaves across the domed door.

Creating line drawings

Having established dimensions for each marquetry panel and taken pictures to match, it was now possible to produce life-sized drawings to use as templates for the marquetry work. Using Photoshop, I was able to convert the coloured images into monochrome (I much prefer working from a non-colour drawing when building my marquetry work) and size the line drawings up to match the physical dimensions of each panel. A local reprographic firm produced the necessary drawings; in most cases the drawings were too big to be produced on my A3 home printer. Sizes of line drawing ranged from the smallest drawer front to the commode top, the latter being over 210 cm (7 ft) long and over 60 cm (2 ft) wide.

Of course accuracy mattered, because the marquetry designs for each panel were drawn by the creator to fit perfectly between the outer borders. For instance, the top panel design was repeated in each of the four quadrants of the panel (Figure 6.5) and had to touch the borders in places. This made precision vital if the marquetry, when cut and laid on the top, was to fit the panel perfectly. The end panels proved a challenge, since they are concave in shape and, as such, the 'flat' photograph was distorted, which altered the dimensions of the panel and its design. I had to take artistic licence and re-draw the elements to make them the right size for the resulting incurved panels on each of the two ends. This applied similarly to the domed door drawing.

The nine long narrow panels that appear between the drawers and doors were also not straightforward, since the marquetry designs were partially hidden behind rows of berries. I had to construct my own drawings for these, which was a challenge since they consisted of a single leaf gradually decreasing in size from the top leaf to the bottom. Once completed, I was able to reproduce nine copies for each of the nine panels around the front and ends of the commode. The leaves shown in Figure 6.6 decrease slightly in width from top to bottom. Rows of brass berries are later added to the two outer edges, while wood-carved berries run down the centre of the leaves. The line drawing shows these extra elements, therefore ensuring that the leaf dimensions, which have to be cut from dyed burgundy veneer, are perfectly correct in size and shape.

* Reproduced by the kind permission of the Trustees of the 7th Earl of Harewood Will Trust and the Trustees of the Harewood House Trust

Chapter 6 | Building a Replica: Diana & Minerva Commode

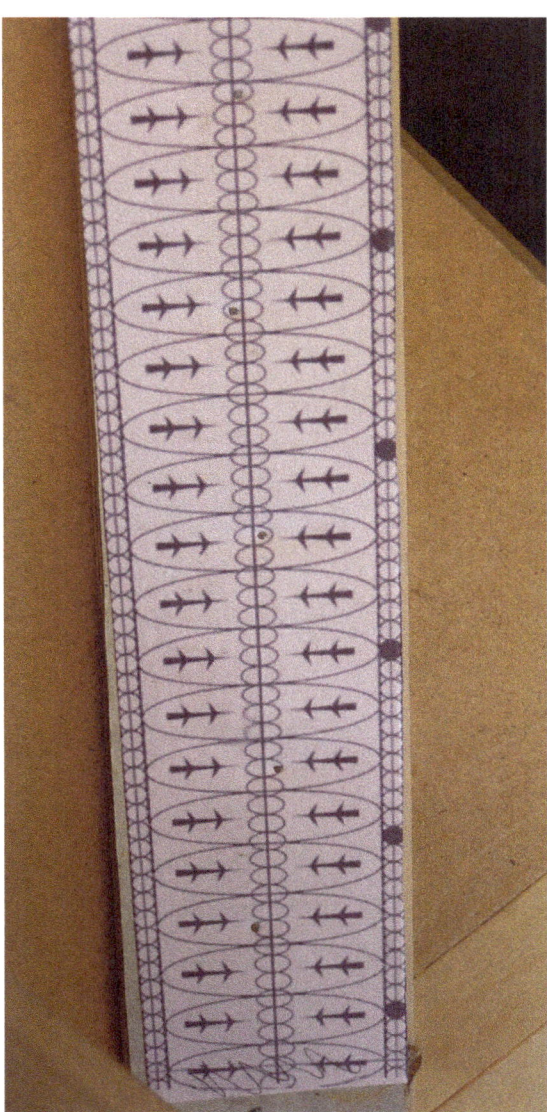

Figure 6.6 Line drawing for panels between doors and drawers.

Tools for the construction

The majority of the marquetry construction was cut by fretsaw and, prior to commencement of this project, I was using my electrically driven model. Fortunately, I discovered evidence that a type of treadle saw was in use across Europe and I decided to have one built for testing. Thanks to a local friend and marqueteur, Malcolm Slater, a few models appeared. These are detailed in Chapter 2. Once tried, the treadle saw became the only saw I used on the marquetry work which demanded the two-part sawing technique.

All the fans were constructed by the template method, which required a small knife (scalpel) and steel straight edge to cut dyed pink veneers against a pre-prepared template design, drawn on a piece of MDF. Compass, protractor and pen helped produce accurate templates to build the various shaped fans throughout the commode. Hot silver sand was heated in my trusty pan to provide the necessary three-dimensional shading. The construction of basic fans is covered in Chapter 3, plus they feature in my previous book – *The Marquetry Course*, still available on-line.

Hollow punches of various sizes were sourced and used to produce berries of the sizes necessary for reproduction.

An inlay knife, made by myself, and featured in Chapter 3 (see Figure 3.1), was used to carry out the necessary inlay work on the domed door. The laurel leaf swags that traverse the door each had to be 'cut in' using this tool. Hot animal glue used with a veneer hammer was also needed in this technique to secure the marquetry to the substrate. My thermostatic glue pot served as the source of heat to melt and mix the animal glue to the correct consistency (Chapter 2 refers). Fish glue was occasionally used where needed, providing an alternative to animal glue. Fish glue is applied cold and evidence shows it was available during the Chippendale period. The glue was used to fix the two incurved marquetry panels to their respective substrates using a vacuum press. Fish glue was used because of its extended open time (1.5 hours), giving me time to position the veneers and marquetry into the incurved panel.

THE MARQUETRY BEGINS: COVERING THE NINE DRAWERS

All of the nine drawer fronts are identical, consisting of swags and drops of laurel leaves, which terminate beneath ribbons. Above each swag sits a half-round fan. These motifs are set into a background veneer of satinwood, with its grain running from top to bottom. The panels are bordered with tulipwood crossbanding. Construction of the fans is covered in Chapter 3 – *Techniques* (see pages 77–79).

Building the laurel leaf swags, drops and ribbons

Green-dyed veneers were used for assembling the laurel leaves, with plain paper glued to the face side to provide a stable veneer during sawing (Figure 6.7). The hot animal glue also seals the grain, aiding the finishing process. Nine green-dyed veneers were each protected with paper on the opposite side, seen in Figure 6.8. Two wasters (to the left) are used to protect the packet during sawing. Figure 6.9 shows the nine matching left and right swag and drop laurel leaves, fretsawn and laid in tray waiting for sandshading.

Sandshading is a very laborious and time-consuming task, and it is easy to see how the end result can suffer. If you overshade, the result may look right at first, but one has to remember that the application of polish darkens the burning at least twofold. I have to trust in my experience and hope that the amount of shade shown (as shown in Figure 6.10) is not too much. Every set of leaves had to be dipped into hot sand – a long and tedious process, but very necessary to achieve a three-dimensional effect. Nine left-hand drops, cut and shaded, are shown Figure 6.11.

Figure 6.12 shows the swags, drops and ribbons laid on the background. A line is drawn around the elements by scalpel and the elements removed. The position of the saw blade shows I am sawing the window here for the fan to be inserted. Figure 6.13 shows me fretsawing the windows for the swags, drops and ribbons. I saw 'up to' the line, not 'on the line'. This provides a tight fit when the elements are inserted.

Figure 6.7 Paper is glued to the veneers to provide stability during sawing.

Figure 6.8 Assembling the packet with nine green-dyed veneers and two wasters.

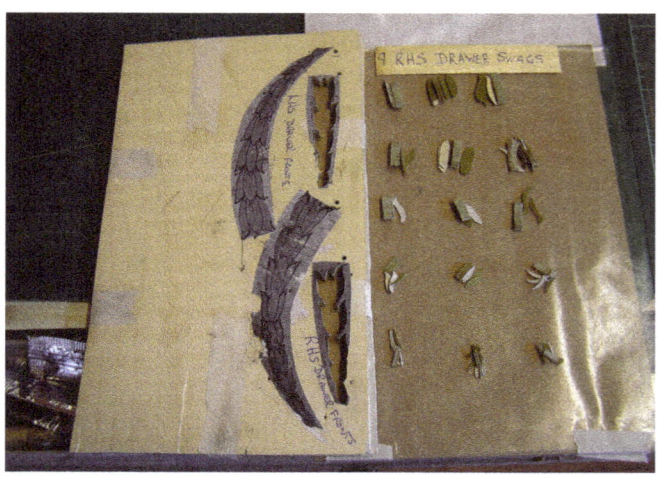

Figure 6.9

CHAPTER 6 | Building a Replica: Diana & Minerva Commode

Figure 6.10 Sandshaded laurel leaves.

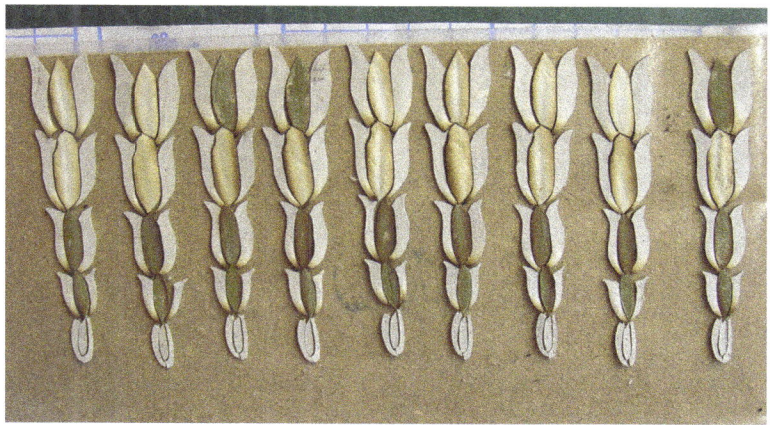

Figure 6.11 Nine left-hand drops, cut and shaded.

Figure 6.12 Swags, drops and ribbons are laid on the background.

Figure 6.13 Fretsawing the windows for the swags, drops and ribbons.

Figure 6.14 shows five of the nine repeats, ready to have the crossbanding tulipwood borders fitted, while Figure 6.15 on the next page shows the central drawer complete with marquetry glued in place.

You can now see how the symmetry is beginning to show, as well as the amazing colours.

Figure 6.14 Five of the nine repeats ready to have the crossbanding borders fitted.

CHAPTER 6 | Building a Replica: Diana & Minerva Commode

Figure 6.15 The central drawer with marquetry glued in place.

Figure 6.16* The left-hand door of the commode, with the central medallion depicting Minerva, goddess of wisdom, war, art, schools and commerce.

Figure 6.17* The right-hand door of the commode, with the central medallion depicting Diana, goddess of hunting and of the moon.

* Reproduced by the kind permission of the Trustees of the 7th Earl of Harewood Will Trust and the Trustees of the Harewood House Trust

CHAPTER 6 | Building a Replica: Diana & Minerva Commode

BUILDING THE MARQUETRY FOR THE TWO OUTER DOORS

Figure 6.18 Our replica panel depicting Minerva.

Figure 6.19 Our replica panel depicting Diana.

The matching doors sit either side of the domed door. The left door (see Figure 6.16) displays the goddess of war, wisdom and art (among other things), Minerva, while Diana, the goddess of hunting and the moon, sits on the opposite door (see Figure 6.17). Each goddess resides in a circular medallion surrounded by a matching circle of laurel leaves beneath a ribbon. Four fans soften the four corners on each door. Like all other panels, satinwood provides the background and tulipwood crossbanding frames the design.

The marquetry on the two doors was a joint effort, with my colleague building the two goddesses using the window method of construction, while I constructed the rest using the template method for the fans and two-part fretsawing for the laurel leaves and ribbons.

I initially decided on the colours of the marquetry for these doors, in collaboration with furniture historian Adam Bowett. We used our past knowledge from working on the Library writing table to work out the colour scheme. We almost got all the colours right, because when the scientific tests and results were declared following Heinrich Piening's visit about a year later, we had chosen the wrong colours only for Minerva's dress and head attire. My colleague was able to make the necessary changes.

Our replicas of Diana (Figure 6.18) and Minerva (Figure 6.19) (following colour correction) show the results of Heinrich Piening's dye colour discoveries, whereas Figure 6.20 illustrates where we got Minerva's colours wrong before learning the results of the scientific tests. This emphasises the value of science and how it makes this replica unique.

Figure 6.20 Our replica of Minverva before correcting the colours.

157

Figure 6.21 Building the corner fans using the template method.

Building the four corner fans

Using the template method as described in Chapter 3, pages 77–79, the four stages as given in Figure 6.21 illustrates the template method of building four matching corner fans. Corner fans are also documented in my first marquetry teaching book, *The Marquetry Course*.

Laurel leaf garland

The garland of laurel leaves surrounding Minerva is cut out of the line drawing (I made a black/white copy of the images in Figures 6.16 and 6.17), in groups of two leaves (see Figure 6.22). A packet of two green veneers is assembled, and groups of two leaves are pasted in number order on to the packet. The numbering identifies the location of each pair of leaves when assembly takes place. Each pair of leaves is sawn out (see Figure 6.23), and then laid in a tray in number order (Figure 6.24).

Figure 6.22

Figure 6.23

Figure 6.24

Figure 6.25

Figure 6.26

Each leaf section is sandshaded prior to assembly (Figure 6.25), and then pushed together to produce tight joints (Figure 6.26).

The figure-of-eight leaves are laid on the satinwood background to mirror the line drawing (Figure 6.27). Using a scalpel, a line is scored around each leaf (Figure 6.28), and then lifted clear. Fretsawing the windows 'up to' the insides of the scored lines ensures tight joints (Figure 6.29).

Each leaf is inserted in the numbered order from the assembly tray (Figure 6.30), providing perfectly tight joints. With all the leaves inserted, a hollow punch is used to fit red berries between petals (Figure 6.31). This is vital because, with satinwood, which is very brittle, very little wood remains after sawing close to the joints where two leaf clusters converge. This in turn creates unsightly holes and clearly this happened to the marqueteur sawing the original. Chippendale had to find a solution for this unplanned event, so he introduced red berries to hide the indiscretions. Luckily, berries do form part of the classic motifs, so our designer remained within the rules of the canon.

Finally, in Figure 6.32 you can see me fretsawing the window into the satinwood background to accept the roundel motif.

Figure 6.27

Figure 6.28

Figure 6.29

Figure 6.30

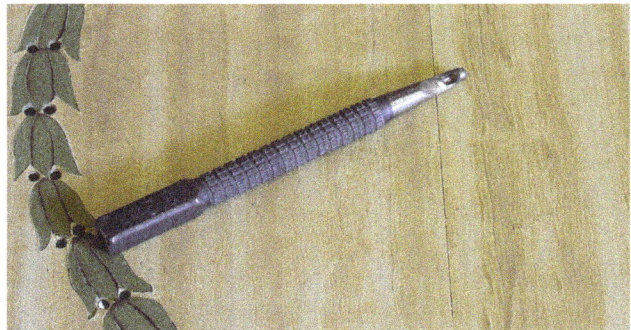

Figure 6.31

Figure 6.32

Figure 6.33 The completed door panels, with only the flesh parts of the goddesses to insert after the panels are glued in place.

Both doors are complete, as shown in Figure 6.33, with only the outer crossbanding tulipwood remaining to be installed. The doors are then ready for gluing to the substrates. Note that the flesh parts for both Minerva and Diana are added after the panels are glued in place.

CHAPTER 6 | Building a Replica: Diana & Minerva Commode

MAKING THE LONG AND SHORT FASCIA PANELS

The long panels reside between the front doors and the short panels between the drawer units. Long and short panels exist on both ends, making eight of each type. While the marquetry is straightforward, most of it, when installed, is hidden behind brass work. However, it has to be cut and installed before the brass work can be fitted.

The upper and lower panels taper, with the widest leaf at the top, decreasing leaf by leaf to the lowest, as can be seen on the original panel (Figure 6.34). The leaves are burgundy in colour, set into a background of satinwood. The blend of colours provides a warm harmony with the brass work.

Packets of four burgundy veneers are prepared, ready for fretsawing, with two packets of four veneers for the long columns, and two packets of four veneers for the short columns. Each leaf is numbered, to enable easy identification when assembling (see Figures 6.35 and 6.36).

The fretsawn leaves are placed in number order in the assembly tray (Figure 6.37). The assembled leaves are glued to the substrate (Figure 6.38), and carved berries are positioned in place, prior to making brass mouldings.

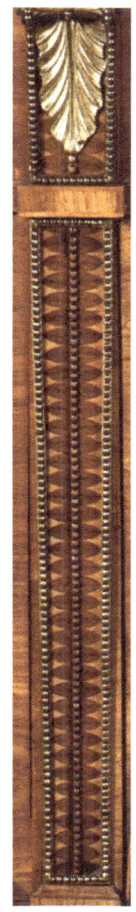

Figure 6.34* One of the original fascia panels.

Figure 6.38 One of the replica fascia panels.

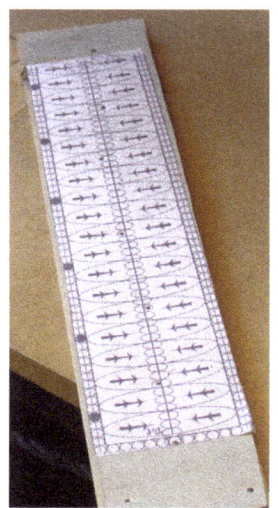
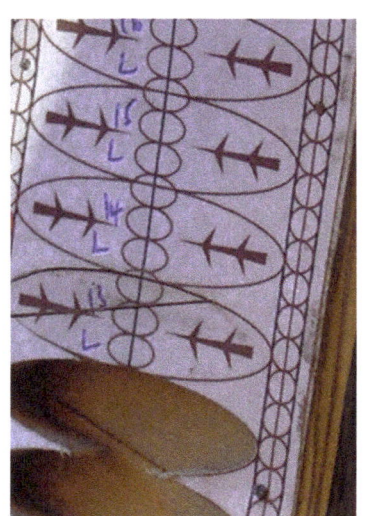

Figure 6.35

Figure 6.36

Figure 6.37

* *Reproduced by the kind permission of the Trustees of the 7th Earl of Harewood Will Trust and the Trustees of the Harewood House Trust*

BUILDING THE TWO INCURVED END PANELS

The two matching end panels proved to be my testing ground for fitting incurved veneers and marquetry. I knew that the ultimate test would be veneering and laying marquetry on the domed door, a challenge I had decided to leave till last. What made these panels a challenge were the quarter matching satinwood background veneers covering the lower panel. The satinwood background on the upper panel which displayed the dummy drawer front was laid with the grain pointing vertically (see Figure 6.39).

The second challenge was the circular guilloche in the centre of the panel. This design demanded total accuracy if it was to be effective. I knew the tendency of the satinwood veneers once they were eased into the curved surface would be to pull apart. Because satinwood is not a very pliable veneer, I wondered if it would present a problem for me. I had a contingency plan in the back of my mind if this happened. I had planned to build the panel up completely and glue the whole assembly to the substrate in one operation.

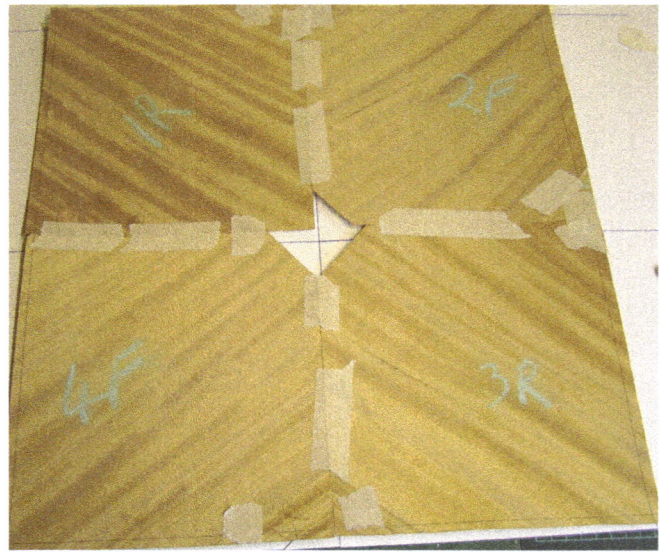

Figure 6.40 Four herringbone veneers create a quarter matching panel.

My plan was to press it into place using my vacuum press. '*But*', I hear you say, '*that's not how it would have been pressed when the original was made*' – and you are right. However, this was pioneering 'suck it and see' time and to glue it in place piece by piece using hammer-veneering for the first time on a incurved surface was, for me, at this stage, a step too far. I chose the modern option.

With hindsight, given what was to follow, when I did use the original technique on the domed door, I now know I could have used the original methodology here. That's the learning curve this project brought and who would have it any other way?

Clearly, cutting the satinwood veneers was the place to start, and accurate measuring was the order of the day. Measuring incurved surfaces has to be done carefully so I 'mapped' out the substrate by drawing in the outer borders of crossbanding, till I had only the central area open to map the four quarter-matching panels.

You will note that the grains on the four central panels are book-matched, providing a herringbone effect from the centre, radiating out to the four sides. Figure 6.40 show four quadrants fitted showing two sides (2F & 4F) with the 'face' side showing and the opposite (1R & 3R) with the reverse side showing. This is to create

Figure 6.39 One of the completed incurved end panels.

a quarter matching effect by the face sides being lighter in contrast to the reverse sides. The effect is caused by light refraction of opposing grain directions.

While the quarter match effect is not visible on this image, I can assure you it will be when polish is applied. Note I have used chalk to identify each quarter panel. This is normal practice as chalk is easily removed with a damp cloth.

After fretsawing four acanthus leaves from a packet of four green veneers (Figure 6.41), using my trusty treadle-saw, I sandshaded them to create the animation. You can see the 3D effect even with the paper covering the shaded area, in Figure 6.42.

I laid the sawn acanthus and laurel leaves onto the satinwood background, carefully positioning them to give the best quarter effect (Figure 6.43). I then scored around the leaves with a scalpel, allowing me to fretsaw the windows (Figure 6.44).

I now have the floral marquetry and corner fan inserted into the satinwood background on one quadrant (Figure 6.45).

Using a hollow punch (Figure 6.46), I created the right sized holes to accept red berries. Like the laurel leaves on the two front outer doors, these were to hide broken veneers where two leaves converge.

Figure 6.41 Fretsawing four acanthus leaves from a packet.

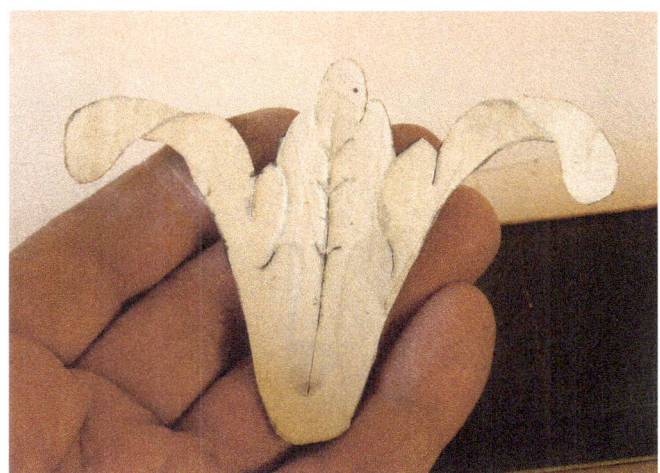

Figure 6.42 One sandshaded acanthus leaf.

Figure 6.43 Sawn acanthus and laurel leaves laid onto the satinwood background.

Figure 6.44 Windows fretsawn after scoring round the leaves.

CHAPTER 6 | Building a Replica: Diana & Minerva Commode

Figure 6.45 Floral marquetry and fan inserted into the background.

Figure 6.46 Punching the holes for the red berries.

Building the challenging guilloche

I saw this motif as a very challenging task in marquetry terms. The intertwining rope effect would only look right if it was geometrically exact. The line drawing in Figure 6.47 shows all the elements that make up the motif. I had to make two, since each end panel holds the same design. I built a veneer packet (see Figure 6.48), consisting of four dark green, two white holly and four light green veneers, with wasters top and bottom of the pack and design pasted to the top. This would make two guilloches from one sawing.

First I drilled pilot holes in the centre of each roundel (see Figure 6.49). Next, starting at the centre (Figure 6.50), I fretted the central parts of the floral motif. This retained the strength of the packet to allow the outer parts to remain stable. Note the nails in the packet on the outside of the design. Next, I made the right decision to fret out the roundels (Figure 6.51), before removing the central floral piece. Again this retained stability within the packet.

The floral arrangement was now sawn and assembled (see Figure 6.52), and you can see the tonal contrast that

Figure 6.47 Line drawing of the central guilloche.

Figure 6.48 Veneer packet for the guilloche.

CHAPTER 6 | Building a Replica: Diana & Minerva Commode

Figure 6.49 Drilling pilot holes in the centre of each roundel.

Figure 6.50 Fretsawing the central parts of the floral motif.

the two different shades of green produce. The centre will be filled with a cluster of red berries; this time the berries are purely for a decorative purpose. Note also the veins I have sawn up each leaf. The aim of this was to give artistic realism, just as the designer intended, and this was how the original was produced by the marqueteur of the day.

The next step was the delicate stage, since I had to install two stringers, one either side of the guilloche. I then had to insert the floral green centre such that it fit and filled the central area fully; it was a perfect fit (Figures 6.53). Next I had to insert red veneers into the numerous triangular gaps, both between the green assembly and between the guilloche, and the two stringers. The result is shown in Figures 6.54 and 6.55.

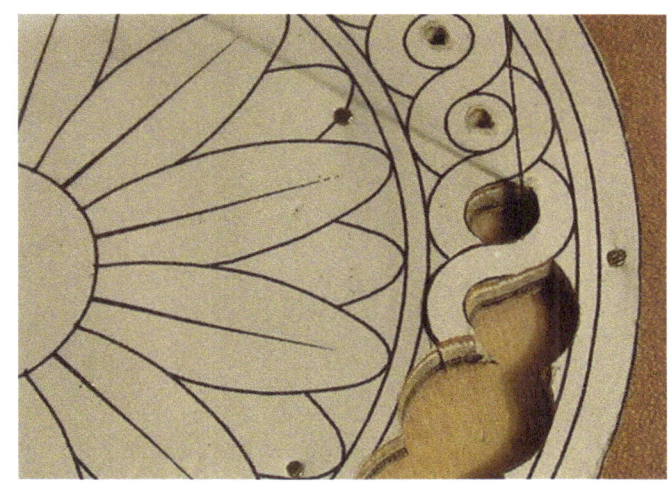

Figure 6.51 Fretting out the roundels.

Figure 6.52 Floral arrangement sawn and assembled.

Figure 6.53

With the final addition installed – a green circular border to both guilloches – I was more than satisfied with the outcome. I knew they would stand out loud and clear against the satinwood background veneers.

With the two matching panels crossbanded with tulipwood, they were now ready for gluing to the substrate (Figures 6.54 and 6.55).

The coloured glue you see across the laurel leaves in Figure 6.56 is fish glue coloured with satinwood dust to fill any gaps that might occur when the veneers are forced open when stretched across the incurved panel. I also applied extra veneer tape across the front to help tighten the joints during pressing.

The panel was now safely in the vacuum press. I used a soft fabric (see Figure 6.57) between the bag and the veneers to cushion any uneven thicknesses that might occur between different veneers. It seemed to work well. The work was kept under pressure for 12 hours, the statutory time for pressing fish glue.

Figure 6.54 The completed left motif.

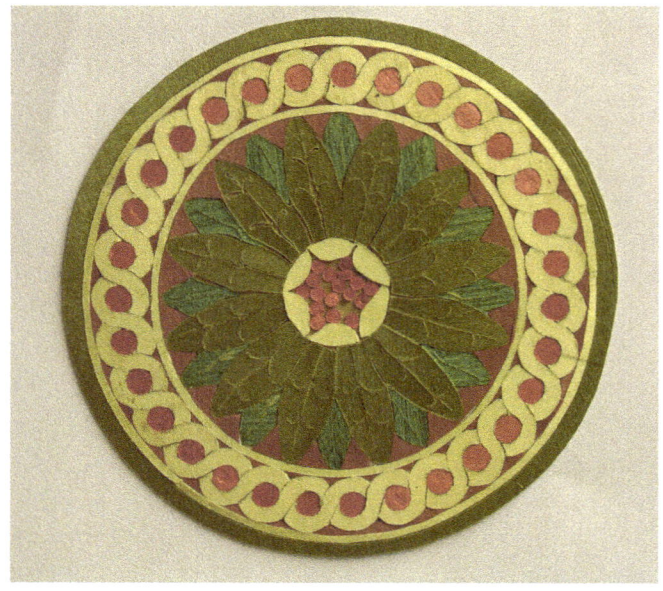

Figure 6.55 The completed right motif.

Figure 6.56 Fish glue coloured with satinwood dust is applied to fill any gaps that might occur when the veneers are stretched across the incurved panel.

Figure 6.57 A soft cloth is used to cushion the veneers in the press.

CHAPTER 6 | Building a Replica: Diana & Minerva Commode

THE COMMODE TOP

Figure 6.58* The top of the original commode, showing no trace of the colours that would have made it so spectacular.

Figure 6.58 shows Chippendale's largest panel, measuring 2200 mm (7 ft 4 in) wide, 600 mm (2 ft) deep. The marquetry has lost all of its original colours. My replica will change all that, allowing me to bring the original colours back to life. Heinrich Piening's spectronomy tests will unfold as the new build takes place. If you have been impressed so far with the views of the previous panels, then wait until I unfold the secrets of this amazing top.

The 40-flute, two-tone fan dominates the centre, with each of its pink flutes set into white borders and surrounded by a ring of foliate green leaves with white and green stringers. Inside the fan a ring of red berries surrounds two-tone green foliage set into a padauk border and a white floral ring with more berries filling the centre. It's almost impossible to imagine those colours as we see the fan shown here in Figure 6.58, but those are the colours I will use to reproduce it along with the remaining greens, yellow, burgundy, reds, purple, lilac and white for the remaining elements. Add to that the gold-coloured satinwood and the multi-coloured tulipwood border, and you are in for a kaleidoscope of colours that not even the most vivid imagination could comprehend.

You can see from the design in Figure 6.58 that the pattern repeats itself in each of the four quadrants. The design follows the symmetry and style of the classic movement. Yet one aspect of the design bothered me greatly. I had never, until making this copy, been able to work out why the table is divided by a straight lined diamond that bisects the marquetry in this manner. The classic style is about movement, grace and symmetry, and not straight lines, yet here we are looking at a diamond that dominates the top.

This puzzle demanded an answer and, fortunately during the reconstruction of this top, I found it. *Read on!*

Creating a line drawing

It took several attempts to get the line drawing to match the precise dimension of the top, but with the help and patience of a local reprographic firm I was able to obtain a drawing that mirrored the precise dimensions and layout of the motifs of the original (see Figure 6.5 on page 152, where I describe the process of creating my line drawing).

The first task was to cut, arrange and join together the satinwood background. As you can see from the picture taken in my workshop, shown in Figure 6.59,

* *Reproduced by the kind permission of the Trustees of the 7th Earl of Harewood Will Trust and the Trustees of the Harewood House Trust*

the top is sub-divided into four quadrants. Two of the diagonally opposite corners show the 'face' side of the veneers (the darker pair in the picture) and the opposite two (the lighter coloured) show the reverse sides of the veneers. It is called quarter matching and it is very important to maintain this effect. Light refraction hitting the grain at two different angles causes the phenomenon, and when the veneers are polished, the effect is even more impressive.

As you can see from the picture, the central 40 two-tone fluted fan is complete. Therefore it's time to build the marquetry, starting with this fan.

Building the central fan

The fan was constructed by the template method, as all other fans are made. However, one additional technique is necessary because each flute consists of two veneers, and it is the second veneer that is added which requires the window method to achieve its installation. The step-by-step procedures below explain.

The fan is 300 mm (12 inch) in diameter. With 40 flutes it meant each flute was separated every 9° around the circumference of the circle. The protractor and compass made the drawing accurate (Figures 6.60 and 6.61). Fortunately I had a large homemade compass that spanned the dimensions easily. The large compass keeps the measurements constant. Here, the white background flutes are being laid using the pre-drawn template.

Pink flutes were sandshaded along one edge (see Figure 6.62). One window was cut into the white veneer using the wood template shown in Figure 6.64. This

Figure 6.59 The satinwood background in my studio.

creates a window for the pink veneer to be slid under the window, scored, cut out and inserted: the window method (see Figure 6.63).

Using the wood template, each window would be exactly the same size. Figure 6.65 shows me installing a stringer held in place with a ring of red berries. I am using sticky-back plastic to hold them in place. The original marqueteur would have used hot animal glue, gluing one berry at a time. Stringer and berries in place, each berry is covered with protective paper on the face side (see Figure 6.66) and Figure 6.67 shows the central floral design fretsawn and assembled. This is the exact design used on the end panels, which surrounds the guilloche shown on page 166. Black wax has been pressed in between the ring of berries to fill the gaps.

Figure 6.60 Protractor marks out the 40° flutes.

Figure 6.61 Large compass draws inner and outer circles.

CHAPTER 6 | Building a Replica: Diana & Minerva Commode

Figure 6.62 Sandshaded pink veneer for the flutes.

Figure 6.63 Pink flutes installed by the window method

Figure 6.64 Cutting the windows using a wooden template.

Figure 6.65 Installing the stringer and berries.

Figure 6.66 One red berry turned over to reveal red colour.

Figure 6.67 The completed central fan.

169

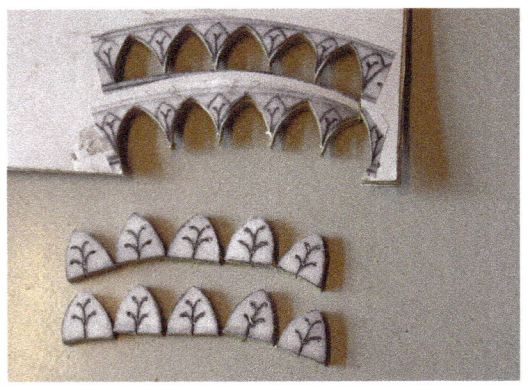

Figure 6.68 Fretsawn laurel leaf tips.

Figure 6.69 Large and small laurel leaves in order.

Laurel leaf tips (large) were fretsawn to form the outer border of the fan (Figure 6.68). Large and small laurel leaves (Figure 6.69) were kept in order to fit from where they were sawn.

To summarise the construction of the outer border seen at 6.70:

* Padauk triangles fitted into the ends of each flute, using the window method.
* White stringer fitted around padauk triangles.
* Two-tone green foliage fitted around stringer.
* Black triangles installed between leaves.
* White stringer fits around black triangles 6 mm green banding fit to white stringer.
* Green banding cut from one sheet of veneer.

All components are held together with veneer tape attached to the face side. You are looking at the reverse side that eventually will be glued to the substrate.

Figure 6.70 Reverse side of completed fan.

Creating four matching acanthus leaf elements

Because the four quadrants are a mirror image of each other, at least where the acanthus leaves are concerned, I was able to create a packet of four green veneers so that I could fretsaw all four simultaneously from one sawing. However, it was not that straightforward because the corners are quarter-matched, meaning that the diagonally opposite corners match each other, while the opposite diagonal corners are displayed in reverse. To achieve this, two of the four green veneers have to be reversed in the packet when it is assembled (shown in Figure 6.71).

I traced the acanthus leaves from one quarter of the original photocopy, so that I knew they represented the actual shape and style of the initial drawings. The tracings are placed on the packet so that the grain of the green veneers travels up each leaf, as seen in Figure 6.72.

The leaves are fretsawn (Figure 6.73). For acanthus leaves that sit in pairs around the central fan, I made up two green veneers for this packet, because these acanthus leaves are only book-matched, not quarter matched like the other foliage (Figure 6.74).

Figure 6.75 is a display showing book-matched acanthus leaves (numbered 1 and 2) and quarter-matched acanthus leaves (numbered 3 to 10). At this

CHAPTER 6 | Building a Replica: Diana & Minerva Commode

Figure 6.71 Packet for acanthus leaves.

Figure 6.72 Acanthus leaf tracing.

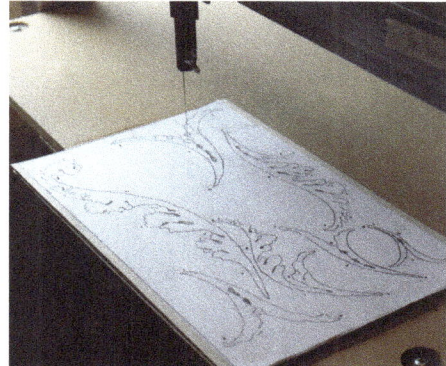

Figure 6.73 Fretsawing the leaves.

Figure 6.74 Book matched acanthus leaves fretsawn.

juncture I make no apology for reminding you of the purpose of packet fretsawing – to create symmetry. Perfect repetitive images are achieved every time, as displayed here. The true quarter-matched effect is achieved simply by reversing two of the four veneers in the packet. When placed into the four quadrants, all four elements will be in the correct orientation, and all face-side up, as in Figure 6.75.

Figure 6.76 shows white protective paper glued onto the face sides, showing the quarter-matched herringbone effect of the top. The paper is applied for two reasons: first to protect the veneers from splitting during sawing, and, a secondary, yet important reason, to seal the satinwood to improve finishing at the final stage.

Figure 6.77 shows me fixing the master tracing of the entire top onto the satinwood background. By holding the tracing with tape to the top, it allows me to slide fretsawn elements underneath, making sure they are

Figure 6.75 Display of the fretsawn acanthus leaves.

correctly located, as seen in Figure 6.78. I like this method because it means I control the positioning throughout by sliding each fretsawn element under the tracing paper. This I repeated for all the acanthus leaves on all four quadrants. At this stage I was not interested in any other elements of the design.

Figure 6.76 White protective paper glued to the top.

Figure 6.77 Fixing the master tracing to the veneer.

Figure 6.78 Sliding the fretsawn elements into place.

Figure 6.79 All the acanthus leaves in position.

All the acanthus leaf elements are now in place on all four quadrants, Figure 6.79. At this stage they are held in place with tabs of masking tape.

That is as far as I can go now, because I need to make and install the decorative diamond arrangement, and position the fan exactly in the centre.

Making the decorative diamond

The four lengths of bandings each consist of rows of laurel leaves, with two red berries set in between each leaf node. They are set into a background veneer of purpleheart. A white boxed stringer placed either side borders the banding. Only fretsawing can achieve this construction, since purpleheart is far too hard to cut free-hand with a craft knife. Thirty-nine laurel leaves exist in each strip. Each strip is 480 mm (18 inch) in length and 15 mm (9/16 inch) wide. Figure 6.80 shows four strips made up, with only the first on the left complete with berries and stringers. Here's how I made the borders:

I made up a packet of four green-dyed veneers 510 mm (20 inch) long and 18 mm (11/16 inch) wide, with a waster on either side. With the design pasted on top, I was able to produce four rows of sawn laurel leaves. The 156 inner leaf sections were sandshaded to create the all-important 3D effect to each row.

Holding the purpleheart intact during assembly was a tricky operation, since there was very little left of it after sawing the laurel leaves. I reduced the width to 15 mm on all four completed bandings, then adding stringers to each side. I deliberately made the purpleheart

CHAPTER 6 | Building a Replica: Diana & Minerva Commode

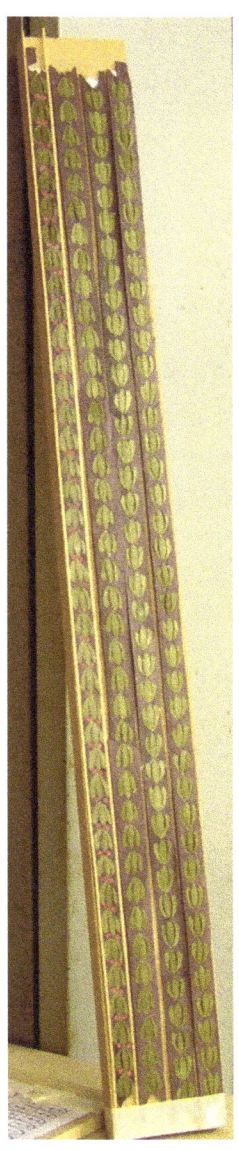

Figure 6.80 Four strips showing full length.

Figure 6.81 The diamond's defining moment.

background wider than needed, because I expected it to be a problem as just explained, and also it allowed me to trim the width against one long steel straight edge.

I now needed to position the diamond around the central fan using the original line drawing as a guide.

It was at this precise moment that it hit me! There, staring me in the face, in Figure 6.81 was the reason for the inclusion of this unplanned additional element.

The marqueteur constructing the original top was faced with an impossible task, as I was, because the marquetry elements waiting to be sawn into the satinwood background would not fit into the throat of his or my fretsaw. The throat of the fretsaw is the distance between the fretsaw blade and the frame of the saw. In the case of a treadle-saw, there are two throats, one left and one right of the blade, and both the same distance. Figure 6.82 shows the background veneer section measuring 650 mm (2 ft 2 inch) across one herringbone satinwood section, which the marqueteur had to fretsaw. After installing the diamond, that measurement was reduced to 450 mm (1 ft 6 inch) (see Figure 6.83), which was clearly the throat distance of the marqueteur's saw.

Figure 6.82 Background veneer too long!

Figure 6.83 Diamond reduced length to allow fretsaw work.

My own treadle saw only had a throat of 300 mm (1 ft), so I had to have a new saw constructed with a new throat of 450 mm (1 ft 6 inch). For the original marqueteur, and for Chippendale, two solutions were possible. These were to either build another, larger treadle fretsaw, with a throat of 650 mm (2 ft 2 inch), or insert something into the design that had the effect of shortening these herringbone sections to meet the constraints of the existing saw. It is at this stage that another situation beckons.

As I have previously considered in Chapter 3, maybe an independent firm, who operated in the capital city, performed the marquetry work. This means that the client (Chippendale) had no jurisdiction over them, and therefore could not insist they built a larger saw. He was left with no alternative but to find another solution to minimise the length of the herringbone segments to allow fret work to continue, and get his precious commode completed. A narrow, straight lined diamond, which he skilfully and artistically designed solved the practical needs of the marqueteur.

On other large marquetry panels, on earlier commissions, the trend had been to insert oval bandings to reduce background veneers to fit the throat of the fretsaw, so Chippendale was familiar with these demands. I suspect he thought that by creating quartered panels that were arranged in the herringbone style, the dimensions would suffice for fretsawing needs. It is also very clear to me that an oval decorative band could not be used here, because there was not enough room for one. It was with sheer luck that he managed to accommodate the diamond and reduce the background sizes sufficiently to accommodate fretwork. At last I had the answer to a question that had puzzled me ever since seeing the commode. The classic design followed the artistic theme of style and symmetry where movement and motion worked hand-in-hand to achieve a flowing stylistic theme across all elements. The straight line played no part in such a movement, but in this case the physical needs outplayed the artistic. Seeing his solution is also rewarding because he could have just included a diamond consisting of four stringers, which would have had the desired solution. We know our designer always looked for artistic excellence, and his decorative banding was a joy to both construct and view, despite the unwanted straight lines. My own opinion suddenly changed, and I was filled with respect for how he achieved this difficult, yet necessary, unplanned alteration.

My friend Malcolm Slater duly made me a larger treadle saw, increasing the throat from 300 mm (1 ft) long to 450 mm (1 ft 6inch). Without it, I could not have completed this project. At least I now know the size of saw the original marqueteur had in his workshop, and now I have the same.

As you can see from Figures 6.82 and 6.83, more motifs have been added, and I would like to show you their construction.

Making two acanthus leaves that sit either side of the fan

A packet of two light-green veneers and two smaller dark-green veneers are assembled and sawn, Figure 6.84. The outer tips will be sandshaded to give 3D effect, shown in Figure 6.85, while the remaining two-tone leaves that cluster round the fan are shown in Figure 6.86.

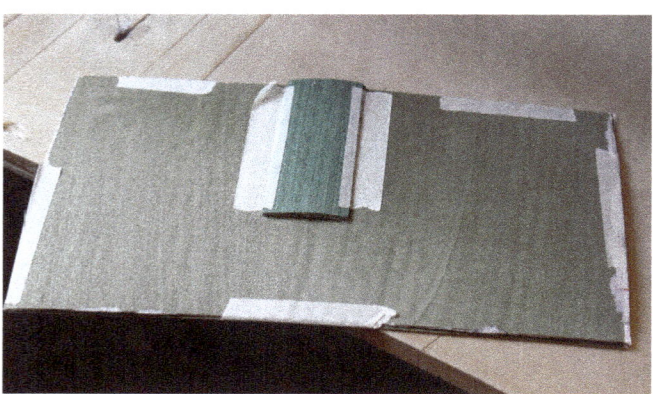

Figure 6.84 Packet for the acanthus leaves.

Figure 6.85 Assembly of both green veneers. Two tips need sandshading.

CHAPTER 6 | Building a Replica: Diana & Minerva Commode

Figure 6.86 Foliage ready for inclusion.

Figure 6.87 Miniature vase shapes.

Figure 6.87 shows miniature vase shaped elements cut from a yellow-dyed veneer, with red berries around the tops. Black filler compound is used to fill the minute gaps between the berries.

Plumages in burgundy and green, cut, sandshaded and assembled, ready for adding to the design are shown in Figure 6.88.

Ready to commence installation of all elements

I started by getting the diamond positioned accurately (see Figure 6.81), so that all the inner and outer components fitted into the space created, making sure that the central fan also fitted perfectly in place. Positioning the diamond was the most taxing part, because at the four points where the diamond met, the berries had to match and appear to join together naturally. Once in place and held with masking tape, I was able to position and mark the other elements within the diamond.

Figure 6.89 shows how the elements have been laid on the background, a line scored around them with scalpel, then lifted clear, for sawing out. Figure 6.90 shows the background veneer lifted from Figure 6.89. The picture is not sharp enough to highlight the scored lines, but please trust me when I say the lines are there and I did fretsaw up to them. I taped the veneer to a waster to protect it during sawing.

Next, I scored the anthemion, which nestles into the point of the diamond, and the two plumages on either side. You can just make the anthemion out below the two straight lines. The picture in Figure 6.91 shows the location where the background was taken, while Figure 6.92 shows where the windows are sawn out to take the corner anthemion and two plumages.

Figure 6.88 Plumages in burgundy and green.

Figure 6.89 Positioning the elements within the diamond.

Figure 6.90 Background from Fig. 6.89.

Figure 6.91 Windows waiting for sawn insert at Fig. 6.92.

Figure 6.92 Corner anthemion and two plumages to be sawn into equivalent windows.

By turning the central panel over to reveal the reverse side, in Figure 6.93, I got to see the impact of colour for the first time. It was like finding a hidden treasure! Here, before me, was a taster of Thomas Chippendale's creative genius, simply stunning and beautiful. It took my breath away, forcing me to stand alone in my workshop, in total silence, as I tried to take in what I was seeing. All thoughts of the straight-lined addition were swept aside, as I viewed a creation consisting of artistry, classicism, colour and sheer splendour. I noticed the purple anthemion nestled into the corner where the diamond terminated with its white plumage below. On either side, splaying acanthus leaves burst across the diamond border, striking out into the wilderness of

Figure 6.93 First glimpse of the completed diamond.

Figure 6.94 A striking cameo.

protective white paper (Figure 6.94). It was mesmerising. The use of purpleheart for the diamond background was a carefully selected choice, since its natural colour complements the dyed purple used to make the anthemion.

I was witnessing an artistic master at the top of his profession, offering his skills for all to see and enjoy. But I was the first person to see it, standing alone, as I was in my workshop. I wanted to dash out into the street and shout long and loud about my findings – tell the world what genius I had unfolded, by piecing together the coloured woods he had merged together into a classic design some 250 years ago. It spurred me on to want to add more work, more colour, more artistry, by using the skills my late mentor, Tommy Limmer, had first planted into my craving hands, some 15 years earlier. How immensely proud he would have been to see what I was now witnessing.

This cameo shot, in Figure 6.94, stands out like a lighted beacon, surrounded by a white morning fog. It is shouting to its surround to catch up, and join in the carnival of colour, which beckons beneath their protective papers. What greater aspiration could I wish for as I was spurred on to complete the remaining work.

My gratitude went out to Heinrich Piening for identifying the original dyestuffs and their stimulating colours. Without his new technology, what I was seeing would and could not have happened. I thought also of the immense help I had received from Melissa Gallimore at Harewood House, and how she would react to seeing these images. Could these stunning colours ever be seen standing against the original commode, made for and held at Harewood, by our country's greatest furniture designer? So many thoughts flashed through my head on this day, but reality made me turn to the facts as they stood, and logic told me to continue working on the rest of the replica, using the skills I had developed and the encouraging results I had so far achieved.

My new treadle saw

Following the discovery of the fretsaw size, my new version was built and delivered, shown in Figures 6.95 and 6.96. I could continue with the work. I am indeed grateful to Malcolm Slater for his skilled work in making and delivering the new larger model. A 900 mm (3 ft) rule laid across the table shows the 450 mm (18 inch) throat.

As you can see, the footplate is hinged at the toe end and not the heel end. The first model was hinged at the heel end and I found my calf muscle soon ached. Simply moving the mounted plate to the toe end removes that problem; I still use this very model today.

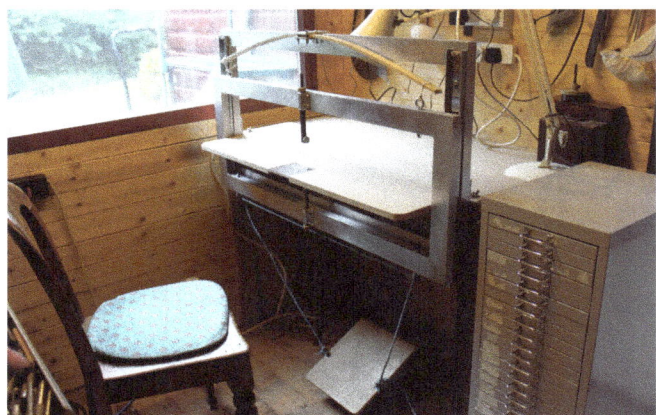

Figure 6.95 My new treadle saw.

Figure 6.96 Larger 450 mm (18") throat.

Figure 6.97 Motifs ready for insertion into background.

Figure 6.98 Scored lines and pilot hole.

Fretsawing background veneers outside the diamond

With the diamond now in place and my new, larger-throated fretsaw made, I could start work on the background veneers outside the diamond design.

The elements you see in Figure 6.97 have been laid on the background, scored around with a scalpel, removed (shown above the elements), and taken to the fretsaw. Figure 6.98 shows scored lines created by the scalpel, and used to fretsaw along. A pilot hole is needed to thread the saw blade through.

Figure 6.99 shows one acanthus leaf window sawn. The leaf and waster are removed, as seen here. The remaining scored lines to be sawn are just visible.

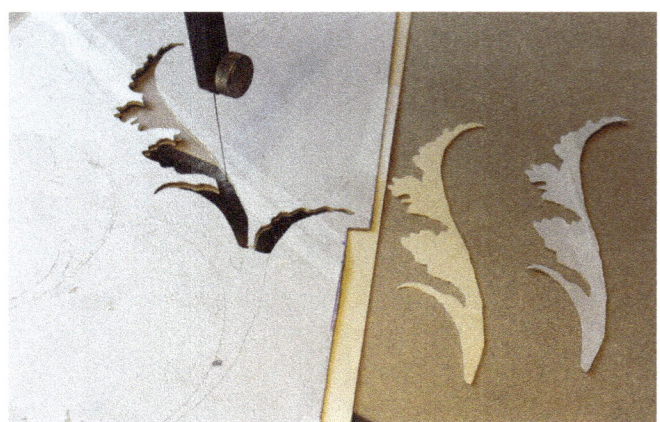

Figure 6.99 One acanthus leaf sawn.

Forming circular stringers

A different and refreshing technique to use on the next aspect of the build, bending stringers has always been a joy to perform, ever since my erstwhile mentor taught me the tricks of the trade. If he wanted to bend a stringer only slightly, and providing it was white wood, and not dyed, he would run it through his mouth, sucking it along the length, for a few minutes to soften it. In most cases it had the desired effect.

It taught me a lesson about improvisation, and I have used it on rare occasions. However, I much prefer my more healthy modified approach, using a hot bath and/or dry heat. In this instance, I use dry heat supplied by my hotplate, which I use to heat sand. By looking around my workshop I usually find a metal object that is fit for purpose. In Figure 6.100, an old broken metal torch happened to be the perfect diameter for the circular stringers, which I needed to wrap around the four acanthus flowers placed in each of the four quadrants of the design. Figure 6.101 sees a tin can doing the same job, while Figure 6.102 shows one stringer installed. Heat bending makes the tasks possible at every attempt, and you are in control throughout.

In Figure 6.103, we see all components inserted into the background, showing the coloured acanthus flowers in each quadrant with their stringers tightly around them.

It is clear from Figure 6.104 that an ellipse would not have fit into the four-quadrant design, leaving our designer no alternative but to use this straight lined bisecting diamond. You are looking at the reverse side of the top, which will eventually be stuck down on to the substrate. All that is left to do now is fit the dyed green inner border and the outer tulipwood crossbanding border.

CHAPTER 6 | Building a Replica: Diana & Minerva Commode

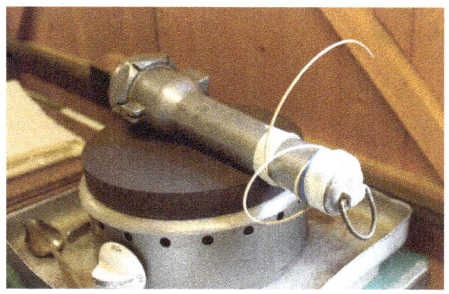

Figure 6.100 Bending stringers.

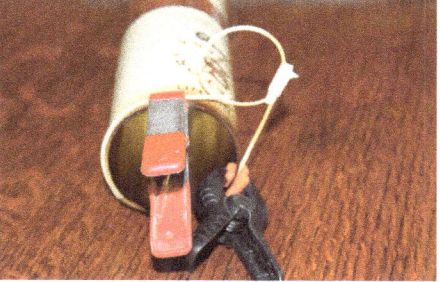

Figure 6.101 A heated tin can.

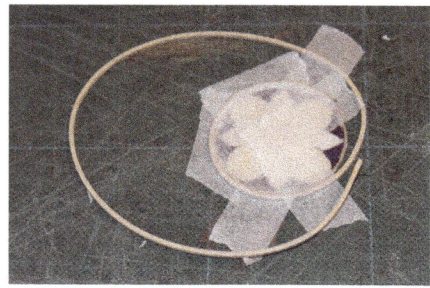

Figure 6.102 One string installed.

Figure 6.103 Top complete and protected with tape.

Figure 6.104 The completed commode top.

At this stage I had to move the work into my house, because the winter of 2010 was approaching and I could not maintain the right temperature both day and night in my workshop. Damp conditions are not conducive to veneering work. The warmth and comfort of my house provided a rarely used lounge and the answer to completing this final stage of build. How lucky I was to have a fully devoted and supportive wife, who fully understood my dilemma. As she said, teasingly, at least I get to see you more. A timely reminder that woodworkers and their workshops habitually create seclusive environments. A pang of guilt crossed my mind. Now seven years later and still writing this book, I reflect on my wonderful late dear wife and the 54 happy years we shared together. While it is now over four years since she passed away, I am never without her presence and strength pushing me forward to fulfil my passion for this absorbing craft. I am proud to share my thoughts about her greatness of character, and unwavering love and support she gave without condition.

Fitting the green-dyed borders and tulipwood crossbanding

To mark out the width of the green border, I adapted my marking/cutting gauge to get the width even along the curved line. Figure 6.105 shows the tool modified, with two matching half-round beadings pinned either side of the marking tool. This provides equilibrium once the gauge has been set for the fixed distance. A uniform gap along the curved edge is achieved as the tool traverses along the edge of the table. The gauge can be turned around 180 degrees if a flat surface needs scribing. I found it more accurate to scribe the line with a pencil, as seen here, rather than cut through the scored line with the gauge loaded with a cutting blade. I used a scalpel to cut through the pencil line manually.

Tulipwood is an attractive veneer, with its multi-striped colours (see Figure 6.106), yet also a difficult wood to work with, because of its extreme hardness. I used a fretsaw to cut across the grain on the shaped ends, and a veneer saw and straight edge for the straight cuts. Fortunately, the cuts to join two lengths together are with the grain. To achieve these cuts where two tulipwood veneers overlapped, I used a 50 mm (2 inch) wide steel plane blade and a hammer, as seen in Figure 6.107. The blade must be very sharp. It encourages me to think that perhaps the same type of hand tools were made, or modified, and used on the original construction.

At last, the final borders were in place and the panel was complete. It had taken about a year from when I first started and that included waiting for a second fretsaw to be made and installed. As a retired pensioner, time was not of the essence, since I did not work long hours, nor even a five-day week, so one year was quite acceptable.

Figure 6.105 My adapted marking/cutting gauge.

Figure 6.106 Tulipwood sample.

Figure 6.107 Plane blade used to cut joints in tulipwood.

Figure 6.108 Seeing the finished top for the first time.

With the panel now fully bordered, it was with great pride and anticipation that I was now ready to view the underside, to see the full extent of the colourful design. This time I was not alone. My dear wife stood beside me in our lounge as I lifted the base to expose the underside of the marquetry and other veneers, shown in Figure 6.108. She gasped, then went silent for quite some time. The silence was deafening. She walked from left to right, never taking her eyes from the scene. After what seemed like eternity, she eventually looked at me with a meaningful gaze and said, *"No wonder you've been locked into this work all this time, I now see why: it's beautiful."* With that she went into the kitchen, put the kettle on, and made a cup of tea. No further words were needed.

My own artistic observations matched those spoken just then: it was beautiful. Speaking honestly, I never imagined it would have such an impact. A kaleidoscope of colour, tonal balance and ultimate symmetry lay before me. I had to acknowledge to myself that this was all my own work, performed with historically accurate tools and techniques, as used by the original marqueteur. A feeling swept over me that I had emulated all he put before me, yet what I was looking at was done by my own hands and was, I hope, equal to anything the original tactician achieved.

On a technical basis, the image shows all the colours and the symmetry that the designer always sought to achieve. The diamond now becomes an acceptable inclusion, even more so now I know the trauma it must have caused at the time. His solution stands testament to his creative genius. Future opinions about the diamond, following my discovery, may create interesting discussions about its technical inclusion: how it was conceived, whether other options could have been taken, and so on. The path taken by the diamond is clear to see, inasmuch as it just made it through the tiniest gaps left by the quadratic design. Clearly there was no room for the traditional ellipse he used on other large panels, and on previous and subsequent commissions, and seen in Chapter 8.

Another solution, which would have achieved completion of the top without the addition of the diamond, would have been to build a four-foot treadle saw. That, for whatever reason, was clearly an option not available to our designer. Perhaps it strengthens the belief that marquetry work was performed by independent workshops within the capital city, where a decision regarding a larger saw was outside Chippendale's authority. It does however throw up the need for a larger-throated fretsaw, since much of the marquetry work for furniture produced by the large firms along St Martin's Lane was on furniture intended for stately homes, where large-sized furniture was common place. We have seen in Chapter 2 where a replica four-foot treadle saw was made in Germany around the 18th century, so it is not unreasonable to assume that larger versions eventually arrived in workshops across the rest of Europe. We know there are no constraints for building and using a four-foot treadle saw and, had one been available, Chippendale could have omitted the reducing ellipses and, in this case, the diamond to overcome the smaller saw's limitations.

Gluing and sanding the top

It is at this point that I took up an offer to have the top pressed professionally in a hydraulic plated press and also belt-sanded. The offer was too good to refuse. Mark Forster, Director of SPA Laminates, Leeds, took the top and, using PVA glue, he held it under one of his presses overnight. Some days later, I was able to watch as one of his staff, Glen Blair, expertly belt-sanded the surface, removing all the protective paper and got all veneers down to one level. I had witnessed marquetry panels sanded this way on many occasions in Sorrento, Italy, during my many visits. This time I was witnessing my own work undergoing the process. Watching was a nerve-wracking experience, but Glen was an experienced belt-sander, so I entrusted my work to his safe hands.

The alternative to this option would have been for me to press it using the hammer-veneering technique, as used to press the original. While this would have been technically correct for making this replica, I have to confess my reluctance to commit my inexperience to such a demanding task. Yes, I know how to hammer-veneer, and would not flinch from doing so on small manageable panels, but this mammoth panel was a step too far for me! One has to recognise one's own limitations and be honest about taking alternative decisions.

Images of the top panel and its original, scientifically proven colour scheme

The marquetry top, shown in Figure 6.109, displays all its original colours as planned by Thomas Chippendale, and accomplished by the unknown marqueteur in 1773. This reproduction captures the same polychromatic impact that the original owner intended.

The left-hand side, seen in Figure 6.110, captures the colouring and symmetry of the quadratic theme which carries through to the right-hand side shown in Figure 6.111. Three burgundy anthemions (see Figure 6.110, far left and Figure 6.111, far right) are almost faded out of sight on the original commode, so it is good to have the scientific proof of their colour, replicating the honeysuckle flower, as it is called today.

Note the cut-out on the front edge: this is to follow the shape of the front, as will become obvious when the panel is installed. Like the left side, the herringbone effect of the quarter matching satinwood is prominent now a first coat of sealer polish has been applied.

The two-tone circular fan (Figure 6.112) placed at the centre of the panel really does dominate, with its bold statement radiating as it does to all four parts of the classic design. To show off my proud construction, a close-up (Figure 6.114), highlights the central floral theme and the classic band of berries perfectly lined within curved stringers.

Looking at the top panel, I am reminded that it was less than 20 years since I took up the craft for the very first time. Such a rewarding and pleasurable journey was made possible by a mentor and friend who unearthed a

Figure 6.109

Figure 6.110 Three burgundy anthemions (seen far left).

Figure 6.111 Similar athemions (far right).

Figure 6.112 View of diamond surrounding the circular fan.

hidden talent, releasing a passion and energy that has never diminished.

Seeing the whole panel laid out in these images reminds me of the rewards of using two-part fretsawing, which are there for all to see and enjoy. It is a great source of satisfaction to see tight joints between mating edges, and to achieve total symmetry between the four quadrants. Even to construct the diamond banding was a challenge and, as already stated, I now take on a different, more complimentary view of its necessary existence. These are the rewards that make you want to emulate Chippendale's work time and again. I hope my results inspire marqueteurs to take up the saw and the knife – but *not* the laser – and start building classic designs the way I have built them.

Figure 6.113

Figure 6.114 Close-up of the central motif – the ultimate examination of marquetry work!

TODAY'S MARQUETRY TECHNIQUE

I take this opportunity to talk about today's approach to producing commercial marquetry, using computer numerical controlled (CNC) machinery, a subject high on my agenda. I am assured by professional companies within the UK that they cannot find a professional marquetry practitioner, who, like me, produces handmade work. One such London based firm assured me I was the only person in the UK still practising and producing hand-fretsawn reproduction antique work.

The thought of that, if true (and I have no reason to challenge it) fills me with despair. Does it mean I can be replaced by a machine to perform work equally as accurate and stylish as mine? There are mixed answers to this statement: yes, I can be replaced by a machine; yes the work will be as accurate; yet no, it will never be as stylish.

CNC programming works where a design, drawn by Computer Aided Design (CAD) resides on a computer database. The CNC reads the CAD, translating it to drive a remote laser, which in turn follows the paths on the CAD to cut through veneers to produce a precise replica of the initial design. So far, the human hand has not touched this process. Because the laser can cut so precisely, gaps between mating joints are non-existent. A tiny, almost indistinguishable, burn mark results along the mating joints. Now the human hand is required, to piece together the cut marquetry elements and surrounding background veneers. The result is a 'perfectly' cut display on every production. In addition to this, it costs pennies, compared to the high labour costs of handmade marquetry.

The change happened during the past ten years, and I cannot see my 'hands-on' world ever returning. I have, however, to warn those who tread this modern path, pointing out its drawbacks. CNC and Computer Aided Manufacture (CAM) do not – and never will – match the stylish and artistic results illustrated in this publication and, more importantly, in museums and stately homes where 17th and 18th century marquetry is on display. When comparing today's computer-driven marquetry against the handmade equivalent, produced by the techniques as used in this reproduction, the latter will, I believe, win hands down. The reason is that the computer system cannot replicate the style and artistry generated by human hands, both in the design stage and the application that follows. One reputable London-based restorer told me recently that, after receiving CNC/CAM driven fretwork, it had to be deliberately 'distressed' to make it look handmade. This was because the delivered work was 'too perfect' and 'too mechanical' – so much so that it looked false and out of place with its surrounding handmade equivalents. I understood what he was saying. My opinion, and standard saying on such marquetry, is that it produces marquetry to send you to sleep. If this book achieves nothing else but to revive an interest in handmade work, in marquetry, cabinet work, wood-turning, and wood-carving, I will be satisfied as both practitioner and writer.

So why is handmade much better? To answer this we have to look at how the work is performed. To start with, designs are hand drawn. Imagine comparing a Van Dyke or a Botticelli painting alongside a CNC generated copy. A Chippendale or Ince and Mayhew marquetry commode is no different. Like the painter, the marquetry designer selects the woods and dyed colours to paint the images within the design. From that, the marqueteur carefully selects each piece of veneer, checking grain direction and figure to give maximum impact to each element. Accurate knife or saw work ensures the initial artistry is retained. Every curve and curl of a acanthus leaf has its own personality, planted there by the designer's hand and retained by the marquetry sawyer. Embellishment, like sandshading and engraving is applied to provide more animation.

Today these secondary applications tend to be omitted on laser-produced work because of labour costs. Handmade motifs such as acanthus leaves, laurel leaves, vases, fans, ribbons, swags, anthemions and guilloches come alive when competently and lovingly constructed by dexterous hands using classic techniques.

I can assure you the commode panel I have just completed will echo not only the original commode, but would also echo Chippendale's original drawings, if it was possible to locate them. The personality and the soul of the work is retained throughout each process, and the end result is testament to that.

DECORATING THE DOMED DOOR

I deliberately left this panel to the end for two reasons: first, because I knew it would be the most testing technically and, second, because I needed time to improve my skill level. Having completed the commode top, I felt that my skills had reached an all-time high. That, for me, is a pleasing statement to make. Now approaching the age of 80, I doubt I am going to get any better than this!

Whether that meant I could carry out a new technique for the first time successfully remained to be seen. I knew I was excited about starting it, which was a positive in my favour. I had researched the techniques I would be using and, although I had seen them being applied by skilled artisans during my many visits to Sorrento, Italy, this was a first for me.

In Chapter 2, I explain what the inlay technique demands, and how I discovered where it was used on the domed door and on the drawer fronts. I did not emulate the technique on the drawer fronts, simply because I had not discovered its use till after I had completed them.

Inlaying and hammer-veneering

I would be required to carry out the inlaying technique to apply some of the marquetry across the incurved dome. This operation required me to make a specialist inlay knife and master the hammer-veneering technique, again as described in Chapters 2 and 3. I am sure that the step-by-step illustrations, as I carry out the work, will help you understand and follow the practical aspects of the technique.

Hammer-veneering is still carried out today by some marqueteurs, and it is a good skill to have up your sleeve, especially on concave and convex surfaces. I also saw it applied to laying parquetry work onto jewellery boxes when on a visit to the Alhambra Palace, southern Spain. In the palace, a small marquetry shop was selling marquetry and parquetry decorated jewellery boxes and, inside the shop, the public was allowed to watch the marqueteur at work. I watched him laying parquetry pieces individually by smearing a spot of hot animal glue with his finger on to the veneer, then pressing it in place on the box, using his small veneer hammer. He was using the stick-as-you-go method, which I discussed in Chapter 3. This is a useful method, providing you know the

Figure 6.115*

dimensions of the pattern and the area it is applied to. It gives you total control of the work at every stage and, more importantly, it provides immediate adhesion.

The dome door construction

Plan of action

The black and white image of the original domed door, Figure 6.115, allowed me to look at the plan of action. This stage of the project demanded twelve stages of work and, for the most part, for them to be completed in the order I have shown below:

1. Hammer-veneer eight satinwood segments to dome.
2. Build the half-round fan.
3. Fretsaw the laurel leaf swags and drops.
4. Make nine flowers using the window method (made by my colleague).
5. Inlay swags, drops and flowers.
6. Hammer-veneer the half-round fan.
7. Fit crossbanding tulipwood across the bottom of the door.
8. Build the two triangular designs on the fascia panel.
9. Build the small circular fan at the centre of the fascia panel.
10. Build the crossbanding tulipwood on fascia panel.
11. Glue the two matching panels in one operation, using animal glue and clamps.
12. Build the marquetry for the raised arch that sits above the dome.

* Reproduced by the kind permission of the Trustees of the 7th Earl of Harewood Will Trust and the Trustees of the Harewood House Trust

My colleague built the nine tiny daisy flowers in Step 4, leaving me to execute the remaining eleven action points. However, before I did anything on the list, I decided to make up a model to allow me to practise hammer-veneering, since it had been some years since I last performed it, and then only on a flat surface.

The dome was a different challenge because I knew I would be experiencing, for the first time, compound angles trying to pull the veneers where you do not want them to go.

In the case of this dome, three different angles are present across its surface: vertical, horizontal and diagonal, with each angle pulling against the other two. I tried to recall my physics teaching and the formula used to calculate compound angles. Since over 50 years had passed since my college days, I decided not to explore the theoretical, but concentrate on the practical, and have the experience of seeing the resulting conclusions. All the same, it gave me a good feeling to realise I was about to apply my earlier, theoretical learning and see the practical results for myself. The exercise also allowed me to test out my new tool, the inlay knife, by performing the inlay technique.

Practice model

My incurved model, shown in Figure 6.116, allowed me to hammer-veneer satinwood with hot animal glue. While not an exact copy of the domed door, the model did present compound forces enough for me to practise on. After fretsawing the laurel leaf swag, I laid it across the satinwood, Figure 6.117. After scoring round the swag, I was able to use the inlay knife and small hammer to cut along the scored lines (see Figure 6.118).

I was encouraged and excited by how easily the knife followed the scored line, with consummate accuracy. The bevels I had placed on the point of the knife made it easy to twist, both left and right, as the path of the inlay dictated.

Figure 6.116 My incurved practice model.

Figure 6.117 Fretsawn swag laid on the model.

Figure 6.118 Cutting along the scored lines.

Figure 6.119 Hot water brushed on.

Chapter 6 | Building a Replica: Diana & Minerva Commode

Figure 6.120 The cavity for the swag exposed.

Figure 6.121 Hammer-veneering the swag into the cavity.

It was now time to remove the satinwood area where the swag would sit, and to do this I applied heat and water by using a small unused glue brush dipped in hot water and held on the area I wanted to remove (see Figure 6.119).

With the cavity exposed (Figure 6.120), I used the wedge-end of the hammer to hammer-veneer the swag into the cavity (Figure 6.121).

I found the practice piece very easy to perform. The inlay knife performs unbelievably accurately and is very easy to use. I can't believe the result gained at the first attempt. Because I had filed bevels on to the point of the knife, both in front and the back of the blade, the tool followed the twisting line easily and accurately. Equally, the hammer-veneering technique was simple and effective. The inlays are small, so only the tiniest amount of glue is needed to secure the swags to the cavity. I felt very confident now to take on the real work.

Step 1. Hammer-veneering eight satinwood segments to the dome

I made a paper model of the elements that appear across the dome (see Figure 6.122) to see how the different elements would both fit across the panel and be in line with each other. Note how the eight segments are joined together, indicated by the faint lines below the laurel leaf vertical drops. The lines converge at the fan but, more importantly, they converge where every other flute meets its partner flute. This provides a continuing joint line from the laurel leaf swags through each satinwood segment and continuing through the fan flutes. Without this continuity of line the whole design loses meaning and purpose.

Building a life-sized model was part of my training from my mentor, the late Tommy Limmer. His teaching was: *"If you can't draw it to scale, or build a model to scale (as in this case) and make it work – it will never work"*. This is

Figure 6.122 Paper model of the elments appearing across the dome.

advice I use in all my marquetry panels. The only parts of the design missing are the tiny daisies, which fit where the nine laurel leaf swags converge under the outer edge of the door. I know these will fit and the space I have left is catered for on the model.

It is clear to see from this model that the dome is relatively flat at the bottom, but increases height gradually at the start until its steepest climb occurs where the swags exist. That is the reason why the swags are where they are. They break the satinwood segments at the steepest point of the dome, thereby taking the strain out of the wood and reducing the pull of the compound angles that bear down on the assembly. It is wonderful to realise our intrepid designer knew all about compound angles, and the proof is that he reduced the sizes of each satinwood segment across the horizontal plane, then placed the marquetry to eliminate the vertical pulls. Collectively, the two placings also reduced the diagonal pulls as well. Oh what a designer, conscious of physics (even though the word was not in use until the end of the 19th century) and the effects on shapes like this, yet more than capable of applying a practical solution. The existing dome has survived intact for over 250 years, and stands as living proof of his designing genius.

With these thoughts and seeing the mock model before me, I was more than ready to start the greatest test of my short, yet ambitious, marquetry experience. Having tested my inlay knife on the practice model and realised I had the touch and skill to undertake such a challenge, I could not wait to get started. My confidence and excitement was overflowing, so that I knew it was going to work before making the first cut with knife or saw. I felt like an artist looking at a blank canvas (see

Figure 6.123 Using dividers to map where the satinwood segments would go.

Figure 6.123), yet with the finished picture firmly planted in my mind.

Using dividers I mapped out where the eight satinwood segments would lie. I then made an oversized paper model of one segment, using it as a template to cut eight matching segments to cover the dome. I deliberately cut the segments oversized, so they would overlap each other when glued to the dome using the hammer-veneering technique. By laying the paper model on my stack of satinwood (Figure 6.124), I was able to select the best figuring to place side by side and give the best overall effect, both vertically and horizontally across the domed surface.

Figure 6.125 shows where I cut across each veneer, where the swags would be inlaid. This created two separate parts to each segment. The two central segments were glued in place using my veneer hammer. It is important to glue both sides of the veneer as it

Figure 6.124 Full length of satinwood veneers.

Figure 6.125 All eight satinwood segments glued in place.

makes it more durable when pressure is applied from the hammer. The surplus glue scrapes off easily while it is still soft. I found it better to create the joints with a steel rule before applying glue. I realise this is not the normal method, but I found from experience that working on a curved surface changes the rules of application. The standard method is to glue both veneers in place, overlapping each other, then cut through both veneers while the glue is workable and pull the surplus pieces free.

We now see all segments glued in place, and this is where I have to confess my indiscretion. I was so intent on performing the hammer-veneering technique I forgot to take photographs. You can see where I cut each segment along the lines where the marquetry swags would be inlaid. This made hammer-veneering possible and confirms how the original was also glued. I tried bending full-sized segments into the dome, and even with hand pressure, the veneer cracked across the steepest part of the shape, i.e. where the swags reside.

All satinwood segments were first protected with paper glued down with animal glue. This provided stability to the veneer during installation. The last segment on the right in Figure 6.125 illustrates this.

I decided to build the half-round fan next, making it ready to be installed at the bottom centre of the door.

Step 2. Building the half-round fan

I used a paper design to create the template onto a sheet of MDF (Figure 6.126). This allowed me to build the flutes of the fan following the template method (Figure 6.127). I have included a few images here to show the staged construction.

The 16 flutes are sandshaded on one edge (Figure 6.128), then built to the lines on the board and, at this stage, held together with veneer tape (Figure 6.129).

On completion, I used a roll of blue electrical tape to draw the scallops at the ends of each flute (Figure 6.130). The roll of tape just happened to have the correct

Figure 6.126 Paper design for the half-round fan.

Figure 6.127 Template for building the fan.

Figure 6.128 Sandshading the flute veneers.

Figure 6.129 Building the flutes across the template.

Figure 6.130 Electrical tape, the right diameter for curves.

curve profile for the scallops. I believe in improvisation: if it works, use it.

I fixed a sheet of white holly to the outer edges of the fan and, using a scalpel, hand-cut a shaped stringer across the ends of each flute (Figure 6.131). Holly is the marqueteur's favourite wood to cut, whether by knife or saw. Clearly the same opinion applied when the original fan was built. It proves the point that what works remains unchanged. What a pity holly sliced into veneers is rarely available commercially these days. Figure 6.132 shows stringers all in place.

To build the half-round floral centre, two green veneers of different tones are needed, shown in Figure 6.133. The packet is seen here being fretsawn on my treadle saw (Figure 6.134). The paper pattern to the right is placed under a sheet of sticky-back plastic to allow the sawn parts to be located in their correct positions.

The floral design is fretsawn and seen assembled, (Figure 6.135). Small berries punched out from a red veneer are inserted between two stringers around the outer edge (Figures 6.136 and 6.137).

I fretsawed fine veins in each acanthus leaf to echo the original construction (Figure 6.135). To highlight the veins against the green-dyed veneers required mixing a black pigment combined with fish glue (Figure 6.138) and pressed into the back of the floral leaves. Veneer tape fixed to the face side captured the pigment (Figure 6.139).

Figure 6.131 Cutting the white stringer.

Figure 6.132 Stringer installed.

Figure 6.133 Two contrasting veneers for packet.

Figure 6.134 Foliage fretsawn and placed on copy on the right.

CHAPTER 6 | Building a Replica: Diana & Minerva Commode

Clusters of red berries are installed in the central part of the floral arrangement (Figure 6.140). Finally, to border the fan, bright-red padauk is used for the scallops, which sit up to the white holly stringer.

The final marquetry, assembled (Figure 6.141), sits in the bottom centre of the display and will be hammer-veneered as one piece of marquetry. The whole assembly is held together with white paper held down with animal glue on the face side. This final picture was taken before I applied the black pigment to the floral centre.

Figure 6.135 Foliage in place.

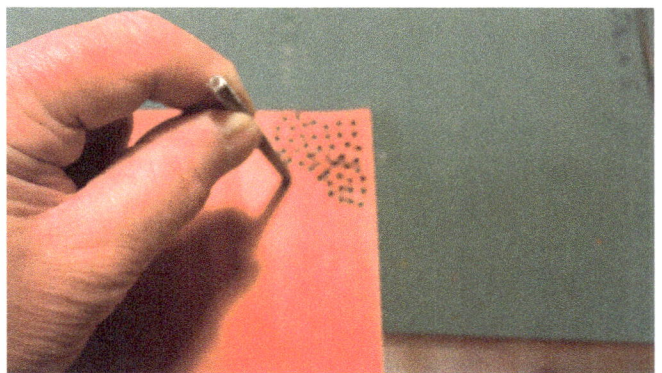
Figure 6.136 Punching red berries.

Figure 6.137 Installing berries.

Figure 6.138 Pigment and fish glue.

Figure 6.139 Central motif fitted.

Figure 6.140 Leaf veins infilled with black mastic.

Figure 6.141 The half-round fan completed.

Step 3. Fretsawing the laurel leaf swags and drops

It is very important at this stage that I declare a deliberate change between the way Chippendale shaped the laurel leaves for his domed door and the way I have formed mine. On Chippendale's original, he designed the swags and drops to consist of one solid veneer. The discovery, which I made on the original work, applied not only to the domed door, but also to the drawer fronts. I built my replica with the same shaped swags, but instead of using one solid veneer, as seen in Figure 6.142, I cut each laurel leaf with three separate sections, which allowed me to sandshade the central petal, thus matching the drawer fronts I had previously constructed and installed. By doing this I maintain the rule of the canon that I set great store by, namely symmetry.

I did replicate Chippendale's shape of the swags, giving them rounded edges as seen in Figure 6.143. This was a deliberate move, since the rounded shape (as it seemed) makes it easier for the inlay knife to follow the line. Since this was my first experience of the technique, I had to follow the lead of the original work.

The reason I did not cut the swags from one solid veneer, as in the original, was that I knew it was possible to hammer-veneer multiple pieces of marquetry in one operation, providing they were held together with tape. The proof of this was the half-round fan. The fan was assembled as one complete unit, held together (in my case) with veneer tape. In the original, all elements would have been held together with paper and hot glue. So the question remains: why were the original swags cut from one solid veneer?

Figure 6.142* Detail from Chippendale's original door.

The answer is expediency. Chippendale knew he could replicate sandshading and make the solid veneer look as if it was built from three separate pieces by the application of artwork. This is evident when you look at the swags on the central drawer. They were cut as one solid veneer, yet when the artwork is added to the laurel leaves, they look as though they have three separate sections. I know from experience that the longest process of producing life-like laurel leaves is by the application of sandshading. Chippendale had to look for the fastest way to get the job done, without compromising quality. Here, as on many occasions, artwork became his saviour.

Steps 5, 6 & 7. Using the inlay knife

My inlay knife, shown in Figure 6.144, with its larger bevel front and smaller at the back of the point, I believe, echoes the knife used to inlay the original work. My small tack-hammer pushes the knife forward along the scored line (Figure 6.145). The degree of accuracy and ease of use is amazing. Having bevels front and back of the point of the knife makes turning and control of the line easy. Even subtle changes of angle are not a problem to the performance. I'm very impressed.

I found that a small glue brush, dipped into a pan of very hot water, eventually softened the glue, allowing it to be removed (see Figure 6.146). I used an old towel beneath the brush to absorb surplus water. With patience the veneer soon came loose and a small pointed knife teased it free (Figure 6.147).

At this stage, I also cut away the surplus satinwood to prepare for the insertion of the completed fan (see Figure 6.148).

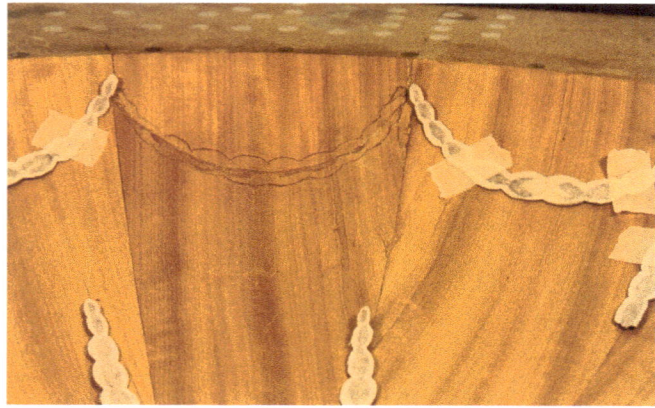

Figure 6.143 Swags with rounded edges.

* *Reproduced by the kind permission of the Trustees of the 7th Earl of Harewood Will Trust and the Trustees of the Harewood House Trust*

Figure 6.149 shows all eight swags plus the half-round fan inlaid using the hammer-veneering technique. The fan, with its multiple small parts all held together with veneer tape, was laid very easily with hot glue and a veneer hammer.

I apologise for not producing pictures of this process, but being so apprehensive of the technique, which was new to me, I completely forgot about the camera work. On a project of this magnitude, one discretion, I hope, is forgivable.

Figure 6.144 My bevelled inlay knife.

Figure 6.145 Cutting through the line.

Figure 6.146 Hot brush softens the glue.

Figure 6.147 Inlay is released.

Figure 6.148 Cutting outer curve to accept the fan.

Figure 6.149 Using profile scraper to remove paper and surface glue.

I also started the clean up, using a cabinet scraper with a convex profile to match the domed shape. The scraper is seen to the right side of the fan in Figure 6.149.

That just left the eight-laurel leaf drops, and the eight tiny daisy flowers above each swag, to complete the inlay work.

Overall, so far, I was more than pleased with the result, and while more remained to be done – and one should never assume the finishing processes will not be a problem – I felt encouraged with my efforts so far.

Step 8. Building the two triangular designs on the fascia panel

It was now time to turn to the fascia panel above the dome, and cut and prepare the elements of the two matching triangular designs that reside left and right above the dome. Set between the two triangles, a single white circular fan creates a small yet appealing motif, perhaps suggesting a celestial body illuminating its surroundings. This is only the second time I have seen the designer use undyed white holly for the flutes of a fan. In all other designs he has used dyed pink. The image shown in Figure 6.150 allows you sight of the finished door, but it may be useful to see some of the challenges and techniques I encountered while building the various elements.

I began by creating a full-sized line drawing, from which I could fretsaw two matching sets of scrolling acanthus leaves to fit in each of the two triangles. Looking for symmetry (which, as you now know, always dominates my thinking when looking at his designs), fretsawing both scrolling acanthus leaves from one veneer packet will always achieve my goal. The other matching elements include an anthemion in the centre of the curved line, two plumes below and two single acanthus leaves below the plumes. Two corner fans sit in the 90-degree corners, which I planned to build from one template.

Figure 6.151 shows the paper copy used to create the two matching diamond shaped designs. The various elements that make up the triangles are two matching sets of acanthus leaves laid out on the satinwood background (protected with white paper). In Figure 6.152, you can see that I have already cut out one of the windows. The scrolling acanthus leaf is waiting to be scored and sawn.

Figure 6.150 The finished domed door prior to mounting and polishing.

Four stylised acanthus flowers, shown in Figure 6.153, consisting of lilac and white petals and yellow centres, represent the colours found in nature and replicated by Chippendale.

Corner fans

The final part of the triangular sections was the two matching corner fans, which I built from one template. Figure 6.154 shows the first stage, while Figure 6.155 shows the fans completed, with floral centres and the statutory padauk scallops to form the outer borders.

Figure 6.151* Full-sized drawing of the triangular section of the fascia.

Figure 6.152 Cutting the acanthus leaves.

Figure 6.153 Stylised acanthus flowers.

Figure 6.154 Corners fans built using the template method.

Figure 6.155 Completed corner fans.

* *Reproduced by the kind permission of the Trustees of the 7th Earl of Harewood Will Trust and the Trustees of the Harewood House Trust*

CHAPTER 6 | Building a Replica: Diana & Minerva Commode

Figure 6.156 Drawing out the template for the fan.

Figure 6.157 Chisel used to profile the ends of the flutes.

Step 9. Central 16-fluted circular white fan

The template was drawn out to scale on MDF (see Figure 6.156), and strips of white holly were sandshaded along one edge to give the 3D effect. A half-round carving chisel was used to profile the ends of the flutes, (Figure 6.157). Perhaps the same tool was used to shape the original! The fan was then laid on fascia to judge the size (Figure 6.158), and the floral centre was let in with a single red berry (viewed from the back in Figure 6.159).

Two 1 mm boxed stringers were wrapped around a metal pipe (Figure 6.160), which was heated over my hotplate to shape them (approximately) to the required diameter. One boxed stringer and red berries are placed around the stringer (Figure 6.161). A second stringer

Figure 6.158 The fan is laid on the fascia to judge the size.

Figure 6.159 Red berry let into the centre of the fan.

Figure 6.160 Stringers being shaped.

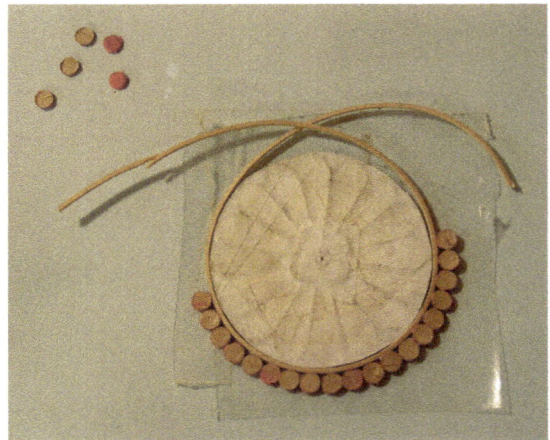

Figure 6.161 Stringer and berries being placed round the flower.

CHAPTER 6 | Building a Replica: Diana & Minerva Commode

Figure 6.162 Second stringer added.

Figure 6.163 The central fan finished.

keeps the berries intact (Figure 6.162). A scarf joint joins the stringers together invisibly. Note the inner stringer still needs pushing together where the scarf joint has sprung apart at about 8 o'clock on the circle.

The finished motif is looking good (Figure 6.163). The delicate sandshading provides adequate 3D effect, and the stringers and ring of red berries balance perfectly. When polished, it should stand out as a shining star.

Steps 10 & 11. Fitting the tulipwood crossbanding and gluing to door

The tulipwood crossbanding, which surrounds the door, has to point to the centre of the panel from all sides. Over the domed shape, this means that only short strips at a time could be laid, so that the overall effect remained uniform across the shape. You can see by the intervals of white tape, in Figure 6.164, just how short the strips are across the domed edge. The finished effect should be a continuous effect of straight lines all radiating equally to the centre of the dome. Because the figure of tulipwood provides distinctive straight lines, it makes it easier to achieve the finished effect.

To protect the marquetry veneers across the dome, I covered it with card shaped to fit. I did not want any damage occurring while tools and materials were worked above it. Clamping the finished fascia marquetry was the only way to hold it down while the glue dried (see Figure 6.165). Fish glue was used, which needs twelve hours bonding time. This glue, being reversible, offers future conservators/restorers the opportunity to lift veneers using heat and water.

Figure 6.164 Second stringer added.

Figure 6.165 Using clamps to hold everything in place.

Figure 6.166 The raised arch.

Step 12. Build the raised arch that sits above the dome

Figure 6.166 shows the raised arch made from MDF that sits on top of the crossbanding. The arch is decorated with floral marquetry. A curved solid wood satinwood stringer will be set either side of the raised arch to border it, prior to mounting it on the door. The arch, seen here, without the stringing borders, is 15.87 mm ($5/8$ inch) wide and 6.35 mm ($1/4$ inch) deep.

I fretsawed a packet of six dyed green veneers to produce large half laurel leaves (Figure 6.167) and small half laurel leaves (Figure 6.168), which sit in between the larger leaves. Figure 6.169 shows the larger half leaves arranged around the circumference of the arch, leaving space for the interleaving small leaves (Figure 6.170). The tiny triangle left after installing the small leaf is filled with a black veneer, providing depth to the arrangement. The veins fretsawn on the larger half leaves will be filled with

Figure 6.167 Large laurel leaves fretsawn.

Figure 6.168 Small laurel leaves sawn.

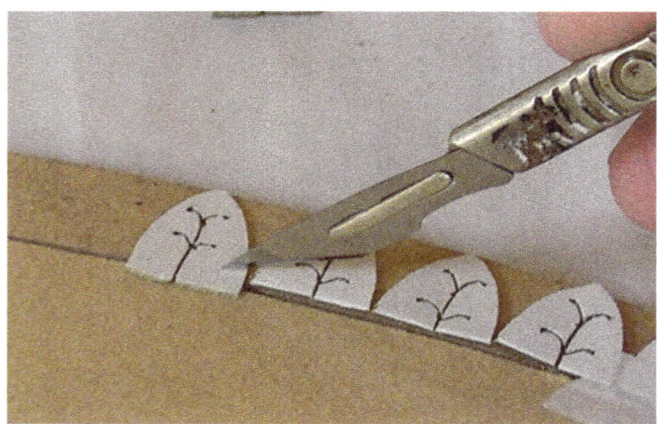

Figure 6.169 Leaves set in place around raised curve.

Figure 6.170 Small leaves dropped in place.

black mastic to provide the artistic medium, as applied to the original.

My dilemma

It was at this stage that I realised I had created a problem for myself. The laurel leaves on the domed door did not match the shape of the laurel leaves on the three drawers. The former had rounded sides to each leaf, intended to be like the original, to make inlaying easier, whereas the leaves on the drawers were pointed at each leaf end.

In my defence, the laurel leaves on the drawer fronts were made and installed before I discovered the solid veneer type application used on the domed door. Nevertheless, my penchant for symmetry meant I could not ignore this fact and I therefore took the bold step of changing the swags and drops on the domed door. I now knew I could inlay more intricate shapes with my inlay knife, so I felt confident I could achieve these changes.

Redrawing new swags and drops

The first step was to redraw the laurel leaves and create a new line drawing to fretsaw from. I found this fairly straightforward and, as you can see from Figure 6.171, the newly designed swags are much improved on the old. The outer petals have pointed ends and match the drawer swags. The sandshading is also less harsh than the first set – another lesson learned. In Figure 6.172, eight matching swags are fretsawn from one cutting and you will also notice that, this time, I remembered to use the camera and photograph the inlaying technique using the inlay knife and hammer, and the application of hammer-veneering.

I was able to redraw the new laurel leaves slightly larger than the old, and thus they created a new and clean line outside the old swags. This allowed me to cut the new line with the inlay knife, as you can see in Figure 6.173. The new design, now inlaid, Figure 6.174, is an improvement on the old design, and the sandshading is

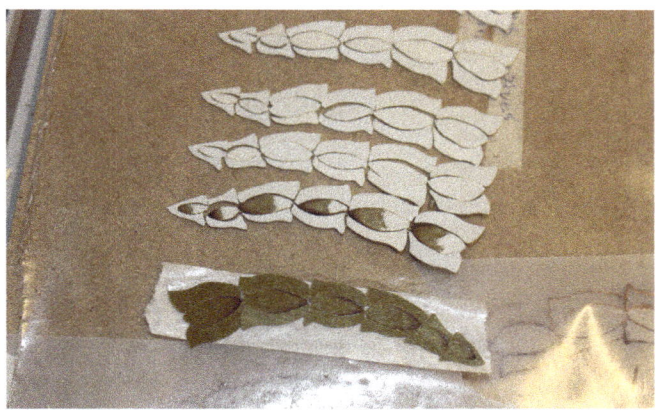

Figure 6.171 The replacement laurel swags.

Figure 6.172 Eight matching swags fretsawn.

Figure 6.173 New swag line cut.

Figure 6.174 New swag inlaid.

Figure 6.175 Inlays tried for a fit.

Figure 6.176 Hammer-veneering with hot glue.

much more natural. Green-dyed woods are not easy to sandshade, being all too easy to over-shade, thereby spoiling the final appearance.

The cavities for the drops are created and the inlays are tried for a fit (Figure 6.175). In Figure 6.176, you see me hammer-veneering them with hot glue. Because of the curved surface, I found my small tack hammer served best as a veneer hammer.

The excess glue is quickly removed with warm water while it is still workable. It really is a very controllable way to work. It may look a mess with all the hot glue stuck to the surfaces, but it is easily and quickly cleaned up. The glue also acts as a sealant by filling the grain, which aids and improves the finishing process.

Figure 6.177 shows the dome with all swags and drops replaced. Please note it is the veneer tape that holds the swags and drops together during hammer-veneering, as seen on the three drops still papered. Once the glue has set, the paper is scraped off with a convex cabinet scraper.

I hand-sanded the dome first using 120 grit paper, followed by 180 grit, and finally 400 grit paper wrapped round a sponge-sanding block. This allowed the paper to keep in contact across the dome.

I am very proud of this work; it has been the greatest challenge of my marquetry career, and I am sure no other panel will ever top this for personal satisfaction.

Figure 6.177 The dome complete with all swags and drops replaced.

CHAPTER 6 | Building a Replica: Diana & Minerva Commode

COMMODE FINISHED, COMPLETE WITH BRASS MOUNTS

With the addition of artwork to the marquetry, brass mounts installed and polish applied, thanks to the skilful work by my colleague, it gives us great pride and joy to display the final work. These images were taken while the commode was on public display in Newby Hall,

Our commode provides one of the showpieces of Newby Hall's 'Chippendale Tercentenary Exhibition of 2018'. It is also fitting that our replica of Chippendale's iconic piece should be shown in public for the first time during this 'Chippendale 300' milestone year.

Figure 6.178
Resplendent polychromatic replica, showing brass mounts between drawer units and around the legs.

Figure 6.179
Highly figured satinwood to the domed door and profiled solid satinwood mouldings below.

CHAPTER 6 | Building a Replica: Diana & Minerva Commode

Figure 6.180 Top panel displaying the now acceptable diamond separator.

Figure 6.181 Central drawer with repeating fans and swags, framed with brass acanthus leaves and berries on each pillar.

Figure 6.182 Minerva door panel.

Figure 6.183 Diana door panel.

CHAPTER 7

BUILDING A REPLICA 3: PIER TABLE TOP

INTRODUCTION

Having completed my work on the replica Diana and Minerva commode in late 2012, I assumed that was the end of my hands-on experience with the great man's creations. In 2015, however, to my surprise and delight, I was approached by The Chippendale Society to make a replica marquetry top belonging to a pier table made initially for Harewood House in 1772. The table was made to fit into the Robert Adam designed circular Dressing Room, and, because of the shape of the room, it was made with a curved back. It was also made to fit between two mirrors, and for that reason cut-outs were made (*after* delivery to the house) at both ends of the curved back to accommodate the mirror frames, clearly visible in Figures 7.3 and 7.4. Communication between Adam's 'house fitters' and the Chippendale workshop had not taken place, since the two cut-outs had to be made 'on-site'. Not the most auspicious beginning for such a prestigious commission!

Figure 7.1* *Curved back pier table made for the circular dressing room at Harewood House.*

* Reproduced by the kind permission of The Chippendale Society

CHAPTER 7 | Building a Replica: Pier Table Top from Harewood House

Amazing historical events

The table remained in its circular dressing room for 72 years, but in 1844 Harewood House received a complete remodelling by York-based architect Sir Charles Barry. The circular dressing room was removed, and since no other site could be found for the table, because of its curved back, it became surplus to requirements and was placed in storage in the loft above the stable block at Harewood. Black paint was applied to the legs and plinth to protect the delicate carvings and paints.

In 1976, some 130 years later, it re-emerged in the estate joiners' workshop, with a gluepot stuck to its top. One of the joiners (now retired) who worked in the workshop at the time told me that he remembered the table well, but in those days staff were not allowed into the house, so they had no idea what a piece of Chippendale furniture looked like.

Even though the table had been held in storage for that time, it is still perhaps surprising that it could eventually become used as a workbench! While such an event seems incredible, I can understand how this came about. When the table was first discovered, the plinth and legs were coated with the Victorian black paint; in addition, over 130 years of dirt and grime had accumulated on the top, masking the marquetry work. This event makes a wonderful human story, one that could and does happen to all of us. One popular UK television programme called *Cash in the Attic* deals with celebrities and members of the public who raise money from artefacts found in their lofts and garages by taking

Figure 7.2* Table as found in the loft of the stables.

them to auction. The Harewood story is no different – except perhaps on a grander scale.

The table, in its rather distressed condition, was sold for £8800 at Christie's, London, on 1st April 1976 and purchased by Simon Redburn on behalf of The Chippendale Society. A restoration programme followed, with the late David Hawkins appointed to carry out the necessary repairs to the marquetry and harewood background veneers. Hawkins took four years to complete the work, and some of the details are included in his book *The Techniques of Wood Surface Decoration*. Whether because of time and effect of light, the veneers (sycamore) used to replace the damaged harewood have dramatically changed colour, and the polish applied (not by Hawkins) is most uncomplimentary to the piece.

Figure 7.3* Pier table top showing where the gluepot had been stuck to the right-hand end – heating the glue to free the pot clearly removed most of the marquetry work.

CHAPTER 7 | Building a Replica: Pier Table Top from Harewood House

Figure 7.4* Right-hand end of the table top, showing the damage to the marquetry work when the gluepot was removed.

A second restoration programme

Another restoration programme was initiated in autumn 2015 by The Chippendale Society to analyse and correct the current state of the table. Ian Fraser, Honorary Conservator to The Chippendale Society, and I were asked to draw up a programme, which would include not only restoring the original table, but also building a replica copy. I realised that we also had to identify the colours of the original dyestuffs used on the marquetry work, and the type of paint used on the plinth and legs. To this end, I approached scientist and conservator Dr Heinrich Piening to come over from Germany to perform the necessary tests on the original piece.

Prior to his arrival, I advised the Society that the uneven polish on the table could seriously hamper the spectrograph readings – a problem Heinrich had encountered on the top of the Diana and Minerva commode when he tested that for dyestuffs back in 2007. It was agreed to remove the polish and Ian Fraser performed this work in early November 2015. I was concerned that the artwork would be removed as well as the polish, so a small area was tested to see what happened. Through this one small sample we made yet another new discovery.

Discovering engraving work

Ian and I were astounded to find that the artwork was not applied by paint and brush, which, when applied, sits under the polished surface, but that the decoration was applied by engraving. The quality of the engraving was astonishing and clearly performed by a skilled professional engraver.

For me, this discovery opened up new thinking about the other commissions, because I had identified surface decoration by paint and brush on the middle drawer of the Diana and Minerva commode, as shown in Figure 3.73 on page 83. This indicates that two methods of applying artwork were in operation, one by brush and paint applied to the surface of the marquetry and the other by engraving into the marquetry and filling with wax crayon. It was beginning to point to two distinct and separate operatives, since engraving is a very specialist skill, while painted artwork requires less.

I have already identified instances of drawer fronts being farmed out to external marqueteurs whose methodology was to inlay the marquetry, after first gluing the background veneer to the substrate. The discovery of both engraving and surface decoration shows that our designer was openly prepared to accommodate both methods. It is not immediately obvious, when looking at marquetry decoration, which method is used, since the quality of each application is skilfully applied. On this evidence, one can assume the designer selectively employed engraving, based on cost, the customer and its eventual location. Chapter 8 shows each known commission closely examined, and in that chapter I will be in a position to identify who performed the various aspects of the marquetry artwork.

The whole ethos of this research is built on dealing with discoveries as they occur. It's clear that the more intervention one encounters, as in this project, the more discoveries one makes and the more questions they raise about the origins of work. Examining engraving versus artwork raises questions as to who performed them, and why use two similar decorative methods when one would suffice. I suspect the answers are that engraving achieves a more artistic result, but is more costly to apply, whereas artwork can be applied by a less skilled workshop, thus

* By kind permission of The Chippendale Society

speeding up production and keeping costs down. Our designer was also a businessman, so production time, cost and quality all had to be taken into account.

Discovering dyestuffs and paints used on the original table

Figure 7.5 shows the original plinth and legs of the pier table afte the black Victorian paint was removed. Three paints were used as backgrounds to the applied fretwork: blue and pink colours on the legs and red behind the frieze on the plinth. These colours complement the white hand-fretted and carved motifs.

To find out the true colours used in the marquetry, and the type of paint used on the frieze and legs, my colleague, Heinrich Piening, travelled from his native Bavaria to Leeds in November 2015 to test for dyestuffs and paint type used. He was also able to establish the veneer type used for the harewood background as highly figured sycamore with a ripple effect.

Filming the work while building the replica

My brief, as detailed by The Chippendale Society, was not only to build a replica marquetry top, but also to record the event on film while doing the work. The reasons for making the film were two-fold: firstly, to make the filmed record available for viewing on my website and secondly, for use at the Tercentenary Chippendale Exhibitions being staged in 2018.

The filming was in itself a challenging prospect, since marquetry is not a craft that is over and done with in a matter of a few days or even weeks. Months of detailed work would be needed to create the marquetry on a table of this stature, making filming an interesting and time-consuming proposition. Fortunately, I already had past experience in this matter, and was confident of being able to put together filming sequences to capture a meaningful storyline that would, when edited, provide useful visual footage of the whole process.

I also had to remember to photograph the stages of construction for inclusion in this book, as the illustrations on the following pages will demonstrate!

Figure 7.5* *The original plinth and legs after removing the black Victorian paint, with three paints used as backgrounds to the applied fretwork: blue and pink on the legs and red behind the frieze.*

INVESTIGATION AND PREPARATION

I began by making close a examination of the original marquetry and veneering. The two matching end panels and the central panel were veneered with 'harewood' veneers for the background foil. I know that the process called harewood is sycamore veneer dyed with sulphate of iron, because I have used the process for the past twenty years on sycamore and other different timbers. I later learned, following Heinrich's dye tests, that logwood (campeachy) dye was also used, along with sulphate of iron, on the original harewood. I also discovered that the central panel consisted of four lengths of dyed harewood, each over 1200 mm (4 ft) long – clearly too long to fit into the throat of a fretsaw, which means the marquetry was all inlaid.

It was at this point that I recalled David Hawkins' book, mentioned earlier, where he recorded finding knife marks on the substrates when restoring marquetry to the original table. This meant the harewood veneers would need to be glued down first, before the fretsawn marquetry elements could be positioned in their correct locations. Each element of the marquetry then had to be 'inlaid'. It also meant I would have to lay the harewood veneers by the hammer-veneering technique, as used to lay the original.

Engraving

When all marquetry was in place and levelled, it would have to be engraved, which requires removal of slivers of veneers using an engraver's tool known as a burin (see page 86). After sanding and levelling, engraving could commence. Since the polish had now been removed from the original table I was able to examine the engraving on it more closely. It is clearly finer than that achieved by artwork applied by paint and brush.

In addition, further decoration is applied by the use of sandshading. All in all, the quality of workmanship on this table is exceptional and the original marqueteurs have set the standard for me to emulate. A daunting challenge indeed! I have only scant experience of performing inlay work, which was on the domed door of the Diana and Minerva commode replica. That was miniscule compared to the challenge ahead of me on this classic piece measuring over 1800 mm x 600 mm (6 ft x 2 ft). Engraving would be applied by a professional engraver, as it was on the original. Engravers were, and still are, skilled artisans capable of engraving metals applied to gunstocks and on furniture as applied to ivory and veneers. In the mid-1770s in London, engravers would offer their skills to all those trades as a contractual arrangement. To give some indication of the timescale to engrave this table, a local engraver and colleague, Malcolm Long, estimated a week to complete the work. Journeymen were paid by the day in the 18th century, so their rates of pay would have been known across the furniture-making businesses. Regardless of the rate applicable at the time, the cost for this single aspect of the decoration is perhaps one reason why engraving was used selectively by Chippendale, who clearly only applied the medium to special commissions.

The project team and plan

A project of this length and magnitude, embracing not only the complex marquetry, but also continuity of filming, demanded a very strict project plan. The success of the plan would depend on my constant discipline in achieving each target. This plan was written, vetted and adjusted till the working parties involved with the different processes agreed that it reflected each action. Those involved in the project team were: Ian Fraser (Conservator, Leeds Museums and Galleries), Heinrich Piening (Scientist/Conservator), Malcolm Long (Engraver), Jack Metcalfe (Marqueteur). Three committee members of The Chippendale Society completed the working party: Adam Bowett (Honorary Chairman), James Lomax (Honorary Curator) and David Bower (Honorary Members Secretary).

I should add here that this was not a professionally based project, where contracts would be needed to set out who would pay for items such as labour costs. This was because I, as the leading player, would be carrying out my work free of charge. That also applied to Ian Fraser, who was contributing in a much lesser timescale. This is because we are both members of The Chippendale Society. Also, I am not a professional and therefore do not charge for my work, no matter for whom I do it. However, the services of conservator/ scientist Heinrich Piening and engraver Malcolm Long would have to be taken into account.

Creating a life-sized paper template of the marquetry top

A life-sized paper template was necessary because I needed an exact copy of the background and border veneers. We achieved this by turning the existing table upside down onto a sheet of heavy-duty cardboard and drawing around the outer edges. I was then able to take measurements of the key parts of the design. These included the border veneers and the two dividers that divide the top into three separate panels.

I was able to measure the two matching oval fans with their decorative borders. This allowed me to make up all the oval wooden templates, which I would need later to build the fans using the template method. Making templates would allow me to map the component parts exactly, and then to cut and apply the parts to the new substrate.

Cutting the solid wood substrate

Using 25 mm thick high-quality birch plywood for this purpose, Ian Fraser was able to cut and shape the plywood to match the original size and shape. Ian reduced the two ends and front edges by 1 mm so that when they were covered with 1 mm thick border veneers the original dimensions of the base would be achieved. Here, in Figure 7.6, I have already fitted the tulipwood around the edges and positioned the harewood background veneers to the centre panel, but not, as yet, glued them down.

Creating an exact line drawing of the marquetry work

Figure 7.7 shows me tracing the entire table's marquetry, which proved to be an inspiring experience. Using a loupe to give me the best view possible, I was able to trace every motif accurately.

I had not prepared myself for the unexpected thrill it gave me to suddenly fulfil the role of the artisan I had so admired and emulated for the past twenty years. As a non-artist, I found myself drawing acanthus leaves, and realising for the first time how each leaf bears it own personality. Every laurel leaf was an individual because the original designer's artistic hand made it that way. I was able to replicate his artistic genius simply by drawing along the lines he himself had created. I was totally absorbed by the experience, feeling in some way at one with the creator.

I traced one complete copy of the centre panel and one copy of the matching end panels. Using the tracings, I took them to an industrial photocopier, who produced paper copies for use on the construction of the marquetry. I do realise at this stage, that in order to get copies of Chippendale's original drawings, the 'prick and pounce' technique was used as detailed in Chapter 3 (see page 56).

Figure 7.6 Table substrate shaped and bordered with tulipwood.

Figure 7.7 Tracing the original marquetry.

CHAPTER 7 | Building a Replica: Pier Table Top from Harewood House

Figure 7.8* Heinrich testing for dyestuffs on the original marquetry, November 2015.

Figure 7.9 Colour scheme for marquetry to central panel.

Testing for dyestuffs using UV-VIS spectronomy

Heinrich Piening was commissioned to test all the marquetry elements and background veneer for identifying the dyestuffs. In total 90 readings were taken of the marquetry elements. Also, Heinrich tested the type of paint used for the colours on the legs and plinth.

Creating colour drawings based on Heinrich's findings

Having received the dye results outlined in Chapter 4 (see Table 4.3 on page 101), I was able to create a colour scheme, based on the tracings I had made of the original top and photocopied to paper drawings. Figures 7.9–7.11 show the colour scheme I was aiming to follow. Drawing the designs and colouring in the original motifs began to excite me and I could not wait to get into using the veneers and building the designs.

The old familiar feelings were returning and energising my passion for the type of marquetry I love. It was good to be immersed again in this new challenge. My head, hands and heart were fully engaged again, and it was a good feeling to be back in my workshop working with wood after a five-year break.

Figure 7.10 Colour scheme for matching end panels.

Figure 7.11 Lovely corner 'cameo' shot.

209

VENEERS FOR THE MARQUETRY WORK

The dyed veneers chosen for the marquetry took some time to collect. The chosen tones had to blend into the silver/grey harewood background veneer and give the best colour contrast. The three shades of green, in particular, proved a problem. In the end I had to choose veneers I would not normally choose to work with, because they were ultra thin and very open grained. On the positive side they offered the best tonal qualities and most importantly were colourfast. They are a product from workers in Milan, Italy, who guard their secret into how they achieve permanent colourfast very closely.

The veneer type was magnolia and sliced to 0.6 mm in thickness. This is very thin, but I have worked with 0.7 mm thick veneers for the past twenty years, so that was not such a problem. The problem was the open grain. I realised I could get round the wood chipping problem when fretsawing and knife cutting by protecting the face sides of the veneers with hot animal glue and paper, as I always do, but how would it affect the engraving work?

I made up a small panel with green veneer attached and sent it to engraver Malcolm Long for tests. He said the engraving tool chipped the woods due to the open grain and suggested we polish the work, prior to engraving to a mirror finish, which Ian Fraser did and sent it back to Malcolm. The result was perfect. Malcolm said he was still able to take a small sliver of veneer, but because the grain was now filled with polish no chipping occurred. Having come across this problem before, Malcolm knew how to solve it. I love working with professionals who have had the same hands-on experience.

The engraver working on the original marquetry would not have experienced this problem, because holly veneer was used for the marquetry. Holly is one of the tightest grained temperate hardwoods available. It is just a pity that no one dyes holly today. The reason why dyers dye woods that they can slice to 0.6 mm thick and are open grained is because this speeds up the dye penetration. Today's industry is all about cutting down production time, which in turn cuts costs, so quality takes a dive, I'm afraid.

The dyed colours shown in Figure 7.12 provide the best match to the findings made by Heinrich. There are three shades of green, yellow, two shades of red, and burgundy.

In addition, the solid woods shown in Figure 7.13 consisted of tulipwood, harewood, padauk, steamed beech, berberis, pear and holly. Blue and green dyed stringers were also identified.

Making 'harewood'

We knew from Heinrich's analysis that he had found both iron and logwood when he tested the harewood on the original table. What we had to decide was the tonal value of the colour. For that, we carried out a series of tests using different strengths of the two dyes, this time using measured quantities of iron sulphate and logwood to see if any tonal differences were achieved. We used 200 ml of distilled water for each test given in Table 7.1, soaking in a cold bath for two days (21/22 March 2016).

Figure 7.12 Palette of dyed colours used on the pier table replica

CHAPTER 7 | Building a Replica: Pier Table Top from Harewood House

Figure 7.13 Solid woods used on the pier table replica

Table 7.1 Test quantities used for making harewood

1.	iron sulphate 10 grams	+ logwood 6 grams
2.	iron sulphate 10 grams	+ logwood 8 grams
3.	iron sulphate 10 grams	+ logwood 10 grams
4.	iron sulphate 10 grams	+ logwood 20 grams
5.	iron sulphate 5 grams	+ logwood 2 grams
6.	iron sulphate 10 grams	+ logwood 2 grams
7.	iron sulphate 15 grams – **the favoured result**	+ logwood 2 grams
8.	iron sulphate 5 grams	+ logwood 4 grams
9.	iron sulphate 10 grams	+ logwood 4 grams
10.	iron sulphate 15 grams	+ logwood 4 grams

To dye large sheets of sycamore we needed fifteen litres of distilled water, and based on the above results where only 200 ml were used, we calculated the following quantities of iron sulphate and logwood.

iron sulphate 15 grams + logwood 2 grams per 200 ml

for 1 litre =	5 × 15 = 75 grams iron sulphate
	5 × 2 = 10 grams logwood
for 15 litres =	75 × 15 = 1125 grams iron sulphate
	10 × 15 = 150 grams logwood

Armed with the dye quantities, we were ready to dye the lengths of ripple sycamore I had procured from my supplier (see Figure 7.14). I found by experimentation that the logwood chips had to be protected from direct contact with the veneers, because they stained the wood. To achieve this, I secured the logwood chips in a muslin bag allowing the dye to escape through the cloth, while protecting the veneer surfaces from contact with the logwood (see Figure 7.15).

Figure 7.14 Dye bath holding de-ionised water, with iron sulphate mordant and logwood dye ready to be added.

Figure 7.15 Iron sulphate and logwood immersed in de-ionised water. Muslin bag is seen floating to the right.

CHAPTER 7 | Building a Replica: Pier Table Top from Harewood House

Figure 7.16 Harewood veneers drying out over dye bath.

Figure 7.17 Ian Fraser hammer-veneering the harewood veneers to the substrate (glue pot can be seen top right).

The veneers were soaked for two days and nights, after which full penetration of the dyes had taken place. The veneers were then suspended over the bath to dry (see Figure 7.16).

Hammer veneering harewood background veneers to the substrate

The central panel requires the harewood veneers to be glued down before the marquetry elements could be added. The ancient method known as 'hammer-veneering' would achieve this (see Figure 7.17). The four harewood veneers required for the centre panel are applied oversized, such that they overlap each other and the glue allowed to dry. The following day, joints are cut through with straight edge and knife, then heated and wetted, to allow the joint to be opened to remove the excess waste. Similarly the edges that meet the outer borders are cut and trimmed. Outer border veneers are then applied and glued in place, to frame the central panel.

Many people find the name 'hammer-veneering' confusing. The hammer, shown close up in Figure 7.18 and being used by Ian Fraser in Figure 7.17, is really a squeegee tool, used to apply downward pressure onto the veneer in order to squeeze out excess glue while it is still hot and workable. The four lengths decrease in width (as seen and as per the original) and overlap where they join. I was now in a position to sand off the protective paper and expose the newly laid harewood.

Figure 7.18 Veneer hammer showing brass inlay along its edge

With the central panel veneers in place, the process of inlaying the marquetry motifs began. The next few sections of this chapter present a selection of motifs being first fretsawn, then inlaid into the harewood background. I then go on to show similar photographs of the two matching end panels.

DYEING AND INSTALLING THE GREEN AND BLUE STRINGERS

The photographs on this page show the various stages of dyeing and installing the green and blue stringers into the veneer.

Figure 7.19 shows 1.5 mm square stringers dyed green, plus 1 mm square stringers dyed blue. At the top of the photo you can see sections of unused water pipes, with wine corks to seal ends, which I used as dye baths. The shorter pipe was used for the blue stringers, needed later in the project.

Figure 7.20 shows green stringers dyed for installation to the central panel. I used indigo carmine for the blue and berberis chips for the yellow to obtain the green dye (see Chapter 4 for descriptions and recipes for both dye products.)

Figure 2.21 shows the circular inlay routed out using a Dremel drill with a special screw-on router attachment made by Stuart McDonald in the USA (see Figure 7.22). I used a 1 mm router bit (not shown). A hand-made router could have been used to route out the original stringer inlay. An example of a hand-made router is shown in the Roubo engraving in Figure 3.11 on page 55.

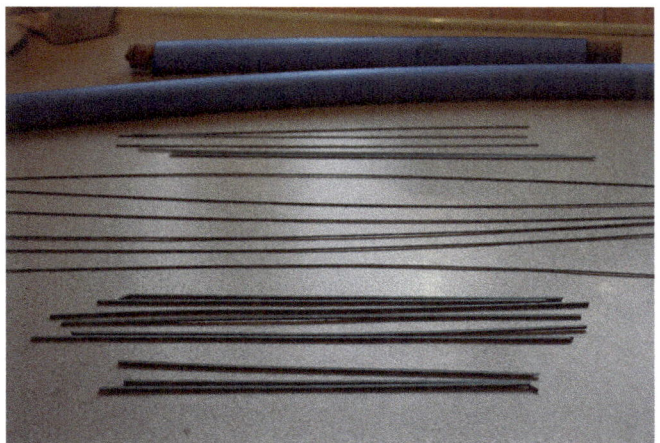

Figure 7.19 1.5 mm square stringers dyed green, plus 1 mm square stringers dyed blue.

Figure 7.20 Green stringers dyed for installation to the central panel.

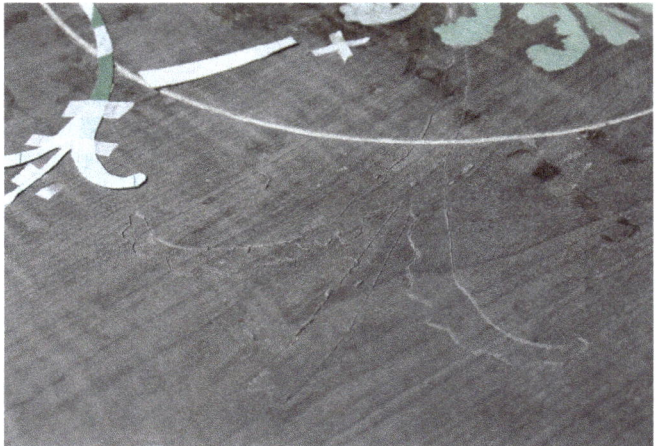

Figure 7.21 The circular inlay installed after routing out.

Figure 7.22 Dremel drill with a special screw-on router attachment made by Stuart McDonald in the USA.

INSTALLING THE GARLAND OF 80 LAUREL LEAVES & SWAGS

Figures 7.23–7.31 show the creation of the garland of laurel leaves that surrounds the green stringer, now inlaid into the routed groove as just shown, together with the swags of acanthus leaves.

It was interesting to find that the 80 laurel leaves were all individually shaped. I had fully expected that the 40 leaves on the right would match the same on the left. However, this proved not to be the case – my hero never fails to amaze me! So, if no two leaves are alike, that is how I will reproduce them.

Figure 7.23 Line drawing cut up into small groups of laurel leaves and pasted on top of the packet of one light green veneer and two wasters.

Figure 7.24 Packet fretsawn, consisting of 80 leaves in total.

Figure 7.25 Half the laurel leaves (40) sawn and placed on sticky-back plastic with each leaf numbered on white 'waster leaves' on the outer edges. The procedure is repeated for the other 40 leaves.

Figure 7.26 Inlaying 80 laurel leaves – see pipette and cup of water ready for removing harewood with a heated spatula (not in shot) following inlay knife work.

Figure 7.27 Two large acanthus leaves forming a packet of two dark green veneers.

Figure 7.28 Two acanthus leaves fretsawn and two wasters alongside.

Figure 7.29 End of each leaf is sandshaded to give a three-dimensional effect when installed.

Figure 7.30 Shaded end of leaf and inlay knife marks clearly visible.

Figure 7.31 Acanthus leaf inlaid and paper removed. The veneer does not sandshade well (burns black instantly), which is a concern.

It is important to declare at this stage that sand shading the magnolia veneers was proving problematic, as Figure 7.31 shows. The open grain of the wood results in the veneers overburning – and in rapid time. By this time I had had three attempts at shading the acanthus plumage that sits in the centre of the design. I therefore decided to leave this feature until all other elements were in place. Then perhaps I would find a way round the problem before making another attempt.

CHAPTER 7 | Building a Replica: Pier Table Top from Harewood House

ACANTHUS FLOWERS MADE WITH BERBERIS WOOD

Finding berberis wood on the original table, and used for the two-acanthus flowers that flank the central acanthus plumage, was a refreshing experience. Finding the wood to use on the replica, however, proved more challenging. Walking around my neighbouring areas and looking into gardens told me how common the berberis bush is as a garden plant. I even found a couple of gardens showing just the bright yellow stump, indicating that the bush had recently been cut down. My enquiries with the owners, however, drew a blank as in each case the bush had been chopped up and taken to the tip. I was beginning to give up the search when an ex-neighbour who had moved to a new house only a few months before invited me to her house warming party. Walking around the garden I found the tell-tale bright yellow stump. Nervously, I asked my friend if the bush had been chopped up and destroyed, but she said, 'No, not yet, it's in the garage waiting to go to the tip.' My heart leapt – and there, lying on the garage floor, was the most handsome trunk. When I told my ex-neighbour why I wanted it, she was delighted to find it being put to unique use. My search was over.

Figure 7.32 shows ten sawn veneers after running the log through a band saw, then further thinning on a belt sander. This brought each veneer down to 1.5 mm thick. I would need to route the finished flowers into the substrate since they were thicker than the harewood background. I loved the banana yellow and could not wait to see them converted into marquetry art. I had one concern, regarding the colourfastness of the wood. The wood is yellow because it is affected by the main colouring agent, berberine, a yellow, crystalline, bitter alkaloid. We know that vegetable dyes, in general, are not colourfast, so while the wood will lose its colour eventually, I decided to perform a test to determine how long. I placed and taped a small sample of the wood into the south-facing window of my workshop on 1st June 2017. While recognising that this was an unnatural test, it would give me some indication as to the degree of colour loss and then perhaps determine how long the colours would last when protected with polish and hidden from direct sun rays.

Figure 7.33 shows the sample first exposed on 1st June 2017 and photographed on 1st December in the same year. The sample on the right shows new, fresh berberis, while the left sample shows the discolouring effect after a six-month exposure to direct sunlight. Since most of this test was made over the summer period, it escalated the process somewhat unfairly. However, I do know that the marquetry veneers used on the door panel of the Harewood Library writing table, as detailed in Chapter 5, shows that all the colours were lost after only ten years' exposure, and our research shows that berberis dye was used on some of those woods. Therefore, if we multiply this test by a factor of 20 (6 months times 20 = 120 months), we reach 10 years. I reiterate from the findings of the door panel in Chapter 5 just mentioned, we can be reasonably certain that 18th century marquetry work would lose its initially vibrant colours after ten years exposure. This occured despite extra

Figure 7.32 Thin sawn veneers seen placed between thin spacers before placing into my press to keep flat prior to using.

Figure 7.33 Berberis sample showing effects from UV light pollution

protection such as covering furniture with damask covers when houses were not occupied, because it is not just UV light that is the main cause of colour loss, but air pollution (oxidisation) affects it as well.

Building the flowers

Figures 7.34–38 illustrate the process of building the flowers using my precious berberis wood.

Figure 7.34 Fretsawing joint between two sections, using grain orientation to give the spiral effect when complete. Engraving lines, seen within each leaf, will be added later.

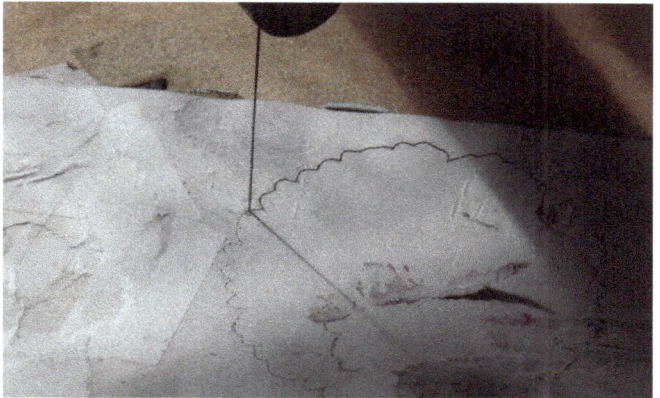

Figure 7.35 Sawing around the outer edge of the flower (now complete), after scoring with a scalpel. The line I am following is just visible.

Figure 7.36 Both flowers sawn into the harewood border, viewed from the underside.

Figure 7.37 The packet made up for the two red centres ready for fretsawing

Figure 7.38 Routing the substrate for inlaying berberis flower.

Figure 7.39 Flower inserted into substrate (wrong way up) to show the effect.

BUILDING THE TWO END PANELS

The beauty of the classic movement is that it allows designers to switch from one style to another within the same construction. Such is the case on this iconic table. The central design is quite masculine in its content with large bold acanthus leaves and central plumage, while the outer matching panels house pink fans surrounded by the most delicate swags I have ever encountered. Set into each of the four corners of the outer panels are multicoloured floral and acanthus leaves and flowers surround tiny pink oval fans. It is most definitely a truly feminine statement. We know the piece was designed for a lady's dressing room, so despite the two contrasting themes, the designer did not disappoint.

Building the central fans using the template method

Figures 7.40–7.46 show the process of building the central fans using the template method and setting the fans into an oval background with borders and stringing. I found, when sandshading the pink veneers, that the leading edge burnt jet black. Fortunately, I was able to cut this away, leaving a lighter shade of black suitable for building the fans.

Figure 7.40 Building the fan, using the template method, as discussed in Chapter 3.

Figure 7.41 All flutes installed and held together with veneer tape.

Figure 7.42 Cutting a white stringer around the flutes freehand with scalpel (image is of the reverse side) – face side covered in veneer tape to hold woods together while cutting fine stringers.

Figure 7.43 Fretsawing the oval shape around the padauk scallops.

Chapter 7 | Building a Replica: Pier Table Top from Harewood House

Figure 7.44 Using a measured spacer to draw the width of banding on the pear veneer and determine the space between the two blue stringers.

Figure 7.45 Outer blue stringer bent around the banding. Fish glue is used to bond stringer to pear veneer. Masking tape holds the stringer in place overnight.

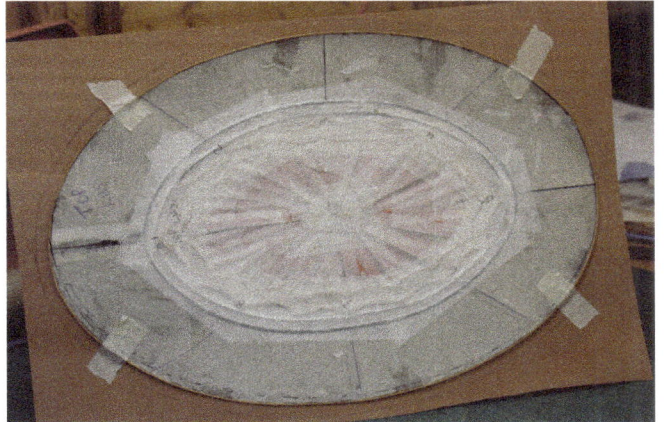

Figure 7.46 Fan with two blue stringed banding is now cut into eight sections of harewood, then circled with a steamed beech banding between two white stringers.

Cutting the harewood background to the outer panels

In Figures 7.47–7.52 you can see how I built up the background of the two outer panels using harewood veneers before gluing the completed panels to the substrate.

Figure 7.47 Ten outer harewood veneers cut and taped together. Each veneer is positioned with the grain pointing to the centre of the panel. Note the pins inserted to top edge to maintain location when gluing in place.

Figure 7.48 Central oval fan and outer harewood background cut and shaped. The central oval assembly is located on the harewood background and rotated towards the inner panel by 4 degrees. The same applies to the other end panel.

Figure 7.49 The outer veneers are glued to substrate using liquid hide glue, a modern version of animal glue, now available in a dispensing bottle.

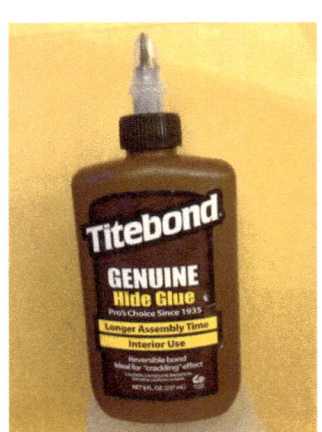

Figure 7.50 Liquid hide glue in a bottle: simply stand it in hot tap water for ten minutes and it turns liquid. The addition of urea creates the condition. The glue is still fully reversible. What my hero who built this original table would have given for this product!

Figure 7.51 Each oval assembly is glued into the harewood outer veneers. Note the black pen mark, seen at past 6 o'clock, marking the 4 degree offset from centre.

Figure 7.52 Of course pressure is needed after applying the liquid glue. Here I used a redundant classic marquetry panel, built some years ago and now used for pressing, as seen here. No wastage in my workshop!

Installing the swags of laurel leaves

The swags that surround the central oval fans on the two end panels are the tiniest ever used by Chippendale. For the marqueteur of the day, that was not a problem. He used holly veneer, the most stable and tight grained wood. I was using magnolia, the most open grained wood I have ever encountered, and it was at this stage that I realised it was going to present a big problem.

Each laurel leaf consists of three sections, one central and two outer sections. During fretsawing, the outer sections broke up, since they were not large enough to maintain stability. Despite applying protective paper glued with animal glue to the face side, I lost more outer sections than I saved. There is an alternative method of sawing laurel leaves, which gives the impression of three sections. It is by using a technique called 'blind cuts' as used on a pair of pier tables made for Harewood House and featured in Chapter 8.15 (see Figure 8.15.3), plus Chapter 3, Figure 3.24, page 59, where each image shows two fretsaw cuts made half way into each laurel leaf; the saw is then drawn back to give the impression of three sections. I know this is a departure from the original method used on the table top I am reproducing, but I cannot change the open grained woods because they matched the colour scheme, which is the most important reason for making this replica copy. Similarly, each laurel leaf is sandshaded on the original, but these open-grained veneers will not sandshade successfully, because of their minute size. I will get round this dilemma by applying shading with the addition of artwork at the polishing stage.

Using fish glue and a new applicator

Up to this point I had been gluing marquetry into the cavities with hot animal glue, because it is the way the original marquetry was glued. However, it became clear that the end panels consisted mainly of small, delicate elements. It was around this time that I watched a TV demonstration of marquetry applied by a marqueteur and friend – Quentin Smith, Chairman of the Staffordshire Marquetry Group here in the UK. Quentin was using a tiny glue bottle which had the tiniest pin in the top acting as the stopper. It is called 'Fine Tip PVA Glue Applicator' made by Anne Read, shown in Figure 7.53.

I found it on the internet and immediately ordered a pack of four bottles. I filled it with fish glue, which was used during the 18th century for gluing metal and ivory work to substrates. It is fully reversible, and I found another advantage during inlaying on the end panels as you will read about below. The bottle and its tiny pin stopper has one small challenge, namely it takes a while to thread the pin back into its tiny hole in the top of the bottle – the stopper has to be replaced after every use to stop the glue blocking the hole. I put up with this small inconvenience as the benefits were far more important.

Another aspect of gluing is worth mentioning. I realised that all reversible glue reacts to applied heat instantly. By using my heated spatula, as seen in Figure 7.56, the heat applied to the fish glue after only a few seconds, fully bonded the insert. This worked perfectly because the items being glued were small in size and therefore the small spatula was large enough to cover the work. The spatula now has a dual role: not only heating the background veneer to create the windows, but also inlaying the motifs with fish glue.

Figure 7.53 Fine tip PVA Glue Applicator made by Anne Read.

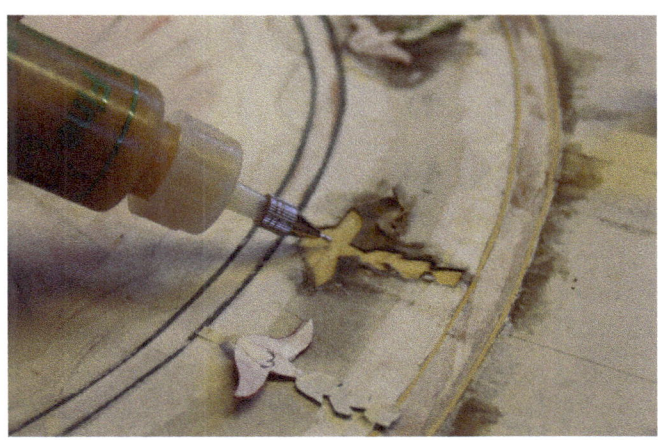

Figure 7.54 Applying a thin bead of glue across the window.

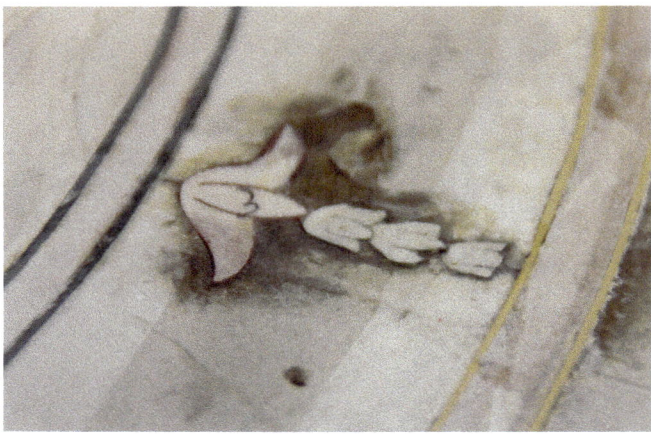

Figure 7.55 Insert placed into window.

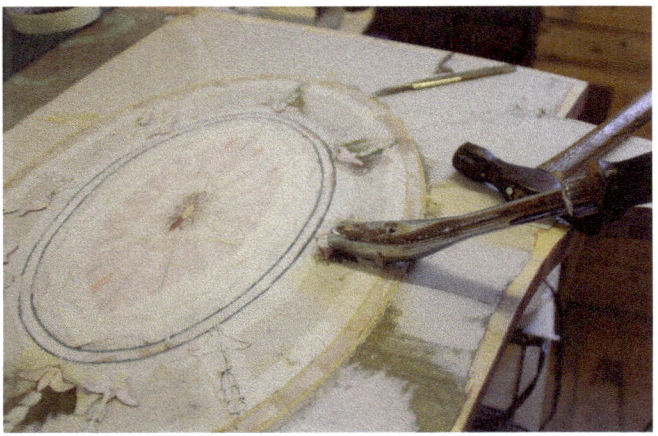

Figure 7.56 Using a heated spatula both to heat the background veneer and to inlay the motifs with fish glue.

Figure 7.57 All eight vertical laurel leaf drops inlaid. Now to repeat the exercise for the intermediate swags.

Figure 7.58 Windows removed and fish glue applied from the fine tip bottle. It is so precise and easy to apply.

Figure 7.59 shows all swags and flowers installed. I came across another problem with the open grained magnolia. I tried sandshading each leaf only to find it turned into black carbon in a matter of seconds and because the leaves are so small, it ruined the intended purpose. I decided to adopt yet another technique used on Chippendale designs, that of applying artwork prior to polishing.

Fitting tulipwood crossbanding around the table

It was important to border the panels at this stage, in order for the marquetry I wanted to install next to fit correctly in each corner. Tulipwood is not the easiest of woods to work with tools, because of its extra hardness. A further difficulty was that none of the surfaces had straight lines so each short section had to be cut with a knife, for which purpose I used a scalpel, although a sharpened section of a hacksaw blade would have done the same job in the 18th century. Figure 7.60 shows the finished effect – it gave me great encouragement to see my work at last framed and only four corner decorations remaining to fit on each panel.

Building the corner decorations

My colour chart, reproduced in Figure 7.61, shows the sixteen different elements needed to complete each corner design. The count includes the two yellow berries, but not the four red dots in each of the two acanthus flowers seen on the left and right sides of the design.

Figure 7.59 All swags and flowers installed.

Figure 7.60 Tulipwood crossbanding fitted.

CHAPTER 7 | Building a Replica: Pier Table Top from Harewood House

Figures 7.62–7.76 illustrate the process of building the corner decorations.

Figure 7.61 Colour chart showing the corner design planned for each of the eight corners across the two end panels.

Figure 7.62 Acanthus leaves.

Figure 7.63 Double acanthus leaves, C scrolls, and small acanthus stems.

Figure 7.64 Red flowers large and small.

Figure 7.65 Assembling small double layer fans. First (top) layer installed here.

Figure 7.66 Second (under) layer added.

223

Figure 7.67 Blue stringer added around the fan.

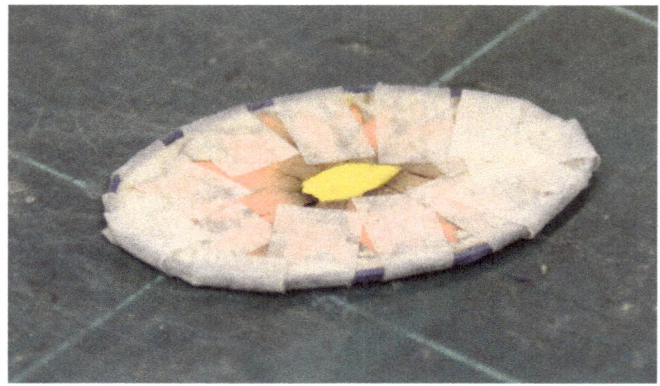

Figure 7.68 Stringer held in masking tape while fish glue sets.

It's worth noting here that I had to sandshade both layers of the tiny fans and, for it to be effective artistically, the shading had to be as delicate as possible. I had already found that magnolia burnt black on the leading edge, which meant I had to avoid that during the build. Fortunately, because I built these fans by the window method I was able to slide the shaded pink veneer past the burnt edge and use the lesser-shaded areas. Figure 7.69 illustrates the result. If only I could do this when building the plumage in the centre of the table, a task which I was leaving until all other elements had been installed.

Figure 7.69 Double layer oval fan showing delicate sandshading giving a perfect 3D effect. The thin blue stringer frames the assembly.

Figure 7.70 The author using his trusty inlay knife and tack hammer.

CHAPTER 7 | Building a Replica: Pier Table Top from Harewood House

Figure 7.71 Close-up of inlay knife showing bevelled sharp point.

Figure 7.72 All elements lifted clear.

Figure 7.73 Water and heat (spatula) applied to inlaid sections to soften the glue below and lift from substrate.

Figure 7.74 Filling cavities with fish glue from the mini glue bottle.

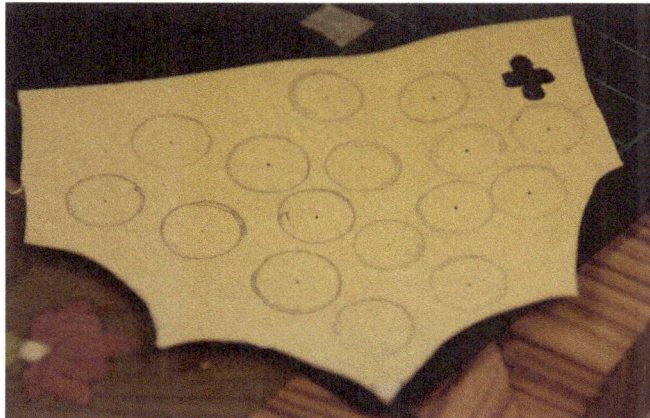

Figure 7.75 Marking the small circular flowers which reside in the two C scrolls. I will punch in the four red berries after all is glued in place.

Figure 7.76 I decided to cold press rather than use heat from the spatula. Fish glue takes 12 hours to bond when cold.

Chapter 7 | Building a Replica: Pier Table Top from Harewood House

Figure 7.78 Right-hand panel complete.

Figure 7.77 Left-hand panel complete. Sandshading is added to the swags of laurel leaves on both panels by using applied artwork.

REBUILDING THE CENTRAL PLUMAGE

The final challenge was to try and rebuild the central plumage (for the fourth time) and to sandshade the vertical plumes without turning the woods into carbon dust. I took advice from my friend and colleague Heinrich Piening, who suggested I shade them and then, during the polishing process, tone down the black colour with colour tints. He assures me it is a normal process in conservation, so I bow to his superior knowledge. Unfortunately, he is based in Germany, but I was able to pass the process of finishing and polishing to a trusted professional polisher, Phillipa Barstow, whom I have known and respected for many years.

On my first attempt to build and shade the central plumage, the resulting sandshading was unacceptable, since the edge of the green-dyed veneer, when submerged into the hot sand, turned jet black and, in places, produced carbon dust which, in parts, removed the firm edge of the green veneers. This totally removed the purpose of sandshading. Given this dilemma, I chose to adopt a more restricted method and decided that the engraving process, when applied, would produce the overall 3-D effect. As we will see on the following pages, I was almost correct, although the tinting of the black shading also played its part in the process. Heinrich's explanation as to what caused my dilemma and disappointment is given in his email to me early December 2017 thus:

Slice cut veneer can work different to historical veneer, especially when it is heated up. You can have the same problem with the synthetic dyes; some of these are thermo-chrome and change colour under different temperatures, so they are tricky when they are heated.

Heinrich calls the modern dyes, as used in Milan, Italy, 'synthetic'. Here in the UK we call them 'aniline dyes'. Heinrich went on to offer me holly veneer, dyed green, to overcome the problem. I explained to him that my main purpose in choosing the synthetic or aniline dyed stock, from Italy, was to achieve colour retention. He fully understood my reason, but his scientific explanation was good to hear and learn.

By early December I had re-sawn the central motif, sandshaded the veneers and inlaid it to the centre panel. It is worth noting here that green-dyed veneers react much worse than any other colour when applied to hot sand. Perhaps it is the combination of the two synthetic components, whatever they are, or just one of them that is the most thermo-chrome. Chapter 4, page 123, covers the subject of synthetic dyes. Figure 7.79 and the resulting tinted and engraved image in Figure 7.80 show the 'before and after' of my labours. I am truly indebted to Heinrich Piening for his timely and effective solution to my problem, and to Philippa Barstow, polisher/finisher, for applying the tinting treatments.

Figure 7.79 Plumage changed showing the over-burning of the sandshading.

Figure 7.80 Plumage now tinted to tone down the over-burnt green dyes and engraving added to achieve the desired result

CHAPTER 7 | Building a Replica: Pier Table Top from Harewood House

THE REPLICA TABLE TOP COMPLETE

Figure 7.81 shows the full panel polished and engraved following two years of research and build. I trust you appreciate the tonal results of the chosen colours, and how the original table would have looked when first delivered to Harewood House in 1772.

As seen here, the kaleidoscope of colours speaks for itself. Despite the challenges presented with the magnolia veneers, I am delighted to achieve my initial goal to replicate the colours and hues discovered through Heinrich Piening's spectrographic analysis.

I am also indebted to the professional help throughout the construction of this challenging design. These are: Heinrich Piening, conservator/scientist; Ian Fraser, conservator; Malcolm Long, engraver; and Philippa Barstow, polisher. Without their knowledge and expertise, these end results, seen here, would not have been possible.

Figure 7.81 The completed tabletop after polishing and engraving. Because of the open grain of the marquetry veneers (magnolia), the engraving had to be performed after the polishing was applied. This allowed the polish to fully fill the grains and prevent chipping when the engraving tool was applied. The image of the central plumage shows how the engraving work provides the 3-D effect, along with a lesser, but necessary, shading where needed.

Similarly, the engraving to the laurel leaf swags on the two end panels provides the necessary shading, which I could not achieve with hot sand on such tiny areas. The engraver also changed the single leaf into three leaves by extending the joint lines. This was done on my request to overcome the technical problem I had experienced when fretsawing the leaves. The subject is covered on page 220.

CHAPTER 7 | Building a Replica: Pier Table Top from Harewood House

Figure 7.82 Berberis engraved to give it shape and symmetry.

Figure 7.83 Floral corner arrangement with miniature fan, plus part of the green swags below showing the engraving effects.

Figure 7.84 Closer view of the central panel.

229

Chapter 7 | Building a Replica: Pier Table Top from Harewood House

Figure 7.85 Matching end panels looking resplendent and very feminine in their replica colours befitting a table made for the Ladies Circular Dressing Room at Harewood House in 1772.

CHAPTER 8

GALLERY OF CHIPPENDALE'S MARQUETRY FURNITURE

INTRODUCTION

This final chapter provides a detailed illustrated gallery of all the known marquetry commissions made by Thomas Chippendale Senior. This book does not include commissions following his retirement in 1776, when his son, Thomas Chippendale the Younger, ran the firm. Where possible, I have put the furniture in chronological order, so that you can see not only the development of the maker's designs, but also the advancement of both the materials and the marquetry techniques. As you read through the pages, moving from piece to piece, you will, I hope, be struck by how the designs mature artistically, and, at the same time, how marquetry techniques improved as previously unused working methods were introduced.

For each commission I have endeavoured to provide the provenance of the piece, where known, along with technical data regarding the construction and methodology of the marquetry techniques used. In total I have included 21 commissions, covering a seven-year period, starting in 1768/9 and finishing in 1775.

To put into context the output of work from the firm's workshops during the productive years, I have summarised all the major commissions in Table 8.1 on the following page, showing start and finish dates, as well as the duration of each commission. This table gives some indication of the firm's workload and output, not only in terms of the customers receiving marquetry-decorated furniture during this period, but also customers who were supplied with other non-marquetry furniture and associated household fittings.

Table 8.1 reinforces the unrivalled output of furniture and fitting that the Chippendale workshop produced, with over 700 items emerging from his workshops during his tenure, 1754–76, far outstripping any of his rivals.

Figure 8*

* By kind permission of the Private Collector

Chapter 8 | Gallery of Chippendale's Marquetry Furniture

Table 4.3 Major commissions arising after the publication of Chippendale's Director

Commissions	1754	1755	1759	1762	1763	1766	1767	1768	1771	1772	1773	1776	1779
Director Editions (year of publication)	1st	2nd		3rd									
Dumfries House, Ayrshire				7 years									
Wilton House & Pembroke House, London				14 years									
Nostell Priory, Yorkshire							19 years						
Foremark Hall, Derbyshire							7 years						
Harewood House, Yorkshire							30 years						
Mersham-le-Hatch, Kent								12 years					
David Garrick's three London homes									10 years				
Burton Constable Hall, Yorkshire									11 years				
Goldsborough Hall, Yorkshire										5 years			
Newby Hall, Yorkshire											7 years		
Paxton House, Berwickshire												30 years	
Thomas Chippendale retires													
Death of Thomas Chippendale													

Red areas denote events & commissions by Thomas Chippendale.
Green areas denote commissions continued by Thomas Chippendale the Younger.

Medium- to long-term commissions illustrate the firms' workload during the marquetry years 1770–75.
Some short-term commissions (not shown) were also in the firm's work programme.

The seven preceding chapters will, I hope, have advanced your understanding of marquetry to a level where you can recognise why different techniques needed for assembly were developed and how each technique came to be performed with consummate skill and dexterity.

This collection clearly illustrates the diversity our designer achieved in meeting the demands of his clientele. You will see a wide variety of home furnishings, elegantly designed and constructed to the highest order, ranging from a games table, to dining room, lounge, library and bedroom furniture.

Marquetry-decorated furniture became the order of the day during the 1770s, and Chippendale and his London based rivals each produced marquetry designs based on the neo-classical style. It is certainly the case that central 'finishing' firms controlled and provided the marquetry decorations for each of these furniture manufacturers. In the case of Chippendale's furniture, I have established that two external firms were employed to perform the marquetry and other finishing applications. One was a large undertaking, where marquetry and all other finishing processes were undertaken, as detailed in Chapter 3 (see pages 85–86). The other was a much smaller operation, performing small commission services, in particular marquetry inlay work, and artwork, as applied to drawer fronts. Both these situations will become apparent during your journey through this chapter.

I hope you will enjoy this final and 'revealing' journey of discovery, where Greek and Roman mythology was one artistic medium of the period. However, our intrepid designer had the vision to include a current, landmark event into his marquetry design – an inclusion that until now has remained concealed, until my timely and tantalising discovery.

Read on and discover …

CHAPTER 8 | Gallery of Chippendale's Marquetry Furniture

8.1 PEMBROKE 'GAMES' TABLE ~ NOSTELL PRIORY, 1769

The Pembroke games table, made for Nostell Priory and invoiced 3rd July 1769 suggests this was Chippendale's first entry into serious marquetry work. While occasional small compass rose motifs appeared on earlier furniture, they were not a prominent feature of the furniture and for that reason I have discounted them in this collection.

The marquetry – or, to be more precise, parquetry (geometric designs) – applied to this table is found inside the drawer and no external decoration was made (see Figure 8.1.1). The table was invoiced by the maker as:

"To a very neat Pembroke Table of fine yellow and other woods with a very good Backgammon Table fitted as a drawer & good Locks & Casters &c. £7 10s

A Set of Ivory Men & Ivory Boxes and Dies £1 10s"

In addition to the backgammon fitted to the inside of the drawer, a chessboard was fitted to the underside of the drawer, as seen in Figure 8.1.2. The ivory chessmen with their boxes and backgammon counters have not survived. The 'yellow wood' referred to by Chippendale is the name he gave to the wood 'fustic' (*chlorophora tinctoria*) from the family moraceae, a tree found in the

Figure 8.1.2* Chessboard concealed on the underside of the drawer.

West Indies and South America. The timber would almost certainly have arrived in England with the early imports of mahogany from the same regions. Other timbers endemic to those regions were also to feature in the production of Chippendale's marquetry furniture as we will discover later in this chapter.

Fustic or 'yellow wood' was his first attempt to find a golden/yellow coloured veneer that would support and highlight marquetry work on future commissions. However, experience was to force Chippendale to stop using it around 1770/1 simply because of its short colour life. The bright golden yellow timber soon faded when exposed to light and disappointingly turned a dull brown colour. Chippendale would certainly have witnessed the colour loss transformation within the first year or two from point of delivery.

Tulipwood crossbanding provided borders to the fustic panels across the three leaves of the table.

The photograph shown in Figure 8.1.3, of the loss of tulipwood to one corner, offers an insight into the thickness of the veneer. This gave me my first evidence of veneer sawing, matching the descriptions by Roubo (see Chapter 3), whereby veneers were sawn from the log to a thickness of between 1.2 and 1.4 mm. What we see on this table is veneer reduced to 1 mm following

Figure 8.1.1* Pembroke games table.

* By kind permission of Nostell Priory © The National Trust

Figure 8.1.3* Loss of veneer to this corner provides evidence of the 1 mm veneer thickness which became a consistent feature on all Chippendale marquetry furniture.

sanding, levelling and with the addition of polish. This finished thickness remained consistent throughout the following six years. In most cases veneer thicknesses are easily measured by pulling out doors and drawer fronts to expose the leading edges of the facing veneers. On tables without doors and drawers, the veneer thickness can be seen along the horizontal edges of tables.

The two board games contained within the single drawer provide an early insight into high-quality parquetry work. Because the woods used on each side of the drawer have remained hidden from daylight for most of the time, the colours are still fresh and vibrant. On the chessboard, African ebony is used for the black squares, while sycamore is evident with its tell-tale 'lace' figure shown in Figure 8.1.5. What is amazing is the lack of contamination of black dust leaching from the ebony into the white sycamore. African ebony is the worst wood in the world for leaching its black dust into adjacent veneers when sanding is carried out, yet here there is no evidence of any discolouration on the sycamore squares. One other wood that leaches its colour badly is padauk. Both veneers were used regularly by Chippendale yet in my researches, I have not found a single instance of ebony or padauk leaching their colour. The reason for this is that the woods are first sealed with hot animal (hide) glue on the face side and covered with protective paper. The glue, brushed onto and into the surface, fills the grain. I replicated this practice on numerous occasions during the construction of the Diana and Minerva Commode and not once did either wood show any signs of colour leaching.

The reason why both woods cause problems with today's marquetry techniques is because face surfaces are not sealed with any glue prior to sanding. Instead, a sanding-sealer base polish is applied in an attempt to stop leaching. In my experience it is not a foolproof cure, as some coloured dust does tend to escape into surrounding woods.

This provides another example of how we can learn from the techniques of the past. I am sure that 18th century woodworkers were fully aware of the pitfalls of working with ebony and padauk, since dust leaching

Figure 8.1.4* Africa ebony and sycamore veneers used for the squares.

Figure 8.1.5* Note the lack of staining/leaching on the sycamore squares.

Figure 8.1.6* Ebony background supporting mahogany and sycamore points (triangles). Two game areas separated by herringbone tulipwood and matching narrow.

Figure 8.1.7* Cupped shape of the drawer sides to make removal of the checkers possible.

occurred when working with the two timbers in the solid form – for example, when turning these woods on a lathe the amount of dust stained the clothing and hands of the wood turner.

The backgammon board is set into the base of the drawer unit and consists of natural woods (not dyed) on African ebony background with alternate triangles known as 'points', made up of mahogany and sycamore (see Figure 8.1.6). The board is divided down the centre with the 'bar' separating the two playing areas used by the players. The bar areas on both sides consists of tulipwood cut at 45° forming a quarter-matching herringbone arrangement. A tulipwood crossbanding, with holly stringers at each side, separates the four playing areas from the herringbone arrangement.

Note the 'cupped' shape of the drawer sides (Figure 8.1.7), purposely provided to allow 'checkers' to be removed in a sliding action by the players. Had the sides been vertical, players would have had to try and pick out the checkers. Here we have yet another example of Chippendale's attention to detail and awareness of the possible pitfalls when setting a board game into the well of the drawer.

* By kind permission of Nostell Priory © The National Trust

8.2 HARRINGTON COMMODE ~ c.1770

This commode first came to my notice when it appeared at auction at Sotheby's, London, on 7th December 2010. It was sold for a staggering £3,793,250, setting a new record price for a piece of furniture. It was sold by order of the trustees of the late 10th Earl of Harrington. The last association with the piece is its final location at Elvaston Castle, Derbyshire where it formed part of a collection, formerly owned by the Earls of Harrington. Further intriguing historical records suggest a more compelling provenance linking the Harrington dynasty to Edwin Lascelles, who became 1st Baron Harewood and built Harewood House. Here I refer to notes taken from the Sotheby's catalogue of 7th December 2010.

Unfortunately the original commission or the point at which this commode entered the collection of the Earls of Harrington currently remains undiscovered. It would appear unlikely that it was commissioned by the Stanhope family; both William Stanhope, the 2nd Earl of Harrington (1719–79), and Charles, his son and later 3rd Earl (1753–1829), were military men without substantial wealth, the 2nd Earl dying with considerable debts, embroiled in legal negotiations.

However, a possible introduction of the commode into Harrington ownership is through the marriage of the 3rd Earl to Jane Fleming (1755–1824), eldest daughter of Sir John Fleming, 1st Bart. (1701–63) of Brompton Park, Middlesex, and Jane Colman (1732–1813), a niece of the 8th Duke of Somerset. Upon her father's death in 1763,

Figure 8.2.1* The Harrington commode.

* By kind permission of Sotheby's London

Chapter 8 | Gallery of Chippendale's Marquetry Furniture

Jane Fleming inherited an extraordinary £100,000 fortune. Her mother subsequently married Edwin Lascelles, later 1st Baron Harewood (1713–95), one of Chippendale's most important patrons. They had no children of their own and as such there is an intriguing and tempting connection between the current commode and Lascelles.

Charles Stanhope married Jane Fleming on 23rd May 1779, barely more than six weeks following the death of his father and his accession as the 3rd Earl of Harrington. The new Countess of Harrington generously settled her new husband's debts and re-purchased the former Harrington London home, Harrington House in St. James's Stable Yard, where Robert Adam had previously been commissioned for a design for a Dressing Room circa 1770 which was probably executed (see Howard Colvin, A Biographical Dictionary of British Architects, 1600–1840, 3rd Edition, Yale, 1995, p. 57).

Shortly before her marriage Jane Fleming's mother, now Jane Lascelles, commissioned a portrait of her daughter from Sir Joshua Reynolds, now held in the collection of The Huntington Library, California. This is of interest as this picture is known to have reverted to the Countess of Harrington upon the death of her mother as other pieces may have done so. Edwin Lascelles' will stipulated that his widow was to retain all the 'Pictures and furniture which belonged to her before our marriage, or which she has since purchased or acquired, in which ever of my houses the same may be'. Furthermore, the Countess' mother, Jane, Baroness Dowager Harewood bequeathed '...all my Jewels Watches Rings Trinkets Gold and Silver Plate useful and ornamental China Pictures Prints and all my household Furniture Books Linen Carriage live and dead Stock and other effects...in and about my houses in Portman Square and Sunning Hill (not before specifically bequeathed) In trust for my dearest beloved Jane, Countess of Harrington...' (extract of Probate of Will [22 Feb 1811] of Jane, Baroness Dowager Harewood, 14 May 1813, held in Derbyshire Record Office, Matlock, D664 M/F 22).

Unfortunately no further documentary evidence has surfaced regarding the pieces that were bequeathed by the Baroness Dowager Harewood. Whether this commode once furnished one of her and Edwin Lascelles' homes may escape conclusion. Other important furniture was and is however evident in the Harrington Collection where it is unknown at what point it was acquired, in particular a large part of the famed Palm Room suite by Vardy supplied to the 1st Earl Spencer for Spencer House, some of which was sold by the 11th Earl of Harrington at Sotheby's London on 8th November 1963.

Figure 8.2.2* Close-up of classical vase on one of the two doors. Note also the stylised anthemion mount embracing the two doors.

This George III commode is gilt-lacquered and brass-mounted, with woods consisting of fustic, rosewood, tulipwood and marquetry built from dyed holly. The piece was catalogued by Sotheby's *"as believed to be almost certainly made by Thomas Chippendale"*.

I discussed its construction with Simon Banks, of Dingwall & Banks, furniture restoration specialists based at Constable Burton Hall, North Yorkshire. Simon was commissioned by Sotheby's to examine the piece prior to its sale and produce a 'Condition Report'. After seeing the images shown here and reading Simon's report, I had no doubt that this commode came from Chippendale's workshops, based in St Martin's Lane, London.

The commode is in characteristic rococo style, with the mounts showing rams' heads, scrolls, acanthus foliage and a single anthemion embracing both front doors. The marquetry motifs are of matching vases on the doors (see Fig 8.2.2.), with guilloche borders across the drawers and dummy sides, and the garland of laurel leaves suspended

* By kind permission of Sotheby's London

CHAPTER 8 | Gallery of Chippendale's Marquetry Furniture

Figure 8.2.3* View of one of the side panels, showing the garland of leaves suspended by a riboon.

from a single ribbon to the side panels (see Fig 8.2.3.). This is a feature I myself had built on the Diana and Minerva commode to frame the two goddesses that give the commode its name.

The choice of the background veneer – 'fustic' or 'yellowwood' as Chippendale called it – not only endorses the identity of the maker, but dates it closely to c.1770/1. We know that fustic ceased to be used by Chippendale after that date.

The final comparison with other Chippendale works, which adds weight to its provenance, is best given, not by myself, but from Sotheby's catalogue of December 2010. It states:

The final decade of his life culminated in what is arguably his greatest commission, a neoclassical triumph, for Sir Edwin Lascelles at Harewood House, Yorkshire. The serpentine form of the present commode slightly predates many of Chippendale's most celebrated neoclassical pieces, the rectilinear furniture at Harewood, and the renowned commode supplied for Melbourne House, London (now at Renishaw Hall, Derbyshire) in the early 1770s. However, there are undoubtedly similarities in the design and treatment of the marquetry to his Harewood commission, the rosette-centered interlaced banding found to the frieze here is almost identical in design to the bandings on the metamorphic library steps at Harewood, whilst the ribbon-tied bellflower garlands on the sides of the current commode are very similarly conceived to those on the famous dressing-commode (Diana/Minerva) supplied to Lascelles. The urn to the front doors of the current commode closely resembles the design of the urn on the central lower panel of the widely published Panshanger cabinets, which also share the concave sides, ram-mask mounts and oak-leaf wreaths to the frieze that are apparent on the Harrington commode. The similarities to the commode supplied to Viscount Melbourne for the house designed by Sir William Chambers on Piccadilly are also evident when compared with the current example. The concave sides are once again flanked by ram-headed mounts above which sit near identical scroll-topped capitals issuing four pendant husks. The marquetry to the sides displays rosettes within concave-sided lozenges as apparent to the top of the Harrington commode. Furthermore, the commode supplied by Chippendale for Lady Winn's Bedchamber at Nostell Priory, Yorkshire, whilst of a slightly more rococo form, displays similarly shaped and double-crossbanded doors, with a fustic ground and likewise a rosette-centered top with foliate scrolls to the sides inset into the magnificently figured fustic veneers. Direct comparison must be made with the commode in the Lady Lever Art Gallery, illustrated by Lucy Wood, Catalogue of Commodes, London, *1994, no. 20, pp. 180–190 along with a commode, possibly the pair to the Lady Lever example, sold Christie's London, 6 July 1995, lot 152. Whilst straight fronted, both these commodes display a similarly conceived form, a drawer (in the Harrington example this is a false drawer) over a pair of cupboard doors, flanked by similar mounts to those on the current commode. The feet on these two are very similar in form to the Harrington commode and also appear on The Messer Commode, although in this instance in carved mahogany and not embellished with gilded mounts, sold Christie's London, 5 December 1991, lot 130. These all derive from a design by Chippendale held in the Metropolitan Museum*

* By kind permission of Sotheby's London

CHAPTER 8 | Gallery of Chippendale's Marquetry Furniture

Figure 8.2.4* Commode top marquetry.

of Art, New York City, The Rogers Fund, 1920 [20.40.2(61)] and also a design that was published in the 1762 (third) edition of his Gentleman and Cabinet-Maker's Director, no. LXVIII, as designs for 'A French Commode' and reproduced in Peter Ward-Jackson, English Furniture Designs of the 18th Century, London, 1958, pl. 92. In Chippendale's notes to this design he comments 'The Ornaments may be Brass; That on the Right hath two Doors, which represent Drawers, and a long Drawer above: ' Chippendale's own inspiration appears to have derived from Louis XIV's reign in France and the designs of Jean Berain (d.1711) who published a design for a commode with strikingly similar foot in L'Oeuvre Complet de Jean Berain, Paris, n.d., pl.88.

The top of the commode, shown in Figure 8.2.4, displays a central fan with a ring of interlocking leaves. Four back-to-back anthemions are positioned in the four quadrants of a star shaped banding running north, south, east and west around the fan. The star-banding is tulipwood crossbanding with white stringing either side. The star-banding was to appear again on the end panels of the Diana and Minerva commode. A wider circular banding is added with the most precise guilloche I have ever seen, displaying the most delicate sandshading on each end of the 128 tiny twists of the guilloche motif. This guilloche is quite perfect, and not only am I convinced that this is a Chippendale piece, but I do believe I am witnessing the skilful hand of my trusted journeyman marqueteur, whose sumptuous work appears time and again throughout this marquetry collection.

However, there is also a practical reason for the inclusion of the guilloche banding. It was put there not solely as a decorative element, but also to reduce the size of the background veneers in order for them to fit the throat of the fretsaw. We will encounter this time and again, because we have to remember that most of Chippendale's furniture was made for large establishments and therefore the pieces themselves were large. This commode measures 89 cm (2 ft 11 in) high, 140 cm (4 ft 7 in) wide, and 65 cm (2 ft 1½ in) deep. I have been able to work out that the fretsaw used by this marqueteur had to have a throat capacity of 51 cm (1 ft 8 in). While these measurements show the mathematical results of the fretsaw throat, in practice, a slightly shorter throat can be accommodated, by slightly turning up the ends of a packet to clear the throat while sawing in a motif. This means a fretsaw having a throat of 450 mm (1 ft 6 inch) would be capable of achieving all the sawing needed on this commission. I already know that the fretsaw used to build the top of the Diana and Minerva Commode had a throat of 450 mm (1 ft 6 inch), meaning that the same saw would also achieve these cuts.

* By kind permission of Sotheby's London

Chapter 8 | Gallery of Chippendale's Marquetry Furniture

Figure 8.2.5* Internal shelves and back of doors revealing black rosewood veneers.

Looking at the top of the commode (in Figure 8.2.4), we can work out that the diagonal distance between the back corners (both left and right) and the outer circumference of the central fan is approximately 60 cm (2 ft). This meant that the background veneer had to be reduced into manageable sizes – hence the outer guilloche banding. It's always rewarding to me to be able to identify a Chippendale piece by technical engineering attributes, and not just by the design.

In Figure 8.2.5 we see the interior of the commode showing two shelves. Simon Banks' condition report tell us of two doors folded back, veneered with black rosewood and now enclosing two conformingly veneered slides (referring to the shelves). This is the only occasion I have seen Chippendale use rosewood veneer in this manner, but it's not surprising since the veneer was still in vogue.

Engraving

Simon Banks' condition report did not cover the technique of engraving, which was clearly used on this commission. This is understandable since engraving is a technique Simon would have encountered before and its inclusion on this work did not affect the condition of the piece. However, having had the advantage of examining all the known marquetry commissions built by the designer, it eventually became clear to me that engraving was reserved for his most prestigious works. Of the twenty plus marquetry-decorated pieces of furniture to emerge from the Chippendale firm, I have only identified five where the more expensive decorative medium was deployed. The remaining pieces received surface decoration, as explained in Chapter 3.

We know engraving was employed to decorate the marquetry foliage, and on this work the acanthus leaves are engraved with very fine lines, gouged out by the engraver's burin tool, which removes tiny slivers of veneer to give the effect of veins. Similarly fine lines exist on each laurel leaf, which together form the garland surrounding the two matching vases on the doors, and also on each petal of the starflowers within the guilloche on the dummy drawers. I would go as far as to say it was done by the same engraver who applied this technique to the table made for the circular dressing room at Harewood in 1772. Clearly, this commode was supplied with only the best and most expensive techniques, indicating the client's choice for quality and appearance.

8.3 BUREAU DRESSING TABLE ~ HAREWOOD HOUSE, 1770

This bureau dressing table was originally made for Harewood House, but acquired by the Victoria & Albert Museum in 1928, where it remains today.

The piece represents an early example of classic expression, and bears resemblance to other marquetry elements produced during the same period. You could say that, on this piece, Chippendale gave an indication of the range of standard motifs he was planning for future works. The vases used on the two outer door panels were to be reproduced on the Harewood Library writing table, while the two torches on top of each vase reappear three years later on the Panshanger cabinets. The swags and drops of laurel leaves across the drawer fronts would be repeated on the Diana and Minerva Commode, while oval and circular fans abound throughout the collection.

In producing this bureau, Chippendale also chose the two species of wood he would consistently use over the next five years as the most suitable background foils for his creations. Satinwood and Indian rosewood are both used to good effect, yet future work sees him using just one or the other. The crossbanding surrounding each panel is tulipwood, a choice that was not to change on the rest of his commissions.

These three tropical hardwoods, along with mahogany, purpleheart, padauk and ebony, together with temperate species – holly, sycamore, maple, and ash from across Europe – formed the nucleus of species for the following five years. I firmly believe that one of the secrets of his success was the constraints placed upon him by the limited availability of woods coming into the country at the time. You could argue that the types that were available happened to be the best species, not only in terms of colour, texture and figure, but also, as time has proved, because they were free from inherent faults and diseases likely to cause short- or long-term problems. Only on three earlier pieces, namely the Pembroke table and Lady Winn's commode, both made for Nostell Priory, and the Harrington commode (covered earlier in this chapter) did he use West Indian fustic as the background foil for the marquetry work.

Figure 8.3.1* Bureau dressing table.

* *By kind permission of the Victoria & Albert Museum, London*

CHAPTER 8 | Gallery of Chippendale's Marquetry Furniture

Figure 8.3.2* Mechanical mirror set in drawer unit.

The bureau converts into its dual role as a dressing/writing table when the mechanised mirror is raised and the opened drawer exposes inbuilt containers providing for writing materials such as stationery and inkwells and narrow compartments for filing notepapers.

The marquetry displays knife/template work on both the twelve-fluted fan shown on the centre door panel, and the circular nineteen-fluted oval fan on the top.

Two-part fretsawing is clearly evident in the motifs, on the two matching outer doors, while I suspect the inlay method may have been deployed on the laurel leaves applied to the drawer front. I later prove that drawer fronts were sent to a different finishing house from the one that applied to the rest of the commode Holly is used for all the motifs, with padauk used around the fan flutes.

The surface decoration was achieved with sandshading and artwork applied by brush.

* By kind permission of the Victoria & Albert Museum, London

8.4 COMMODE ~ NOSTELL PRIORY, c.1770

This superb commode was made for Lady Winn's bedchamber, Nostell Priory, Wakefield, Yorkshire. This fully provenanced work may well have been Chippendale's final fling with the rococo movement. Figure 8.4.1 shows the serpentine front and heavy use of brass mounts down each of the two front legs and feet. Here we see the rococo lines still evident, even though they are not as pronounced and 'fussy' as designs found in the *Director*.

On subsequent works the serpentine front and curved legs are, in the main, replaced with flat fronts and straight upright legs. That aside, I love the whole shape of this piece. The sweeping scroll across the base of the doors complements the gentle sweep of the legs. The two door panels, with marquetry set into a background veneer of fustic, are perfectly framed to their respective door shapes by the addition of three 'quartered' or 'broken corners', with the fourth corner elegantly pointing downwards towards the legs to complete the scrolled sweep across the door bottoms. For me, it's that fourth corner that makes the whole design balance. Had Chippendale used a quartered corner as in the other three, it would not have worked. Such attention to detail where it mattered most!

The whole design is pure classical: the vase with its Greek key handles, a guilloche strap and topped by an anthemion. Swags and drops of laurel leaves are suspended from a ribbon. Here, our designer was making his statement, expressing his passion for the movement that Robert Adam had placed into his hungry artistic hands on his discovery of the movement during his grand tour of Pompeii and Herculaneum.

Tulipwood crossbanding surrounds the panels, and brass gilded acanthus leaf mounts provide the perfect frame. Fustic veneer was chosen, I imagine, because of its rich yellow colour that complements the dyed green laurel swags and ribbons above the two oval medallions, each displaying a matching vase.

Figure 8.4.1* Rococo-style Commode with fustic ground veneers.

* *By kind permission of Nostell Priory © The National Trust*

CHAPTER 8 | Gallery of Chippendale's Marquetry Furniture

Figure 8.4.2* Oval medallion close-up.

The choice of fustic veneer was not a success, I believe, for two reasons:

- Firstly, the veneer soon lost its bright yellow colour, as exposure to light turns it to russet brown.
- Secondly, the wood is very unstable, and there is evidence of small clusters of stress cracks appearing. A close-up of one of the oval medallions is seen in Figure 8.4.2, highlighting the small clusters of stress lines, seen as wavy dark lines across the surface.

The vase is set into an oval garland of leaves trapped between two green stringers, providing evidence that the green dye still exists, whereas the laurel swags around the vase have lost their green colour completely. The stringers have retained their colour because they would have been dyed green using the dyestuff saffron. We know this because green stringers are also present on the Harewood Library writing table (described in Chapter 5), which were tested using UV-VIS spectromony. It also confirms the assumption that stringers were most likely dyed in bulk with saffron by outside specialist dyers. Saffron, even today, is an extremely expensive dye and it would have been uneconomical to use it to dye sheets of veneers in the 18th century. Saffron produces a yellow dye which is both lightfast and colourfast. The addition of indigo (blue dye), which turns yellow to green, does not affect the chemical qualities of the saffron.

The top has two cut-outs at the back (see Figure 8.4.3), which were made to fit into window jambs. However, the notches were wrongly cut, much to the annoyance of Sir Rowland Winn, the owner, whose

Figure 8.4.3* Commode top displaying oval fan and the two wrong cut-outs at the back.

* By kind permission of Nostell Priory © The National Trust

CHAPTER 8 | Gallery of Chippendale's Marquetry Furniture

reputation for making life difficult for Chippendale is well documented. Sir Rowland's tardiness in settling bills made life intolerable for Chippendale, causing him to write repeated letters for settlement of accounts in order to pay his workmen. At one stage, Chippendale wrote to Sir Rowland stating that *"I could hardly keep myself out of jail and I have not a single Guinea to pay my men with tomorrow."* Sir Rowland, however, viewed the cabinet-maker with disdain, and repeated mistakes and late delivery of work did not help to improve relationships. The Nostell contract spanned 19 years (1766–85), during which Chippendale struggled to accommodate Sir Rowland's unrelenting demands.

The oval fan seen at Figure 8.4.4 was probably dyed pink to suit the female owner. Padauk is used to border the scallops at the ends of flutes. Green stringing bandings are placed inside and around the fan. The twenty-fluted fan was assembled by knife. The veneer was holly and when assembled its thickness would have been about 1.2 to 1.4 mm, making it easy to knife-cut. A template was drawn up on a wooden board, making sure that the design showed wider flutes to the left hand and right hand sides, and narrower flutes above and below. A smaller oval fretsawn leaf design completes the centre. Stylised acanthus leaves topped with purple anthemions are fretsawn to left and right of the patera, seen in Figure 8.4.5.

It is interesting to see a large tulipwood oval banding placed between the fretwork and fan. The reason for this is not decorative, but merely to break up the fustic background veneer into manageable sizes to fit the throat of the fretsaw. To the right of the photograph in Figure 8.4.5, the central joint is clearly visible where matching leaves of fustic are used to cover the surface. It is my belief that the oval banding was not in the initial design, but added after the marqueteur pointed out the constraints of his fretsaw throat. This in itself raises further questions, because I firmly believe this marquetry was cut and assembled by the two-part fretsawing method, suggesting that his marqueteur did know of the technique before the calamity caused by the packet fretsawing technique on the Harewood Library writing table (see page 129). I am sure that if the tulipwood banding had not been forced on the designer, he would have added something much more decorative. The banding looks out of place and clumsy and lends weight to the assumption that it was included for purely practical reasons.

Regardless of these observations, we know that Chippendale was not to use fustic again during the following five years, for the reasons outlined above.

Figure 8.4.4* *Oval fan built by the template method.*

Figure 8.4.5* *The straight line joining the two fustic background veneers are clearly visible between the two matching sides of the acanthus marquetry work. The joint continues from the anthemion to the outer crossbanding.*

* By kind permission of Nostell Priory © The National Trust

CHAPTER 8 | Gallery of Chippendale's Marquetry Furniture

8.5 PIER TABLES (PAIR) ~ HAREWOOD HOUSE, 1770

Made for the dining room at Harewood House, this magnificent pair of matching tables, *en suite* with pier glasses, illustrate Chippendale's supremacy as a designer. The lavish carved and gilded base and pier glass are partly based on a drawing of a pier glass held in the Victoria & Albert Museum. The marquetry top with its flamboyant content is set into a background of Indian rosewood, narrow satinwood banding and tulipwood crossbanding borders. The marquetry elements are cut from dyed holly.

Figure 8.5.2* Border of repeating oval paterae.

From a technical aspect, the 53 repeating oval paterae, which form the elaborate border, display yet another example of Chippendale deliberately changing a standard design to solve a logistical need. To explain further, I believe that the row of 53 oval paterae started out to be oval fans consisting of a number of flutes joined together with straight lines, with each flute terminating at a scalloped end, as seen on the large half-round fan at the back of the table (Figure 8.5.2). As previously explained, these designs, made from a pre-drawn template, would have been constructed individually, with each flute cut by a small craft knife against a steel straight edge. On these two matching tables, Chippendale had a logistical problem to solve. It is my belief that he wanted to introduce 53 repeating fans around the border, on each of the matching tables, making a combined total of 106 assemblies. To make those individually would have been time-consuming, so in order to speed up production, I think he changed the

Figure 8.5.1* Pier table made for the dining room at Harewood House.

* Reproduced by kind permission of the Trustees of the 7th Earl of Harewood Will Trust and the Trustees of the Harewood House Trust

CHAPTER 8 | Gallery of Chippendale's Marquetry Furniture

Figure 8.5.3* Rounded flutes drawn for packet fretsawing.

'fans' into 'paterae' with rounded petals. This departure allowed the motif to be constructed in multiples by the two-part fretsaw method, thus achieving uniformity, yet permitting mass production, meaning it would have taken less time than it would have taken to build fans by the single knife and template method.

This change of mind clearly illustrates another example of Chippendale 'the designer' working hand in hand with his marqueteur to overcome a logistical problem. In addition to this, I can also see that the stylised paterae were sawn from packets of dyed pink veneers, just as would have been used to construct the fans. We know he used pink dyes for fans on other commissions, confirmed by the dye results made by Heinrich Piening using UV-VIS Spectronomy.

The evidence of multiple sawing lies in the obvious variances between one oval and another as they sit side by side around the border. On close inspection of Figure 8.5.3 and counting full ovals from left to right, ovals 4 and 8 share identical shape, while 2, 5 and 7 are a matching set. By mixing up the completed assembly, the marqueteur achieved uniformity while maintaining the natural 'hand-made' features. Each petal is also sandshaded and it is possible to identify different shades of burning from one patera to another.

The acanthus leaves that surround each oval are also produced by the two-part method. When each assembly is sawn and sandshaded, they are laid onto the rosewood background, scored around the edges with a small craft knife, then the resulting windows are fretsawn out, ready for the elements to be inserted. Fretsawing the windows is time-consuming, we know, but much less time-consuming than building them individually by the knife and template method. The stylized paterae are totally in keeping with the classic movement.

Figure 8.5.4 shows the repeat foliage within the border consisting of green acanthus leaves. Inside the border further acanthus leaves terminate in two 'C' scrolls that wrap around two stylized acanthus flowers, each depicted with alternate lilac and white petals. An anthemion flower stands between the green foliage. Larger anthemions, dyed burgundy, stand between the larger oval paterae. The result is a very colourful display embracing greens, pinks, burgundy and lilac-dyed holly, along with natural white holly, all set into a background of black to violet-coloured Indian rosewood.

Engraving

It's interesting to find evidence of engraving work on the central acanthus leaves. Engraving was reserved for the most prestigious commissions, and clearly Chippendale felt these tables warranted such expensive application. I have also found engraving used on the Diana and Minerva commode, the curved table and the Lunar table, all made for Harewood House, as well as the Harrington Commode. This departure clearly illustrates the high esteem the designer had for these sumptuous tables, making them fit to grace any room.

Figure 8.5.4* Matching oval around border.

* Reproduced by kind permission of the Trustees of the 7th Earl of Harewood Will Trust and the Trustees of the Harewood House Trust

CHAPTER 8 | Gallery of Chippendale's Marquetry Furniture

8.6 LIBRARY STEPS ~ HAREWOOD HOUSE, 1771

To accompany the Harewood Library writing table, folding library steps were made for the same room. Shown here in Figure 8.6.1 in the original setting, the steps, when open, reveal a mahogany frame of three ladder steps and a safety handrail. When folded (Figure 8.6.2), the steps convert into a long stool; the padded seat (upholstered originally in black leather) has undergone recent restoration work in red leather.

The veneers consist of Indian rosewood background, surrounded by a narrow satinwood banding. Tulipwood crossbanding centralises each panel, and further tulipwood is added in herringbone design down the legs of the stool.

The central panel shows a circular fan set into a garland of laurel leaves and tied with a ribbon. Two large and impressive anthemions embellish further laurel swags and ribbons.

Finally, a broad guilloche border is added at the top and bottom of the piece. Small brass medallions add further decoration. While the marquetry is of lesser quantity than other commissions, the quality is still supreme.

I had this piece tested for dyes, as I did the matching Library writing table at Temple Newsam House. Using the results of the UV-VIS Spectronomy analysis carried out by Heinrich Piening in 2008, I was able to identify the different colours used. The results of this analysis are shown in the impression in Figure 8.6.4, produced by photographer Ted Clements using Photoshop. Note that only the marquetry colours were tested and reproduced, so one has to imagine the original and natural multi-coloured tulipwood surrounding the panel.

The piece has a very striking appearance and would have made an impressive companion to the writing table in the first Earl's impressive library at Harewood House in 1771.

Figure 8.6.1* Library steps (opened).

Figure 8.6.2* Library stool (folded) steps closed, showing the decorative guilloche framing the panels above and below.

* *Reproduced by kind permission of the Trustees of the 7th Earl of Harewood Will Trust and the Trustees of the Harewood House Trust*

CHAPTER 8 | Gallery of Chippendale's Marquetry Furniture

Figure 8.6.3* Marquetry seen on the side panel.

Figure 8.6.4* The Library steps coloured to match the scientific findings performed by Heinrich Piening in 2008.

* Reproduced by kind permission of the Trustees of the 7th Earl of Harewood Will Trust and the Trustees of the Harewood House Trust

CHAPTER 8 | Gallery of Chippendale's Marquetry Furniture

8.7 LIBRARY WRITING TABLE ~ HAREWOOD HOUSE, c.1771

Made for Edwin Lascelles' Library at Harewood House, and now held at Temple Newsam House, Leeds, the table epitomises everything that the classic movement represents; style, grace, symmetry and form emanate from this majestic masterpiece. The work I did in reproducing two of the panels was, for me, an invaluable opportunity to uncover Chippendale's previously kept secrets. Because Chapters 4 and 5 of this book cover much of the detail about the piece and its construction techniques, I will resist adding much more here, other than to point out two important aspects: namely, the uniform width of crossbanding border that surrounds each panel of the table, and the impressive side panels as detailed below.

As described in Chapter 5, the marquetry made for the four matching doors proved to be too large for the panels it was intended for, and it would not have been possible to reduce the width of the borders because it

Figure 8.7.2* Both acanthus leaves cut off short by approximately 10 mm, the calamity that changed a working practice for ever – see Chapter 5, page 129

Figure 8.7.1* Note the consistent width of the crossbanding borders around doors and end panel: important for maintaining continuity and balance of one panel with its neighbouring panels.

250

* By kind permission of the Leeds Museums and Galleries

CHAPTER 8 | Gallery of Chippendale's Marquetry Furniture

Figure 8.7.3* One of the two matching end panels.

would make each panel out of balance with its neighbouring panel. Here you can see the reason for maintaining continuity and uniformity of line. The arrows used on the two pictures opposite clearly illustrate the dilemma confronting the cabinet maker. The piece, intended to be positioned in the centre of the room, allows the user to sit either side, since the two sides mirror each other perfectly.

The matching end panels (Figure 8.7.3) display the most flamboyant acanthus leaves, spreading out from the majestic 56-fluted fan like matching ostrich feathers. This two-tone fan is the largest ever used by the designer and consists of white outer flutes, with red or pink centres. Green dye was used for the acanthus leaves and the garland of laurel leaves surrounding the fan which are separated by a ring of berries cast in brass.

Figure 8.7.4* Ram's head superbly chased in brass work.

* By kind permission of the Leeds Museums and Galleries

8.8 SIDEBOARD PEDESTALS (PAIR) ~ HAREWOOD HOUSE, c.1771

Two sideboard pedestals were made *en suite* for the dining room furniture of Harewood House, each decorated with rosewood and satinwood, together with elegant gilt brass mounts (see Figure 8.8.1).

The decoration consists of marquetry oval fans on each side of the pedestal base, enclosed in a Greek key design. Lead-lined urns are fitted in both vases above, one intended as a plate warmer and the other for rinsing utensils during meals, with a pot cupboard inside each pedestal base.

The inclusion of a Greek key design adds a geometric element, which is both attractive and balances the overall classical theme. It's also fitting that Roubo wrote and illustrated how the design was pieced together. Whilst Roubo's illustrations are explicitly clear, his written explanation struggles to achieve clarity, resulting in the reader being left to work out the methodology from studying the engraved images. (I have covered the process of building the Greek key design in Chapter 3 *Techniques*, see page 75.)

Indian rosewood quarter-matching on all four sides of each pedestal base is laid diagonally to create a stylised herringbone effect (see Figure 8.8.2). The decorative banding that forms the Greek key is made of satinwood surrounded by white stringers on both sides. Pinkish/red oval fans on each side provide a central medallion feature, while satinwood crossbanded borders surround each oval fan. Finally, a tulipwood crossbanding border completes each panel.

The top of each pot cupboard is also decorated with the same motif as the side panels (Figure 8.8.3). Here we see the herringbone effect of the quarter-matching rosewood background veneers.

Elegant brass work completes the effect in the form of rams' heads on each corner, with laurel leaf swags hanging beneath matching anthemions surrounded by acanthus leaves and 'C' scrolls, finally terminating in an acanthus flower – altogether truly sumptuous.

These panels ooze the classic style, harmony, balance and symmetry, exemplifying perfectly the ideals of the classical canon. We can only imagine what a striking impression these pieces would have made when all the colours were present.

Figure 8.8.1* One of the matching pair of eye-catching pedestals.

* *Reproduced by kind permission of the Trustees of the 7th Earl of Harewood Will Trust and the Trustees of the Harewood House Trust*

CHAPTER 8 | Gallery of Chippendale's Marquetry Furniture

Figure 8.8.2* The Classical design of the panels of the pedestal base showing perfect symmetry.

Figure 8.8.3* The top of the pedestal base, using the same Greek key design.

* Reproduced by kind permission of the Trustees of the 7th Earl of Harewood Will Trust and the Trustees of the Harewood House Trust

CHAPTER 8 | Gallery of Chippendale's Marquetry Furniture

8.9 PIER TABLES (PAIR) ~ MUSIC ROOM, HAREWOOD HOUSE, 1771

Made *en suite* with pier glasses, for the music room at Harewood House, these two magnificent tables and matching glasses show carving and gilding of supreme quality. One could be forgiven for assuming that this display of craftsmanship would have satisfied our intrepid designer, but having completed the work shown here, the tables were further embellished with marquetry of equal workmanship.

My investigation of the way the marquetry was put together on these matching tables reveals startling evidence of two 18th century techniques:

- **Overlaying** – I had previously discovered the use of the overlaying technique when I lifted the veneers on the door panels of the Harewood library table, described in Chapter 5, but this piece gave further and undeniable confirmation. One would be excused for assuming that marquetry applied to tables of such large dimensions, as these are, would be inlaid into background veneers previously glued to the substrates. This was not the case; on these tables we first witness a deliberate choice to 'overlay' the marquetry through the two-part fretsawing technique, rather than 'inlay' with an inlay knife.

- **Mass production marquetry** – These tables reveal another feature not previously seen on other pieces of furniture made in this period, namely the use of of mass production marquetry on a relatively large scale. Two-part fretsawing and mass production techniques are described in Chapter 3, *Techniques*, supported by clear pictorial proof.

Figure 8.9.2 gives a complete bird's eye view of the marquetry on the table tops. The flamboyant design is a fitting match for the ornate carving and gilding on the tables and glasses above.

Figure 8.9.1* Table and matching mirror glass of the highest order. One of two made for the Music room at Harewood.

* Reproduced by kind permission of the Trustees of the 7th Earl of Harewood Will Trust and the Trustees of the Harewood House Trust

CHAPTER 8 | Gallery of Chippendale's Marquetry Furniture

Figure 8.9.2 View of the marquetry table top and its flamboyant design.*

UV-VIS Spectronomy

In 2008, I commissioned Heinrich Piening to travel from Germany to Harewood House in order to test this piece and establish the dyestuffs used to create the range of colours originally chosen. This analysis uses UV-VIS Spectronomy, which is detailed along with results in Chapter 4. Using these results, a simulation of the top with its original colours was produced using Photoshop, shown in Figure 8.9.3, together with a section of the border in Figure 8.9.4.

Figure 8.9.3 Photoshop-produced simulation of the top showing the original colour scheme of green foliage and pink floral work and the oval fan with pink flutes bordered by a guilloche of white set around red berries. Rings of red berries surround the guilloche.*

*Reproduced by kind permission of the Trustees of the 7th Earl of Harewood Will Trust and the Trustees of the Harewood House Trust

CHAPTER 8 | Gallery of Chippendale's Marquetry Furniture

Figure 8.9.4* Simulation of colours used for the border elements and also a clearer view of the marquetry and its colours.

The repeating border design consists of the following elements, starting at the bottom corner far right:

- back-to-back 'S' scroll in pink
- green acanthus leaf standing on a red berry
- a blue strap linking the two S scrolls
- finally, a green seed-pod supporting a green laurel leaf.

The pattern then repeats around the circumference of the table. In each corner a burgundy anthemion, coloured with the dye campeachy, covers the mitred corners. The rosewood background matches the background used on the top, but in the case of the border the grain points at right angles to the central background, forming a crossbanding effect. An inner banding of satinwood with white stringing separates the border from the inner veneers, and tulipwood crossbanding is fitted around the outside of the table.

For the blue colour, I would make up a packet of 10 veneers and fretsaw 9 repeats of the design. If you look at Figure 8.9.4, you will see that only a tiny blue strap is needed in the design. For the red dyed veneer, only one sheet is required. This is because the red berry is produced, not by fretsawing, but with a hollow punch.

The central panel is quarter matched with some of the best examples of fretsawn acanthus leaves to be seen on Chippendale's furniture. The original green dye is still visible on most of the leaves, giving a hint of 'early-spring' realism to the foliage.

The central oval fan has 48 flutes, which originally had pink centres with white borders. Some of the flutes have been over-sandshaded as you can see from the dark burn marks in Figure 8.9.2. The green colours of the borders inside and outside the flutes are still visible. A second, yet smaller, 20 fluted patera sits in the centre.

Surrounding the fan, a guilloche motif is added, which would have consisted of white 'S' turnings and red roundels.

Other motif features include four 16-petalled acanthus flowers at the ends of each 'C' scroll, depicting alternate petals of lilac and white.

Despite some over sandshading in places, the marquetry on these tables is expertly executed. The strong evidence of original colours adds ghostly realism, complementing the extraordinary moulded brass work for which this exquisite *en suite* arrangement is noted.

Engraving

Extensive engraving was applied to the foliage as would be expected on works of such high calibre. Our flamboyant designer did not disappoint; neither did the quality and skill of the engraver.

Following the UV-VIS Spectronomy tests performed on this table, which revealed the coloured dyes used on the marquetry work, the image seen at Figure 8.9.3 offers a stunning reminder of the splendour of these matching tables. When set into the elaborate and expressive brass work to the frieze, legs and *en suite* pier glasses, the full ensemble would have made a truly majestic impact.

* Reproduced by kind permission of the Trustees of the 7th Earl of Harewood Will Trust and the Trustees of the Harewood House Trust

8.10 PIER TABLES (PAIR) ~ DINING ROOM, HAREWOOD HOUSE, 1771–2

Made for the dining room, these two matching tables are comparatively plain compared to other marquetry pieces in the Harewood collection, and perhaps reflect the room they were intended for.

Set into black Indian rosewood, the marquetry is clean and simple, consisting of a half-moon fan at the back of the table with four smaller paterae around the front semicircular edge (see Figure 8.10.2). Both fan and paterae are constructed from holly, most probably dyed pink, with the swags of laurel leaves dyed green. Red berries are let into the swags of laurel leaves, which terminate at stylised green acanthus leaves. Wide green dyed holly surrounds the central fan and forms a border along the semicircular edge. Equal widths of rosewood and tulipwood complete the border arrangement.

Engraving work has been applied to the half round paterae, which run around the curved edge of the table, and also to the laurel leaf swags. Seeing engraving on these less ambitious commissions leads me to suspect that perhaps the marquetry firm themselves decided on the type of surface decoration to be applied. It is certainly true that engraving does provide a more impressive appearance to the finished effect, compared to the lesser effect of surface artwork as applied by brush.

The frieze and legs are painted in a very attractive turquoise colour and, complementing the choice of colour, fretted and carved classical motifs are mounted with 3 mm thick white holly veneers.

Figure 8.10.1* Pier table made for the dining room at Harewood House.

* *Reproduced by kind permission of the Trustees of the 7th Earl of Harewood Will Trust and the Trustees of the Harewood House Trust*

CHAPTER 8 | Gallery of Chippendale's Marquetry Furniture

Figure 8.10.2* Marquetry set into Indian rosewood with tulipwood crossbanding border.

* Reproduced by kind permission of the Trustees of the 7th Earl of Harewood Will Trust and the Trustees of the Harewood House Trust

CHAPTER 8 | Gallery of Chippendale's Marquetry Furniture

8.11 SALON COMMODE ~ HAREWOOD HOUSE, c.1772

This attractive and colourful commode was supplied by Thomas Chippendale to Edwin Lascelles, 1st Baron Harewood, for Harewood House, c.1772. It was initially planned for the White Drawing Room, which later became the Green Drawing Room and is now called the Cinnamon Room. Figure 8.11.2 shows the commode in position in the original White Drawing Room.

The commode was loaned out to Temple Newsam House, Leeds for an exhibition on Thomas Chippendale as part of the Festival of Britain, from 8th June to 15th July 1951. Figure 8.11.3 shows the original exhibition catalogue. There is also an exhibition label still fixed to the back of the commode, shown in Figure 8.11.4. I was fortunate to receive black and white photographs, taken while the commode was on show at the exhibition in 1951 (see Figure 8.11.5).

Figure 8.11.2** Commode in the former White Drawing Room.

Figure 8.11.1* Salon commode made for Harewood House, c.1772.

* Reproduced by kind permission of Ronald Phillips Ltd
** Courtesy of Country Life Picture Library

CHAPTER 8 | Gallery of Chippendale's Marquetry Furniture

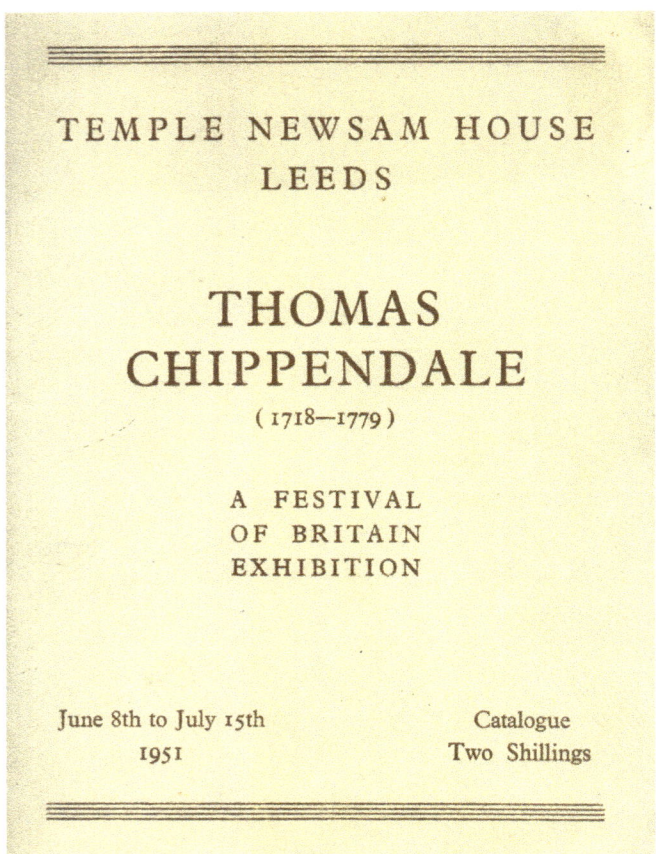

Figure 8.11.3* Catalogue of the Chippendale exhibition mounted in 1951 at Temple Newsam House as part of the Festival of Britain celebrations.

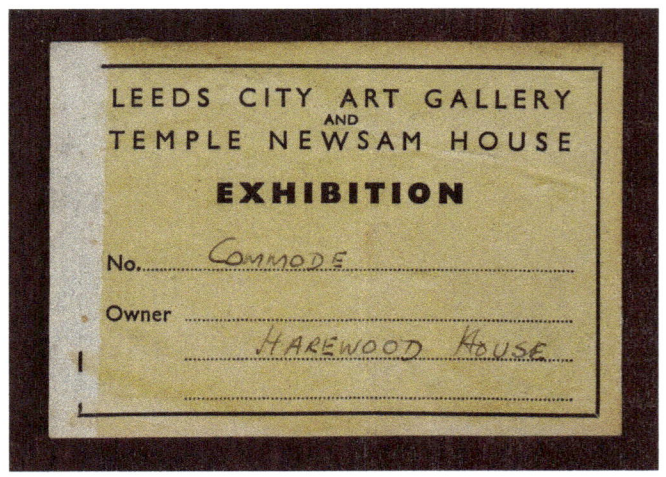

Figure 8.11.4* Exhibition label on the back of the commode.

The commode was subsequently acquired directly from the 7th Earl of Harewood, KBE, in the 1960s for a private collection in London, England. The commode is now the property of Ronald Philips Ltd, Antique Dealer, Mayfair, London.

This commode first came to my attention while I was working with my colleague, Heinrich Piening, at Ronald Phillips furniture workshop in Mayfair, London. As you can see, the marquetry and veneering is exposing the almost true dyed marquetry colours and the near true colour of the satinwood background veneers. This was the first time I had the enormous pleasure of seeing what a Chippendale piece looks like in its near original polychromatic condition. To add to the joy of seeing the colours in 'the flesh' as it were, Heinrich was able to perform UV-VIS Spectronomy tests on the colours to identify the dyestuffs originally used (see footnote, page 263).

The commode is veneered with satinwood background and tulipwood crossbanding borders on each panel, with two purpleheart panels on the commode top and the central door. These can be clearly seen in Figure 8.11.6.

The dimensions of the piece are: height 88.5 cm (34 ¾ in); width 154 cm (60 ¾ in); depth 64.5 cm (25 ½ in), with a stylish serpentine sweep across the front, created by three incurved drawer units at either side of the outward curving central door. The sweep is completed by pointing down to the four legs on each corner. Stylish incurved side panels complete the serpentine style.

Figure 8.11.5* Photograph of the commode taken during the Festival of Britain exhibition in 1951.

Reproduced by kind permission of Ronald Phillips Ltd

CHAPTER 8 | Gallery of Chippendale's Marquetry Furniture

Figure 8.11.6* Purpleheart panels on the top and central door.

Clearly, restoration work has been carried out at some time in the commode's history. Close examination of the 1951 photograph in Figure 8.11.5 shows that restoration had already taken place prior to the exhibition, because artwork does not appear to be present on this image, indicating that it had already been removed during restoration.

Removal of artwork proves that it was applied with paint and an artist's brush onto the surface of the veneers; hence, when the polish is removed, the artwork is removed also. Had engraving been used, removing the polish would not have affected the engraved lines, since engraving cuts into the veneer creating a permanent cavity. In previous and later commissions where drawer fronts exist, the marquetry panels were, in some cases, engraved. On this piece, however, that was not the case, and it soon became clear that all the marquetry was inlaid followed by the application of artwork to all panels as just described. In Figure 8.11.7, we see the green dyed laurel leaves devoid of any artwork.

Figure 8.11.7* Green dyed laurel leaves devoid of artwork.

* *Reproduced by kind permission of Ronald Phillips Ltd*

CHAPTER 8 | Gallery of Chippendale's Marquetry Furniture

Figure 8.11.8* Top panel showing highly figurative satinwood veneers on background

The top panel, shown in Figure 8.11.8, consists of highly figured satinwood surrounding an elliptical purpleheart central medallion. Green-dyed swags surround the central panel, and we can see that the swags are again devoid of artwork, revealing that they are formed of one solid veneer. The artwork, when applied, would have shown that the swags formed individual leaves.

It is interesting to see the satinwood with its highly figured feature. This matches perfectly with the dressing commode (see section 8.12 of this chapter, pages 264–265), and the secretaire (see section 8.13, pages 266–268), both made in 1772, the same year as this piece. It is my belief that the same batches of veneers were used for all three commissions. Strikingly, purpleheart medallions also feature on both the secretaire and the dressing commode. I do not suggest that this commode was intended for the same room as the other two commissions, but similarities in both veneer and motifs, together with the use of similar techniques, suggest common design elements.

The end panel, shown in Figure 8.11.9, is disappointingly not covered by any marquetry work, except for an ellipse made from a decorative banding of tulipwood. The ellipse was clearly inserted to provide access for fretsawing, but marquetry work is not added, which suggest misunderstandings between

Figure 8.11.9* Tulipwood ellipse reducing panel inserted, but for what reason?

* Reproduced by kind permission of Ronald Phillips Ltd

marqueteur and designer. If this was intentional, however, it is the only time a panel is provided and left empty.

The stylish brass mounts on the two outer corners display a ram's head above a swag of laurel leaves, with a long bold sweeping acanthus leaf below, resembling a 'cravat'.

The central door terminates at the bottom with the most stylised creation ever to appear on any of Chippendale's marquetry-decorated furniture productions (see Figure 8.11.10). It consists of a central trophy, with lid, supporting swags of acanthus leaves at either side. This motif is suspended below, and linked to, a metal frame with captive rings to the right and left ends, supporting a rope of acanthus leaves wrapped around the metal frame and terminating with knots at each end.

This is an extremely elaborate item, and one that I would suspect was expensive to produce.

Finally, Figure 8.11.11 illustrates two of the four legs terminating in brass feet representing ram's hooves, with each foot supporting a single acanthus leaf stylishly representing the 'sock' above the 'shoe'.

For me, it has been a golden moment to come across this piece and see what is clearly a high-class design, skilfully constructed by a talented marqueteur, using high-quality materials throughout.

Figure 8.11.10* Brass mount below the central door.

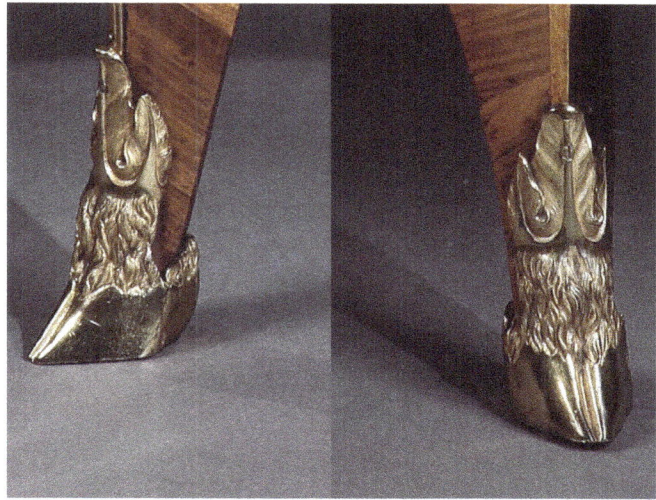

Figure 8.11.11* Brass feet representing ram's hooves.

Footnote: Dye results

The dye results obtained using UV-VIS Spectronomy tests described on page 260 are not given because they did not indicate any new dyestuffs not already identified on earlier pieces. In addition, sight of the original colours is there for all to see, as outlined in these pages.

* Reproduced by kind permission of Ronald Phillips Ltd

8.12 DRESSING COMMODE ~ HAREWOOD HOUSE, 1772

Made to match the secretaire described in the next section (8.13), this piece was decorated with the same highly figured satinwood. The main difference from the secretaire is that the medallion on the top of the dresser is circular in shape, compared to an ellipse on the secretaire. The medallion on the front panel displays a 'painting' of the three graces, made to look like ivory set into ebony. The painting throws up interesting theories about the reasons for this disappointing choice of medium. On other furniture made for Harewood, Chippendale did not hesitate to include ivory. Perhaps this piece was not considered important enough to merit the ultimate material. Another reason could simply be one of expediency and cost.

The oval fans on the outer door panels are faultlessly constructed with a knife, using the template method, with fretsawn centres of acanthus leaves made to look like an added three-dimensional carving. As with the secretaire, the hand of the same marqueteur is evident throughout.

The top (see Figure 8.12.2) shows a matching medallion of similar design to the front, where purpleheart is again used for the background. A circular fan, in this case, is preferred to the painting.

The matching side panels either side of the central medallion (see Figure 8.12.3) show diamonds, into which are sixteen pointed paterae cut from dyed green holly. Throughout, the green dye is still faintly visible. The

Figure 8.12.1* *This handsome dressing commode was made to match the secretaire described in the next section.*

* *Reproduced by kind permission of the Trustees of the 7th Earl of Harewood Will Trust and the Trustees of the Harewood House Trust*

CHAPTER 8 | Gallery of Chippendale's Marquetry Furniture

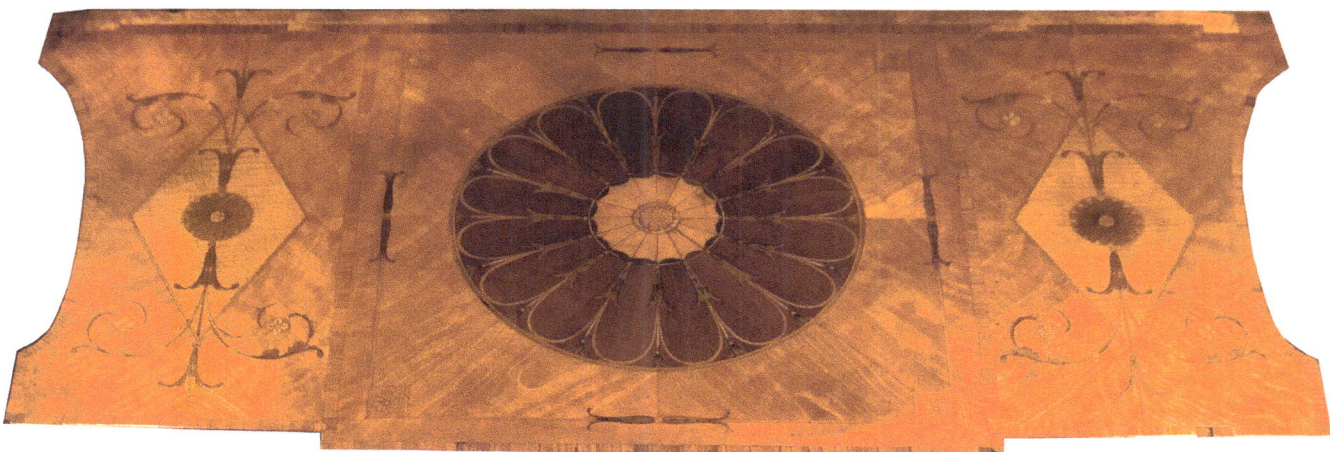

Figure 8.12.2* *Dressing commode top.*

veneer used within the diamond area is figured (ripple) sycamore. The narrow diaper banding was added to reduce the overall size of the panel so the four outer quadrants of satinwood background would fit into the throat of the fretsaw. Above and below the patera, radiating green acanthus leaves terminate with 'C' scrolls wrapped around tiny acanthus flowers of lilac and white petals. Tiny white plumes bisect the acanthus fronds.

The drawer fronts, like all other commissions where drawers exist, are inlaid with artwork added to give foliage effect. Artwork is also added to the rest of the piece, instead of the more costly engraving technique. Some of the artwork has eroded away both on the drawers and the other panels. Maybe restoration work took place at some time in its history. None of this distracts from the overall classic marquetry work nestled into the best figured satinwood I have ever seen.

Figure 8.12.3* *Side panel of the commode top, showing the narrow diaper to reduce satinwood background sizes.*

* Reproduced by kind permission of the Trustees of the 7th Earl of Harewood Will Trust and the Trustees of the Harewood House Trust

8.13 FALL-FRONT SECRETAIRE ~ HAREWOOD HOUSE, c.1772

The first thing that strikes you when you stand in front of this secretaire is the beauty of the figuring of the satinwood veneers. I have to ask myself whether perhaps the marquetry workshop received a new shipment of timber when this and the matching dresser commode (see section 8.12) and the commode (see section 8.11) were made. The colour and figure surpass any of the other pieces to come out of Chippendale's workshop. The attractive quarter panelling on the two front panels is initially, for practical purposes, to reduce the panel to manageable sizes for fretsawing, but it also provides a secondary artistic feature. This marqueteur knew all about using veneers at differing angles to give maximum impact, because he gave the impression of 'raised panels'. By adding a border of satinwood cut on the 'cross grain' to all four sides, it makes the two panels (upper and lower) appear chamfered, when in fact they are perfectly flat. Even the cross-grained tulipwood that surrounds the chamfer does not spoil the illusion. An interesting new addition is the repeat diaper pattern (a chequered parquetry pattern as used in architecture) on the upper frieze. On both panels he introduced South American purpleheart to form the central medallions, containing a classical vase in the lower half and a reclining figure representing 'learning' in the upper half.

Interestingly, the purpleheart has retained some of its original colour, whereas the species grown today tends to turn brown in colour shortly after exposure to light. Does this suggests that the soil structure in the 18th century was different from today's, or that logging, drying and cutting processes contributed to producing better species?

The quality of the marquetry is superb and clearly performed by our now recognisable marqueteur, whose talented hands we see yet again. The work on the lower medallion shown in Figure 8.13.2, with its vase set into macassar ebony, surrounded by loops of C scrolls and anthemions, speaks for itself.

While the vase is constructed in isolation with the knife, it would have been let into the background with a fretsaw. Ash is used for the body of the vase, with the delicate fluting on the underside being perfectly sandshaded. The tiniest rows of berries indicate the use

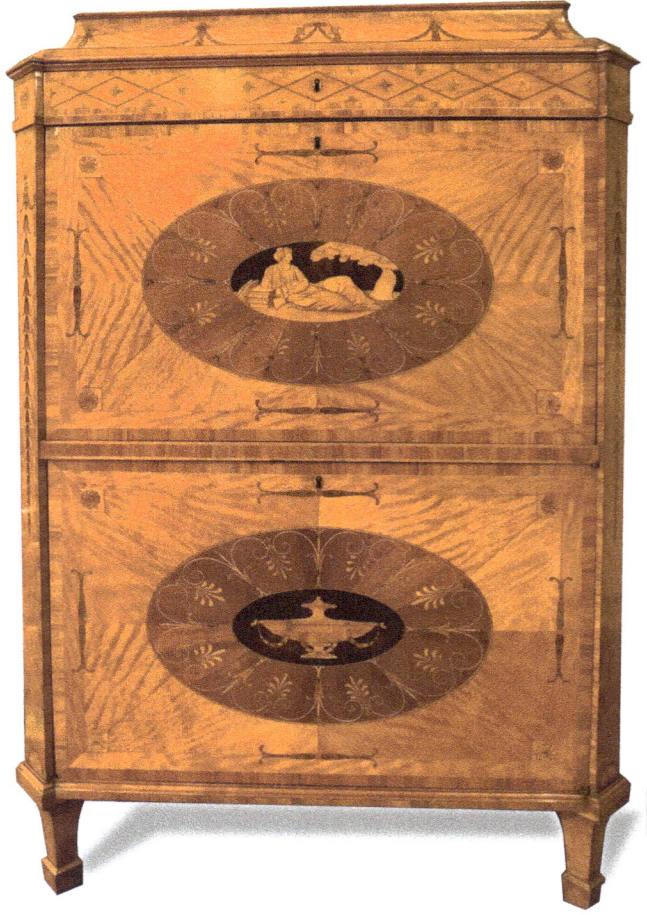

Figure 8.13.1* Fall-front secretaire.

of a very small metal punch made to achieve such perfect uniformity. The looped scrolls and anthemions, however, could only have been cut with a fretsaw; purpleheart is far too hard a veneer to be cut freehand by a knife.

The construction of the two oval medallions reveals some interesting discoveries, and it's worth looking closely at the methods that were used to build it. You can see that the purpleheart background is made up from 16 equal segments, with the grain pointing to the centre of the oval on each segment. If we now examine the 'C' scrolls closely, we see that they differ in size and shape. The smaller ones are used on the north and south (four each side) axis and the larger size on the east and west (four each side) axis. The scrolls east/west had to be

* Reproduced by kind permission of the Trustees of the 7th Earl of Harewood Will Trust and the Trustees of the Harewood House Trust

CHAPTER 8 | Gallery of Chippendale's Marquetry Furniture

Figure 8.13.2* *Lower medallion showing classical vase, set into ebony with purpleheart surround supporting scrolls and anthemions.*

slightly bigger (elongated) to match the ellipse. To create the marquetry, two designs were used: one smaller (NS) and one bigger (EW), with some duplicate copies made available, as will become clear.

First, 16 leaves of purpleheart and 16 leaves of holly are cut 'oversize' at this stage, with the grain running along the length. Protective paper is glued to the 'face' side of each veneer, using hot animal glue. Two packets for north and south scrolls are made up of four purpleheart and four holly (not dyed). Two of each veneer are placed into the packet with the paper face-up, and the other two with paper face-down. Waster veneers are placed on top and below the packet, and the design pasted onto the top waster. Nails are driven in around the outer edges to secure the packet. The design is pasted to the top. The 'C' scrolls are fretsawn, maintaining a 1.5 mm width throughout the scroll. After separating the packet, the four holly scrolls and purpleheart pieces are assembled together, trapping the scrolls in place. The two reversed sets are opened up to form a 'book' match to the two facing sets. In that way matching back-to-back scrolls around the design are achieved, as is shown at Figure 8.13.2.

Two other packets for east and west scrolls are built as described, until all 16 scrolls and backgrounds are ready to be assembled into an ellipse. To achieve this we revert to our trusted template method of construction. Just as we build elliptical fans, so this elliptical fretwork is built. The 16-fluted ellipse is drawn onto a block of wood (MDF in our case) and each segment of purpleheart with its scroll is placed onto the template and, using a straight edge and knife, the segments are joined together. Because the initial design was very accurately drawn, the scrolls will meet perfectly at the sides of each segment. Finally, the eight anthemions, acanthus leaves and tiny rings connecting the scrolls are fretsawn independently and placed in position onto the purpleheart background. After scoring around the elements, the windows are sawn out, thus allowing the elements to be inserted.

* Reproduced by kind permission of the Trustees of the 7th Earl of Harewood Will Trust and the Trustees of the Harewood House Trust

The upper panel is a repeat of the lower, except that the pictorial theme is of a reclining figure with books of learning, sitting beneath a tree. Delicate sandshading provides the necessary depth to the composition.

The marquetry on the side panels consists of a vase on the lower and a profiled silhouette head on the upper (Figures 8.13.3 and 8.13.4 respectively). The vase, cut with both knife and saw, and assembled in isolation prior to fretsawing into the background, displays some very delicate shading on the fluted lower half of the vessel. A mixture of ash, holly and sycamore is used. The lid of the vase shows a 'twist' effect to the coned shape – a feature seen before on the vases on the Harewood Library writing table (see section 8.7).

On the upper side panel, a garland of rope or decorative cord is wrapped around the profiled head forming swags beneath. This decorative motif illustrates an interesting technique. To give the effect of a plaited rope, art work is applied, perhaps before the wood has been sealed with a base polish. Normally artwork is applied after sealing the wood, and before applying the top coats of polish. In that way the paint sits on the polish without it bleeding into the wood. In this case the marqueteur wanted to achieve a plaited rope or cord effect, so the paint may have been applied to the bare wood, thus allowing it to bleed slightly to give that plaited stringy appearance. The straight drop piece on the right shows the bleeding very clearly. Here we can see the artistic side of a marqueteur, constantly searching for realism, perhaps through experimentation or by having learnt from previous experience. While today, many non-professionals reject the additional use of artwork, we have to accept the importance it held in the production of 17th and 18th century marquetry throughout Europe. The medium became known as 'painting in wood', indicating that the use of exotic hardwood background, dyed coloured veneers and artistic art work created the classic style that still, in my opinion, leads the field in wood surface decoration.

Figure 8.13.3* Vase on the lower side panel.

Figure 8.13.4* Profile head surrounded by swags of braided rope or cord, artistically painted with applied artwork.

* Reproduced by kind permission of the Trustees of the 7th Earl of Harewood Will Trust and the Trustees of the Harewood House Trust

8.14 PIER TABLE ~ HAREWOOD HOUSE, 1772

Made initially for the Circular Dressing Room at Harewood House, the table is unusual in design, because it was shaped with a curved back to match the curve of the room. The back incorporates two cut-outs, profiled to fit around two wall mirror frames. This was an unplanned event because the wall mirrors and frames were already *in situ* when the table was delivered. The two corners had to be sawn out, and marquetry work and crossbanding borders relaid while on site. Whether this required a cabinetmaker and marqueteur to make the trip from London to Yorkshire is unknown. The trip would have taken days by horse-drawn carriage, plus the same to return. An alternative possibility is that Chippendale turned to his previous employer, Richard Wood in York, to fix the problem. Chippendale had good relations with Wood with whom, it is believed, he spent

Figure 8.14.1* Table top showing curved back and cut-outs to fit around window frames.

Figure 8.14.2* Curved back pier table, showing highly decorative turned and carved legs, and fretwork and carving to the plinth.

* *Reproduced by kind permission of of The Chippendale Society*

CHAPTER 8 | Gallery of Chippendale's Marquetry Furniture

Figure 8.14.3* Close-up of left-hand side following minor restoration and re-polishing

his formative years learning the trade of cabinetmaking, carving and turning, not to mention furniture design. It is therefore feasible that Wood provided on-site workers as and when required.

The table is also unusual in its veneer choice, because the background veneer is sycamore, chemically treated with iron sulphate and logwood dye to create 'harewood'. (Chapter 2, page 26 explains the historical background to the name, and Chapter 7 shows how the chemical treatment was carried out.)

Because the table forms part of my major replica project, detailed in Chapter 7, I only want to cover the most salient feature of the original table in this chapter.

Image 8.14.2 shows the highly stylish turned legs and shaped plinth, with their painted backgrounds of blue and pink on the legs and red on the plinth. Attached to each of the legs we see, starting at the top, carved white anthemions set into the capitals against blue painted backgrounds. Below, a plume with a ring of berries sits in the centre, followed by swags of laurel leaves and oval paterae consisting of raised acanthus leaves set between each swag. At the base of each leg, a further ring of berries exists between two stringers. The leg then widens with a fluted band set against blue painted background, followed by another ring of berries to a spiral column, more berries, and finally the foot of the leg consisting of a ring of acanthus leaves.

The plinth, with its red painted background, is decorated on the front and two matching ends. At the top of the plinth a moulded border of 'egg and dart' is repeated along the length of the three sides. Below is a fretted and carved design, similar to the marquetry design used to border the matching pier tables in the Music Room at Harewood (see section 8.9). The design consists of repeat back-to-back 'S' scrolls, terminating in tiny acanthus flowers. In the spaces between the scrolls are alternating designs of three laurel leaves and a single acanthus leaf. These motifs repeat around the three sides of the plinth.

Figures 8.14.3 and 8.14.4 are close-ups of the marquetry top following some minor sympathetic restoration to the veneers, and re-polishing, carried out by my colleague Ian Fraser, Conservator at Leeds Museums and Galleries, and Honorary Conservator to

* Reproduced by kind permission of of The Chippendale Society

Figure 8.14.4* Close-up of right-hand side following minor restoration and re-polishing

The Chippendale Society. The immediate improvement is seen where some of the original colours of various marquetry elements have emerged, including both dyed and natural woods used in the construction. Previous restoration carried out by David Hawkins after the discovery of the table in 1964 in the Harewood joiners' workshop had faded significantly . In addition, the polish applied then was inferior, to a point where most of the marquetry work was masked in a pool of uneven lacquer. Chapter 7 outlines the damage the table had sustained while in the joiners' workshop at Harewood, mostly affecting the right-hand end, but to some lesser part the central panel. Most of the left hand end is original.

Now visible are red plumes on the centre panel and the four pink small oval fans to both end panels. Smaller red flowers are visible on the ends of the swag, surrounding the large oval fans to the two matching end panels. On the ends of the flutes of the two oval fans, red coloured padauk is clearly visible on the scallops and finally the tulipwood crossbanding borders truly stand out to frame this majestic commission.

Footnote

As custodians of our English heritage we all have a responsibility to foster and maintain our past. The late David Hawkins and his partner Fred Drewitt demonstrated great dedication and skill in the restoration programme carried out at the time of the table's rediscovery in the 1960s. Credit is also due to The Chippendale Society for doing what was necessary to place this important piece back into the public domain, where it belongs. Regardless of how the unfortunate damage to the table occurred, this important historical work now stands testament to the principles of conservation and restoration. It is immensely rewarding to see this splendid and unique table fully re-restored and displayed prominently in Temple Newsam House, for all to enjoy.

My replica copy offers scientific evidence of the woods and dyes used on the original work. Thanks are due to Dr Heinrich Piening and his revolutionary UV-VIS spectronomy technique, which enable me to replicate the colours on the copy seen in Chapter 7.

* Reproduced by kind permission of of The Chippendale Society

CHAPTER 8 | Gallery of Chippendale's Marquetry Furniture

8.15 PIER TABLES (PAIR) ~ HAREWOOD HOUSE, 1772

This pair of matching pier tables was made for the Breakfast Room at Harewood House. What makes this piece interesting to me is the designers use of holly for the background foil. This is only the third time he selected this very white, smooth textured and figureless veneer as the background foil to the marquetry top. The marquetry elements were, as always, holly dyed into the appropriate colours. With ageing, and the effect of light and air pollution, the holly used for the background foil now takes on a golden tone, enough to deceive the untrained eye into thinking it is satinwood.

The legs and frieze display exquisite carving and gilding work, consisting of small florets set into roundels, separated by acanthus leaves around the frieze. Raised paterae on each side of the capitals above each fluted leg support the table (see Figure 8.15.1).

The marquetry work to the top has a repeat border surrounded by a rosewood crossbanded border to the inside and tulipwood crossbanding on the outside (see Figure 8.15.2). Evidence of both repeat fretwork and knife construction of the fans can be clearly identified. The six oval fans that form an arc around the table are cut and assembled using the template method, where each flute, after cutting, receives sandshading before assembly.

The use of holly as a background foil, instead of the usual choice of satinwood or Indian rosewood, raises questions about the designer. It could be argued that the Breakfast Room did not require furniture of the stature we see made for more formal rooms, and therefore this offered an opportunity to cut costs on materials. Chippendale knew only too well the limitations of holly, inasmuch as it is completely devoid of figure and grain, whereas sycamore or maple, which we see used on other commissions covered in this chapter, provide a range of alternative figurative decorations, including quarter-cut

Figure 8.15.1* *Pier table for Breakfast Room at Harewood House.*

* Reproduced by kind permission of the Trustees of the 7th Earl of Harewood Will Trust and the Trustees of the Harewood House Trust

CHAPTER 8 | Gallery of Chippendale's Marquetry Furniture

Figure 8.15.2* Pier table top showing holly background and interesting mix of techniques.

ripple, figured crown-cut or the same species treated as harewood. For a man normally keen to maximise his design work, I find his use of holly quite interesting, making me believe that he was under pressure to reduce costs at this stage. Holly was perhaps the most used veneer at that time because of the increased demand for coloured marquetry work, indicating that stocks were high and competition for sales between stockists may have kept the price down. We find holly used as a background foil on two other commissions: the matching Panshanger cabinets made initially for Melbourne House and now at Firle Place, Sussex, and the Renishaw commode, again made initially for the same client at Melbourne House, now at Renishaw Hall, Derbyshire. Both are featured later in this chapter.

Closer inspection of the marquetry work reveals the way the swags of laurel leaves below each oval fan have been sawn. If you look carefully, you will see that each leaf is not three leaves, but made to look like three leaves. This is a smart way of avoiding sandshading. You can see that the fretsaw blade has travelled up each side of the 'central' leaf then turned around 360° leaving the tell-tale black hole. In fretsawing terms, this is called a 'blind cut'.

Likewise, the twelve four-leaf florets that appear in the outer border are cut in a similar way from one sheet of veneer. In this case, a larger blind cut is used between each leaf, and again filled with sawdust and glue to give the illusion of sandshading. Blind cut filled with glue and sawdust prior to assembly is a normal fretsawing technique, adopted prior to and subsequent to these examples. While most of our marqueteur's endeavours were to eliminate gaps in marquetry work, here was a perfectly acceptable opportunity to use a cut that provided the artistic needs.

While applauding the marqueteur's ingenuity in this instance, I am more hesitant when examining the eight florets that form the centres to each oval fan. They are fretsawn from a packet of green-dyed holly veneers. Close examination of them reveals that they are cut as one solid piece, with artwork added afterwards to try to give the illusion that the leaves are separate. These short-cuts do suggest either naivety, or that the marqueteurs were under considerable pressure to produce work under very rigid time constraints. In view of the overall high quality work of this piece, I tend to support the latter explanation.

Having said all that, this table fills me with admiration, since it demonstrates a selection of skills, each of which illustrate the variety of techniques that can be used to achieve an impressive appearance. Studying these practices and analysing them, as my experience has allowed me, provides the most complete teaching medium one could hope for. I firmly believe that the best way to move forward in one's education of marquetry work, is to look backwards and study the past, and there is no better period in which to find answers than the mid-18th century. We have also to recognise the

* Reproduced by kind permission of the Trustees of the 7th Earl of Harewood Will Trust and the Trustees of the Harewood House Trust

CHAPTER 8 | Gallery of Chippendale's Marquetry Furniture

Eight florets sawn as one veneer with artwork added to provide the all-important animation.

Figure 8.15.3* Close up showing blind cuts during fretsawing.

Four leaf florets fretsawn as one piece of veneer, using four blind cuts, filled with sawdust and glue to provide the animation.

Here we can see the blind cuts of the fretsaw around both sides of the central leaf. Also note the tight joints between the leaves and the background, proving the use of two-part sawing technique.

impact that expertly executed techniques have on the overall composition, making this table so viewable and admirable.

It is worth asking, at this juncture, whether the replacement technique of Computer Aided Design and laser-driven marquetry work can achieve the same superb results. Will 'modern' productions last the next 300 years and – as we are seeing – attract the huge, seven-figure prices that are achieved by the works of this eminent designer and craftsmen, who performed such high-class techniques?

* *Reproduced by kind permission of the Trustees of the 7th Earl of Harewood Will Trust and the Trustees of the Harewood House Trust*

CHAPTER 8 | Gallery of Chippendale's Marquetry Furniture

8.16 HORSESHOE TABLE ~ BURTON CONSTABLE HALL, 1772

Unique in Chippendale's marquetry furniture, the horseshoe table has no apparent reason for its singular shape, except that it was perhaps made to fit into a bay window. It was also supplied with a leather damask cover and fitted with drawers, suggesting it could have been used either for writing or as a dresser.

The marquetry design is relatively plain, and of limited content, yet revealing a technique that astounds me. Set into a ground veneer of dark coloured Indian rosewood with tulipwood crossbanding, it suggests the piece was intended to be used by the man of the house. Chippendale reserved the use of gold coloured satinwood for backgrounds where pieces were intended for the lady of the house.

The central oval and the two outer circular fans are constructed with two woods. Sycamore is used for the central flutes, where the distinctive 'lace' figure is evident, and I'm reasonably sure that ripple ash (ash quarter-cut which offers a striped figure) has been used for the outer parts of the fan. The inner flutes are holly dyed pink. The line of laurel leaves linking the three motifs is holly, more than likely dyed green. Four fluted legs each terminate in spade feet, with inset rosewood panels and satinwood borders on each of the four sides. The spade feet with the same marquetry pattern was replicated on the Diana and Minerva commode the following year.

Each of the two matching circular fans at each end of the table and highlighted here in Figure 8.16.2 has been constructed using the 'window' method. Clearly, the solid sheet of ripple ash used to border the 19 flutes is evidenced by the grain and striped figure running through the surround from the top of the design to the bottom. On the upper right-hand side, six cracks appear in line with each other suggesting that the veneer suffered a stress fracture following construction, which traverses in a straight line. Also, the outer borders on each flute are not separate pieces jointed down the centre as in later two-toned fans; they consist of one sheet of veneer. The 19 inner flutes consist of individual pieces, identified by the grain running along the lengths of each

Figure 8.16.1* *Horseshoe table in Burton Constable Hall, Humberside.*

* *Reproduced by kind permission of the Burton Constable Hall Foundation*

275

Figure 8.16.2* Construction by the window method.

Figure 8.16.3* Construction by the template method.

piece. This indicates to me that this motif was constructed by the 'window method', but the cutting was done with a fretsaw and not with a knife. There is a telltale dark line between all of the inner and outer flutes, plus the joints between the two pieces on each flute are not clean, tight and straight, as they would have been if a straight edge had been used to cut them. So how was it built?

The answer is: by the window method. A paper pattern glued onto the sheet of ripple ash allows each 'window' for each flute to be sawn out following the lines on the pattern. A piece of holly (possibly dyed pink) is held under the resulting windows, one flute at a time. The holly is rotated till the grain runs along the length of the window. By scoring and cutting through the insert with a craft knife, each flute is added. Prior to insertion, each piece is sandshaded along one edge to form the three-dimensional effect. Unfortunately, on these two fans, not all the pieces were sandshaded, and those that were are sometimes shaded on the wrong edge. Despite the poor quality of cutting and shading, we are seeing the window method for the first time.

I find it amazing to discover a technique used in 1772 that up till now had its origins firmly placed in the 20th century. Are we witnessing here the true origin of the method and discovering, yet again, another example of my marqueteur's innovative genius?

The oval fan, shown in Figure 8.16.3, clearly shows construction by the template method. The knife cuts are much improved from the previous circular fan, simply explained because the cuts are made along a straight edge. The 18 flutes are each pre-cut into strips with the grain running along its length. Each piece is sandshaded along one edge, and clearly these have been shaded correctly, evidenced by the excellent three-dimensional effect achieved throughout. The template method is clearly explained in Chapter 3, and this example was constructed by that sequence of steps. Conversely, the floral motif in the centre would have been cut by fretsaw and inserted after the flutes were assembled. You will note that the stringing separating the flutes from the centre is very uneven. The scallops at the ends of each flute are cut from padauk, which is a common choice of veneer on nearly all Chippendale's fans. This quirky, yet pleasing piece of home furniture, demonstrates that no request was turned away, with our designer amply demonstrating his ability to meet any order, while maintaining the classic theme in its architectural and marquetry décor.

* Reproduced by kind permission of the Burton Constable Hall Foundation

CHAPTER 8 | Gallery of Chippendale's Marquetry Furniture

8.17 DIANA AND MINERVA COMMODE ~ HAREWOOD HOUSE, 1773

One of the stars of the collection is the Diana and Minerva commode, so called because of the inlaid medallions representing the Roman goddesses of hunt and arts respectively. It was made for the State dressing room at Harewood House, and described by Chippendale himself as:

> *A very large rich Commode with exceedingly fine Antique Ornaments curiously inlaid with various fine woods – drawers at each end and enclosed with foldg doors, with Diana and Minerva and their emblems curiously inlaid & engraved, a cupboard in the middle part with a cove door, a dressing drawer in the top part, the whole elegantly executed & varnished, with many wrought brass antique ornaments finely finished £86.00.00.'*

At £86, the work was, at the time, the most expensive ever recorded for a piece of cabinet furniture, which in itself is evidence of the high esteem Chippendale placed on the work. The feature of the cabinet has to be the coved door, or domed door as it's referred to in woodworking circles today. Whether you're a joiner, cabinetmaker, architect or just an admirer of antique furniture, the construction of the door, curving both top-to-bottom and side-to-side simultaneously, offers plenty to talk about. As a marqueteur, my challenge was to add marquetry and veneers to the incurved surface, using the same materials and techniques as were used on the original. I hope those challenges are answered fully in Chapter 6, where I show how it was achieved.

As we have just seen, Chippendale called the commode 'very large' and, at 2200mm (7ft 4in) wide, 600mm (2ft) deep and 600mm (2ft) high, this gives us a better understanding of the size of the task he faced with its design and construction. Since the reconstructed replica is fully detailed in Chapter 6, I will not repeat the technical aspects here. It is interesting to note however, that the colour scheme of the piece (green and gold) perfectly matched Robert Adam's splendid decoration for the State dressing room, with green damask on the walls, secured around the room with a gilt ornamental

Figure 8.17.1* Diana and Minerva commode, made in 1773.

* *Reproduced by kind permission of the Trustees of the 7th Earl of Harewood Will Trust and the Trustees of the Harewood House Trust*

CHAPTER 8 | Gallery of Chippendale's Marquetry Furniture

Figure 8.17.2* *The domed door of the Diana and Minerva commode*

border in burnished gold. It was clear that this work was made as a 'showpiece' to complement a State room that cost over £1000 to complete. Today, the commode resides alongside the state bed, which itself has been fully restored in the same two colours.

As with other period furniture, the original colours of the dyed woods representing the marquetry work have all but disappeared. The background satinwood still retains its gold appearance and, in some respect, age has given it a warmer, more mellow tone than when first laid. Some evidence of the green dye is still visible on the top of the commode, proving that some dyes do last despite exposure to light and air. We have seen from the dye analysis (Chapter 4) that different tests detected different dye pigments for producing the same colours. Perhaps this is the reason why some dyes fade and others remain colour-fast. Certainly the results clearly suggest that our designer did not dye veneers, nor did he apply dyed veneers to his cabinetwork. These services were most likely supplied and fitted by a company or companies who specialised in both marquetry and all other finishing processes, as discussed in Chapter 3. Chapter 4 covers the colour spectra taken from the UV-Spectronomy tests I had done prior to building the replica marquetry as seen in Chapter 6.

* Reproduced by kind permission of the Trustees of the 7th Earl of Harewood Will Trust and the Trustees of the Harewood House Trust

8.18 PANSHANGER CABINETS (PAIR) ~ FIRLE PLACE, 1773

Two matching china cabinets of majestic proportions and truly ambitious marquetry represent the very best of Thomas Chippendale's classic statement. The pieces, owned by the 8th Viscount Gage and his family, reside at Firle Place, Sussex. Initially, there were doubts regarding provenance to Chippendale, but evidence linking their ancestry to Lord Melbourne, one of Chippendale's wealthiest customers and the subsequent movement of the pieces that follow, comes from Christopher Gilbert's comprehensive publication, *The Life and Work of Thomas Chippendale* (page 264):

> *At last it is possible to offer evidence which establishes the case for accepting Chippendale's authorship and gives them the status of credited masterpieces. Lord Cowper of Panshanger inherited Brocket Hall in 1869 and the property was leased as a furnished house until his heirs sold it in 1923. It is a reasonable assumption that he sold certain items from the collection to his own seat nearby before letting the hall, and it seems likely that he transferred these majestic cabinets which can thus, at long last, be associated with a premier Chippendale commission. Their ultimate provenance may even have been Lord Melbourne's house in Piccadilly.*

The cabinets were probably made for the use of Lord Melbourne's wife, Elizabeth, at their London townhouse, Melbourne House, now Albany in Piccadilly, around 1773. They subsequently came to Panshanger, Hertfordshire, via her daughter Emily, who married the 5th Earl of Cowper, of Panshanger. This famous house held many remarkable works of art as well as some exquisite furniture, but the collection was finally dispersed equally between the remaining daughters on the death of their mother, Lady Desborough, in 1952. Imogen, wife of the 6th Viscount Gage, received as part of her inheritance the pair of Chippendale cabinets, which were moved to Firle, where they remain today.

I am delighted to be able to include these two cabinets in this book, not just because of their supreme standing in Chippendale's prestigious marquetry collection, but because of the conservation work the two pieces received in 1982 by the late David Hawkins, whose report and staged photographs, now the property

Figure 8.18.1* One of the pair of Panshanger cabinets.

of Viscount Gage, first came to my notice in January 2007. Sadly, David Hawkins died in October 2006, aged 84, before I had the chance to meet him. His book *The Techniques of Wood Surface Decoration*, published in 1986, is still a source of great inspiration to me as an educational tool towards understanding marquetry techniques down the ages. The book, although now out of print, is still

* *Reproduced by kind permission of the The Firle Estate Trustees* available in some libraries. Hawkins was an expert and highly respected furniture restorer, specialising in 18th century marquetry furniture. Prior to restoring these two cabinets he had restored the damaged pier table made for the circular dressing room at Harewood House (see Chapter 7).

Hawkins' restoration of the Panshanger cabinets took five months to complete (October 1983 to February 1984), and saw the two pieces skilfully restored to their current pristine condition. Damaged marquetry was skilfully lifted and restored. In particular, missing tulipwood crossbanding had to be sourced and matched in figure and colour to blend into the existing, so that on my visit to Firle Place in 2007 I found it impossible to spot the new from the original. Hawkins' cleaning of the marquetry work revealed some of the original dyed veneers. Some artwork was exquisitely reworked and the two cabinets finally repolished. The legacy that Hawkins has left us will hopefully aid future students of furniture history and technology to understand the working practises of 18th century journeymen. The discoveries he made about Chippendale's construction of marquetry are both revealing and educationally beneficial. In particular, I am delighted to add that my own findings (formed prior to seeing this work) are fully endorsed in his restoration report.

Prior to examining his report, let's take a look at the finished work in some detail, as these cabinets will always attract academic and technical interest to students studying this period of furniture design. It is also a guide to other custodians, who may have specimens in need of restoration, to witness that sympathetic and skilful conservation not only enhances the work structurally and artistically, but revives vital, but hitherto hidden origins. The Panshanger cabinets are, in my opinion unique, and provide the very best example of 'design and build', especially now that we can add the results of Hawkins' restoration programme.

Basic construction information

The two cabinets are identical in size and design, measuring 2470 mm (8' 1¼") high, 1370 mm (4' 6") wide at the back, 1130 mm (3' 8½") wide at the front, and 550 mm (1' 9½") deep at the base. They form the tallest pieces of all the Chippendale known marquetry collection. The single glass door reveals shelves for holding chinaware, while the two incurving side doors

Figure 8.18.2* Incurved side door revealing storage shelves.

provide further shelving. The lower cabinet has three drawers, two small (left and right) and a larger central drawer. Dummy drawers fold around the two incurved sides. Three cupboard doors match the three drawers above, with the central door revealing three draw units of varying depths, with mahogany fronts and drop handles.

The veneers used for the marquetry are holly, dyed in a variety of colours, plus padauk. The veneer used as the background foil throughout is natural undyed white holly. Tulipwood provides the crossbanding throughout. Timbers used are: pine for the carcass and mahogany for the visible timbers – doors, drawers, shelves etc. Gilbert referred to the background veneer as satinwood, while Hawkins said it was sycamore, a simple mistake to make on both parts, since aged holly mellows to the same colour, but I have no doubt as to the correct species.

* Reproduced by kind permission of the The Firle Estate Trustees

CHAPTER 8 | Gallery of Chippendale's Marquetry Furniture

Figure 8.18.3* Three doors below three drawers form the lower half of the cabinet.

The second change, evident on these drawers, show that engraving and not artwork was applied to the marquetry work, both on the outer wreath and the inner patera, plus the central drawer seen at Figure 8.18.5. This is very strange, because it is the first time I have seen engraving to marquetry on drawer fronts. What makes it even more confusing is that the rest of the marquetry work across both cabinets displays surface decoration applied with artwork. The only explanation I can come up with is that our intrepid designer took the drawers, as normal, to the smaller marquetry operative for them to 'inlay' and apply artwork. However, for some unforeseen reason, they were two-part fretsawn and engraved.

Drawer marquetry technique

The two outer drawers mark a departure from the normal practice adopted to apply marquetry. Instead of inlaying the motifs with the inlay knife, followed by adding artwork by brush and paint, these drawers were installed by using the two-part fretsawing technique. How I am able to prove this departure from the normal practice applied to other drawer units is two-fold. First, Hawkins said he did not find any knife marks on either of the two cabinets but, more importantly, there is visual proof that inlaying was not used. If you look at the laurel wreath applied to the drawer at Figure 8.18.4 you will notice the wreath is too large for the background it is applied to. Above the key escutcheon the laurel leaves are too large to fit inside the border, caused by the design being over-sawn by the marquetry cutter. The uniform border surrounding the drawer had to be a standard width to balance with the other drawers across the front. Had the background and borders been glued in place first, as is the case with other commissions, the laurel wreath would have fit within the borders, because the inlayer would have had to make it fit. This is similar to the mistake made on the door panels of the Harewood Library writing table, as identified in Chapter 5.

Figure 8.18.4* Marquetry laurel wreath surround inner floral patera to two outer drawers.

Figure 8.18.5* Central drawer shows that the marquetry design fits perfectly between the four surrounding borders.

*Reproduced by kind permission of the The Firle Estate Trustees

CHAPTER 8 | Gallery of Chippendale's Marquetry Furniture

Figure 8.18.6* Familiar hand of my intrepid marqueteur, easily recognised on this half-round fan arrangement.

Figure 8.18.7* A classic vase applied to the central door.

Seeing the feature illustrated in Figure 8.18.6 fills me with joy, because it is, in my view, undoubtedly the hand of my intrepid marqueteur. In addition, engraving work is added to his creation. For me, this gives confirmation of the authorship of this work. When one sees the joint creation of London's leading designer and the leading marqueteur, no other proof is required.

The vase seen on the central door (shown in Figure 8.18.7) is expertly sawn by the two-part system. When new, one can imagine green foliage, perhaps a red vase base and a burgundy anthemion at the top. A very similar vase is found on the front door of the Renishaw commode, which, like these cabinets, was initially made for Lord Melbourne's London home.

David Hawkins' restoration

I cannot end this report without some mention of the David Hawkins restoration programme and his comprehensive photography and comments during the programme. In total, Hawkins, in his report, provides over 200 images and written observations. His photographs (colour prints) and report were loaned to me by Viscount Gage in 2007. I had the photographs digitally converted and it is my hope that they can be stored in The Chippendale Society archive for future research purposes. It would be wrong for me not to include a small taste of the findings pertinent to my own research and this publication.

I am delighted that David Hawkins took the step to first remove, then restore the artwork. The cabinets needed cleaning and it was not possible to do this effectively that without loss of original animation. Animation, or artwork, provides the all-important final artistic effect, adding depth and realism to the designs.

Figure 8.18.8* Close up of ram's head on right-hand side head prior to cleaning.

* Reproduced by kind permission of the The Firle Estate Trustees

CHAPTER 8 | Gallery of Chippendale's Marquetry Furniture

Figure 8.18.9* Part of lamp base removed and turned over, exposing toothing to both substrate and underside of veneers. This improves the bond for the glue.

Figure 8.18.10* Ram's head reversed after lifting exposing more toothing.

Figure 8.18.11* Artwork lost during cleaning.

Figure 8.18.12* Artwork exquisitely restored.

In the world of furniture restoration, there is a wealth of expertise among those able to perform this work, and it is vital that this precious aspect of conservation is not ignored. In my long research of other custodians of Chippendale's (and other leading providers') marquetry, I have all too often found that the opposite has been the case. If marquetry or cabinetwork becomes damaged, it gets repaired; artwork should be treated no differently. It is an essential component of the aesthetic *and* monetary value of the furniture – remembering that Chippendale's furniture, today, can realise seven figure sums when placed under the auctioneer's hammer!

Figure 8.18.13* Rams' heads, lamp base and torchère after restoration.

* *Reproduced by kind permission of the The Firle Estate Trustees*

 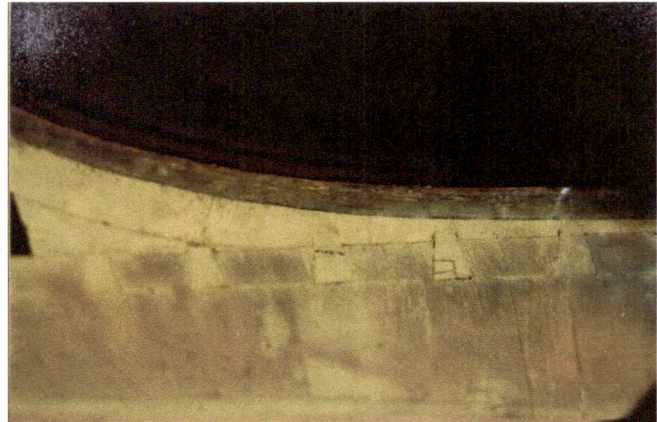

Figure 8.18.14* Images of the two cabinets, as seen looking up from the base, showing how coopering is achieved to the incurved panels seen at Figures 8.18.1 and 8.18.2.

The two photographs in Figure 8.18.14 were taken from the base of each cabinet looking up and along the bottom edge of the panels. I would not normally include cabinet-making details, but these two images provide historical evidence of the two cabinets' construction. They not only confirm how incurving panels were constructed in the 18th century, but they also suggest that the two matching cabinets were perhaps made by two different journeymen. This is not unusual, as both journeymen would work from the same design using their own individual methods, but making sure that the final external results matched.

From the previous pictures and comments, you will have seen how sympathetic and talented conservation work can enhance and recapture the vibrancy of timbers and exquisite marquetry that were only visible when new. The inspiration these cabinets now bring to visitors at Firle Place is testament, initially, to the valiant decision by Viscount Gage and his trustees to make the assignment possible. They are determined to protect and display these superb cabinets for the enjoyment of future generations. The legacy left by David Hawkins is now also preserved for all to benefit from. His acknowledged skills, and the discoveries he made at the pinnacle of his career, are captured as a technical and aesthetic reference for the future.

The evidence found within this conservation project further informs my own research. I am now totally convinced that the marqueteur who worked on previous known commissions such as the Renishaw commode and the highly prestigious Diana and Minerva commode at Harewood House, also worked on these superb cabinets. All three commissions bear the technical 'signature' of the skilled journeymen who transformed these majestic designs into supreme examples of 18th century craftsmanship.

* Reproduced by kind permission of the The Firle Estate Trustees

8.19 PEMBROKE TABLE ~ NEWBY HALL, 1775

In the early hours of Friday 29th June 2007, shortly after the photograph of this table shown in Figure 8.19.1 was taken, thieves broke into Newby Hall and entered the room where the table was kept. Tragically, the table was stolen, and it looked as though the table would never return to Newby. This was clearly a targeted robbery, since no other items were taken. Thanks to persistent and patient detective work, however, the table was traced and recovered some years later. The table is back where it belongs, allowing visitors to Newby Hall to admire the quality of this classic piece.

This dreadful event illustrates the dilemma facing custodians of our cultural and artistic heritage across Britain. On the one hand, stately home owners are prepared to open up their homes for the public to enjoy and share these masterpieces, but at the same time this gives an opportunity to those with malicious intent. As someone who values our country's heritage and collections, I am simply thankful to see the table returned to its rightful owner.

Made in 1775 for Newby Hall, it is the only recorded Pembroke table decorated with marquetry to the outer surfaces. A Pembroke games table was made for Nostell Priory (described in section 8.1 of this Chapter), but the marquetry on that piece existed only inside the drawer. The marquetry is set into a ground veneer of Indian rosewood, which is impressively quarter-matched on the central leaf. With tulipwood crossbanding around the edges, the table has one drawer which is almost as long as the length of the table. Four tapered legs terminate on casters. The use of Indian rosewood suggests the table was made for the man of the house, since Chippendale exclusively deployed this masculine timber for the male gender.

The table top consists of a central oval fan whose flutes are clearly cut by knife following the template method. Tiny florets are artistically added around the fan, a feature not previously used by Chippendale. Four matching quadrants of laurel leaves which decrease in size surround the fan. These are fretsawn from four leaves of green holly, then opened up to produce a quarter-match around the fan. Small red berries are added at leaf joints and engraving provides further animation. Ribbons terminate the garlands at each end and stylised anthemions decorate each of the four corners.

The matching drop leaves of the table display smaller oval fans, linked by acanthus leaves to tiny circular florets. Of all the pieces in Chippendale's collection, the sandshading throughout this piece is the most consistent and evenly applied that I have seen.

Figure 8.19.1* *The prized Pembroke table now back where it belongs at Newby Hall.*

* *Reproduced by kind permission of Newby Hall, Ripon, North Yorkshire*

CHAPTER 8 | Gallery of Chippendale's Marquetry Furniture

Figure 8.19.2* Table opened out to reveal an illusion of a 'deep trough' caused by the quarter matching background veneers.

Figure 8.19.3* Close-up of central fan and garland of laurel leaves surrounding.

What struck me first when this table was opened fully, as seen in Figure 8.19.2, was the three-dimensional effect of the quarter-matching Indian rosewood veneers applied to the background. It looks as if the table forms a 'deep trough', with the applied marquetry appearing to float in space above it. A quite remarkable illusion. I have seen a similar illusion achieved before, by the same marqueteur, when he applied satinwood background veneers to the secretaire at Harewood House (see section 8.13, page 266). On that occasion he made the panels appear raised up, because the chamfered borders were placed at right angles to the central veneers, to give the three-dimensional appearance.

The marquetry on this Pembroke table is sublimely constructed. Each fan is built using the template method. The garland of laurel leaves surrounding the central fan bears similarity to the decoration used on the pier table made initially for the circular dressing room at Harewood House in 1772, described in Chapter 7. There is extensive use of engraving on the foliage, pointing to the high status the designer placed on this commission.

* Reproduced by kind permission of Newby Hall, Ripon, North Yorkshire

Figure 8.19.4 shows the marquetry applied to one of the two matching side panels. A central oval fan is beautifully sandshaded, with a centre of repeat florets surrounding a cluster of berries. Each flute of the fan terminates with black scallops, which is a departure from previous practices, where padauk has always been the favoured veneer.

Swags of laurel leaves, positioned sideways, provide an interesting alternative way of enclosing this motif. Between each laurel leaf two berries are placed, but not for decorative reasons; they are put there to cover holes that develop after fretsawing the rosewood backgrounds, which in turn causes breakages of the veneer at these tiny unstable joints. I experienced the same dilemma when building similar motifs on the replica Diana and Minerva commode, described in Chapter 6. I realised that the designer placed the berries to hide the unavoidable holes that develop on these delicate joints. I imagine the berries would be dyed red and the swags green, with the central fans perhaps dyed pink or red. The remaining acanthus leaves would be dyed green.

The enlarged image of the central panel (see Figure 8.19.3) allows us to examine some of its fascinating features. The central fan again is sandshaded well, giving a perfect three-dimensional appearance. In a new style of design, not before used, each flute consists of one veneer of dyed holly (perhaps pink or red) with stringers bisecting the ends to form scallops. Another new addition is the single acanthus leaf protruding from between each flute, with three berries in decreasing sizes pointing out towards the garland of laurel leaves.

The centre of the fan matches those of the two outer fans, with a border of repeat florets surrounding the neatest uniform cluster of berries I have ever seen. I think they may be a result of delicate artwork.

Outside the fan, the garland of laurel leaves is engraved, with two berries placed between each pair of leaves. This time the berries are purely for decoration and not to hide unplanned holes. I know this because the berries, as you can see, are not placed at joints where breakages occur. The garland terminates at each end with ribbons. Finally, stylised anthemions are placed at each corner with more acanthus leaves terminating in C scroll and acanthus flowers.

Figure 8.19.4* Close up of one side panel.

Because of the year this table was made (1775) – just a year before Chippendale Senior retired – I am led to wonder whether his son had a hand in the design of this table and, in particular, its marquetry. If this is true, it is testament to the younger partner's skills and evidence that perhaps he was being encouraged by his father to become more involved at the designing stage. The introduction of new features, just discussed, would support this assumption. If I am right, Thomas Senior would have been assured that the Chippendale future was in safe hands when the senior partner finally bowed out.

* *Reproduced by kind permission of Newby Hall, Ripon, North Yorkshire*

8.20 RENISHAW COMMODE ~ RENISHAW HALL, c.1775

Renishaw Hall, situated in North Derbyshire, is home to the Sitwell family. The commode, while not a proven attribution to Chippendale's workshop, is unquestionably accepted into the collection on both stylistic and constructional grounds.

Further information suggesting authorship is given in Christopher Gilbert's book (*The Life and Work of Thomas Chippendale*, page 21) relating to furniture made for Lord Melbourne's residence, Melbourne House, Piccadilly, London. Lord Melbourne was one of Chippendale's most prominent London clients. Gilbert talks of a visit to Melbourne House by Thomas Mouat of Garth in the Shetland Isles, c.1775. Mouat was taken on a conducted tour of the house by Thomas Haig (partner to Chippendale), and in Mouat's subsequent vivid account of his impressions of the tour, he mentions seeing *"a Commode table of inlaid work, cost £140"*. Gilbert states that:

> *"Haig, it appears, was not averse to boasting about the cost of furniture supplied by the firm, and if his figures are to be believed, some of the items were vastly more expensive than comparable pieces supplied to Harewood about the same time".*

At a cost of £140, this commode is now recognised as his most expensive piece of furniture. There are a number of striking similarities with other marquetry pieces, not least the celebrated Diana and Minerva commode made some two years earlier for Harewood House at a cost of £86. Not only do the design elements have similar features, but the dimensions of the two pieces, internally and externally, closely match. Clearly the same designer's drawing (rod) was used to construct the carcass. This observation is another strong indication that it came from Chippendale's workshop.

The obvious difference between the two commodes is the central door – the Renishaw displaying a 24-fluted flat oval panel, whereas the Harewood version displays a coved door. One more significant difference between the two commodes is the background veneer. Satinwood was used on the Harewood version, while white (undyed) holly was chosen for this work. It's interesting to note the similarities in tonal values between the two woods, now that age has mellowed the holly to a golden tone. Certainly the designer, with full knowledge of timbers of the day, would have previously seen evidence of this on

Figure 8.20.1* The Renishaw commode, displaying medallions emblematic of architecture and sculpture

* With very kind permission of Mrs Alexandra Hayward

CHAPTER 8 | Gallery of Chippendale's Marquetry Furniture

Figure 8.20.2 *The Renishaw commode is included in the background of the famous Sitwell family prtrait of 1900 by John Singer Sargent.*

aged and polished holly and noted the tonal similarities. I have good reason to suggest this, because holly is used again as the foil on the two matching glass china cabinets, better known as the Panshanger Cabinets (described in section 8.18), which also display the same tonal effect. The Panshanger cabinets are also linked stylistically to this commode by the use of the vases, both situated on their respective central door panels. While the change of background veneer is explainable, the choice of the crossbanding border is consistent with all other commissions using multi-coloured, multi-striped tulipwood.

Figure 8.20.1 shows two outer doors with two medallion figures representing architecture (right) and sculpture (left). The figures are let into figured (ripple) sycamore, treated with sulphate of iron to turn the veneer a silver-grey colour, which marqueteurs worldwide refer to as 'harewood' (see Chapter 2, page 26). This kind of silver/grey stained wood was only used twice during the firm's existence. The other occasion was on the pier table made for the circular dressing room at Harewood and featured in Chapter 7. The two figures on the Renishaw commode are completely different from those on the Harewood commode, suggesting a change of decorative style. Similarly, some of the motifs display a change of design style, quite different to that for which Chippendale is consistently recognised. Was this the younger member of the family firm flexing his designing skills on this commission? I have already hinted that Chippendale the Younger might well have designed the marquetry on the Newby Hall Pembroke table, made in the same year as this piece and described in section 8.19. If so, in my opinion, he passed the test with honours.

The acanthus leaves and 'C' scrolls on the central door above the central fan display symmetry and harmony with the rest of the panel in which they sit, including the brilliantly designed and constructed vase of the central door, a close copy of the vase found on the Panshanger cabinets. Evidence confirming authorship of a piece of furniture usually depends initially on proven documentation, such as a bill of sale or an entry in the original household inventory of contents. Where this does not exist or cannot be traced, authorship can sometimes be attributed on stylistic grounds. To date, the latter applies to this work.

The top of the commode, shown in Figure 8.20.3, holds a mirror, positioned in the centre of the top, where normally it would have been veneered and covered with marquetry. I find it a rather strange addition to the piece,

Figure 8.20.3 *Commode top displaying a mirror, requested perhaps by the original owner to display silverware*

* *With very kind permission of Mrs Alexandra Hayward*

but perhaps it was installed to reflect ornaments, such as a classic ornamental silver salver, allowing the mirror to show off its underside.

In general, the marquetry on this commode is of the highest order, and for that reason I have included here a selection of close-ups for you to admire the workmanship.

Figure 8.20.4* Commode top end panel.

Figure 8.20.5* Close-up of fan and central patera.

The two matching outer panels of the commode top consist of an oval fan, most likely dyed pink/red, with deep red padauk veneers used for the scallops at the ends of the 20 flutes. The use of padauk to depict the scallops was a regular choice by the designer. The centre of the fan displays a delicate 32-pointed patera (see Figure 8.20.5), matching the same as used on the table made for the Circular Dressing Room at Harewood in 1772 (described in Chapter 7). The delicate and artistic sandshading applied to both examples is, without doubt, the work of one marqueteur. The close-up shows the illusion that two 16-pointed fans reside one behind the other. I have first-hand experience of building this design, because I had to construct eight of them, as seen in my replica curved pier table (see Chapter 7).

The central radiating sunburst fan with its 24 flutes is most impressive and clearly demonstrates the accuracy that knife cutting offers over fretsaw work when straight lines are needed. The detail on the vase and its decorative elements is sublime. I am convinced that whoever cut this vase and the central patera also constructed much of the marquetry on the Diana and Minerva commode, as well as the near-replica vase on the Panshanger cabinets discussed earlier. For me, recognising a craftsman's dexterous work is as good as recognising an individual's handwriting and offers further proof that this commission emanated from the same workshop.

The end panels (see Figure 8.20.7) illustrate the use of fretsawn and craft-knife cut marquetry. The colour scheme chosen by the designer and depicted in dyed holly consisted of green foliage and pink fans, set against white holly background. Each panel is bordered with multi-coloured, multi-striped tulipwood crossbanding. Add the very shiny brass mounts (when they were new) and the Renishaw commode would have been a highly impressive and colourful production. The end panels

* With very kind permission of Mrs Alexandra Hayward

CHAPTER 8 | Gallery of Chippendale's Marquetry Furniture

Figure 8.20.6* The 24-fluted radial sunburst patera. The central vase closely matches the one on the Panshanger cabinet.

again show a striking resemblance to the Diana and Minerva commode. The marquetry with its corner fans and garland of laurel leaves to the lower panel, plus the laurel swags surrounding the half-round fans on the upper dummy drawer fronts, complements the brass mounts on the corner columns. The casts of the brass ram's head appear on the Harewood Library writing table described in section 8.7. The legs and their brass mounts of acanthus leaves are again almost identical to the Harewood piece.

Above the central patera, a satyr mask depicting a lion's head is cleverly shaded around the face (see Figure 8.20.8), and the use of ash veneer for the lion's mane and ebony for the eyes provides the perfect ghostly image. You may also notice the use of clusters of berries lying in the fronds of the acanthus leaves at either side of the mask. The same feature was used on the two outer doors of the Diana and Minerva commode, to fill tiny holes caused by fretsawing unstable veneers at leaf joints. Such artistry, timelessly captured and repeated, provides compelling evidence that this piece was designed and made in the Chippendale workshop.

Fig 8.20.7* One end panel showing similarities to the Diana and Minerva commode end panels.

* *With very kind permission of Mrs Alexandra Hayward*

Figure 8.20.8* Satyr mask depicting a lion's head.

We know that Chippendale's son was being groomed to take over the family firm, possibly as early as 1771, and in 1775, when this piece was made, Thomas Senior was only a year away from retirement. It's also a logical piece for the father to pass onto his son, since the senior partner had already designed and installed the Harewood version two years earlier, and it was perhaps appropriate to let his son cut his designing teeth on a near-matching piece. One would also expect to see the same classic themes continued, since Chippendale the Younger had been raised on and trained in those well-proven, well-executed design elements.

In most father–son relationships, however, there is also a case for individualism, in which the younger partner did not disappoint. One could argue that the younger partner perhaps also had a voice in setting the final fee for the piece. Seeing the financial difficulties his father had experienced before him, young Thomas was perhaps encouraged to introduce new and improved production costs, and the suggestion of £140, if this figure can be proven, does suggest a change of company policy around this period. I am confident that the technical discoveries made during my research provide sufficient evidence that this commode did indeed have its origin in Chippendale's London workshop.

* With very kind permission of Mrs Alexandra Hayward

CHAPTER 8 | Gallery of Chippendale's Marquetry Furniture

8.21 THE 'LUNAR' TABLE ~ HAREWOOD HOUSE, 1775

This breathtaking table, made initially for the Yellow Drawing Room at Harewood House (but subsequently sold in 1965 and now in a private collection) was, I believe, Thomas Chippendale's final contribution at the end of an illustrious career. The ambitious and thought-provoking design, the flawless marquetry and chased engravings to the ivory work are some of the finest examples of artistry and craftsmanship I have ever seen. You may think that is praise enough to heap on any one piece, but in addition I believe I have made a ground-breaking discovery which, if true, adds extra historical significance to this table. I have renamed this table from its earlier name: 'The Emblematic Table' to 'The Lunar Table' based on my hypothesis to be discussed later in this chapter. First, however, let's examine and enjoy this masterpiece.

The table, when delivered to Harewood House on the 1st December 1775, was lovingly described by Chippendale as:

"A large Circular table of fine yellow Sattin wood with Antique Ornaments curiously Inlaid with various other fine woods and Emblematic Heads in Ivory very finely Engraved and varnished, on a very rich Carved frame with ornaments highly finished in Burnished Silver and varnished £60".

This glowing description clearly illustrates the status he awarded this table yet, 'curiously' (to use his own popular phrase), he describes this half-round piece as a 'circular' table. Perhaps, as seen in Figure 8.21.1, and prior to writing this entry in his bill, he had seen the table reflecting against the mirror-glass, in the Yellow Drawing Room.

We know he reserved the use of ivory only for the very best commissions, and the engravings on the emblematic heads and throughout the marquetry work are exquisitely chased. I fully endorse Christopher Gilbert's claim regarding its standing as the finest

Fig 8.21.1* The lunar table: reflected in the mirror glass it becomes 'circular'.

* *Reproduced by kind permission of the private collector*

CHAPTER 8 | Gallery of Chippendale's Marquetry Furniture

Fig 8.21.2* The lunar table: the six hand-carved oval shaped fluted legs and the plinth were originally covered in burnished silver and varnished.

example of English marquetry furniture. As a practising marqueteur, I have not seen anything to equal it.

Chippendale retired the year after making this table and I believe he regarded the table as his 'swan song'. This piece encompasses all Chippendale knows and loves about the classic movement. The rules and laws of the canon are fully adhered to, and the design captures the style and symmetry that characterise the movement.

Furthermore, our 'marqueteur journeyman' displays the finest craftsmanship ever seen on a piece of English furniture. The choice of woods, the fretsawing, sandshading, assembly, and the most delicate and artistic engraving add up to sheer perfection – to a point where I can, for the only time in my experience, state that the workmanship on this iconic table is flawless.

Figure 8.21.2 shows the stylish legs and frieze which were burnished silver when new, but later changed to gold by the present owner. The legs are oval in shape and are expertly carved with flutes running the length of the leg, broken with projecting paterae along the length. The frieze is vertically fluted and again decorated with carved paterae.

The top consists of a satinwood ground veneer, with mythical representations of classic themes set into four radial windows of purpleheart background. Five ivory heads separate the windows and, above, radial swags and ribbons enclose a stylistic lunette fan with a sixth ivory head at its centre. The whole work is bordered in repeat foliage, patera and anthemion design, with tulipwood crossbanding to the outer edges. Delicate sandshading on the flutes of the lunette-shaped fan demonstrate assembly by template and knife. The clean tight joints of the ribbons and stylised anthemions are a product of fretsawing of the highest precision.

The five ivory heads across the radial surface are set into an ebony background, with each emblem bordered by the finest and most perfectly inset stringer (0.5 mm wide) I have ever seen. The joint in each stringer is only visible under a magnifying glass. Outside the stringer, a uniform ring of berries (originally coloured red) surround each emblem.

I have formed a theory as to how the circular ebony backgrounds and their ultra thin stringers were formed. I imagine the ebony circles were formed from a block of ebony whose grain ran across the face of the circle. The ebony block would have been turned on a pole lathe until the required diagonal dimension was achieved. The block of ebony needed only to be approximately 3 inches long. Once the turned block was uniform in diameter along its length, it was sanded while still on the lathe and a layer of holly veneer was wrapped and glued around the circumference of the block using hot animal glue. The joint in the veneer was achieved by overlapping the ends of the veneer and cutting a straight joint with a sharp craft knife against a straight edge. A hot iron would help to soften the animal glue and form a tight joint along the length of the veneer. The veneer would then be gradually sanded on the lathe; applying only short

* Reproduced by kind permission of the private collector

intervals of sanding such as not to heat up the glue below and cause the veneer to come loose. The delicate sanding would continue until a uniform thickness was achieved along its length, approximately 0.5 mm. Finally, each roundel of ebony (six in total) with its intact stringing was sliced from the block while still on the lathe, using a narrow parting tool. Each ivory insert, first fretsawn into shape, is laid on the ebony roundel, now protected with plain paper held in place with hot animal glue and aligned, before scribing around the ivory shape with a fine craft knife. The ebony is then fretsawn to provide the perfect 'window' for the ivory shape to fit. The full assembled insert is laid on the satinwood background and a similar window sawn for the circular ebony, now intact with ivory head and outer stringer, to be inserted. A ring of red berries produced from a hollowed metal punch is added around each roundel. Final sanding would take place once the completed top is glued to the base. Because animal glue exists on the surface of the ebony, no dust contamination can occur during sanding. Finally, the ivory heads are engraved with a burin engraving tool, then in-filled with a black wax, to show the necessary facial details. The finished engravings illustrate the high skill of the engraver in getting details artistically right.

Four radial windows set across the table represent Roman mythological images, each depicting a different classical movement. The far left window (Figure 8.21.3) shows a triangle, tambourine and pipe, symbolising music and dance. The captive rings around the triangle are particularly well cut. The green dyed wood is holly. I think the tambourine and pipe are cut from boxwood which, like holly, has no visible grain feature. It's these panels that display the finest marquetry cutting techniques I have ever witnessed.

The second radial panel (Figure 8.21.4) displays the lyre, trumpet and laurel wreath – the symbols of poetry. The lyre and trumpet are cut from ash, but the strings of the lyre, cut perfectly straight and uniform would most probably have been either holly or boxwood, because they are both close-grained woods, ideal for cutting stringers. The shell decoration on the top of the lyre is beautifully sandshaded and piped with the finest stringing around the outer edges. The laurel leaves are also sandshaded to show some curling, while delicate engraving adds artistic realism.

Figure 8.21.3* Symbols of music and dance.

Figure 8.21.4* Symbols of poetry.

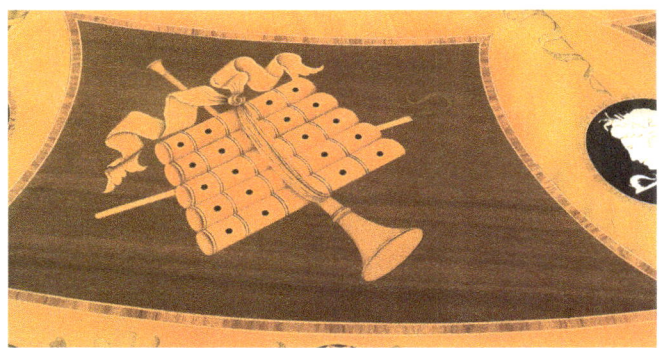

Figure 8.21.5* Symbols of heroic and pastoral poetry.

Figure 8.21.6* Symbols of love and learning.

* *Reproduced by kind permission of the private collector*

The panel at Figure 8.21.5 shows the shepherd's crook, pan pipe and trumpet, which are symbols of heroic and pastoral poetry. The pan pipe and the ribbons are cut from boxwood, but the trumpet is ash. The double fine lines added to separate the musical sections along the pipe are expertly engraved.

The final panel (Figure 8.21.6), with its torch, quiver and arrows, illustrates symbols of love and learning. The torch is again ash, while the quiver and arrows are boxwood. There is good use of dyed green, mixed with some non-dyed woods to add realism to the arrows' feathers.

This delightful little 'cameo' (shown in Figure 8.21.7) on the right-hand end of the table illustrates the consistent quality of the work. The oval patera, the single acanthus leaf, followed by the ten decreasing laurel leaves are symmetrically perfect. Again, delicate and precise engraving adds the artistry. The image also captures the neatness of the tulipwood crossbanding arranged around composite angles. The marquetry complements the carved legs and frame, and the overall condition after 230 years is truly amazing.

During Chippendale's working life, he had witnessed many contrasting movements affecting art, poetry and music, as well as within his own domain of interior architecture. His initial designs, embracing first the Gothic then the Chinese, led into his mastery of the classical, which always included a host of mythical images. This table was his final chance to display all he had seen, learned and practised and, by doing so, demonstrate through marquetry and engraving that he fully understood the true meaning of an architectural movement that shaped not only his furniture, but his life.

The Lunar Society

This table and the construction I have just explained and illustrated was to be the closure of this book, and a few years ago I would have been proud to end it here. But as I have already stated, a further story has to be told, following a discovery I made after reading a fascinating historical book called *The Lunar Men*, written by Jenny Uglow. The historical events within the book provoked, for me, questions regarding elements of the furniture and fittings destined for the Yellow Drawing Room at Harewood. Perhaps a cohesive programme was purposefully planned at the design stage, hinting that an untold story lurks within the room's original purpose. Does this table perhaps tell a fascinating secret story through its marquetry and ivory images? Its creator leaves enough clues to help piece together the events and achievements of a host of remarkable men who influenced our future.

The 'Lunar Men' were a group of 18th century philosophers and businessmen based in and around Birmingham. They met monthly at each other's houses on the Sunday nearest the full moon, so that the path home would be lit for them following their lengthy deliberations. These men and their unique discoveries and inventions undeniably formed part of the driving force for the Industrial Revolution that was already underway. Their names sound like a list from *Who's Who* of 18th century industrial pioneers. They include:

Figure 8.21.7* Table - shaped end and corner detail.

* *Reproduced by kind permission of the private collector*

Figure 8.21.8* Four ivory heads depicting from left to right: Air, Earth, Water and Fire.

James Watt, the inventor of the steam engine; Josiah Wedgwood, perhaps the finest potter that ever lived; Joseph Priestley, preacher/philosopher who discovered oxygen and nitrogen as by-products of fire and air; Erasmus Darwin (grandfather of Charles), doctor, poet and philosopher, whose book *The Botanic Garden* preceded his grandson's theory of evolution; Scotsman James Keir, chemist, inventor and industrialist; Thomas Day, poet whose dedicated efforts to end Britain's slave trade preceded those of William Wilberforce; and finally Matthew Boulton, industrialist, whose manufactory at Soho, Birmingham perhaps produced some of Chippendale's and Robert Adam's brass and ormolu mounts. Boulton also manufactured Watt's steam engines. These philosophers and industrialists, who worked together between 1765 and 1803 had, as we will see, close connections with the Lascelles family who owned Harewood House.

As already described, the plinth and legs of this table (like the matching girandoles and mirror glasses) were burnished silver, a decoration not previously used by Chippendale and never used again. The lunette shapes and choice of material are significant, because I believe that collectively they are part of a deliberate tribute towards the Lunar Society, the burnishing meant to invoke the silvery moon. Yellow damask on the Drawing Room walls was again a deliberate choice since it made the perfect foil for the silvered furnishings.

However, it is when we look at the four ivory heads to the right and left of the central head that we see a distinct connection with the achievements of the Lunar Men and their inspirational discoveries and inventions.

Reading from left to right (Figure 8.21.8), the ivory heads depict 'Air', represented by a bird in flight, followed by 'Earth', a figure wearing the mural crown, a symbol representing notable achievements of outstanding significance. On the right-hand side we have 'Water' (symbolised by a fish) and, far right, 'Fire' showing the roman god Vulcan holding a fork. These four profiles – air, earth, water and fire – represent the ancient elements, the very elements that formed the basis for the inventions and products that emerged from the scientific and industrial activities of the Lunar Men. Earth provided the clay for Josiah Wedgwood to produce his ceramics, while fire heated his kilns. Air and fire allowed Joseph Priestley to experiment and discover oxygen (called 'phlogiston' – a name he carried to his grave) and the gases nitrogen and hydrogen, with assistance from chemist, inventor and industrialist James Keir. Water and fire combined to produce steam, helping James Watt to experiment and produce the first working steam driven engine. And finally, all four elements allowed Matthew Boulton to manufacture his ormolu and brass mounts, as well as coins for the Royal Mint, since each needed the base mineral extracts from the earth, as well as fire, air and water to forge the end products.

In addition, the four radial panels described earlier and the fifth ivory head (Figure 8.21.9) depicting poetry, possibly suggest a tribute to poets and philosophers Erasmus Darwin and Thomas Day and their contribution to the Lunar Society.

The final element on the table is the lunette fan shown in Figure 8.21.10. The very word 'lunette', meaning 'little moon', has the same Latin origin as 'Lunar'. I believe the image was deliberately intended to allude the moon, and I now have evidence to support this. How provocative the designer was to show 'Pan' –

Figure 8.21.9
The fifth, central ivory head, with the harp depicting poetry.*

* Reproduced by kind permission of the private collector

Chapter 8 | Gallery of Chippendale's Marquetry Furniture

Figure 8.21.10* The central lunette fan, along with the green ribbons showing dye retention.

or perhaps a Lunar Man emerging from darkness into the light of the moon – ignorance into enlightenment. To create this effect, he deliberately placed the ivory figure jumping out of the lunette fan, suggesting either the mythical Pan or a Lunar man emerging from darkness into the light of the moon. Dare I suggest an 'artistic scenario' was deliberately included here, by using the satyr figure seen representing half man-half goat. How teasingly evocative to embrace mythology with reality!

Further evidence in support of my hypothesis comes from a paper written by Eric Robinson, entitled 'Matthew Boulton and the Art of Parliamentary Lobbying' (*The Historical Journal*, Vol. 7, No. 2 (1964), pp. 209–29, Cambridge University Press). Watt's 'Fire-Engine Act' of 1775 recalls Mathew Boulton approaching Members of Parliament (MPs) to ease the act through parliament. One of the MPs named was Edward Lascelles, then MP for Scarborough, and cousin of Edwin Lascelles, 1st Baron Harewood. (Edward Lascelles was to inherit the Harewood fortune on Edwin's death and in due course became 1st Earl of Harewood.) Clearly the Lunar Men were known to the Lascelles family. Watt's Fire-Engine Bill received Royal Assent on 22 May 1775. Watt's steam engine was labelled a 'fire engine' because of the coal fire in its belly.

The Lunar Society was formally established between February and May 1775, and Chippendale delivered this pier table and the silvered wall furniture to Harewood on the 1st December in the same year.

It is my hope that by disclosing my hypothesis, more evidence will emerge regarding the outline plans for the decoration of the Yellow Drawing Room, which will make possible further discovery of contemporary events influencing Chippendale's designs.

Dyes used on the Lunar table

Following my research and analysis of dyestuffs used in the 18th century, as detailed in Chapter 4, I can now offer my final contribution showing you what this table looked like when first delivered. Seeing the results of the colours, electronically painted using Adobe PhotoShop, is truly stunning (shown in Figure 8.21.11). As the illustration shows, the legs and plinth were re-burnished gold by the current owner. The stunning reproduction of the marquetry work shows the dye 'madder' used for the red swags. Burgundy dye, 'campeachy', was used to depict the four anthemions above the red swags, proving that nature is perfectly replicated. The dye kamala was used to depict the archer's bow in the far-right radial panel, proving that reality was the byword, since English bows were usually constructed from yew, a distinctive orange-coloured timber.

All the foliage is coloured green as one would expect, including the bows of ribbons at the back of the table, where the original green dye is still visible. Interestingly, the lunette fan at the back of the piece had no trace of dye, offering the final and compelling evidence towards the interpretation of the table's symbolism I have just given. On this and all other commissions, a pink dyed

* *Reproduced by kind permission of the private collector*

CHAPTER 8 | Gallery of Chippendale's Marquetry Furniture

Fig 8.21.11* The lunar table, with the original vibrant colours of the marquetry recreated electronically.

veneer was always used to represent fans. Clearly, Chippendale chose plain white holly veneer for this fan for a particular reason – in my view because he wanted to display a lunette image to recognise the achievements of the newly formed Lunar Society.

For Thomas Chippendale, this was his final contribution, capturing the essence of his life's journey in one brilliant creation. It was the iconic masterpiece, eloquently expressed using the products that nature provided and becoming his final masterclass, an object lesson in design and build from the most expressive period of furniture design. He was the consummate designer, whose name is now recognised worldwide. His gifted, yet unnamed, marqueteur, who brought his creations to fruition, had the most fertile mind and dexterous hands, which are and always will be my permanent inspiration.

I hope that this journey I have shared with you through Chippendale's marquetry furniture has proved fascinating and fulfilling and that, like me, you are intellectually stimulated by the skills and artistry produced by two talented minds. I trust that those responsible for the future of this remarkable collection continue to treasure and protect its integrity.

As a final word, I have to recognise a proud and talented Yorkshireman, motivated by his own aspirations, which took him from obscurity to the brink of greatness. A man selflessly, yet proudly offering his talents to anyone gracious enough to receive them. Through the expressive marquetry work, I'm reminded of the skills I have gained from a man whose genius I have studied, touched, written about, taught and finally replicated. But as I stand alone in the Yellow Drawing Room at Harewood, I'm reminded of the challenges he has encountered, taken on and ultimately overcome. For me, his journey has been wholly inspirational and, in particular, his marquetry designs represent the best of their period. No other competitor of his time matches his artistry. For all this, I consider myself lucky to have realised a skill I found late on in my life, allowing me to endeavour to emulate his most eloquent designs. The reproductions given in this book are proof of the joy I have experienced, shared and celebrated, just as my intrepid designer offered his own achievements during his own expressive life, which stand as a lasting legacy into the future.

* Reproduced by kind permission of the private collector

INDEX

acanthus 128
   flower 144
   leaves 134–135, 170–172, 174–175
acidity 104
Adam, Robert (architect) 11, 15, 16, 19–20, 277, 203
alkalinity 104
alum (aluminium potassium phosphate) 90–92, 104–105
   alum trade 90–92
   recipes 105
animal glue 31–32, 153
anthemions (honeysuckle) 102, 142
aqua-fortis 95
artwork 28, 83–84, 85–86
ash 26, 119–124

bandings 82
Banks, Simon (furniture restorer) 46, 60–63, 237
barberry 95, 101, 106
Barili, Antonio (wood inlay artist) 46
Barry, Sir Charles 204
beech 119–124
bench. *See* marquetry cutter's bench
Benson, William (apprentice/foreman) 9
berberis 216–217
bevel cutting 44, 64
birch 119–124
birch (masur) 26
Boulle, André-Charles 24, 34
   packet fret-sawing 58
Boulton, Matthew (industrialist) 297–298
Bowett, Adam (furniture historian) 26, 126, 148, 157, 207
boxwood 26
brass mounts 201
brazilwood 93, 96, 101, 112
burin 86
Burton Constable Hall, Yorkshire 19, 80, 232
   Horseshoe table 80, 275–276

campeachy (logwood) 96, 101, 102, 116
chevalet (marquetry donkey) 42–44, 134

The Chippendale Society 271, 203, 204, 205, 206, 207
Chippendale, Catherine (née Redshaw) (wife) 9
Chippendale, John (father) 9
Chippendale, Thomas 'the Younger' (son) 9, 99–100, 231, 232, 289, 292
Christie's, London 204
Circular dressing room pier table (Harewood House) 203–230, 269–271
classic style 15–16, 18–21
cochineal 97–98, 101, 102, 115
colours
   of dyed holly veneers 27
copper 104, 121
crossbanding 145–146, 180–182, 197
curcuma 101, 109

Darwin, Erasmus (philosopher) 297
Day, Thomas (poet) 297
Diana and Minerva commode (Harewood House) 83–84, 277–278
   dyes used on 101
   replica 124, 149–202
   UV-VIS Spectronomy tests 99–100
diapers 264
dragon tree 96–97
Dumfries House, Ayrshire 232
dyes and dyeing 89, 93–102
   recipes 106–108
   synthetic 123–124, 227
   Weber's recipes for dyeing 94–96

ebony 25
   problems with leaching 28–29
Elvaston Castle, Derbyshire 236
engraving 86, 146, 240, 247, 256, 207

fans 153, 158, 168–170, 189–191, 196–197
Feinberg, Simon 126, 148
Firle Place, Sussex 273
   Panshanger cabinets 279–284
fish glue 32, 153, 221
Foremark Hall, Derbyshire 232

Fraser, Ian (conservator) 120, 126, 148, 270, 205, 207, 208, 210, 212
fretsaw 153
    blades 44–45
    invention of 33–34
fretsawing 131, 136, 138, 155, 192
fustic 107
    colour fading 233, 244

Gage, Viscount 279, 282
Garrick, David 232
The Gentleman and Cabinet Maker's Director 10–11, 232
Gilbert, Christopher (author) 279, 280, 288, 293
gimbarde 55
glue 31–32
    fine tip glue applicator 221
Goldsborough Hall, Yorkshire 232
Greek key design 74–76, 252
guilloche 140–141, 164–167

hammer-veneering 48–49, 185, 187–189, 212–217
harewood 26–27, 119–124, 270, 210–212
Harewood House, Yorkshire 19, 20, 232
    and airewood 26–27
    Bureau dressing table (1770) 241–242
    Circular dressing room pier table 269–271, 203–230
    Diana and Minerva commode 83–84, 277–278
    Dining room pier tables (1770) 246–247
    Dining room pier tables (1771-2) 257
    Dining room pier tables (1772) 272–274
    Dressing commode (1772) 264–265
    Library steps (1771) 248
    Library writing table 125–148, 250–251
    'Lunar' pier table 293–299
    Music room pier tables (1771) 68–76, 254–256
    Salon commode (c.1772) 259–263
    Secretaire (c.1772) 266
    Sideboard pedestals (c.1771) 252
    UV-VIS Spectronomy tests 99–100
Harewood, 1st Baron 126, 147–148, 236, 237, 238, 250, 259, 298
Harewood, 1st Earl of 298
Harrington commode (c.1770) 236–240
Hawkins, David (conservator) 271, 204
    Panshanger cabinets restoration 279, 282–284
henna 101, 113
Herculaneum 11, 16

hide glue 220
Hill, Joyce (professor of Anglo-Saxon history) 26
hollow punch 47, 63, 81
holly 27
    dyeing veneers 98
Horseshoe table (Burton Constable Hall) 275–276

indigo 94, 95, 101, 117
ink
    indelible 122–123
inlay 52–55
    echnique 53, 83
inlay knife 24, 45–46, 52, 53, 153, 185, 192–194
intarsia 46, 55
iron gall ink 122–123
iron sulphate 104, 122
    use in making harewood 119–124, 210–212
ivory 27, 264, 297

journeymen 51

kamala 101, 111
Kauffmann, Angelica (painter) 20
Keir, James (chemist, inventor) 297
kerf mark 128
knife cutting 45

L'Art du Menuisier (Roubo) 13–14
Langlois, Pierre (cabinet-maker) 99, 100, 101
Lascelles Edwin. *See* Harewood, 1st Baron
Lascelles, Edward, MP for Scarborough.
    See Harewood, 1st Earl of
laurel leaves 130, 154
    garland 158–163
    swags and drops 143, 154–157, 199–202
leaching 28–29, 234
Leeds Museums and Galleries 125
Leonardo da Vinci 35
    water-driven auto-feed reciprocating saw 35
Library steps (Harewood House) 248
    UV-VIS Spectronomy tests 99–100
Library writing table (Harewood House) 250–251
    dyes used on 101
    replica door panel 125–148
    UV-VIS Spectronomy tests 99–100
The Life and Work of Thomas Chippendale
    (Christopher Gilbert) 279, 288

line drawing 167–168
logwood 96, 101
    use as red dye 96
    use in making harewood 210–212
Long, Malcolm (engraver) 207, 210
'Lunar' pier table (Harewood House) 293–299
    dyes used on 101
    UV-VIS Spectronomy tests 99–100
Lunar Society 296–298

madder 101, 114
magnolia 210
maple 26, 119–124
marquetry 52
    dyes used in 89–124
    mass production 254
    materials used in 25–32
    techniques 51–88
    tools used in 33–50
marquetry cutter's bench 34
marquetry donkey (chevalet) 42–44
Martin, Elias (painter) 54
Melbourne House 238, 273, 288
Melbourne, Viscount 238, 279, 288
Mersham-le-Hatch, Kent 232
modifiers 104
mordants 89, 104. *See also* alum, tin chloride
motifs used in the Classic style 20–21
mounts 201
Music room pier tables (Harewood House) 254–256
    dyes used on 101
    UV-VIS Spectronomy tests 99–100

neo-classicism 15–16
Newby Hall, Yorkshire 19, 232
    Pembroke table 285–287
    UV-VIS Spectronomy tests 99–100
Nostell Priory, Yorkshire 19, 232
    commode 243–245
    Pembroke games table 233–235
Nymphenburg, Schloss 103
oak gall ink 123
old fustic 107
on-the-line, off-the-line 60
Otley 9, 11
overlaying 254

packet fretsawing 58–59
padauk 25
    problems with leaching 28–29
Panshanger Cabinets (Firle Place) 279–284
parquetry 24, 65, 233
Paxton House, Berwickshire 232
pear wood 119, 121
Pembroke games table, Nostell Priory 233–235
Pembroke House, London 232
penwork 85–86, 146–148
Piening, Heinrich (conservator) 12, 89, 99–102, 103, 120, 124, 150, 249, 255, 271, 205, 206, 207, 209, 227, 229
Pompeii 11, 16
poplar 119–124
prick and pounce 56
Priestley, Joseph (scientist) 297–298
purpleheart 25, 241, 266–268

Rannie, James (business partner) 9–10
Ravenna 15–16
Redshaw, Catherine (Thomas' wife) 9
Renishaw Hall, Derbyshire
    Renishaw commode 238, 273, 282–284, 288–292
Ronald Philips Ltd, Antique Dealer 260
Rose, Joseph (plasterer) 19
rosewood 25
    problems with leaching 28–29
Roubo, André Jacob 13–14, 55
    fretsaw 33
    gimbarde 55
    hammer veneering 48–49
    harmmer veneering 65
    marquetry cutter's bench 34
    sandbags 49
    veneer cutting 29–31, 233–234
router 55

saffron 101, 110, 244
sand bags 49
sanding 182
sandshading 28, 136–137, 154
satinwood 25
    problem with breakages 63
shoulder knife 46, 54–55
Sitwell family 288, 289
Slater, Malcolm 153

smoke tree 107
Sotheby's, London 236–237
Speak, Martin (polisher, lecturer) 147–148
St Martin's Lane, London, premises in 9, 10, 18
stick-as-you-go technique 65–76
stringers 82, 178–180, 213
sycamore 25, 26, 119–124
synthetic dyes 123–124, 227

tannin 121
template method 77–79, 153, 168–170, 218
Temple Newsam House, Leeds 125, 250, 271
    Chippendale Exhibition 1951 259–261
    UV-VIS Spectronomy tests 99–100
tin chloride 104
    recipe 105
treadle saw 35–42, 153, 177
tulipwood 25
turmeric 95, 109

UV-VIS Spectronomy 12, 99–102, 150, 248, 255–256, 260

veneers
    Chippendale's selection of 25–26
    veneer hammer 48–49
    veneer production 29–31, 233–234
Victoria & Albert Museum, London 241, 246

Watt, James (inventor) 297–298
Weber, Peter (cabinet-maker and ebonist) 93
    recipe for harewood 119–121
    recipes for dyeing 94–96
Wedgwood, Josiah (potter) 11, 297–298
weld 101, 108
wig tree 101, 107
Wilton House, London 232
window method 80, 276
Winn, Sir Rowland 244–245
Wood, Richard (carver, cabinetmaker) 9, 269

young fustic 101, 107

Zucchi, Antonio (artist) 20